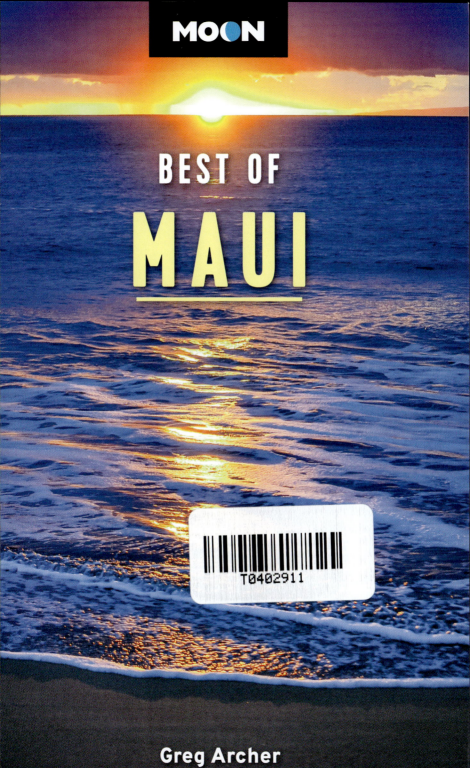

MOON

BEST OF
MAUI

Greg Archer

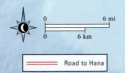

CONTENTS

WELCOME TO MAUI 7
Best Week in Maui 9
Regions of Maui. 17
Need To Know 18
Planning Tips 20

BEST OF THE BEST 25
Best Beaches 26
Best Hikes 27
What to Eat and Drink 28
Best Views 29
Best Scenic Drive 30
Best Snorkeling and Diving... 31
Best Surfing 32
Best Adventure Sports 33
Best Family Fun 34
Top Souvenirs 35
Native Hawaiian
   Culture on Maui 36
Traveling Sustainably 41

SOUTH MAUI 43
South Maui 3 Ways 47
Orientation and Planning ... 52
Highlights 52
Best Beaches 57
Scenic Drives 65
Best Hikes and Walks 65
Snorkeling and Diving 68
Surfing. 75
Other Water Sports 78
Biking 78
Golf 79
Bird-Watching. 80
Spas and Wellness 81
Shopping 83
Food 85
Bars and Nightlife. 91
Lodging 92
TRANSPORTATION. 94

WEST MAUI 97
West Maui 3 Ways 101
Orientation and Planning ... 105

Highlights 105
Best Beaches 113
Scenic Drives 117
Best Hikes and Walks 117
Snorkeling. 119
Scuba Diving 124
Surfing. 127
Kayaking and SUP 129
Sunset Cruises. 133
Whale-Watching 135
Other Water Sports 136
Adventure Sports 136
Golf 138
Spas and Wellness 139
Shopping 140
Food 140
Bars and Nightlife. 145
Lodging 149
TRANSPORTATION. 150

CENTRAL MAUI 153
Central Maui 3 Ways 157
Orientation and Planning ... 162
Highlights 162
Best Beaches 167
Scenic Drives 169
Best Hikes and Walks 170
Surfing. 172
Other Water Sports 172
Biking 173
Horseback Riding. 174
Bird-Watching. 175
Zip-Lining 176
Helicopter
   and Flightseeing Tours..... 177
Golf 178
Shopping 180
Food 181
Bars and Nightlife. 184
Lodging 186
TRANSPORTATION. 188

HALEAKALĀ AND UPCOUNTRY 191

Haleakalā and
Upcountry 3 Ways 195
Orientation and Planning 199
Highlights 199
Scenic Drives 213
Best Hikes and Walks 213
Biking 218
Horseback Riding 220
Bird-Watching 221
Adventure Sports 222
Spas and Wellness 222
Shopping 223
Food 225
Lodging 228
TRANSPORTATION 231

THE ROAD TO HANA AND EAST MAUI 233

The Road to Hana and
East Maui 3 Ways 238
Orientation and Planning . . . 244
Highlights and Scenic Drives . . 244
Best Beaches 257
Best Hikes and Walks 261
Surfing 264
Stand-Up Paddleboarding . . . 267
Biking 267
Adventure Sports 268
Helicopter Tours 270
Spas and Wellness 271
Shopping 271
Food 272
Lodging 273
TRANSPORTATION 278

LANA'I 281

Lana'i 3 Ways 286
Orientation and Planning . . . 294
Highlights 294
Best Beaches 298
Best Hikes and Walks 300

Snorkeling and Diving 304
Surfing 306
Biking 306
Horseback Riding 307
Golf 308
Shopping 310
Food 312
Lodging 314
TRANSPORTATION 315

MOLOKA'I 317

Moloka'i 3 Ways 322
Orientation and Planning . . . 329
Highlights 329
Best Beaches 335
Scenic Drives 338
Best Hikes and Walks 339
Snorkeling and Diving 342
Surfing 342
Kayaking and SUP 343
Biking 344
Bird-Watching 344
Fishing 345
Shopping 345
Food 346
Lodging 349
TRANSPORTATION 351

GEOGRAPHY AND LANDSCAPES 353

PLANTS AND WILDLIFE . . . 359

ESSENTIALS 367

INDEX 381

LIST OF MAPS 390

Big Beach at Makena State Park

WELCOME TO
MAUI

There is a prominent Hawaiian saying about Maui: Maui no ka oi, "Maui is the best."

The countless stretches of golden sand are an obvious draw, but sand alone doesn't entice millions of visitors to a dot in the middle of the Pacific. Perhaps it's more than just the thought of relaxing in a lounge chair with a mai tai in hand. Maybe it's also the way the trade winds blow across a beach of black sand. Or it's the hope of a close encounter with a giant green sea turtle while snorkeling off the coast. Maybe it's the way the setting sun reflects in the waters, both fiery and calm in the same fleeting moment.

Of course, Maui's magic is also found in the endless adventures to be embraced on the island. Hike through a thick bamboo forest and find yourself at the base of a waterfall cascading down a rocky cliff. Ride your first wave and feel the thrill of the surf as you glide across a silky blue break. Or wake up at 3am and drive up a dark mountainside in the freezing cold to see the first rays of light illuminate Haleakalā Crater.

No matter what drew you to the island, the secret to Maui's allure lies in the many moments that stick with you long after you've left it behind.

Maui coastline

BEST WEEK IN
MAUI

DAY 1

Given Hawaii's time zone, you may wake up before dawn. Take advantage by catching **sunrise at Haleakalā.** Allow two hours of travel from Ka'anapali or Wailea and plan to arrive 30 minutes before sunrise. Spend the rest of the day relaxing poolside.

Conversely, have a lazy morning at the pool or beach, take a hike into Haleakalā's crater in the afternoon, and catch **sunset at Haleakalā,** a less crowded and similarly beautiful experience, possibly lingering for **stargazing.** (No reservations are required for sunset.)

DAY 2

Tackle another early morning activity: a snorkeling tour to **Molokini Crater,** departing from Ma'alaea Harbor. Finish by 2pm and spend the afternoon relaxing on the beach.

DAY 3

Enjoy the world-famous **Ka'anapali Beach,** where you can snorkel, cliff-jump, play in the surf, or rent a cabana. Afterward, explore the shops in Whalers Village and dine at Monkeypod Kitchen.

sunset from Haleakalā

Maluaka Beach

DAY 4

Catch an early-morning ferry from Ma'alaea Harbor to the island of **Lana'i.** (Book a Jeep about two months prior to your stay.) Spend the morning exploring. Pick a remote beach such as Polihua or Kaiolohia (Shipwreck Beach). Then head back to Lana'i City for a plate lunch at Blue Ginger Cafe. The last boat back to Maui leaves at 5:30pm.

DAY 5

Brunch at Kihei Caffe before making the drive to Makena. Spend the day at **Maluaka Beach,** exploring to the end of the road, and walking the length of the beach just before sunset.

DAY 6

Check out of your hotel. Drive to Pa'ia and begin the day with a stroll down Baldwin Beach, followed by breakfast at Café des Amis. Enjoy the **Road to Hana** at a leisurely pace, taking time to hike to Twin Falls and explore the Ke'anae Peninsula. Check into your accommodations in Hana and enjoy sunset from Hamoa Beach.

DAY 7

Spend the day in rural **Upcountry.** Enjoy breakfast on the lanai at Grandma's Coffee House, followed by a stroll down Thompson Road. Drive to Ulupalakua for a midday wine-tasting, and then double back the way you came to the town of Kula and visit Ali'i Kula Lavender Farm, a sprawling haven filled with 45 varieties of lavender and a gift shop. Finish the day shopping in Makawao and then have dinner at Marlow. Think about how you'll miss Maui—and plan your next visit.

Twin Falls

ITINERARY DETAILS

- While all **summer months** are fine times to experience this itinerary, traveling during the months of September and October means smaller crowds and easy access to all areas.
- Choosing South Maui for **accommodations** is ideal for the first five days of this itinerary, as it allows easy access to a variety of beaches, Central Maui, and routes to Upcountry.
- Accommodations at popular destinations like **West Maui** and **Hana** should be booked in advance, due to popularity.
- **Advance reservations** are also recommended for car rentals (both on Maui and the special Jeep rental on Lana'i) and the Molokini Crater snorkeling tour.
- **Sunrise at Haleakalā** requires reservations, which are available 60 days in advance. No reservations are required for sunset.

the Road to Hana

16   WELCOME TO MAUI

REGIONS OF MAUI

SOUTH MAUI
From the celebrity-laden resorts of **Wailea** to the condo-dwelling snowbirds of **Kihei**, South Maui is all about worshipping the sun and enjoying the procession of beaches. **Makena** remains South Maui's most adventurous area, with snorkeling, scuba diving, hiking trails, kayaking, and some of the island's most photoworthy beaches. Just offshore, **Molokini Crater** offers 100-ft (30-m) visibility and the chance to snorkel with up to 250 species of fish.

WEST MAUI
West Maui pulses with a unique coastal vibe. The historic town of **Lahaina** was once the capital of the Hawaiian kingdom, and it retains a port town atmosphere. Warm weather and mostly dry conditions make this region a spectacular place for outdoor adventure. Snorkel near sea turtles at **Napili Bay,** lounge on the beach in **Kapalua,** ride the zip line above **Ka'anapali,** or hike to **Nakalele Blowhole.**

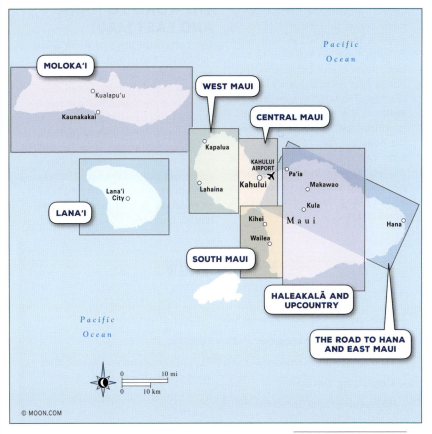

Nakalele Blowhole

CENTRAL MAUI

Central Maui is the island's population center and the seat of county government. Most visitors blow through town on the way to their beachfront resort, but Central Maui has its own set of sights off the regular trail. The twisting road into **ʻIao Valley** is the region's most popular attraction. **Kepaniwai Heritage Gardens** exhibits Maui's multicultural heritage, and down on the shore at **Kanaha Beach Park,** windsurfers and kitesurfers take to the waves along the stretch of Maui's North Shore.

HALEAKALĀ AND UPCOUNTRY

Rural, laid-back, and refreshingly cool, Upcountry is Maui's most underrated zone. Agriculture and produce dominate **Kula,** and everything from vegetables to vineyards and vodka distilleries, coffee, and goat cheese can be found in this rural and relaxing enclave. **Polipoli** is the island's little-known adventure zone, where mountain biking, paragliding, and hiking take place in a forest shrouded in mist. Watch the dramatic sunrise from the frosty peak of towering **Haleakalā,** the sacred volcano from which the demigod Maui famously snared the sun.

THE ROAD TO HANA AND EAST MAUI

The bohemian town of **Paʻia** is as trendy as it is jovial. Surfers ride waves along undeveloped beaches, patrons shop in locally owned boutiques, and the town is home to some of the island's best restaurants. Along the famous, twisting **Road to Hana,** tumbling waterfalls and rugged hiking trails await. The **Pools of ʻOheʻo** spill down cliffs to the sea. The hike through a bamboo forest to the base of **Waimoku Falls** is considered the island's best trek.

NEED TO KNOW

- **Main airport:** Kahului Airport (OGG)
- **Flight time from Los Angeles:** six hours nonstop
- **Time zone:** Hawaii standard time (HST), three hours behind Pacific time
- **Biggest city:** Kahului
- **High season:** mid-December through mid-April

LANA'I

Home to 3,500 residents and one large resort, this island is a playground of outdoor adventure. Learn about the island's history at the **Lana'i Culture and Heritage Center,** and make the journey down to Kapiha'a to see an ancient village settlement frozen in time.

MOLOKA'I

Taking time to explore this island offers a chance to experience the roots of native Hawaiian culture. Take a guided tour into historic **Halawa Valley,** one of the oldest settlements in Hawaii, or enjoy paddling off the sublime southern coast of **East Moloka'i.** Watch the sunset from **Papohaku Beach,** one of the state's longest and most deserted stretches of sand, or climb your way high into the mists of the **Moloka'i Forest Reserve.**

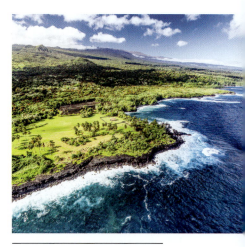

Kahanu Garden on the Road to Hana

Kamaole Beach Parks, South Maui

CHOOSING WHERE TO STAY

IF YOU WANT . . .	REGION
Luxury	South Maui (page 92)
Ocean-view stays	West Maui (page 149)
Affordability	Central Maui (page 186)
Panoramic island views	Upcountry (page 228)
Waterfalls and hikes	East Maui (page 273)
Exclusive resorts and pampering	Lana'i (page 314)
Snorkeling and scuba diving	Moloka'i (page 349)

PLANNING TIPS

SEASONS OF MAUI

Maui might not have four distinct seasons, but it definitely has two—summer and winter.

Summer

During the summer (May-October), areas such as West Maui and North Kihei in South Maui are prone to trade winds that blow most afternoons. While East Maui can see rain during summer, and tend to be five degrees cooler at times than West and South Maui, the rest of Maui's coastal areas can go six months without a single drop. The average temperatures range from the 70s (21-26°C) during the evenings to mid- to high 80s (29-31°C) during the day. Lana'i and Moloka'i temperatures are similar.

Winter

During the winter (November-April), there can be plenty of rain. A winter day on Maui can mean light breezes, sunny skies, and a high of 78°F (26°C), but it can also mean cloudy skies and rain. Experienced surfers will have the best chance of finding **big surf** in winter. Average temperatures on Lana'i and Moloka'i are similar, with cooler temps in the higher mountain areas.

GETTING AROUND MAUI

All flights from the continental United States arrive at **Kahului Airport** (OGG). Numerous car-rental options are available, and to save money, consider renting from an off-site operator rather than a corporate

PROS	CONS
Top quality and best ocean views	High cost
Best sunsets on the island	Overflow of tourists
Lower prices for accommodations and easy access to other areas	Cooler and windier weather with beaches prone to blowing sand
Privacy	Cooler weather, distance to beaches
Scenic and remote	Rural and sometimes rainy
Plush and rejuvenating	High cost
Most pristine ocean setting	Planning and booking ahead is required

chain. During the peak winter season and around Christmas holidays, reserve a rental car well in advance to ensure you get the best price.

The island is most easily explored by **car,** with rentals ranging $450–600 per week. If your schedule is flexible and you aren't in a rush, the most affordable way to travel around the island is the **Maui Bus.** You can buy a day pass for only $4, and routes service much of the island.

MAUI CALENDAR
Spring
PRINCE KUHIO DAY
March 26 is Prince Kuhio Day, a public state holiday observed in remembrance of Prince Kuhio, heir to the throne of the Hawaiian monarchy.

CELEBRATION OF THE ARTS
Toward the end of April, the Celebration of the Arts (www.celebration ofthearts.org) at the Ritz-Carlton hotel in Kapalua begins its monthly spotlight (through December) on various indigenous art forms and cultural traditions. It's an absolute must-visit if you are in town.

LEI DAY
May 1 is Lei Day in Hawaii. There are usually large Lei Day celebrations held in Wailea and various other places around the island.

SEABURY HALL CRAFT FAIR
Upcountry in Makawao, the Seabury Hall Craft Fair (www.seaburyhall. org) is held on the Saturday before Mother's Day and features Hawaiian craft vendors from across the state. With live music, food booths, and hundreds of artists, it's the perfect place to pick up a gift for mom.

MOLOKA'I KA HULA PIKO
The Moloka'i Ka Hula Piko (www. kahulapiko.com) festival in May is perhaps the largest annual event on the island and celebrates the history of the hula at its legendary birthplace in West Moloka'i.

Summer

KAPALUA WINE & FOOD FESTIVAL

One of the largest events in West Maui, the Kapalua Wine & Food Festival (www.kapaluawineandfood-festival.com) takes place over four days in June and is considered the longest-running food and wine event in the United States. The event takes place on the grounds of the luxurious Ritz-Carlton resort and features master sommeliers, seasoned chefs from around the globe, and events such as cooking demonstrations, lectures, themed food tastings, bountiful brunches, and plenty of wine from renowned wineries. Pricing ranges $100-300 for various events, although true foodies can splurge on a festival pass for $1,250-1,400.

KING KAMEHAMEHA DAY

June 11 is King Kamehameha Day in Lahaina. Festivities include a parade through town, crafts, and lots of food and entertainment.

MAUI FILM FESTIVAL

The Maui Film Festival (www.maui-filmfestival.com) typically unfolds over a span of 10 days in June, so check the schedule and consider attending screenings, some of which are held outside under the stars. In recent years, the festival has added events during November and December, too.

MAKAWAO RODEO

Over the July 4 weekend, head for the coolness of Makawao for the annual Makawao Rodeo. Paniolo are an old and important tradition in Hawaiian life. Held at the Oskie Rice Arena, this old-time Upcountry rodeo can't be beat for fun and entertainment. It's accompanied by the Paniolo Parade through town.

ANNUAL LANA'I PINEAPPLE FESTIVAL

Many events on Lana'i are small in scope and akin to a community potluck. However, the biggest event of the year on the island is the Annual

---

May 1 is Lei Day.

Lana'i Pineapple Festival (www. lanaipineapplefestival.com) in July at Dole Park. Ranked among the top 10 specialty food festivals by *USA Today* in 2014, the event features vendor exhibits, games, arts and crafts, live entertainment, an annual food fight, and fireworks after sunset.

Fall

OUTRIGGER CANOE RACES

Moloka'i is well known for its outrigger canoe races, when the island buzzes with visitors from across the Pacific. In September, the **Pailolo Challenge** (www.facebook.com/pailolo) features paddlers who race from Maui to Kauanakakai, and the **Na Wahine O Ke Kai** features all-women paddle crews who race from Hale O Lono Harbor to the neighboring island of O'ahu. In October, paddlers race from West Moloka'i to O'ahu in the **Moloka'i Hoe** (www.molokaihoe.com). More than 1,000 paddlers compete in the event. It's an exciting time to be visiting West Moloka'i.

Winter

HOLIDAY LIGHTING OF THE BANYAN TREE

At Christmas, the holiday lighting of the banyan tree, as well as decorating the Old Courthouse, takes place in Lahaina.

CHINESE NEW YEAR

Chinese New Year (www.visitlahaina. com) celebrations are held in the evening along Front Street in Lahaina and include a lion dance, martial arts demonstrations, live music, food, and, of course, firecrackers.

MAUI WHALE FESTIVAL

The Maui Whale Festival (www. mauiwhalefestival.org) is sponsored by the Pacific Whale Foundation and features live music, festivals, fun runs, and community activities through the month of February. The annual World Whale Day takes place at Kihei's Kalama Park and is the largest event of the festival.

sunset at Ho'okipa Beach Park

BEST BEACHES

MALUAKA BEACH
South Maui
Maluaka is the most happening beach in Makena, where everything from kayaking to snorkeling and stand-up paddling is available. Public restrooms and showers make this a convenient spot for families, and you can walk down the road to historic Keawala'i Congregational Church (page 64).

MAKENA STATE PARK
South Maui
Wide, long, and completely undeveloped, aptly named **Big Beach** is a local favorite that comes alive at sunset. This legendary shore has a lengthy hippie history: Countercultural visitors and nudists should visit neighboring **Little Beach** for Sunday night drum circles (page 60).

D. T. FLEMING BEACH PARK
West Maui
Fleming's offers some of the island's best bodysurfing, beachcombing, and coastal hiking. Public restrooms, showers, lifeguards, and parking make this a family-friendly beach. Surfers flock here in winter to tackle the large swells (page 113).

KA'ANAPALI BEACH
West Maui
Whether you're looking for snorkeling, stand-up paddling, cliff-jumping, or scuba diving, you'll find it at Ka'anapali Beach. This resort district is the see-and-be-seen shore for the island's West Side (page 114).

BALDWIN BEACH
The Road to Hana and East Maui
A North Shore classic, Baldwin Beach is a local favorite for bodysurfing and scenic jogs or strolls. It's flanked by Baby Beach, which families with small children will love for its protected cove, and Secret Beach, which draws hippies and nudists (page 257).

HAMOA BEACH
The Road to Hana and East Maui
If your vision of paradise involves a book, a palm tree, and the sound of waves at your feet, you'll find it at Hamoa Beach, the nicest beach in Hana. Travelers from James A. Michener to Mark Twain have written of the beauty of its sandy shore (page 260).

Hamoa Beach

26 BEST OF THE BEST

BEST HIKES

HOAPILI TRAIL
South Maui
Tucked away in the "deep south," the Hoapili Trail traces the winding footpath of royalty across black fields of lava. This meandering, rugged coastal track is an enchanting time portal to ancient Hawaii and also passes **La Perouse,** a popular surfing spot. Mornings are best to beat the hot sun (page 66).

KAPALUA COASTAL TRAIL
West Maui
Although just 1.75 mi (2.8 km), this short trail encompasses epic scenery, passing some of the most beautiful beaches in the country as well as offering views of Moloka'i and Lana'i (page 117).

SLIDING SANDS TRAIL
Haleakalā and Upcountry
This 12.2-mi (19.6-km) sojourn crosses the floor of **Haleakalā Crater** and weaves past cinder cones bursting with color. Keep an eye out for nene geese and glistening silversword plants. For a real thrill, hike by the light of the full moon (page 214).

TWIN FALLS TRAIL
The Road to Hana and East Maui
This easy-to-navigate hike along the Road to Hana is one of the island's most popular, and visitors traveling with children will especially appreciate the easy access to waterfalls and swimming holes (page 261).

PIPIWAI TRAIL
The Road to Hana and East Maui
If expansive banyan trees, dark bamboo forests, and numerous waterfalls aren't enough of a thrill, this 4-mi (6.4-km) trail in Kipahulu reaches a dramatic terminus at the base of 400-ft (122-m) **Waimoku Falls.** Often regarded as the island's best hike, this should be on every itinerary for a day spent in Hana (page 262).

HALAWA VALLEY FALLS CULTURAL HIKE
Moloka'i
More than just a hike to a waterfall, a trek in Halawa Valley on Moloka'i is a powerful journey to the heart of Hawaiian culture. Halawa Valley is one of the oldest settlements in the Hawaiian Islands. This valley is so sacred it can only be explored with a guide (page 340).

Sliding Sands Trail

BEST HIKES 27

WHAT TO EAT AND DRINK

LOCAL STYLE
The essence of local-style food is found in the form of plate lunch. This hearty meal typically features white rice, macaroni salad, and a choice of protein, such as Hawaiian pulled pork. Consider the pulled pork belly sandwich at **Three's Bar & Grill** in Kihei, South Maui (page 85), or the barbecued pork at **Tante's Island Cuisine** in Kahului, Central Maui (page 182).

HAWAIIAN REGIONAL CUISINE
Hawaiian Regional Cuisine dishes such as poke, Spam musubi, and haupia draw upon the influences of Japanese, Filipino, Tahitian, Chinese, and Portuguese cuisines. Try the exceptional ahi ginger poke at **Merriman's** in Kapalua, West Maui (page 141), or the ahi poke tacos at **808 on Main** in Wailuku, Central Maui (page 183).

fresh-caught mahimahi fish tacos

FISH TACOS
A staple on Maui in almost all restaurants across the island. For added flavor and island style, check out the **food trucks** in Central Maui (page 181).

LAU LAU
This traditional Hawaiian dish is filled with grated pork wrapped in a taro leaf and served with shredded fish. You can experience it at **Hawaiian Regional Cuisine** or **local-style restaurants** in areas such as Kihei and Pai'a (pages 85 and 272).

BIKINI BLONDE LAGER
When in Maui . . . try any number of island-brewed beers, like this lager at **Maui Brewing Company,** with locations in Kihei and West Maui (page 92).

MAI TAI
Although it's available across the island in many venues, you'll want to experience the mai tais crafted by **Monkeypod Kitchen** in Wailea and Ka'anapali (page 88).

BEST VIEWS

HALEAKALĀ
Haleakalā and Upcountry
At 10,023 ft (3,055 m) above sea level, you cannot go wrong here at sunrise or sunset (page 200).

SUNSET ON A KAPALUA BEACH
West Maui
West Maui hot spot Kapalua is filled with beaches, so pick your favorite (page 113). For an unforgettable dinner with grand sunset views, try **Merriman's** (page 141).

WAI'ANAPANAPA STATE PARK
The Road to Hana
This stunning Hana destination has easy beach access and mesmerizing ocean views (page 250).

'IAO VALLEY STATE MONUMENT
Central Maui
Green and lush, this mountainous tropical paradise is not to be missed. The 'Iao Needle itself, an erosional feature that rises 1,200 ft (365 m) from the valley floor, is scenic and the subject of many photos (page 165).

sunrise on Haleakalā

BEST SCENIC DRIVE

THE ROAD TO HANA

Driving Distance: *45 mi (72 km)*
Driving Time: *2 hours without stopping*
Start: *Pa'ia*
End: *Hana*

The island's most scenic drive is along Hana Highway, a 45-mi-long (72-km) stretch comprising Hawaii Routes 36 and 360. Known for its lush rainforests, waterfalls, black sand beaches, and breathtaking ocean views, the route stretches from Pa'ia to Hana, offering travelers unique stops and stunning landscapes that highlight Maui's natural beauty (page 244).

30 BEST OF THE BEST

BEST SNORKELING AND DIVING

MOLOKINI CRATER
South Maui
A crescent-shaped volcanic caldera off the southern coast of Maui, Molokini Crater is home to over 250 species of fish and offers crystal clear waters with 100-ft (30-m) visibility most days of the year (pages 68 and 70).

ULUA BEACH AND MOKAPU BEACH
South Maui
These neighboring Wailea beaches are South Maui's most easily accessible, making them ideal for beginning snorkelers. The rocky point between the two beaches teems with tropical reef fish (page 69).

HONOLUA BAY
West Maui
A world-renowned surf spot during winter, Honolua Bay has the island's best snorkeling during the calm, warm summer. Hawaiian green sea turtles are a common sight, as are parrotfish, octopuses, and the rare spinner dolphin (page 119).

NAPILI BAY AND KAPALUA BAY
West Maui
Within walking distance of each other on the island's northwestern coast, these two bays offer a sandy entry and shallow, protected conditions. Napili has more turtles, while Kapalua has more fish (page 119).

PU'U KEKA'A
West Maui
The island's most famous snorkeling spot, also known as Black Rock, is one of its best. This rocky promontory on the Ka'anapali strip is a magnet for sea turtles and reef fish (page 120).

HULOPO'E BEACH PARK
Lana'i
This Lana'i marine reserve has one of the healthiest reefs in Maui County and fronts a beach ranked as the nation's best. Come face-to-face with multihued parrotfish as they snack on colorful coral, or search the shallows for the humuhumunukunukuapua'a, Hawaii's state fish (page 304).

snorkeling off Maui

BEST SURFING

McGREGOR POINT
South Maui
This is a popular spot for advanced surfers, with the fastest right-hand wave in the world. It's also an ideal area to study surfing techniques. The best time to experience surfing here is afternoons, when the wind picks up (page 76).

HONOLUA BAY
West Maui
Honolua Bay is a place of local legend, with one of the best right-hand waves in the world during winter. If you're an expert surfer—and show respect to locals by waiting your turn in the lineup—you could end up snagging the wave of a lifetime (page 127).

D. T. FLEMING BEACH PARK
West Maui
This Kapalua beach is popular with bodyboarders and is best during the winter. It's less crowded than neighboring Honolua and much more user-friendly, but it is for intermediate to advanced surfers (page 113).

KITE BEACH
Central Maui
Kitesurfing was born here on Maui. While experienced kiters can take straight to the water, schools such as **Hawaiian Sailboard Techniques** provide lessons for visitors who are looking to pick up a new sport (page 173).

PA'IA BAY
The Road to Hana and East Maui
Walking distance from the center of town, Pa'ia Bay is one of the island's only real beach breaks. It's best for intermediate to advanced shortboarding and bodyboarding (page 257).

HO'OKIPA BEACH PARK
The Road to Hana and East Maui
The most popular break on the island's North Shore is also the center of the Pa'ia surf scene. Small waves are acceptable for beginners who are still learning, but during the large swells of winter, this becomes an amphitheater of towering 20-ft (6-m) surf for experts (page 264).

HAMOA BEACH
The Road to Hana and East Maui
More than just a beautiful beach, Hamoa has some of the best surf in East Maui. Intermediate and advanced surfers will find wind swell here any time of the year, even during summer when nowhere else on the island has waves (page 266).

32 BEST OF THE BEST

BEST ADVENTURE SPORTS

ZIP-LINING
Skyline Hawaii
West Maui

From kid-friendly short courses to stomach-churning screamers, zip-lining has rapidly become one of the island's most popular activities. While all companies provide a thrilling experience, Skyline Hawaii in Ka'anapali offers some of the best views (page 137).

PARAGLIDING
Paraglide Maui
Haleakalā and Upcountry

The Polipoli flying location has ideal conditions on a cool mountain slope with views gazing out over South Maui. The instructors at Paraglide Maui will get you soaring (page 222).

MOUNTAIN BIKING
Makawao Forest Reserve
Haleakalā and Upcountry

The slopes of this island are covered in biking trails, and Makawao Forest Reserve has among the best on Maui (page 218).

Moloka'i Forest Reserve
Moloka'i

For serious thrills try the off-road playground of the Moloka'i Forest Reserve (page 344).

mountain biking

BEST FAMILY FUN

WHALE-WATCHING
South Maui
Whale season is officially December-May on Maui, and while there are many charters from which to choose, **Pacific Whale Foundation** stands out for the variety of whale-watching cruises it offers and the expertise of its marine biologists. Children age six and under ride for free (page 53).

MAUI OCEAN CENTER
South Maui
The largest tropical reef aquarium in the western hemisphere, Maui Ocean Center has more than 60 permanent and seasonal exhibits, including outdoor tide pools, a sea turtle lagoon, and the grand centerpiece, an acrylic tunnel beneath a 750,000-gallon (2.8 million-liter) aquarium (page 52).

MOLOKINI CRATER
South Maui
A perfect half-day trip for the entire family—available through numerous charters—takes you just a few miles from Maui's shoreline to snorkel among the island's colorful marinelife at Molokini Crater, where the water is consistently calm and clear (page 68).

OLD LAHAINA LUAU
West Maui
One of the best family outings on the island includes hula lessons for all ages, lawn games, a delicious buffet, and a memorable stage show that reenacts island history, set against an imminently photographable sunset (page 148).

whale-watching off Maui

TOP SOUVENIRS

POLYNESIAN JEWELRY
Maui Master Jewelers in Makawao is the island's leading source for New Zealand bone and jade carvings as well as Tahitian pearl jewelry (page 223).

T-SHIRTS
Island T-shirts abound all over Maui, but there's great variety at **Kihei Kalama Village,** located in Kihei (page 83).

KEYCHAINS, CUPS, AND HATS
These easy-to-pack items are great gifts, and the best ones can be found at **Pacific Whale Foundation,** located at Ma'alaea Harbor Shops in South Maui (page 53).

Tahitian black pearl earrings

Old Lahaina Luau

NATIVE HAWAIIAN CULTURE ON MAUI

When Captain Cook first sighted Hawaii in 1778, there were an estimated 300,000 Hawaiians living in relative harmony with their ecological surroundings. By the late 1800s, the population of Hawaiians numbered about 50,000. Today, more than 240,000 people claim varying degrees of Hawaiian lineage.

POLYNESIAN ROOTS

Early Polynesian history remains an anthropological mystery, but it's believed that they were nomadic wanderers who migrated from both the Indian subcontinent and Southeast Asia through Indonesia, where they learned to sail and navigate on protected waterways. As they migrated, they honed their sailing skills until they could take on the Pacific. As they moved, they absorbed people from other cultures and races until they had coalesced into the Polynesians.

HAWAIIANS TODAY

The majority of people of Hawaiian descent, 240,000 or so, live on O'ahu, where they are particularly active in the hotel and entertainment fields. Ni'ihau, a privately owned island, is home to about 120 pure-blooded Hawaiians, representing the largest concentration of them, per capita, in the islands. The Robinson family, which owns the island, restricts visitors to invited guests only.

The second-largest concentration is on Moloka'i, where 2,700 Hawaiians make up 40 percent of that island's population.

FOOD

Although modern Hawaiian food is extremely meat-based, Hawaiians traditionally were nearly vegetarian, reserving meat for celebrations rather than daily meals. Traditional Hawaiian food can still be found, but a lot of it now is simply considered "local food" and blended with food from other cultures.

For ancient Hawaiians, the ocean was a great source of food, and they cultivated successful land crops such as taro, sweet potatoes, breadfruit, and sugarcane. They raised pigs and chickens for celebratory meals, although they wouldn't make use of the eggs. For more on local-style food and Hawaiian Regional Cuisine, see **What to Eat and Drink** (page 28).

HULA

The hula is more than an ethnic dance; it's the soul of Hawaii expressed in motion. Hula's legendary birthplace is in West Moloka'i. It began as a form of worship during religious ceremonies and was danced only by highly trained men. As time went on, however, women were allowed to learn the hula, and today both genders perform the dance equally.

During the 19th century, the hula almost vanished because the

36 BEST OF THE BEST

hula

missionaries considered it vile and heathen. King Kalakaua saved it during the late 1800s by forming his own troupe and encouraging the dancers to learn the old hula. Many of the original dances had been forgotten, but some were retained and are performed to this day.

Hula is art in swaying motion, and the true form is studied rigorously and taken seriously. Today, hula halau (schools) are active on every island, teaching hula and keeping the old ways and culture alive. Ancient hula is called hula kahiko, and modern renditions are known as hula auana. Performers still spend years perfecting their techniques.

Hula Lessons and Performances

- Old Lahaina Luau (page 148)
- The Shops at Wailea (page 84)
- Moloka'i Ka Hula Piko festival (page 21)

ARTS AND CRAFTS

Since everything in old Hawaii had to be fashioned by hand, almost every object was either a genuine work of art or the product of a highly refined craft. With the colonization of the indigenous population, most of the old ways disappeared, including the old arts and crafts. Most authentic Hawaiian art by master craftspeople exists only in museums. But with the resurgence of connecting to Hawaiian roots as part of the Hawaiian Renaissance, many old arts are being revitalized, and their legacy lives on in a number of proficient artists.

CANOES

The most respected artisans in old Hawaii were the canoe makers. With little more than a stone adze and a pump drill, they built sleek and seaworthy canoes that could carry 200 people and last for generations. The main hull was usually a gigantic koa log, and the gunwale planks were minutely drilled and sewn to the

weaving

sides with sennit rope. Small family-size canoes with outriggers were used for fishing and perhaps carried a spear rack; large oceangoing double-hulled canoes were used for migration and warfare.

CARVING

Wood was one of the primary materials used by Hawaiian craftspeople. They almost exclusively relied on koa because of its density, strength, and natural luster. It was turned into canoes, wood ware, calabashes, and furniture used by the aliʻi (nobility). Temple idols were another major product of wood carving. A variety of stone artifacts were also turned out, including poi pounders, mirrors, fish sinkers, and small idols.

WEAVING

Hawaiians became the best basket makers and mat weavers in all of Polynesia. Ulana (woven mats) were made from lauhala (pandanus) leaves. Once the leaf was split, the spine was removed and the fibers stored in large rolls. When needed these would be soaked, pounded, and then fashioned into various floor coverings and sleeping mats. Intricate geometric patterns were woven in, and the edges were rolled and well fashioned. Coconut palms were not used to make mats in old Hawaii, but a wide variety of basketry was fashioned from the aerial root ʻieʻie.

LEI MAKING

Any flower or blossom can be strung into a lei, but the most common are orchids or the lovely-smelling plumeria. Lei are all beautiful, but special lei are highly prized by those who know what to look for. Of the different stringing styles, the most common is kui—stringing the flower through the middle or side. Most "airport-quality" lei are of this type. The humuhumu style, reserved for making flat lei, is made by sewing flowers and ferns to a ti, banana, or sometimes hala leaf. A humuhumu lei makes an

lei

excellent hatband. Wili is the winding together of greenery, ferns, and flowers into short, bouquet-type lengths. The most traditional form is hili, which requires no stringing at all but involves braiding fragrant ferns and leaves such as maile. If flowers are interwoven, the hili becomes the haku style, the most difficult and most beautiful type of lei.

LEARNING MORE

Bailey House Museum
Central Maui
The museum features authentic Hawaiian artifacts and various events throughout the year. It also offers the best compilation of Hawaiiana literature on the island (page 163).

Native Intelligence
Central Maui
This store in Wailuku not only sells hand-carved jewelry and lei-making supplies, it also offers occasional classes on traditional Hawaiian culture (page 181).

Hui No'eau Visual Arts Center
Haleakalā and Upcountry
This 10-acre (4-ha) estate was built in 1917 and transformed in 1934 into a spectacular center for the arts. Touring the grounds is free, and the gallery hosts the work of local artists and has rotating exhibitions. You can pick up a self-guided tour ($6) of the property or take an hour-long guided tour ($12) (page 204).

Lana'i Culture and Heritage Center
Lana'i
The center features displays pertaining to the days of ancient Hawaii through the end of the Dole plantation. There are black-and-white photographs from Lana'i's ranching days as well as artifacts, such as stone adzes, poi pounders, and a 10-ft (3-m) 'ihe pololu (a wooden spear used as a weapon, similar to a jousting lance) (page 294).

Halawa Valley Falls Cultural Hike
Moloka'i
This memorable tour through a private family-owned property highlights traditional Hawaiian protocol. The presentation offers a better understanding of the region and is filled with historical facts (page 340).

TRAVELING SUSTAINABLY

Sustainable travel is crucial in Hawaii to protect its fragile ecosystems, preserve unique cultural heritage, and ensure that its natural resources remain vibrant and accessible for future generations. Moreover, healthy respect for the island and its nature, people, and culture is essential to a meaningful vacation. Just as each local is an ambassador for Hawaii, every visitor is a representative of the tourism industry. When visitors show respect for these islands, locals take notice. Some general guidelines:

RESPECT THE LAND

In traditional Hawaiian culture, the land is sacred above all. The earth and the sea provide us with sustenance, and to disrespect the land is the ultimate offense. The concept of land ownership is foreign to traditional Hawaiian culture, which sees us as temporary stewards of the land. Pick up your opala (trash), stay off sensitive coral reefs, throw cigarette butts in proper receptacles, and help keep the valleys and shores as pristine as possible.

RESPECT LANDOWNERS' WISHES

Some unscrupulous travel publications encourage trespassing. As a result, far too many visitors walk across private land even when signs tell them not to. Poor behavior and lawsuits have led to restricted access for some formerly public sites. If you see a sign that says Kapu (Keep Out), No Trespassing, or Private Property, please respect the landowners' wishes.

RESPECT THE CULTURE

Hawaii has a culture that is unique in the world, and experiencing it is one of the best parts of visiting the islands. Tourism is the state's largest industry, but ultimately we are guests. Embrace the Hawaiian way of living and slow down for a little while.

RESPECT MARINELIFE

Don't feed the fish when snorkeling! Outside food disrupts their natural feeding behaviors, leading to dependency on human food, which lacks the nutrients they need, and can harm their health. It also disturbs the balance of the marine ecosystem, as fish begin to crowd areas frequented by humans, which can damage coral reefs and reduce biodiversity.

sunset along South Maui's coast

SOUTH MAUI

If one word defines South Maui, it's "beaches." South Maui is graced with dozens of sandy stretches just waiting for your footprints.

The island's longest beach is Sugar Beach; one of its smallest is Pa'ako Cove. The sound of waves lapping against the palm-lined sand is a year-round reality in South Maui. There are enough beaches that a three-week vacation isn't enough time to possibly see them all. Because much of South Maui actually faces west, the end of each day is punctuated by a sunset that somehow outdoes the last.

It's also one of the state's hottest areas, particularly in Kihei, where the smell of coconut oil wafts on the late-morning trade winds. Mornings are for stand-up paddling and snorkeling, and afternoons are for finding a cold drink and settling in for the sunset. At the Maui Ocean Center in Ma'alaea, you can explore the beauty of the underwater world regardless of the conditions outside, and at Molokini Crater, set just offshore, you can snorkel, dive, splash, and swim in Maui's clearest waters.

This is also Maui's fastest-growing zip code, where rows of condos and luxury resorts seem to populate every shore. Despite this hypercharged growth, however, there's still a wild side in South Maui once you venture south toward Makena, where nudist drum circles still take place on the hidden sands of Little Beach, and hiking trails follow a rocky shore that was once the pathway of kings.

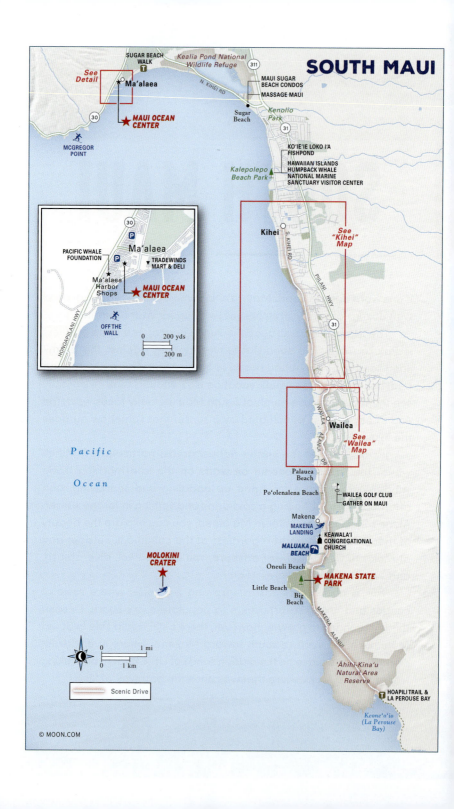

TOP 3

⭐ **1. MAUI OCEAN CENTER:** Surround yourself with sharks, eagle rays, and dozens of fish, all without getting your hair wet (page 52).

⭐ **2. MAKENA STATE PARK:** Enjoy a beach day or take in the glorious sunset along a golden shore (page 60).

⭐ **3. MOLOKINI CRATER:** Immerse yourself in crystal-clear waters at this volcanic caldera, one of the best snorkeling and diving sites in the world (pages 68 and 70).

SOUTH MAUI 3 WAYS

HALF DAY

1 Take a morning walk along **Sugar Beach,** which boasts the longest stretch of sand on Maui. Relish the stunning views of Lanaʻi, Kahoʻolawe, and Molokini in the distance, and check out the paddlers as this spot is home to many canoe clubs.

2 Enjoy a delicious island breakfast at **Nalu's South Shore Grill.** Consider the Heavy Kine Breakfast (two eggs any style, with homemade furikake-garlic breakfast potatoes and choice of Portuguese sausage, applewood-smoked bacon, turkey-apple sausage, or Black Forest ham) or the Island Pancakes.

3 Head to **Maui Ocean Center** for several hours and experience sealife up close in this impressive aquarium setting by the sea. Consider a 60-minute exclusive behind-the-scenes tour led by a dedicated marine naturalist.

4 For a late lunch, nosh at **Paia Fishmarket** in Kihei Kalama Village, then spend an hour perusing the various retail huts.

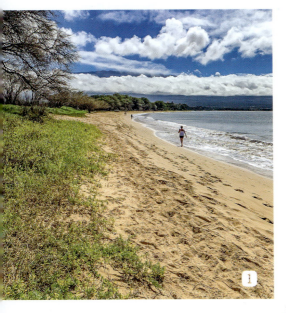

FULL DAY

1 Wake up early and board the *Kai Kanani* for its 6:15am sunrise snorkel. The tour leaves from Maluaka Beach in Makena and gets you out to **Molokini Crater** before all the other boats arrive. Spend an hour snorkeling and enjoy a continental breakfast before returning to the beach at 9:45am, with a full day left to explore. If you get a chance, fill up your reusable water bottle before you depart the boat.

2 You'll next make the drive to the "end of the road," hugging the coast and passing over the island's most recent lava flow. To stretch your legs, hike for 30-45 minutes on the **Hoapili Trail,** stopping to photograph the sandy beaches and watch for dolphins or whales.

3 Back at your car, make the drive to **Makena State Park,** better known as Big Beach, and grab a quick lunch from whichever food truck is parked outside the first entrance.

4 After lunch, spend an hour strolling the beach or watching the local bodyboarders, and drive back to **Maluaka Beach** in Makena if you need to shower off.

5 Next, park in the lot for Ulua Beach and walk to the **Andaz Maui** for a drink at one of their on-site bars, which are popular with locals as well as visitors.

6 Finish the day with a stroll along the **Wailea Coastal Walk,** where you can walk north past Mokapu Beach and watch the sunset from Keawakapu—leaving time to get back to your car before it's completely dark.

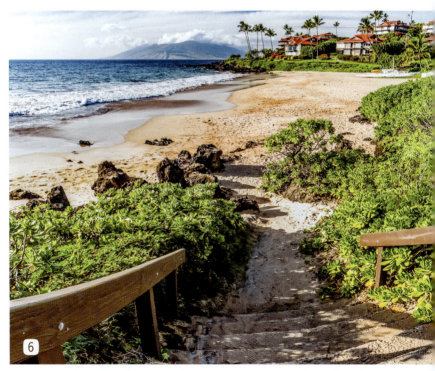

SOUTH MAUI 3 WAYS 49

AVOID THE CROWDS

1 Early risers win, as the best time to beat the crowds is to venture out and explore before 11am. Consider a morning stroll on the **Kamaole Beach Walk.** Starting at Charley Young Beach, the trail connects the trio of Kamaole Beaches and offers scenic coastal views.

2 Spa day anyone? For something truly unique, pamper yourself at **808 Wellness Spa & Healing Center,** where you can begin with a luxury facial, then move on to a 90-minute massage or cranial sacral treatment. You'll float out of the place.

3 **Kihei Caffe** is a fine spot for lunch. The catfish po' boy sandwich, burgers, and fresh salads are among the menu highlights.

4 Plan a tour of **Koʻieʻie Loko Iʻa Fishpond,** a premier destination and an experience that doesn't feel as if you're inundated with hundreds of other people. This remarkable 500-year-old piece of land covers 6 acres (2.4 ha) and produces about 2,000 pounds (900 kg) of fish annually. Private tours are led by knowledgeable guides.

5 Although **Gather on Maui** is best known for cocktails and the wide range of liquors on offer, it's also a great no-wait dinner spot, thanks to its spacious, mostly outdoor, covered dining room. Consider the Maui-style ahi poke, any of the day's fresh catches, or the famous smash burger, made island-style and featuring ground wagyu patties.

ORIENTATION AND PLANNING

ORIENTATION

South Maui runs in a long, narrow column and is never far from the coast. To drive from **Ma'alaea,** the northernmost part, to the end of the road in Makena takes approximately 30 minutes and passes through Kihei and Wailea. The high-end resorts are found in **Wailea,** whereas **Kihei** is laden with oceanfront condos and more affordable options for dining. **Makena** is where the coast gets wild and development disappears, yet it is close enough to the Wailea resorts to reach by pedaling a bike. Kihei, the commercial hub of South Maui, is sandwiched in a strip between **South Kihei Road** and **Pi'ilani Highway,** while Ma'alaea is the site of the harbor and the windy gateway to West Maui.

PLANNING YOUR TIME

South Maui could be either your base for exploring the rest of the island or a sunny, sandy strip of paradise you have no plans to leave. Exploring the wild hinterlands of Makena should take about half a day, enjoying the hiking, snorkeling, beaches, and legendary sunsets. If you aren't staying at one of the Wailea resorts, it's still nice to spend a whole day at one of the popular beaches, strolling the Wailea Coastal Walk and dining at the fancy resort restaurants. If you are staying in Wailea, do yourself a favor and spend one day where you don't leave the resort—just pool time, beach time, and maybe a massage to enjoy the luxurious surroundings. Kihei, on the other hand, deserves two days: two mornings to try out two different beaches and two afternoons to try out two different lunch spots. Ma'alaea requires only a few hours, as the only reason to go is to visit the Maui Ocean Center or catch a boat to Molokini Crater.

HIGHLIGHTS

MA'ALAEA
★ Maui Ocean Center

192 Ma'alaea Rd.; 808/270-7000; www.mauioceancenter.com; 9am-5pm daily; $39 adults, $28 children
Maui Ocean Center boasts the largest tropical reef aquarium in the western hemisphere. This 3-acre (1.2-ha) marine park has more than 60 exhibits and the nation's largest collection of live tropical coral. Small children will enjoy the tidepool exhibits and green sea turtle lagoon. Experience the 54-ft-long (16.5-m) acrylic tunnel beneath a 750,000-gallon (2.8 million-liter) aquarium filled with dozens of rays and sharks, standing in a dry space and watching a tiger shark float right over you, or contemplating how spotted eagle rays look like birds as they buzz circles just a few feet from your head. The 139-seat 3-D dome theater has an adjacent 1,200-sq-ft (111-sq-m) exhibit hall that chronicles the nomadic lifestyle and other behaviors of humpback whales.

The center is also a fantastic resource for learning about native

BEST SUNSET VIEWS

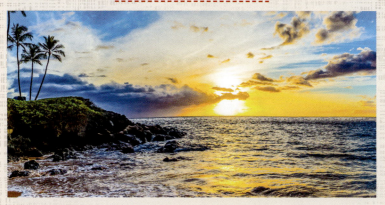

sunset at Ulua Beach

Ulua Beach (page 59) rests just below the Andaz Maui resort, making it easily accessible. Park on Ulua Beach Road, behind the Andaz. A short walk down to the shore and you'll have your pick of places to park yourself. We suggest heading directly to the small beach at the Andaz, where you can enjoy a stellar sunset experience.

Hawaiian culture, with exhibits on everything from Polynesian wayfaring to ancient Hawaiian fishponds. This is one of the island's best attractions for children as well as a rainy-day activity. Its popularity can mean crowds, however, so visit in the morning when the facility opens. There's a self-guided tour through the exhibits, and if you want to have some of them all to yourself, head directly to the last exhibit and work your way backward toward the front. Expect to spend about two hours. Book online for the family pass to save up to 15 percent.

Pacific Whale Foundation

300 Ma'alaea Rd., Ste. 211; 808/249-8811; www.pacificwhale.org

After spending several months feeding off the shores of Alaska, humpback whales migrate to the shallower waters around Maui December-May to mate and give birth. This gives visitors one heck of a water show, with whale breaches, blowholing, and lobtailing. The Pacific Whale Foundation, a non-profit noted for its ocean advocacy, offers a dozen unique whale-watching excursions with team members who have deep knowledge of marinelife. Departures are from Ma'alaea Harbor with standard two-hour morning and afternoon excursions (Nov.-Apr.; $87-187) that include talks by marine biologists and bar snacks.

Specialty tours include the **Ultimate Whale Watch with Experts** (8am Wed.-Mon.; $187 adults, $112

Maui Ocean Center (top); whale-watching with Pacific Whale Foundation (middle); boardwalk at Kealia Pond National Wildlife Refuge (bottom)

children), a three-hour tour led by marine naturalists, with underwater hydrophones to listen for whale songs, downloadable whale photos, and lunch. All trips guarantee a whale sighting; if whales aren't spotted, the foundation offers another trip for free. Become a Pacific Whale Foundation member ($75-1,000) and you'll help play a part in advancing ongoing ocean research. Added bonus: You receive discounts on future excursions and events.

KIHEI

Kealia Pond National Wildlife Refuge

milepost 6, Maui Veterans Hwy.; 808/875-1582; www.fws.gov/refuge/kealia_pond

The road between Ma'alaea and North Kihei passes through a large mudflat that parallels the shore. Most of this area is dry during summer, but on the inland side of the highway is the nearly 700-acre (285-ha) Kealia Pond National Wildlife Refuge. Visit to catch a glimpse of native bird species such as the ae'o (Hawaiian stilt) and 'alae ke'oke'o (Hawaiian coot). Even if you aren't an avid birder, the boardwalk off North Kihei Road is an informative place to stretch your legs and learn about the threats facing the island's species.

Ko'ie'ie Loko I'a Fishpond

726 S. Kihei Rd.; 808/359-1172; www.mauifishpondassociation.org

Inside Kalepolepo Beach Park in North Kihei, the Ko'ie'ie Loko I'a Fishpond is the most prominent example of ancient Hawaiian life between Ma'alaea and Wailea. Estimated to be around 500 years old, it covered 6 acres (2.4 ha) and produced about 2,000 pounds (900 kg) of fish annually. It was formed by rocks passed

SOUTH MAUI

by hand from the uplands to the sea, and thanks to the hard work of the **'Ao'ao O Na Loko I'a O Maui**—volunteers who have been working since 1996 to restore the ancient fishpond—it can be viewed any time by visiting Kalepolepo Beach Park. Contact the organization and inquire about guided cultural canoe trips. Prearrange a visit for a full tour, which varies during the week.

Hawaiian Islands Humpback Whale National Marine Sanctuary Visitor Center
726 S. Kihei Rd.; 808/879-2818; www.hawaiihumpbackwhale.noaa.gov; 9:30am-2:30pm Mon.-Fri.

Next to Kalepolepo Beach Park, the Hawaiian Islands Humpback Whale National Marine Sanctuary Visitor Center is a phenomenal educational resource for anyone with an interest in humpback whales. You can find plates of baleen, krill in a jar, and free binoculars out on the deck to look for the whales in winter. There are also displays on turtles, dolphins, manta rays, and teams that untangle whales. This is an easy stop when traveling from Ma'alaea back to Kihei or Wailea. The Ko'ie'ie Loko I'a Fishpond is in front of the compound, which makes this a fun and educational side trip when visiting Kalepolepo Beach.

MAKENA AND BEYOND
Keawala'i Congregational Church
5300 Makena Rd.; 808/879-5557; www.keawalai.org

In an area of the island that's developing rapidly, there's a timeless beauty to Keawala'i Congregational Church. Set on a palm- and ti-lined cove and bathed in the gentle sound of the surf, Keawala'i was founded in 1832 and constructed in 1855. The original structure was made of pili grass, and this Protestant church served as one of the main centers of worship in southern Maui. The grass was eventually replaced with coral, and in 1856 the church raised $70 to purchase a bell from the United States, then a different country. It took that bell almost three years to travel to Hawaii, and in February 1862 it was lifted into the belfry, where it still hangs today.

Unfortunately, in the mid-1800s, when Makena's streams began to run dry from excessive logging upslope, much of Makena's population

Hawaiian Islands Humpback Whale National Marine Sanctuary Visitor Center (left); Keawala'i Congregational Church (right)

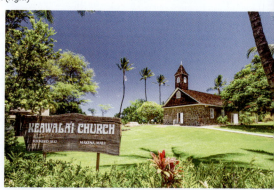

moved elsewhere. Keawala'i slid into disrepair, and when thieves pillaged it in the years after World War II, the community opted to band together to bring the church back to life. Today, after decades of renovations, Keawala'i is as beautiful as at its height. United Church of Christ services are conducted in the Hawaiian language at 10am on Sunday, although visits to the church grounds are possible any time of day.

BEST BEACHES

The morning hours are the best time to hit the beach in South Maui. In the afternoon, the pockets of beaches in south Kihei and Wailea have the best chance of being sunny and calm. Winter months aren't as windy, and this is also when humpback whales can be seen leaping offshore. Is it any wonder so many snowbirds choose to spend the winter here? it's an action-packed hub of surfers, paddlers, and beachgoers soaking up rays.

KIHEI
Kalepolepo Beach Park

Right next to the Hawaiian Islands Humpback Whale National Marine Sanctuary, Kalepolepo Beach Park is Kihei's most underrated beach. What makes this little-visited enclave so special is **Koʻieʻie Loko Iʻa Fishpond**, which has been masterfully restored in recent years by local volunteers. Aside from its rich historical value, the fishpond is great for families with young children since it's a protected area for swimming.

The Cove

Otherwise known as "the surf lesson spot," this beach at the south end of Kalama Park is known for its top-notch people-watching. The beach itself is just a small strip of sand, but it provides a front-row view for watching people surf. There's a volleyball court and shops across the street, and while it isn't Kihei's nicest beach,

Kamaole II (top); Keawakapu Beach (bottom)

BEST BEACHES 57

Kamaole Beach Parks

The Kamaole Beach Parks form the core of Kihei's beach scene. Grassy areas run parallel to the roadway, and all of the parks have showers, restrooms, picnic tables, and barbecue grills for a relaxing sunset meal. The best way to experience these beaches is to stroll along the coast and link all three together. The lava rock headlands can be rough on your feet, and kiawe (mesquite) trees drop thorns, so wear footwear if you walk all three beaches. **Kamaole I** has a beach volleyball court on the north side of the park. The northern end is commonly referred to by locals as **Charley Young Beach,** which can be good for snorkeling. The tide pools between **Kamaole II** and **Kamaole III** are great for exploring, and when you reach the southern end of Kam III, there's a walking trail that runs for 0.75 mi (1.2 km) to the **Kihei Boat Ramp.**

Kam I and Kam II have street parking, whereas larger Kam III has its own parking lot exclusively for beachgoers. Kam III is also the party spot where locals truck in horseshoes, ice chests, and bounce houses for their three-year-old's birthday party.

Keawakapu Beach

Aside from Kam III, Keawakapu is Kihei's most popular beach. This long stretch of sand is more protected from the wind, and a small shop on the north end of the beach rents out stand-up paddleboards, kayaks, and snorkeling gear. This beach is a bustle of snorkelers entering the water and kids splashing in the surf in the morning, and by late afternoon, it changes into the perfect perch for sunset. Snorkeling is best around the north and south headlands, and if you're feeling up for a really long stroll, you can connect with the **Wailea Coastal Walk** at the southern end of the beach.

Wailea Beach

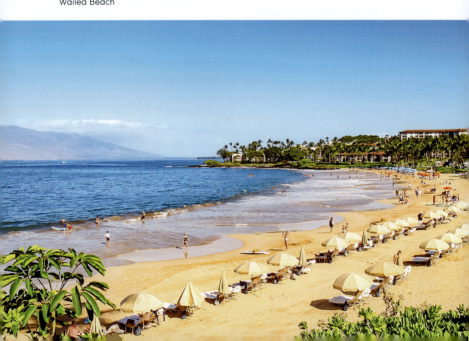

WAILEA

Ulua Beach and Mokapu Beach

Ulua and Mokapu are the northernmost of Wailea's beaches, separated by a small grassy headland. Mokapu is on the north side of the hill, Ulua is on the south, and the point that separates the two is where you'll find the most marinelife and one of Wailea's best snorkeling spots. Thanks to a prime location on a grassy lava point with palm trees and rocks, the vibrant sunsets at Ulua Beach stand out, particularly if there are light clouds. If you're staying at one of the Wailea resorts, you can reach the beaches by strolling along the Wailea Coastal Walk. If you are driving, there are two small public parking lots that fill up early; arrive before 9am.

Wailea Beach

Home to Maui's "see and be seen" crowd, Wailea Beach epitomizes Wailea. Fronted by the Grand Wailea and the Four Seasons Maui, this is a beach where CEOs and professional athletes mingle with regular travelers. The beach is constantly abuzz with activity, such as snorkeling

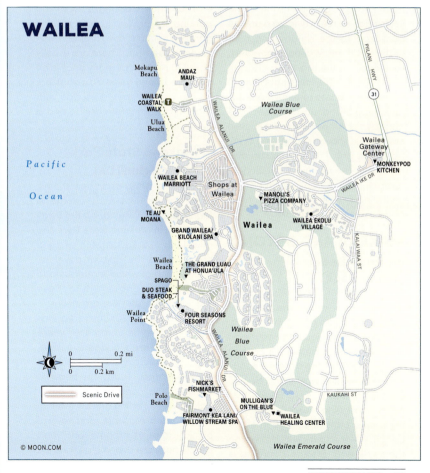

BEST BEACHES 59

around **Wailea Point,** stand-up paddleboard rentals, outrigger canoe tours, and dozens of visitors playing in the surf who are happy to just be on Maui. Despite the private nature of the resorts, public access to the beach is quite easy, as there is a large public parking lot just before the entrance to the Four Seasons. In the parking lot are public restrooms and showers.

Polo Beach

Polo Beach is the southernmost of Wailea's resort beaches and is the southern terminus of the Wailea Coastal Walk. The cloud-white Fairmont Kea Lani dominates the shore, its Arabian spires providing a unique backdrop to the shimmering blue waters. Of all Wailea's beaches, Polo Beach is the most popular with locals because the large public parking area is a convenient place for launching stand-up paddleboards and kayaks. Amenities include public restrooms, showers, and one small barbecue grill. Polo Beach can also be good for boogie boarding in summer, and a small activity booth on the north side of the beach rents paddleboards and kayaks.

MAKENA AND BEYOND

Palauea Beach (White Rock)

Palauea Beach, otherwise known as White Rock, is a perfect spot for snorkeling, scuba diving, swimming, and lounging. Palauea translates to "lazy," and there's ample opportunity to be just that along its white sandy stretches, which are less crowded than at Wailea or Polo Beach, just north. Snorkeling is excellent around the rocky points at either end of the beach, while scuba diving is best on the south end. Boogie boarding is

exceptional during south swells, and when the waters are calmer, they're ideal for wading and swimming—great for kids and adults. While there aren't any restrooms or showers, you can find all those amenities at **Polo Beach,** just a five-minute walk away.

Po'olenalena Beach

Once frequented only by locals, Po'olenalena Beach can now get so busy it's tough to find a space in the potholed parking lot. There are volleyball games on Sunday afternoon, and the beach is a favorite for watching the sunset. On the north end, a small trail leads from the parking lot around a rocky point, bringing you to a cove that isn't visible from the road. There are usually about 10 percent as many people on the cove beach as on Po'olenalena. It's the perfect spot to escape with a beach chair, an umbrella, and a good book.

★ Makena State Park

BIG BEACH (ONELOA)

Among the string of golden shores, none can hold a sandy candle to Big Beach, or Oneloa. As the largest beach in Makena State Park, this mile-long (1.6-km) stretch of sand has avoided the rush of development, much of which is attributed to the grassroots movement to "Save Makena." Sunsets here are stellar.

In the early 1970s this area was a famous hippie commune where hundreds of draft-dodgers, nudists, and dropouts camped out back in the kiawe trees. Today, the beach is family-friendly and is a prime destination for snorkeling and swimming. Lifeguards are on site, and several picnic tables, restrooms, and food concessions are near the parking lot.

LITTLE BEACH

Although Big Beach visitors have since put their pants on, the same can't be said for neighboring Little Beach—the island's official clothing-optional venue, just over the north side of the bluff. There's an anachronistic aura that permeates Little Beach, where simply clambering from one side to the other can transport you back to an era when life was easy and it was hip to be free.

On Sunday nights, the most happening thing in Makena is the **drum circle** at sunset on Little Beach. More of a people-watching spectacle, the event features drummers, fire dancers, hippies, nudists, and curious onlookers. It definitely isn't for everyone, but if you want a bit of counterculture or are up for enlightening conversation, climb the trail to Little Beach in the hour just before sunset. If you plan to stay late, park outside the gate of the first entrance of Makena State Park.

ONEULI BEACH

You did it—you found a black-sand beach. The famous black-sand beach is in Hana, at Wai'anapanapa State Park, and Oneuli Beach in Makena State Park is dark brown and less famous. This hidden spot is a popular place for locals to kick back and fish, and there's good snorkeling at the south end of the bay only on the clearest and calmest days. The main draw, aside from the sand, is the lack of crowds, but note that the access road is potholed and bumpy.

Little Beach at Makena State Park

sunset at Keawakapu Beach

TOP BEACH
MALUAKA BEACH

Directly in front of the Makena Golf & Beach Club, Maluaka Beach is everything you've ever wanted in a beach. Locals refer to it as Prince Beach, since the beach club used to be a hotel called the Maui Prince. You'll find waters perfect for stand-up paddleboarding in the morning, good snorkeling around the north end, fun waves for boogie boarding during the summer, ample parking, restrooms and showers, and a grassy area for relaxing.

SCENIC DRIVES

KIHEI TO MAKENA
Driving Distance: *8.6 mi (13.8 km)*
Driving Time: *30 minutes*
Start: *Kihei*
End: *Keone'o'io (La Perouse Bay)*

Begin this drive from Kihei via South Kihei Road, a beautiful coastal route located on the island's southwestern shore. The road is lined with a mix of charming local shops, restaurants, and beachside parks like Kamaole I, II, and III. These popular beaches are known for their golden sands and clear waters, ideal for swimming, snorkeling, and watching the sunset. The area is lively yet relaxed, offering a blend of natural beauty and laid-back island culture.

South Kihei Road eventually turns to Wailea Alanui Drive as you pass through Wailea-Makena, home to luxurious resorts, world-class golf courses, and stunning ocean views. Keep driving toward the southern end of Makena, and just as the asphalt gives way to a gravel parking lot, you have arrived in a must-see destination known as Keone'o'io, or La Perouse Bay. The lava fields you drove over on the way to La Perouse are remnants of Haleakalā's last eruption. The bay is named for the French explorer Jean-François de Galaup, comte de Lapérouse, who in 1786 was the first European to set foot on Maui at this very spot. As you enter the parking area, there's a stone structure memorializing this event.

Keone'o'io (La Perouse Bay)

BEST HIKES AND WALKS

KIHEI
Sugar Beach Walk
Distance: *5 mi (8 km) one-way*
Duration: *2.5-3 hours*
Elevation Gain: *negligible*
Effort: *easy*
Trailhead: *Haycraft Park or Kenolio Park*

Hiking in Kihei is barefoot sandy strolls down the beach. For the island's longest uninterrupted beach walk, 5-mi-long (8-km) Sugar Beach runs between Kihei and Ma'alaea. You can access the beach from Haycraft Park on the Ma'alaea side, from Kenolio Park on the Kihei side, or at any of the access points along North Kihei Road. It does get windy here in the afternoons.

Kamaole Beach Walk
Distance: *1.5-2 mi (2.4-3.2 km) one-way*
Duration: *45-60 minutes*

Elevation Gain: *negligible*
Effort: *easy*
Trailhead: *Charley Young Beach*

Another popular coastal walk in Kihei connects the trio of Kamaole beaches, following the trails around their headlands. Starting at Charley Young Beach on the north end of Kamaole I (park in the lot on Kaiau Place), you can walk to the south end of Kamaole III along the shore and around the rocky points. Bring footwear as some rocks around the headlands can be sharp.

To extend the coastal walk a little farther, consider the short 0.5-mi (0.8-km) walking path that parallels the coast from the southern end of Kamaole III Beach to the Kihei Boat Ramp. Along the way you will pass informative signs about the coastal dune system and the u'au kani seabirds that nest in the dunes. There are a few benches sprinkled along the walking path for resting or, in winter, watching for whales.

WAILEA
Wailea Coastal Walk
Distance: *3.5 mi (5.6 km) round-trip*
Duration: *2-4 hours*
Elevation Gain: *negligible*

Effort: *easy*
Trailhead: *Ulua Beach*

If your idea of a hike means throwing on some Lululemon, talking on your iPhone, and stopping to pick up some Starbucks, then the paved 3.5-mi (5.6-km) round-trip Wailea Coastal Walk will be your favorite hike on the island. The pathway runs from Ulua Beach to Polo Beach and is undeniably gorgeous, passing a host of native coastal plants put in to revitalize the area's natural foliage. You'll also pass the Grand Wailea, Four Seasons, Kea Lani, Marriott, Wailea Beach Villas, and Andaz Maui. To reach the "trailhead" for the walkway, park in the public lot at Ulua Beach, at the bottom of Ulua Beach Road, or in the public lot on the southern end of the trail at Polo Beach, at the bottom of Kaukahi Street. At the far northern end, the walkway becomes sand and traverses the dunes past Mokapu Beach, where it links to Keawakapu in Kihei. In front of the Marriott, you can watch whales in winter through rented binoculars ($2).

MAKENA AND BEYOND
Hoapili Trail and La Perouse
Distance: *5.5-6.5 mi (8.9-10.5 km) round-trip*
Duration: *3-4 hours*
Elevation Gain: *344 ft*
Effort: *moderate-strenuous*
Trailhead: *La Perouse Bay parking lot*

Hot, barren, and in the middle of nowhere, the Hoapili Trail (also known as the King's Highway) isn't as much about hiking as about stepping back in time, introducing you to a side of the island most visitors never see. The trail was once an ancient Hawaiian walking path reserved for

aerial view of Wailea Coastal Walk

royalty. In 1824, sections of the trail were reconstructed, and the road took on a structure that remains untouched to this day.

To find the trail, drive south on Makena Alanui Road until it dead-ends at **La Perouse Bay parking lot,** 3.1 mi (5 km) past the first entrance to Big Beach. You'll see the trail paralleling the shore and weaving south along the coast. Before you set out, remember that there is no shade and the trail traverses jagged 'a'a lava that's so sharp you'll want proper hiking boots. Since much of this hike is outside cell phone range, it's important to be prepared with food and water. Reduce the chance of overheating by starting early in the morning.

After you've followed the shoreline for 0.7 mi (1.1 km), passing a couple of pockets of sand and sometimes feral black goats, you'll see an abandoned lava rock structure off the right side of the trail. This is the popular surfing spot known as **Laps** (short for **La Perouse**), and on large south swells you can see death-defying surfers riding waves over jagged sharp lava. After the surf spot, the trail climbs 500 ft (152 m) before arriving at a junction and veering off to the left. A sign informs you that you're entering the **King's Highway** and to respect the historic sites. The sign also indicates that Kanaio Beach is 2 mi (3.2 km) ahead.

At approximately 1.5 mi (2.4 km), take the short spur trail down to **Keawanaku Beach,** where you're almost guaranteed to have the beach to yourself. Look for a short lone palm tree springing from the black lava field surrounded by a grove of kiawe trees, then keep an eye out for the trail down to the shore. Although rocky, the trail is

Sugar Beach (top); Kamaole Beach Walk (middle); Hoapili Trail (bottom)

BEST HIKES AND WALKS 67

coral reef formation in Molokini Crater (left); Molokini Crater (right)

noticeable, and if you find yourself asking, "Am I still on the trail?" then you probably aren't. After Keawanaku, the trail continues for 1 mi (1.6 km) to the coast at **Kanaio Beach,** a salt-and-pepper-colored shore of black lava rock and sun-bleached coral. You'll notice the remnants of multiple structures, once part of an ancient fishing village.

Although Kanaio Beach is the turnaround point for most hikers, a sandy road continues from Kanaio Beach and winds along the coast. About 1 mi (1.6 km)—another 20 minutes of walking—from Kanaio brings you to a shore that's completely bathed in bleached white coral, and on the southern end of the "white beach" is an ancient Hawaiian heiau (temple) set out on the point. It looks much the same now as it must have when it was built.

The King's Highway continues to Highway 31 on the "back road to Hana." To reach the highway, however, requires an overnight stay along the trail; camping is permitted along the shore from points east of Kanaio Beach.

SNORKELING AND DIVING

SNORKELING SPOTS
Ma'alaea
★ MOLOKINI CRATER

When it comes to snorkeling, what Ma'alaea is known for is the harbor that serves as the starting point for boats to Molokini Crater, a half-submerged volcanic caldera that rises in 300 ft (90 m) of water. Nowhere else in Hawaii is the water this consistently calm and clear. The back of Molokini Crater drops to almost 300 ft (90 m), but inside the bowl, where snorkel boats tie up, is only about 40 ft (12 m) deep, and the best snorkeling is along the rim of the crater in 15 ft (4.5 m) of water. At Molokini you have a great chance of finding colorful parrotfish, endemic reef species, octopuses, eels, and—if you're lucky—maybe a harmless whitetip reef shark.

Because it's so massively popular, Molokini is a place where it can sometimes seem like there are far more humans than fish. Avoid crowds by booking your trip for as early in the day as possible, and schedule your activity early in your trip, since you'll probably be waking up early anyway with a little bit of jet lag. Nearly all boats leave for Molokini from Ma'alaea Harbor. Three rafts and most scuba-diving boats leave from Kihei Boat Ramp. At Makena, the sailing catamaran *Kai Kanani* departs from Maluaka Beach; its early trip is one of the first to arrive at Molokini.

Wailea

ULUA BEACH AND MOKAPU BEACH

The best locations for snorkeling in Wailea are Ulua Beach and Mokapu Beach, listed together because the rocky point that separates them is where you'll find the most marinelife. Ulua, the southernmost, is more protected and offers a gentle, sandy entry. This is the perfect spot for beginning snorkelers. Morning hours are calm and are the best time for finding turtles. Winter months have the best visibility.

Makena and Beyond

MAKENA LANDING

The best snorkeling in Makena is at Makena Landing. The entry can be a little challenging, but once you make it out past the shallow areas, you'll be glad you made the effort. There are multiple entry and exit points for Makena Landing, the most common being the public parking area off Makena Road.

Once in the water at Makena Landing, hug the coast toward the point on the right, and when you have rounded the tip, you'll notice there is a long finger of lava underwater that extends out toward Molokini. This is what's known as the **South Finger,** and a sea cave here houses green sea turtles. Many snorkel boat operators refer to this area as **Turtle Town,** and unless you want to share the water with 200 other snorkelers, try to be out here before 10am.

If you swim north from the South Finger, you will pass over lime-green coral heads. Keep an eye out for moray eels or the strange-looking flying gurnard. Eventually

morning snorkel off South Maui's coast (top); diving off South Maui (bottom)

SNORKELING AND DIVING 69

SNORKELING AND DIVING TOURS AND RENTALS

NAME	LOCATION	CONTACT INFO
MA'ALAEA		
★ **Trilogy Excursions**	Ma'alaea Harbor, Slip 99	808/874-5649; www.sailtrilogy.com
Four Winds Molokini Maui Snorkel Tours	101 Ma'alaea Rd.	808/879-1571; www.fourwindsmaui.com
Pacific Whale Foundation	300 Ma'alaea Boat Harbor Rd.	808/249-8811; www.pacificwhale.org
Pride of Maui	101 Ma'alaea Boat Harbor Rd.	808/242-0955; www.prideofmaui.com
Maka Koa	300 Ma'alaea Rd., Ste. 225	808/542-3483; www.mauidiveshop.com
KIHEI		
Blue Water Rafting	Kihei Boat Ramp	808/879-7238; www.bluewaterrafting.com
Redline Rafting	Kihei Boat Ramp	808/698-5837; www.redlinerafting.com
★ **Seafire**	Kihei Boat Ramp	808/879-2201; www.molokinisnorkeling.com
★ **Ed Robinson's**	Kihei Boat Ramp, shop at 165 Halekuai St.	808/879-3584; www.mauiscuba.com
Maui Dive Shop	1455 S. Kihei Rd.	808/879-3388; www.mauidiveshop.com
Snorkel Bob's (Kamaole Beach Center)	2411 S. Kihei Rd.	808/879-7449; www.snorkelbob.com
MAKENA AND BEYOND		
★ *Kai Kanani*	Maluaka Beach	808/879-7218; www.kaikanani.com

you'll come to the **North Finger,** another underwater lava formation that houses many turtles. This finger is covered in bright-red slate-pencil urchins that the ancient Hawaiians used for red dye. Eagle rays and manta rays are sometimes seen off the deeper end of the finger.

DIVE SITES
Ma'alaea
★ MOLOKINI CRATER
While Molokini Crater can be a great place to snorkel, to truly experience the crater's magic you have to put on a tank. For experienced divers Molokini ranks among the best dive

ACTIVITY	PRICE
snorkeling tours	Molokini excursion $190 adults, adults-only sunset dinner sail $149 pp
snorkeling tours	Molokini excursion $160 adults, $125 children
snorkeling tours	Molokini excursion $179 adults, Molokini and Turtle Arches snorkel excursion $179 adults
snorkeling tours	five-hour snorkeling excursion $199 adults, Leilani Molokini & Turtle Town Snorkel Tour $199 adults
scuba diving tours	two-tank dive $239 adults
snorkeling tours	four-hour Kanaio Coastline tour $193 adults, two-hour Molokini excursion $119 adults
snorkeling tours	Molokini, Keone'o'io, Kanaio Coast tour $209 adults
snorkeling tours	three-hour Molokini excursion $119
scuba diving	regular two-tank dives $159, advanced two-tank drift dives $179
snorkeling tours, scuba diving	sunset and snorkel tour $249
snorkeling rentals	packages range from basic mask and snorkel ($4 per day) to prescription lenses and fins ($48 per week)
snorkeling tours	two-hour Molokini morning excursion $249 adults, sunrise deluxe snorkel excursion $279 adults

locations around the world, and for novices it's a window into a new aquatic universe. Only certified divers are allowed to dive at Molokini. If you aren't certified but want to experience it from below, sign up for a 20-minute snuba dive to depths of up to 10 ft (3 m).

What makes the crater such an exceptional dive spot is the combination of its pelagic location, where it's possible to see anything, and the multiple dive spots within the crater that cater to a wide range of ability levels. Novices will enjoy either Middle Reef or Reef's End, as depths don't

DON'T FEED THE FISH!

white-spotted toby

Don't feed fish in the ocean for the same reason you don't feed bears in the woods: It isn't their normal diet. The next time you go snorkeling in Hawaii, in addition to looking at the colorful aquatic species, listen to what you hear underwater. The snap, crackle, and pop sounds are the reef fish feeding on algae. When herbivorous reef fish gorge themselves on the outside food you introduce into the water, they become full and stop eating the algae. Consequently, the reef's coral polyps become so overgrown that they struggle to breathe and ultimately die.

Aside from the adverse effect on the coral, larger fish species have been known to drive out the smaller fish species in areas where people feed fish. Many visitors to Molokini notice there are fewer fish than when they visited in the 1980s. This is the reason for the stringent restrictions currently in place.

If that isn't enough to deter you, remember that some fish have really sharp teeth. Many visitors have oval-shaped scars on their fingers from introducing food into the water. For your own safety and the health of the reef, don't feed the fish!

---

usually exceed 70 ft (20 m). **Middle Reef** is home to pelagic species such as jacks and reef sharks, and the sand channel houses curious-looking garden eels. There's also a huge drop-off at the Middle Reef section where it can be easy to exceed your depth.

Similarly, at **Reef's End,** the dive traces the wall of the underwater caldera to the point where it drops off into the abyss. Since this underwater promontory sits on the fringe of the crater, this area offers the best chance of sighting bottlenose dolphins, manta rays, humpback whales, and even the occasional whale shark.

The best and most advanced dive in Molokini Crater is a drift dive of the legendary **Back Wall.** Beginning at Reef's End, divers follow the current along the back of Molokini, where a vertical wall drops 250 ft (76 m) to the ocean floor. If you use nitrox or mixed gases, this is the deepest dive available anywhere in Maui County.

MAUI OCEAN CENTER
192 Ma'alaea Rd.; 808/270-7000; www.mauioceancenter.com

The most unique dive on the island is at the Maui Ocean Center, where you can go diving *inside the shark tank.* As part of its Shark Dive Maui program, certified divers can spend up to 40 minutes surrounded by various species, including hammerhead and tiger sharks. The dive ($350) has a limit of four divers and is only offered on Monday, Wednesday, and Friday mornings. The cost includes the tank and the weight, although divers have to provide the rest of their gear. Although diving at an aquarium might seem like cheating, even some of Maui's most seasoned divers claim it's a great dive. More than just a novelty, this is your best opportunity to be completely surrounded by the ocean's most feared and misrepresented creatures.

HELLDIVER
One of the island's newest wreck dives is a Helldiver World War II airplane that was abandoned by a pilot on a training run off Sugar Beach. When the pilot ejected, his plane sank in 50 ft (15 m) of water, and for the better part of 60 years it sat forgotten in the mudflats. When a local fisher tipped off a Kihei dive instructor that there was probably something down there, the exploratory dive mission yielded a historical discovery that is now property of the US military.

There isn't an overwhelming amount of marinelife here, but many South Maui operators periodically plan excursions to the site, so inquire about when the next outing might be.

BEST TOURS
Snorkeling
TRILOGY EXCURSIONS
Slip 99; 808/874-5649; www.sailtrilogy.com

Trilogy Excursions has been the gold standard for charter boats on Maui for 45 years. Their Molokini trip ($190 adults) is pricier than the budget options, but you get what you pay for: Trilogy boats have only 40-50 passengers, snuba is available as an upgrade, and you get to enjoy a sailing catamaran to feel the breeze in your hair. The trips depart from Slip 99. On Wednesday and Friday, Trilogy also offers the adults-only Captain's Sunset Dinner Sail ($149), focusing on luxury dining and drinking.

SEAFIRE
808/879-2201; www.molokinisnorkeling.com

Seafire offers a Molokini trip ($119) at 7:30am daily on its orange and silver jet-drive raft that not only looks like a Coast Guard boat but is driven by a member of the Coast Guard Reserve. Trips last for three hours, and it's one of the best budget options for reaching Molokini Crater. On the way back toward the Kihei Boat Ramp, you'll stop at a spot along the coast to look for Hawaiian green sea turtles, or maybe even stop at the wreck of the *St. Anthony,* scuttled off the Kihei coast.

KAI KANANI
808/879-7218; www.kaikanani.com

Kai Kanani is the snorkeling boat

SNORKELING AND DIVING   73

SURF SHOPS

NAME	LOCATION	CONTACT INFO
KIHEI		
★ **Maui Wave Riders**	2021 S. Kihei Rd.	808/875-4761; www.mauiwaveriders.com
Big Kahuna Adventures	1900 S. Kihei Rd.	808/875-6395; www.bigkahunaadventures.com
Surf Shack	2960 S. Kihei Rd.	808/875-0006; www.surfshackmaui.com
Boss Frog's	2395 S. Kihei Rd.	808/875-4477; www.bossfrog.com
Island Surfboard Rentals	n/a	808/281-9835; www.islandsurfboardrentals.com
MAKENA AND BEYOND		
Hawaiian Paddle Sports	81 Halekuai St.	808/442-6436; www.hawaiianpaddlesports.com

leaving from Makena, and it features added amenities you would expect from a luxury yacht and top-notch captains. *Kai Kanani* departs directly from Maluaka Beach.

As if that weren't enough, they also offer free transportation to the beach from Wailea resorts. If Molokini was too crowded the last time you visited, *Kai Kanani*'s early morning Molokini charter ($279 adults) departs the beach at 6:15am daily and guarantees you're the first boat at the crater, since it only takes about 15 minutes to motor across the channel. This trip is just over two hours long, and while the second trip of the day ($249 adults) visits the crater when it's more crowded, the fact that it's nearly four hours long, as opposed to two, allows for twice the amount of snorkeling in twice the number of spots. If you're concerned about getting seasick, the journey time from Maluaka Beach to Molokini is much shorter than the journey between Molokini and Ma'alaea.

Scuba Diving

ED ROBINSON'S
808/879-3584; www.mauiscuba.com; 6:30am-5pm Mon.-Fri.
A longtime favorite, Ed Robinson's boasts expertise and quality customer service. Between its scuba lessons and guided shore dives, you can't go wrong here. Standard two-tank dives run $159 per adult. Advanced two-tank drift dives run $179. Inquire about The Adventure X Experience, which includes several options—from snorkeling to scuba.

ACTIVITY	PRICE
surf lessons	one-on-one instruction $150
surf lessons	group surf lesson $95 pp
surf lessons	group lesson up to six people $79 pp, one-on-one $200
snorkeling rentals	snorkeling equipment $25 per day
rental shop	longboards $35 per day/$190 per week, shortboards $25 per day/$160 per week
surf lessons	one-on-one instruction $289, $149 pp for two or more

SURFING

SURF SPOTS

Ma'alaea

OFF THE WALL
Offering the most consistent waves in Ma'alaea, this A-frame, shifty peak breaks directly in front of the harbor wall, and you can usually only surf here in the morning hours before the wind starts howling. To access Off the Wall, park in the dirt parking area

exploring the Makena coast by kayak (left); surfing in South Maui (right)

WATER SPORTS TOURS, LESSONS, AND RENTALS

NAME	LOCATION	CONTACT INFO
KIHEI		
Maui Stand-up Paddleboarding	27-B Halekuai St.	808/568-0151; www.mauistanduppaddleboarding.com
South Pacific Kayaks & Outfitters	n/a	808/875-4848; www.southpacifickayaks.com
WAILEA		
Hawaiian Outrigger Experience	n/a	808/633-2800
Maui Sailing Canoe	n/a	808/281-9301; www.mauisailingcanoe.com
★ **Local Fishing Knowledge**	1215 S. Kihei Rd. Unit D2	808/385-1337; www.localfishingknowledge.com
MAKENA AND BEYOND		
★ **Hawaiian Paddle Sports**	81 Halekuai St.	808/442-6436; www.hawaiianpaddlesports.com
Aloha Kayaks Maui	Makena Landing	808/270-3318; www.alohakayaksmaui.com

at the end of the break wall ($0.50 per hour), and paddle to the shifty peak—which definitely beats jumping off the wall. Expect short but fun rides, and while it isn't the best break on this side of the island, it's a nice place to get wet.

McGREGOR POINT

Half a mile (0.8 km) up the highway in the direction of Lahaina is McGregor Point, the fastest right-hand point break in the world. Although McGregor's rarely gets bigger than head-high, the spot can offer a long wave and is best in the afternoon, when the wind picks up. Parking for McGregor's is in a dirt lot on the road heading toward the lighthouse. Be careful when pulling off the highway as it is a difficult turn. To get down to the shore, you have to clamber down a steep and narrow trail, which can be tough if you're surfing with a longboard. McGregor's only breaks on the biggest of south swells, but it's an island classic when it does.

Kihei

THE COVE

The surf epicenter of Kihei is The Cove, at the southern end of Kalama Park,

ACTIVITY	PRICE
SUP lessons and tours	private lessons and guided tours $249 for one person, $189 pp for two or more
kayaking lessons, kitesurfing lessons	two-hour lessons $89 pp group, $139 pp semiprivate, $179 private
paddling tours, whale-watching tours, outrigger canoe rides	90-minute tour of paddling, snorkeling, and (in winter) whale-watching $149
canoeing tours	canoe tour (including time for snorkeling, paddling, sailing) $185 adults, $145 children
kayak-fishing tours, fly-fishing tours	fishing tours from $129 adult
SUP, kayaking, canoeing, whale-watching tours	SUP tours $249 for one person, $189 pp for two or more; kayak tours $109 pp group tour, $756 total for four-person private tour; $109 pp for whale-watching
kayaking tours	Ultimate Maui experience (including tour and snorkeling) $135 pp

where all of the surf schools give lessons. While the waves are gentle, the downside is that it can get crowded. On some days you'll swear you could walk on water across all the longboards crammed into the small area, but in the early morning hours, before all the surf schools show up, this is still a fun, albeit small, wave. If your goal in Hawaii is to try surfing for the first time, this is where to come.

KIHEI BOAT RAMP

For more advanced surfers, the best wave in Kihei is an A-frame that breaks next to the Kihei Boat Ramp. This is a fickle wave that needs a big southwest or west swell to start working, and you need to be cautious of the boat traffic coming in and out of the harbor area. Access can be tricky, since you're asked to not walk in the sand dune area that runs along the shore. If you're on a longboard and are up for a paddle, you could always paddle from the far southern tip of Kamaole III Beach.

BEST SURF SHOPS

MAUI WAVE RIDERS
2021 S. Kihei Rd.; 808/875-4761;
www.mauiwaveriders.com; 7am-
3pm daily
The shop with the largest presence is Maui Wave Riders, which has a popular surf shop directly across from The Cove. The company also has a Lahaina location and has helped thousands of visitors ride their first wave. Lesson rate is $150 for one-on-one instruction.

OTHER WATER SPORTS

BEST TOURS AND LESSONS

Kayaking and Canoeing
HAWAIIAN PADDLE SPORTS
808/442-6436; www.
hawaiianpaddlesports.com
The top pick for water activities on Maui is the team at Hawaiian Paddle Sports. They're one of only five companies on Maui certified by the Hawaii Ecotourism Association, an organization that sets stringent standards for sustainable and cultural practices. They don't use single-use plastics on their tours (think metal water bottles instead), and they don't touch or disturb marinelife, like pulling octopuses from their holes. Consider kayak tours ($109 pp group tour or $756 for a private tour of up to four guests), outrigger canoe tours ($189 pp), or SUP tours ($249 for one person, $189 pp for 2-5 guests).

Fishing
LOCAL FISHING KNOWLEDGE
1215 S. Kihei Rd. Unit D2; 808/385-1337; www.localfishingknowledge.com
You're in great hands with Captain Jon John. Kayak fishing, fly fishing, and shoreline fishing filter into the mix here, offering a one-of-a-kind experience with a seasoned pro and his staff. These tours are privately guided, offering exceptional excursions and opportunities to fish monster bones, jacks, mahimahi, ono, and more.

BIKING

BIKE ROUTES

Kihei Coastal Ride
For a casual bike ride in South Maui, it doesn't get better than renting a beach cruiser and pedaling to beach-hop, bar-hop, and coolly cruise the paved bike-only strip (2 mi/3.2 km one-way), not worrying about traffic or finding parking. Begin at Kalama Park and head south along South Kihei Road.

Kihei to Makena
For an epic half-day road-biking adventure, ride from Kihei to Makena and the lava-strewn "end of the road" (6.5 mi/10.5 km one-way), where you can cycle across the island's last lava flow and relax at beaches as you go. From the intersection of South Kihei

Road and East Walakahao Road, head south along South Kihei Road.

BIKE SHOPS AND RENTALS
Kihei
SOUTH MAUI BICYCLES
1215 S. Kihei Rd., Ste. MN; 808/874-0068; www.southmauibicycles.com; 10am-6pm Mon.-Sat.

If you're a hard-core cyclist, head to South Maui Bicycles to rent road bikes ($75 per day, $300 per week).

This is a full-service bicycle shop that also offers sales and repairs.

BOSS FROG'S
2395 S. Kihei Rd.; 808/874-5225; www.bossfrog.com; 8am-5pm daily

To beach-hop for a while, beach cruisers begin at $16 per day and hybrid bikes at $30. There are also mountain bikes and proper road bikes. You can also pick up a cruiser at another Boss location in the Dolphin Plaza, across from the southern end of Kamaole II Beach Park.

GOLF

KIHEI
MAUI NUI GOLF CLUB
470 Lipoa Pkwy.; 808/874-0777; www.mauinuigolfclub.com; 6am-6pm daily

Play a relaxing round without shelling out resort prices. The views here look out toward Molokini Crater, and while this course isn't as challenging as the Wailea Gold course, it still provides an enjoyable round. Club and equipment rentals are available from the pro shop, and there's a driving range for working on your stroke before your round. The afternoon trade winds can have a major effect on play, reflected in the greens fees for morning rounds (from $99) and afternoon tee times (as low as $69). To save a few dollars, check the website for online specials. On a winter day with light winds, you can sneak in an enjoyable twilight round after a morning at Molokini Crater. As an added bonus, your first beer at Kono's on the Green—the golf course's 19th hole—is the same price as the score for your round—just present your completed scorecard.

Wailea Gold Golf Course (top); black-necked stilt in the Kealia Pond National Wildlife Refuge (bottom)

WAILEA

WAILEA GOLD GOLF COURSE

100 Wailea Golf Club Dr.; 808/875-7450; www.waileagolf.com

Without question, the Wailea Gold is the best golf course in South Maui, where the pros play when they come to town. The over 7,000-yd (6,400-m) course and 93 bunkers challenge even those with low handicaps. Guests at the Wailea resort complex can play a morning round from $245. Sunset twilight play at 3:30pm can be as low as $125. Club rental and practice facilities are at the main Wailea clubhouse.

WAILEA EMERALD GOLF COURSE

100 Wailea Golf Club Dr.; 808/875-7450; www.waileagolf.com

If the Gold course is intimidating, the Wailea Emerald is far more forgiving. The course isn't quite as long, but it is still a proper resort course with technical challenges and amenities, so you still need to bring your A game. Greens fees are the same as the Gold course.

WAILEA BLUE GOLF COURSE

100 Wailea Golf Club Dr.; 808/875-7450; www.waileagolf.com

Afternoon rates are your go-to here, beginning at $175, with a happy hour/twilight rate beginning at $150 at 3pm onward. Consider the Blue Course Bundle, where you can enjoy greens fees, golf club and shoe rentals, plus a $30 merchandise coupon for just $280 per player.

BIRD-WATCHING

If South Maui had a mascot, it would be the kolea, or Pacific golden plover, since it leaves its summer home in the Arctic for winter on Maui. Those with an interest in Maui County's seabirds should check out the **Maui Nui Seabird Recovery Project** (www.mauinuiseabirds.org).

KEALIA POND NATIONAL WILDLIFE REFUGE

mile marker 6, Maui Veterans Hwy.; 808/875-1582; www.fws.gov/refuge/kealia_pond

For exceptional bird-watching, the Kealia Pond National Wildlife Refuge, between Ma'alaea and Kihei, is nearly 700 acres (285 ha) of open wetlands with over 30 species of birds, including the ae'o (Hawaiian stilt), 'alae ke'oke'o (Hawaiian coot), and koloa maoli (Hawaiian duck). The greatest number of species is found in winter. Short walking trails leave from the visitor center (mile marker 6 on Mokulele Hwy.) into the Kealia Pond area. A short boardwalk from Ma'alaea to North Kihei parallels the shoreline and offers a number of informative placards about the island's native wildlife. The boardwalk takes about 30 minutes to walk to the end and back. It's best to approach from the Ma'alaea side of the road because there's no left turn allowed into the parking lot off North Kihei Road.

MOLOKINI CRATER

Although Molokini Crater is best known for snorkeling, few people know that the 161-ft-tall (49-m) islet is also a seabird sanctuary, home to a healthy population of 'ua'u kani as well as soaring frigates. If you're an avid birder and are planning a trip to Molokini, bring binoculars to check out what's happening above water, not just down on the reef.

ONEULI BEACH
The best place for bird-watching in Makena is at Oneuli Beach by Makena State Park. Although the chances of seeing many species of birds are slim, this coastal wetland area is home to avian species such as the ʻaukuʻu (black-crowned night heron), ʻalae keʻokeʻo (Hawaiian coot), and ulili (wandering tattler).

SPAS AND WELLNESS

KIHEI
808 WELLNESS SPA & HEALING CENTER
2439 S. Kihei Rd.; 808/875-4325; www.808wellness.com; 9am-7pm Mon.-Fri., 9am-6pm Sat., noon-5pm Sun.

There are a handful of places off South Kihei Road to get a relaxing massage. A popular choice is 808 Wellness Spa & Healing Center, which offers a 60-minute traditional Hawaiian lomilomi massage ($125) as well as an aromatherapy massage ($125). Linger longer for a 90-minute massage ($175) to feel truly blissed out.

MASSAGE MAUI
145 N. Kihei Rd.; 808/357-7317; www.massage-maui.com; 8am-9pm daily
Massage Maui is a low-key massage option that offers massages on-site ($125-200) as well as beachfront and outcall services for an additional $20 per service.

Kilolani Spa at Grand Wailea

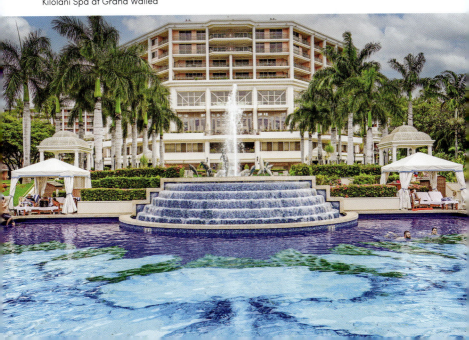

BEACH YOGA

yoga on the beach

South Maui is popular for beach yoga. Nothing is quite as rejuvenating as practicing yoga on the beach, accompanied by ocean views, tropical breezes, and the sound of waves as the sensory backdrop. Standout options include the following.

- **Maui Beach Yoga** (808/385-6466; www.mauibeachyoga.com; $20) goes for memorable toes-in-the-sand yoga experiences, with locations that vary depending on wave and wind patterns. Options include a Group Sunrise Yoga class (around 7am Sat.) and Group Sunset class (around 5pm Mon. and Thurs.). Reservations are required and classes last an hour. Bring your own towel. You can also book a private beach yoga session.

- **Maui Yoga Path** (2960 S. Kihei Rd.; 808/283-9771; www.mauiyogapath.com; $28 per class, $120 for five-class card) holds classes on the tranquil beach in front of the Mana Kai Maui resort, near its popular Five Palms restaurant. This stretch of sand offers sweeping ocean views with glimpses of Molokini Crater. The daily one-hour Sunrise Beach Yoga class is a hit—starting times range 6am-7am during the year, so check the website. Yoga mats and props are provided, and no reservations are necessary.

WAILEA

KILOLANI SPA AT GRAND WAILEA

3850 Wailea Alanui Dr.; 808/875-1234, ext. 4949; www.grandwailea.com; 8am-7pm daily

When it comes to choosing South Maui's best spa, it's tough to beat a 50,000-sq-ft (4,650-sq-m) luxury arena that has recently been revamped into a holistic-focused spa. This palatial spa inside the

Grand Wailea completely redefines the concept of pampering. It's Hawaii's largest spa, and all guests are advised to arrive an hour early to enjoy a casual complimentary soak in the hydrotherapy baths before your treatment. Can't decide among the Roman hot tub, Japanese furo baths, or honey-mango loofah exfoliation? Do them all as a package! Along with an enormous selection of facials and treatment options, there's also a beauty salon and fitness center.

WILLOW STREAM SPA

4100 Wailea Alanui Dr.; 808/875-2229; www.fairmont.com/kea-lani-maui; 8:30am-5pm daily

Down the beach at the Fairmont Kea Lani, the Willow Stream Spa has also been voted among the best in Hawaii, and they work to incorporate plants grown on the property in many massages and services. During the 90-minute Hawaiian hot stone massage, enjoy specific techniques to release and relieve deep-seated tension. This service offers pohaku (Hawaiian stones), which are handpicked by the therapists, who also wrap you in a resort-gown to administer a scalp and face massage. Finish off by rinsing yourself in a rain-inspired shower, and then slink down to the pool.

WAILEA HEALING CENTER

120 S. Kaukahi St.; 808/205-2005; www.waileahealingcenter.com; 8am-8pm daily

A stellar experience all around. Wailea Healing Center is an out-of-resort option that only requires a five-minute drive yet saves almost enough money for a second round. Close to the Wailea Tennis Center, between the Shops at Wailea and the Wailea Gateway Center, this healing zone offers 60-minute massage treatments ($150) that are infused with essential oils, hot stones, and ocean views. Acupuncture, yoga classes, and crystal-bowl sound baths and meditations are also available.

SHOPPING

MA'ALAEA

MA'ALAEA HARBOR SHOPS

300 Ma'alaea Rd.; 877/463-2731

The handful of shops at Ma'alaea Harbor Shops have periodic craft fairs. One of the most popular retail outlets is **U'I Makana** (10am-6pm daily), with a surprising assortment of T-shirts, jewelry, and other island-related gifts.

KIHEI

PI'ILANI VILLAGE SHOPPING CENTER

225 Pi'ikea Ave.; 9am-10pm daily

If you turn up Pi'ikea Avenue between the Azeka Mauka Center and the Long's Shopping Center, you'll quickly come to the Pi'ilani Village Shopping Center, which has the most relevant shopping options in North Kihei. A big draw is the **ABC Store** (808/875-9985; 8:30am-7:30pm daily), which has the best array of snacks and last-minute groceries as well as a surprising variety of men's and women's clothing, shoes, and hats.

KIHEI KALAMA VILLAGE

1941 S. Kihei Rd.; 808/879-6610; 10am-7:30pm daily

The largest concentration of shopping in Kihei is in the Kihei Kalama Village, with over 40 businesses selling a variety of apparel and handmade and locally made products. There are also myriad kiosks and stands where you can get henna tattoos or play a didgeridoo. This shopping area is within walking distance of the Cove Park, where most of the surf rentals take place, so if part of your group is out surfing, you can wander down here for some souvenir browsing while they are on the water.

RAINBOW MALL
2439 S. Kihei Rd.; 808/879-1145; 9am-9pm daily

Rainbow Mall is home to **Maui Fine Art Gallery & Frame** (808/463-9383; www.mauiartframe.com; 8:30am-4:30pm daily), one of the few art galleries in Kihei. In addition to numerous island-themed paintings and ceramics, the frames that encompass the artwork are an art form unto themselves.

WAILEA
While all the high-end luxury resorts have a decent amount of shopping, particularly the Grand Wailea, the majority of retail on this side of the island is at the shopping centers and shops.

THE SHOPS AT WAILEA
3750 Wailea Alanui Dr.; 808/891-6770; www.theshopsatwailea.com; 10am-9pm daily

The Shops at Wailea is a plantation-style shopping complex with wide grassy areas and free hula shows from local halau (hula schools). Inside you'll find art galleries such as **Lahaina Galleries** (800/228-2006) and **Enchantress Gallery** (808/495-4161) accompanying the usual retail shops. For a rare, authentic souvenir, drop by **Mele Ukulele** (808/879-6353), the most established manufacturer of ukuleles on Maui. You can often spot celebrities hanging out in luxury stalwarts such as **Tiffany and Co.** and

---

the Shops at Wailea

Gucci or in restaurants like **Lineage** (808/879-8800).

Aside from the high-end chain stores, you can also find a few island-themed shops offering unique and boutique souvenirs. At **Martin & MacArthur** (808/891-8844; www.martinandmacarthur.com), Hawaiian-made crafts and an assortment of koa woods abound.

WAILEA GATEWAY CENTER
10 Wailea Ike Dr.

Although it doesn't have anywhere near the glitz and glamour of the Shops at Wailea, the awkwardly placed little Wailea Gateway Center still has a couple of boutique shops worth a visit. One of those is **Sweet Paradise Chocolatier** (808/344-1040; www.chocolateonmaui.com; 11am-8pm daily), which will lure you in with the scent of rich chocolate. In addition to an ornate spread of fine chocolates, all the items are made on the island, and some of the cacao is even grown in Hawaii—the only US state where cacao is currently grown.

Nalu's South Shore Grill

FOOD

STANDOUTS
Kihei
THREE'S BAR & GRILL
1945 S. Kihei Rd.; 808/879-3133; www.threesbarandgrill.com; 11am-9pm daily; lunch $12-22, dinner $19-35

One of the most popular venues is Three's Bar & Grill, inside the Kihei Kalama Village. Opened by three chefs who each boast their own culinary specialty—Hawaiian, Southwestern, and Pacific Rim—the restaurant has lunch and appetizer items such as Hawaiian-style ribs and kalua pig quesadilla. Dinner menu entrées feature chicken roulade and a raw bar of sushi and poke. Two daily happy hours (3pm-6pm and 9pm-10pm) feature discounts on both drinks and food, including local faves like sushi rolls.

PAIA FISHMARKET
1913 S. Kihei Rd.; 808/874-8888; https://paiafishmarket.com; 11am-9pm daily; $18-35

In the Kihei Kalama Village, Paia Fishmarket now has a Kihei outlet for their mouthwatering fish burgers ($11-12), and it's a casual spot for grabbing some lunch after a morning of surfing at The Cove.

NALU'S SOUTH SHORE GRILL
1280 S. Kihei Rd.; 808/891-8650; www.nalusmaui.com; 8am-9pm daily; $11-30

In the Azeka Mauka shopping center, Nalu's South Shore Grill is one of the most festive dining spots

SOUTH MAUI FOOD OPTIONS

NAME	LOCATION	CONTACT INFO
MA'ALAEA		
Tradewinds Mart & Deli	20 Hauoli St.	808/242-9161
KIHEI		
★ **Three's Bar & Grill**	1945 S. Kihei Rd.	808/879-3133; www.threesbarandgrill.com
Da Kitchen	1215 S. Kihei Rd.	808/446-3486; www.dakitchenkihei.com
★ **Paia Fishmarket**	1913 S. Kihei Rd.	808/874-8888; https://paiafishmarket.com
Sansei	1819 S. Kihei Rd.	808/868-0780; https://dkrestaurants.com
Fabiani's Bakery and Pizza	95 E. Lipoa St.	808/874-0888; www.fabianis.com
Fat Daddy's Smokehouse	1913 S. Kihei Rd.	808/879-8711; www.fatdaddysmaui.com
★ **Nalu's South Shore Grill**	1280 S. Kihei Rd.	808/891-8650; www.nalusmaui.com
Kihei Caffe	1945 S. Kihei Rd.	808/879-2230; www.kiheicaffe.net
Wow Wow Hawaiian Lemonade	1279 S. Kihei Rd.	808/868-0466; www.wowwowhawaiianlemonade.com
WAILEA		
★ **Monkeypod Kitchen**	10 Wailea Ike Dr.	808/891-2322; www.monkeypodkitchen.com
Duo Steak and Seafood	3900 Wailea Alanui Dr.	808/874-8000; www.fourseasons.com/maui/dining
Nick's Fishmarket	4100 Wailea Alanui Dr.	808/879-7224; www.nicksfishmarketmaui.com
★ **Manoli's Pizza Company**	100 Wailea Ike Dr.	808/874-7499; www.manolispizzacompany.com
★ **Spago**	3900 Wailea Alanui Dr.	808/874-8000

FOOD	HOURS	PRICE
deli	8am-6pm Mon.-Fri., 9am-5pm Sat., 10am-4pm Sun.	$6-9
Hawaiian Regional	11am-9pm daily	lunch $12-22, dinner $19-35
local style	11am-8pm Mon.-Sat.	$8-18
seafood	11am-9pm daily	$18-35
Japanese	4:45pm-9pm Sun.-Mon., 5pm-9pm Tues.-Sat.	$18-44
Italian	2pm-8pm Mon.-Thurs. and Sat.-Sun., 11am-9pm Fri.	$15-28
barbecue	4pm-8pm Wed.-Sat.	$9-25
bar and grill	8am-9pm daily	$11-30
breakfast and lunch	6am-2pm daily	$9-18
natural foods	8am-4pm daily	$8-12
Hawaiian Regional	11am-10pm daily	$15-44
Hawaiian Regional	6am-11pm daily	$32-51
seafood	5pm-8:45pm daily	$18-54
Italian	11am-10pm daily	$13-30
Italian	4pm-midnight daily	$36-58

SOUTH MAUI BARS AND NIGHTLIFE

NAME	LOCATION	CONTACT INFO
KIHEI		
★ Island Art Party	1279 S. Kihei Rd.	808/419-6020; www.islandartparty.com
★ Haui's Life's a Beach	1913 S. Kihei Rd.	808/891-8010; www.mauibars.com
South Shore Tiki Lounge	1913 S. Kihei Rd.	808/874-6444; www.southshoretiki.com
Vibe Bar Maui	1913 S. Kihei Rd.	808/891-1011
Kahale's Local Dive Bar	36 Keala Pl.	808/215-9939; www.kahales.com
★ Maui Brewing Company	605 Lipoa Pkwy.	808/201-2337; www.mbcrestaurants.com
Moose McGillycuddy's	2511 S. Kihei Rd.	808/891-8600; www.moosemcgillycuddyskihei.com
WAILEA		
The Grand Luau at Honua'ula	3850 Wailea Alanui Dr.	808/875-1234; www.grandwailea.com/dine/luau
Te Au Moana	3700 Wailea Alanui Dr.	877/827-2740; www.teaumoana.com
★ Mulligan's on the Blue	100 Kaukahi St.	808/874-1131; www.mulligansontheblue.com
Manoli's Pizza Company	100 Wailea Ike Dr.	808/874-7499; www.manolispizzacompany.com
★ Gather on Maui	100 Wailea Golf Club Dr.	808/875-8080; www.gatheronmaui.com

in Kihei, with great service and terrific atmosphere. Many of the ingredients are local or organic, and the menu includes salads and innovative fish and meat sandwiches. Try the Island Pancakes ($12) for breakfast, a seared ahi club ($15) for lunch, and the Island Style Ribs ($22) for dinner. Order at the counter. There's live entertainment nightly by Maui-based musicians.

Wailea

Prices in Wailea are much higher than in other parts of the island and double the cost in Kihei. You're often paying for master chefs, exceptional service, and unparalleled ambience in world-class resorts.

MONKEYPOD KITCHEN
10 Wailea Ike Dr.; 808/891-2322; www.monkeypodkitchen.com; 11am-10pm daily; $15-44

VENUE TYPE	HOURS
sip and paint	2pm-7:30pm most days
bar and live music	1pm-midnight daily
restaurant and nightclub	11am-10:30pm Sun.-Wed., 11am-midnight Thurs.-Sat.
cocktail bar	7pm-midnight daily
dive bar	10am-midnight daily
brewery, restaurant, and bar	11:30am-10pm daily
sports bar	11am-11pm daily
luau	5pm-8pm daily
luau	4:30pm Mon. and Thurs.-Sat.
pub and live music	2pm-9pm Thurs., noon-9pm Fri.-Sat., 8am-8pm Sun.
bar	11am-10pm daily
restaurant and bar	11:30am-8pm daily

The first restaurant you'll encounter in Wailea approaching from Pi'ilani Highway is Monkeypod Kitchen, the brainchild of renowned Maui chef Peter Merriman. Ingredients are all sourced locally, supporting sustainable farming and ensuring fresh, healthy meals. Dinner options range from hand-prepped pizzas and the popular bulgogi pork tacos in an Asian pear aioli to organic macadamia nut-crusted fresh fish. The craft beer list is the best in Wailea. To save a few bucks, visit during happy hour (3:30pm-5pm). There's live music daily.

MANOLI'S PIZZA COMPANY
100 Wailea Ike Dr.; 808/874-7499; www.manolispizzacompany.com; 11am-10pm daily; $13-30
Wailea's best pizza is at Manoli's Pizza Company, within walking distance from many of the hotels and

SOUTH MAUI LODGING OPTIONS

NAME	LOCATION	CONTACT INFO
KIHEI		
★ **Maui Mango Cottages**	45 Kilohana Dr.	phone number provided at booking; www.mauimangocottages.com
Maui Sugar Beach Condos	145 N. Kihei Rd.	808/851-8855; www.mauisugarbeachcondos.com
Days Inn	2980 S. Kihei Rd.	844/275-2969; www.wyndhamhotels.com/days-inn
Maui Coast Hotel	2259 S. Kihei Rd.	808/874-6284; www.mauicoasthotel.com
WAILEA		
★ **Wailea Ekolu Village**	10 Wailea Ekolu Pl.	866/901-0982; www.destinationhotels.com
Wailea Beach Marriott	3700 Wailea Alanui Dr.	808/879-1922; www.marriott.com
★ **Grand Wailea**	3850 Wailea Alanui Dr.	808/875-1234; www.grandwailea.com
Andaz Maui	3550 Wailea Alanui Dr.	808/573-11234; www.hyatt.com
Fairmont Kea Lani	4100 Wailea Alanui Dr.	808/875-4100; www.fairmont.com
Four Seasons Resort	3900 Wailea Alanui Dr.	808/874-8000; www.fourseasons.com

across from the Shops at Wailea. It serves 14-in (36-cm) thin-crust pizzas with organic and gluten-free options and toppings that include shrimp, pesto, kalamata olives, artichoke hearts, and feta cheese. There are salads, pastas, a selection of 20 wines, and specials at happy hour (3pm-5pm and 9pm-10pm daily).

SPAGO

3900 Wailea Alanui Dr.; 808/874-8000; 4pm-midnight daily; $36-58
At the luxurious Four Seasons Resort, the tables here close enough to the ocean that you can dine to the sound of the waves. Clink glasses beneath the stars and savor the authentic cuisine in a world-famous restaurant. Come here to spoil yourself.

VENUE TYPE	HOURS	BEST FOR
cottages	$195–295	couples, families
condo (vacation rental)	$235–365	couples, families
hotel	$339–565	budget travelers
hotel	$471–533	couples, business travel
condo (vacation rental)	$399–534	couples, families
resort	$782–1,272	families, couples
resort	$997–2,771	families, couples, honeymooners
hotel	$1,151–2,683	couples, families
resort	$1,159–3,659	families, couples, honeymooners
resort	$1,995–10,000+	couples, honeymooners, luxury-lovers

BARS AND NIGHTLIFE

The largest and most popular event in South Maui is the **Fourth Friday** celebration, held 6pm-9pm on the fourth Friday of the month at the Azeka Mauka shopping complex. There are multiple live music performances and beer gardens scattered throughout. It's a surprisingly well organized affair that's fun for the entire family.

STANDOUTS
Kihei
ISLAND ART PARTY
1279 S. Kihei Rd.; 808/419-6020; www.islandartparty.com; 2pm-7:30pm most days; $35-65
For an artistic event that happens most nights, Island Art Party is a unique venue where you can join an instructor-led painting class while

sipping a glass of wine. It's one of the island's best rainy-day activities and is for ages 16 and up.

HAUI'S LIFE'S A BEACH
1913 S. Kihei Rd.; 808/891-8010; www. mauibars.com; 1pm-midnight daily
Haui's Life's a Beach, a.k.a. The Lab, is a rockin' beach bar with an outdoor patio that looks toward South Kihei Road. There's live music on weekends. Other big draws are $2 Taco Tuesdays and karaoke Sunday through Thursday. You can also shoot some pool, watch sports, and people-watch.

MAUI BREWING COMPANY
605 Lipoa Pkwy.; 808/201-2337; www.mbcrestaurants.com; 11:30am-10pm daily
This very popular open-air warehouse restaurant and bar, along with its adjacent brewery, is a big go, especially on weekends. Beyond its stellar brews, it stands out for its Monday-Friday happy hour (3:30pm-4:30pm) with $1 off house beers, $3 off craft cocktails, and $12 pizzas. Live music nightly rounds out the roster. The brewery has 36 of its own beers on tap, tours (check the website for the most updated times), and Advanced Beer Tastings four times a day (call or inquire in person).

Wailea

MULLIGAN'S ON THE BLUE
100 Kaukahi St.; 808/874-1131; www. mulligansontheblue.com; 2pm-9pm Thurs., noon-9pm Fri.-Sat., 8am-8pm Sun.
For live entertainment after the sun goes down, the most popular place in Wailea is Mulligan's on the Blue. This Irish pub is owned by a real Irishman, and periodic performances by award-winning local artists begin at 6pm Friday-Sunday.

GATHER ON MAUI
100 Wailea Golf Club Dr.; 808/875-8080; www.gatheronmaui.com; 11:30am-8pm daily
By the clubhouse of the Wailea golf course—which requires a short drive from the resort strip—this hot restaurant and bar was once known as Gannons. The views are still striking and now the menu has changed slightly, offering exquisite seafood, grass-fed beef, and plenty of specialty cocktails such as the Gather Mai Tai with signature rums. In additional to the extensive wine list, take note of the exceptional array of cocktails and liquors featured here.

LODGING

RESERVATIONS AND TIPS

Because this is one of the most popular areas to stay on Maui, consider making reservations far in advance to lock in the best prices or deals. Summertime and the holidays are peak seasons, so be prepared for more crowds at these times. Early mornings are less crowded on the beach for walkers and joggers.

STANDOUTS

Kihei

MAUI MANGO COTTAGES

45 Kilohana Dr.; phone number provided at booking; www.mauimangocottages.com; $195-295

On the southern end of Kihei, the Maui Mango Cottages are just steps from Keawakapu Beach. The two-bedroom cottage ($195) sleeps 4-5, and the three-bedroom cottage ($295) can accommodate six. This is as close to Wailea as you can get for these rates. Wailea Beach Walk is a 10-minute stroll from the front door. The cottages have kitchens, and in summer, mangoes dangle from the trees.

Wailea

WAILEA EKOLU VILLAGE

10 Wailea Ekolu Pl.; 866/901-0982; www.destinationhotels.com; $399-534

To be walking distance from the beaches of Wailea without the hefty price tag, look into some of the affordably priced condos on the northern edge of the resort. The Wailea Ekolu Village offers one- and two-bedroom condos with included parking and internet, and kitchens. You can often get hefty discounts with advance reservations.

GRAND WAILEA

3850 Wailea Alanui Dr.; 808/875-1234; www.grandwailea.com; $997-2,771

Directly in front of Wailea Beach, the sprawling pink Grand Wailea offers the highest quality and is famous for its pool system and the largest corporate art collection in Hawaii. Families will enjoy navigating the waterslides, rope swings, lazy river, and water elevator. In recent years the resort has instituted numerous cultural programs. Rooms are expensive and amenities lavish.

TRANSPORTATION

While a car is a necessity to go exploring, those who just want to relax on the beach and make sporadic ventures elsewhere can get by in South Maui with a combination of walking, shuttles, public buses, and taxis.

Car

From the airport, head west on Highway 380 to Highway 311, which heads south to Kihei (13 mi/21 km, 25 minutes) and eventually toward Wailea (17 mi/27 km, 30 minutes).

Car Rental

Most people will rent a car at the airport, but if you decide you need a rental car after having already made your way to Kihei, there are local options. One of the most popular car rental options is family-owned **Kihei Rent a Car** (6 Kio Loop; 808/879-7257; www.kiheirentacar.com), which can arrange a free pickup or drop-off at the **Kahului Airport** for rentals longer than five days. The rates are often better than the major corporate competitors. If you would rather get those corporate rewards points, **Avis Car Rental** (1455 S. Kihei Rd.; 808/874-4077; www.avis.com; 8:30am-3pm daily) has an outlet in central Kihei next to Maui Dive Shop and Pizza Madness.

Parking

While South Maui is easily navigable by car, there are parking challenges. Anyone staying at a Wailea resort will likely pay a parking fee upward of $40 per day. Inquire whether your resort has a parking fee and factor this into the cost of the rental. When it comes to parking in Kihei, spots along the street in the Kamaole Beach Park II area can be tough to find in the middle of the day, so either arrive at the beach early or be prepared to do a little walking. Parking at Ma'alaea Harbor costs $0.50 per hour, although you can find a handful of public spots on the northern side of Hauoli Street.

Taxi

To have someone do the driving for you and not worry about parking, directions, or sobriety, the best taxi service in Kihei is **A South Maui Taxi** (808/344-7555; www.asouthmauitaxi.com). Arrivals from the airport are flat-rate: $75 to Wailea, $65 to Kihei, and $115 to Lahaina/Kaanapali. For all other rides, including departures to the airport, a standard taxi meter is used.

Bus

Maui Bus (808/249-2900; www.co.maui.hi.us/bus) operates a number of lines throughout South Maui, and provides service in and between various parts of the island. All rides are $4 per boarding. The Kihei Villager (bus 15) runs between Ma'alaea Harbor Village and Pi'ilani Shopping Center 6am-8:30pm daily with various stops in between. The Kihei Islander (bus 10) runs between Wailea Ike Drive by the Shops at Wailea and Queen Ka'ahumanu Center in Kahului 5:30am-9:30pm daily. If you are trying to get to North Kihei or Ma'alaea, you can transfer at Pi'ilani Shopping Center to the

Kihei Villager (bus 15). The frequency of the buses varies during the year; however, in most cases, buses arrive regularly (every 10-15 minutes) at these shopping centers.

Shuttle

For a ride to the airport, contact **Roberts Hawaii** (808/539-9400; www.robertshawaii.com). Fares run $19-24 per person one-way, depending on where you're staying. Most major resorts tend to offer shuttle pickups from and to the airport; prices vary from free to approximately $75, depending on the resort.

Motorcycle and Moped

South Maui is a popular destination for motorcycle enthusiasts looking to experience the island wind and fresh air. The weather can change quickly, so check the forecast and bring rainwear if needed. Helmets are required by law, but most places offer them for rent or as part of a package. Traffic is tighter in Kihei, so expect more starts and stops.

In the Azeka Mauka shopping center in North Kihei, **Hawaiian Cruisers** (1280 S. Kihei Rd.; 808/446-1111; www.hawaiiancruisers.com; 9am-4pm Mon.-Fri.) offers electric bikes, mopeds, and cruisers ($50-105 per day).

Maui Scooter Shack (1794 S. Kihei Rd.; 808/891-0837; www.mauiscootershack.com; 9am-6pm Wed.-Sun., 9am-noon Mon., noon-6pm Tues.) rents mopeds ($45 per day) and motorcycles ($90-150 per day) and usually offers fair, competitive rates.

LEAVING SOUTH MAUI

West Maui (Lahaina)

From Kihei, take South Kihei Road north and turn left onto North Kihei Road. Continue on to Honoapi'ilani Highway (Hwy. 30) westbound, which will take you along the scenic coastline directly to Lahaina. The 24.7-mi (39.7-km) drive is about 45 minutes. From Kihei, head north on Pi'ilani Highway (Hwy. 31). Merge onto Maui Veterans Highway (Hwy. 311) and continue for about 10 mi (16 km). Follow signs for Kahului Airport, turning right onto Airport Access Road. The drive takes about 20 minutes.

Haleakalā National Park

From Kihei, take Pi'ilani Highway (Hwy. 31) north and continue onto Maui Veterans Highway (Hwy. 311) heading toward Kahului. Turn right onto Hansen Road and follow signs for Haleakalā. Turn right onto Haleakalā Highway (Hwy. 37) and stay on this road as it begins to ascend. This road will take you directly into Haleakalā National Park. The 46.7-mi (75.1-km) drive is about 90 minutes.

Start of the Road to Hana

From Kihei, take Pi'ilani Highway (Hwy. 31) north and continue onto Maui Veterans Highway (Hwy. 311) heading toward Kahului. Turn right onto Hansen Road and right again onto Hana Highway (Hwy. 36). Stay on this road, passing the communities of Pa'ia and Ha'iku, until you reach the Road to Hana mile marker 0 (Hwy. 360). The 27.2-mi (43.7-km) drive is about 48 minutes.

Honolua Bay

WEST MAUI

White sandy beaches, rocky coves, lush valleys, and oceanfront restaurants where the clinking glasses of mai tais and the smooth sounds of a slack-key guitar complement the setting sun—Maui is a magical place.

West Maui beaches are some of the best on the island. In winter, Honolua Bay shapes the kind of legendary right-hand point breaks that attract surfers from across the globe. In summer, this same bay offers some of the island's finest snorkeling, where bright parrotfish, shy octopuses, and curious sea turtles occupy an expansive reef.

Hot, busy, and incomparably historic, Lahaina was once the whaling capital of the Pacific as well as the capital of the Hawaiian kingdom. Today, it's Maui's quintessential tourist town. The name Lahaina translates as "cruel, merciless sun," and, appropriately, almost every day is sunny in Lahaina. As a result, it buzzes with an energetic fervor that draws pedestrians to the streets, fishers to the harbor, and surfers to the breaks offshore.

Whether you're scouring the historic relics of Lahaina, swimming with reef fish at Napili Bay, stand-up paddleboarding along the Ka'anapali shore, or simply enjoying the sunset from an oceanfront luau, this is the Maui you were dreaming of.

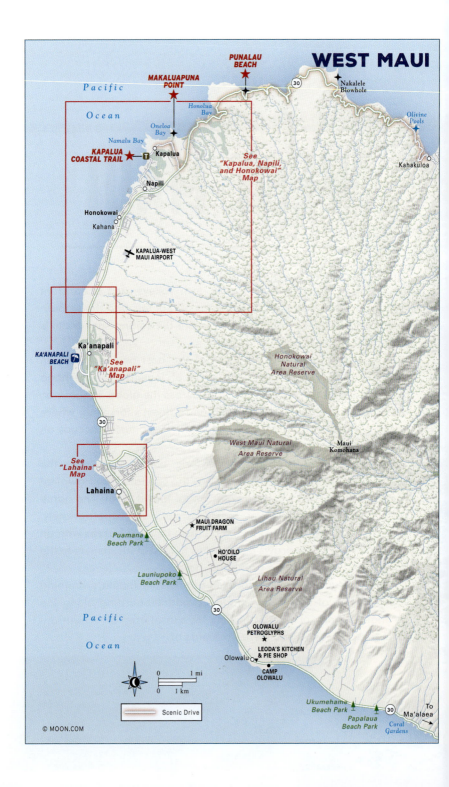

TOP 3

★ **1. MAKALUAPUNA POINT:** Take a short stroll to see the wave-created sculpture and spectacular coastal views (page 105).

★ **2. PUNALAU BEACH:** In summer, this is the perfect spot to find shells and flotsam; in winter, watch advanced surfers ride "The Mill" (page 115).

★ **3. KAPALUA COASTAL TRAIL:** Spend an hour scouring the coast on this luxuriant yet rugged trail, passing some of Hawaii's most beautiful beaches along the way (page 117).

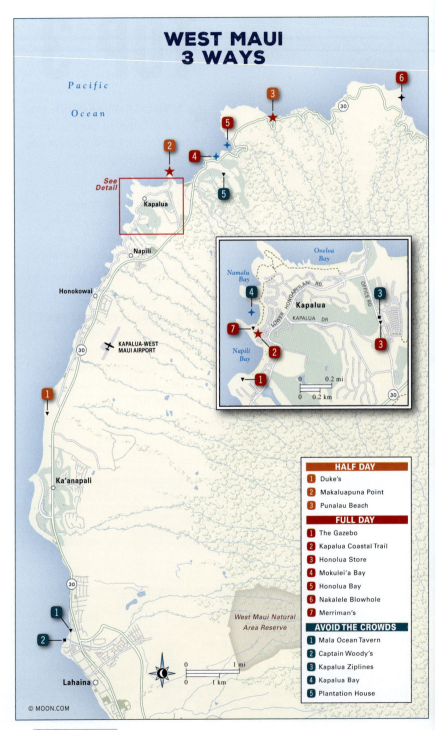

WEST MAUI 3 WAYS

HALF DAY

1 Enjoy a hearty breakfast at **Duke's:** Consider the banana and macadamia nut pancakes or French toast.

2 Drive north to **Makaluapuna Point** (Dragon's Teeth) and experience the unique lava formations overlooking the ocean.

3 Spend a few hours beachcombing and relaxing at the tranquil and scenic **Punalau Beach.**

FULL DAY

1 Get up early and head to **The Gazebo** to be in line for the 7:30am opening and to enjoy a stack of macadamia pancakes.

2 After breakfast, drive up the road to Kapalua Bay and walk off your breakfast on the **Kapalua Coastal Trail.**

3 Having worked up a sweat and soaked up the views, grab lunch at **Honolua Store** before embarking on the adventurous drive north.

4 If you have your own snorkeling gear, stop for an hour at **Mokuleiʻa Bay** and search for octopuses and turtles.

5 Stop to photograph the world-famous **Honolua Bay** when you reach the top of the hill, which offers dramatic views of the iconic half-moon-shaped bay and ocean views of Molokaʻi and Lanaʻi.

6 Continue driving all the way toward **Nakalele Blowhole.** Watch your step as you clamber down to the thundering saltwater geyser.

7 By now it'll be getting late in the day, and you need to make it to **Merriman's** in Kapalua by 7:30pm for cocktails, dinner, and a spectacular sunset (during the winter months you'll want to be at Merriman's by 4:30pm).

AVOID THE CROWDS

1. Enjoy breakfast at **Mala Ocean Tavern** and try the avocado toast or fabulous eggs Benedict.

2. Book a one-of-a-kind private ocean charter with **Captain Woody's** for a personalized snorkeling trip for up to six people. The trip includes snorkel gear, a seasoned guide, and stunning snorkels in the ocean.

3. In the afternoon, see the island from an exhilarating perspective on one of Maui's best zip lines at **Kapalua Ziplines.**

4. Enjoy the sunset without big crowds at **Kapalua Bay,** north of the area's busiest beaches.

5. Dinner awaits at **Plantation House,** where you can order lobster ravioli or Hawaiian short ribs.

ORIENTATION AND PLANNING

ORIENTATION

West Maui, geographically, is an enormous swath of land. It technically begins once you pass through the tunnel and reach **Papalaua Beach,** and stretches all the way to **Kahakuloa** on the island's northern coast. With the exception of tiny **Olowalu village,** there's no development from the time you pass **Ma'alaea** until you reach **Lahaina.** Here you'll find Hawaii's ancient capital as well as restaurants, the harbor, and shops, whereas **Ka'anapali,** just up the road, is lined with world-class resorts. **Honokowai, Kahana,** and **Napili** meld together in a strip of oceanfront condos, and eventually give way to **Ritz-Carlton resort** about 20 minutes north of Lahaina. Past the resort, the coast gets wild and development comes to a halt, and sandy beaches give way to rocky coves and rugged cliffs.

PLANNING YOUR TIME

More people stay in West Maui than any other part of the island, and in many ways, it feels separated from other parts of Maui. Based here, it's easy to make simple half-day jaunts to the beach or go on tropical micro-adventures before lounging back at the resort. For other travelers who aren't based in West Maui, two full days is a good amount of time to experience the area's best sights, with one day spent near and around Ka'anapali and Napili, and another exploring "up north."

From Kahului Airport, it's about 40 minutes to Lahaina and an hour to Kapalua, though as the island grows, the traffic is getting particularly bad—and driving to Lahaina between 3pm and 5pm can often be bumper to bumper. Factor this in if you're trying to get to your 5pm oceanfront luau.

HIGHLIGHTS

KAPALUA, NAPILI, AND HONOKOWAI

★ Makaluapuna Point (Dragon's Teeth)

For spectacular views of the northwestern coast and white-sand Oneloa Bay, take a short stroll on Makaluapuna Point—otherwise known as "Dragon's Teeth." The jagged rocks here have been dramatically sculpted by waves crashing on the coast, and there's a large labyrinth in the middle of the point for silently reflecting on the beauty.

The trailhead is located by the small parking lot at the end of Office Road. Visit without leaving a trace; this point is sacred to Native Hawaiians and access can be controversial (there is a cemetery to the right of the path, beyond the shrubs and trees, and nobody is allowed there accept Native Hawaiians). Stay on the trail out onto the windswept point, and tread lightly.

Honolua Bay

Famous for its exceptional surfing and diving, Honolua Bay is also one

HIGHLIGHTS   105

of West Maui's most beautiful sights. There is a palpable magic in this bay, from the vine-laden valley that leads to the shore and the reef that's teeming with life to the simply legendary right-hand wave that perfectly bends around the point. When visiting Honolua Bay—particularly when the surf is breaking—either stop at the overlook on the north side of the bay after climbing the short but steep hill, or drive down the bumpy dirt road that leads to the top of the bluff. To continue the Honolua adventure on foot, walk to where the dirt road ends, where a very thin trail connects with a network of coastal trails that lead to views of the coast.

Nakalele Blowhole

Eight mi (12.9 km) past the entrance to Kapalua, by mile marker 38, is the famous Nakalele Blowhole, one of the most popular stops along this stretch of coast. It's about a 15-minute drive past the entrance to Kapalua without stopping. On the right days, the Nakalele Blowhole can jettison water upward of 100 ft (30 m) into the air, making it one of

BEST SUNSET VIEWS

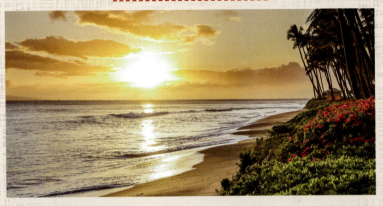

sunset on Kaʻanapali Beach

Between its striking views of the islands of Lanaʻi and Molokaʻi and its easy-access shoreline, **Kaʻanapali Beach** (page 114) remains one of West Maui's best sunset spots.

the most powerful forces of the sea you can witness on the island. Visitors in the past have been killed by standing too close to the blowhole, so pay attention to warning signs in the area.

Park in the dirt pullout at marker 38 or, for even better access, stop 0.5 mi (0.8 km) farther down the road where a trailhead exists at a second dirt pullout, with a trail to the blowhole. The trail to the blowhole is just over 0.5 mi (0.8 km) long, and the last half of the trail becomes a scramble down a moderate scree slope, which is best left to those who are steady on their feet. When you reach the bottom of the rocky trail, turn around and look behind you, facing away from the blowhole. Look closely to find the **heart-shaped hole in the rocks** that's a Maui Instagram or TikTok darling.

Olivine Pools

Past the Nakalele Blowhole, by mile marker 16, the Olivine Pools—traditionally called Mokolea—feature breathtaking coastal panoramas. Even if you don't walk down to the pools, the views alone are reason enough to stop. On rare calm days when the wind is light and the ocean is mellow and smooth, this can be one of the most serene perches on the island. However, the ocean is treacherous here, which makes swimming in the pools risky. Wait to see if any waves are crashing into them. If the ocean is calm and isn't reaching the pools, this is the safest time for swimming or wading. Visitors have died trying to reach the pools, so be aware of your surroundings at all times. If waves are washing into the pools, keep out. Park and follow the trail toward the coast to access the

HIGHLIGHTS 107

Makaluapuna Point (Dragon's Teeth) (top); Honolua Bay (middle); Olivine Pools (bottom)

pools. The trail will fork at a yellow sign that warns about the dangers of continuing. Follow the trail to the edge of the bluff and then proceed down the trail leading to the pools.

KA'ANAPALI

Pu'u Keka'a (Black Rock)

Known to most visitors as Black Rock, Pu'u Keka'a at the northern end of Ka'anapali Beach is a favorite spot for snorkeling, scuba diving, and cliff-jumping. Proceed with care and caution if you want to jump; make sure to leap away from the ledge of the rock.

While this 20-ft (6-m) jump is popular with visitors and locals, the most interesting time of day is about 20 minutes prior to sunset when a torch-wielding, shirtless member of the Sheraton staff scrambles onto the rock and lights a row of carefully placed tiki torches. Once all the torches are lit, his flaming staff is ceremoniously chucked into the water moments before he performs a swan dive off the rock. More than just a creative marketing plan, the ceremony is a reenactment of the sacred belief that this is one of the spots on the island where a person's soul leaps from this world to the next immediately following death. For a prime perch to watch the show, grab a drink at the Cliff Dive Bar inside the Sheraton Maui.

Tour of the Stars

200 Nohea Kai Dr.; 808/667-4727; hotel guests $35 adults and $25 children, nonguests $35

For a truly unique Ka'anapali experience, stand on the roof of the Hyatt and stargaze through high-powered telescopes. Held at 8pm and 9pm every night, the Tour of the Stars allows small groups of 14 people to

108 WEST MAUI

access the roof of the resort and peer through a 14-in (36-cm) reflector telescope with the resort's director of astronomy.

LAHAINA
Front Street

Front Street had long been a sight with its shops, festive restaurants and bars, eclectic street vendors, and sublime views of Lana'i and Moloka'i, especially at sunset. Listed as one of the "Great Streets in America" by the American Planning Association, this premier destination in West Maui is being reconstructed in the wake of the devastating 2023 fires. There is hope that the famous **banyan tree,** at the corner of Hotel Street, and its neighbor, the **Lahaina Courthouse** (648 Wharf St.), will open to visitors by early 2025. Visit www.mauicounty.gov for updates during your trip, or, if you're staying in a hotel in Ka'anapali or beyond, ask your concierge for updates.

Plantation Museum
1221 HI-30; 808/661-3262; 10am-4pm daily; free

To catch a look at a period of Lahaina's history that didn't have to do with whalers, missionaries, or Hawaiian royalty, head over to the Lahaina Cannery shops for a

UPDATES ON LAHAINA AFTER 2023 FIRES

While the rest of West Maui is open and available for tourists to enjoy, Old Town Lahaina was devastated after the fires of summer 2023, and the area is closed until further notice. There are limited sites to experience in and around Old Town Lahaina as the rebuilding process continues, so your best bets would be to visit businesses, beaches, and sites north of Kaeo Place or south of Puunoa Place from Old Town. Lahaina Cannery Mall, near the Old Lahaina Luau, is an ideal spot to park to visit the cannery and its surrounding areas.

Out of kindness and support, refrain from asking servers about the fires. Thousands of individuals lost their homes; assume that everybody you interact with was affected in some way because of the fires. Your presence and support are vital to Maui, and you are welcome. To explore further ways to support West Maui in its rebuilding efforts, consider contributing to **The Maui Strong Fund** (www.hawaiicommunityfoundation.org/maui-strong) or **Maui United Way** (www.mauiunitedway.org/ways-give), two intrepid organizations working hard behind the scenes.

glimpse inside the informative Plantation Museum. There are dozens of old photos showing life during plantation times as well as a video detailing harvesting sugarcane. The Pioneer Mill was the social and economic engine of the West Side for the better part of 100 years, and the plantation days are just as much a part of Lahaina's heritage as harpoons, grog, and bibles. A visit takes only a couple of minutes and is worthwhile.

SOUTH OF LAHAINA
Maui Dragon Fruit Farm
833 Punakea Loop; 808/264-6127; www.mauidragonfruit.com; 8:30am-2pm and 4:30pm-6:30pm Mon.-Fri.
The Maui Dragon Fruit Farm, in the Launiupoko subdivision, makes for a curious combination of agriculture

Pu'u Keka'a (Black Rock) (left); dragon fruit (right)

HIGHLIGHTS 111

THE BANYAN TREE

the Banyan Tree

This magnificent tree is the most recognizable landmark in West Maui. You can't miss it at the corner of Hotel and Front Streets because it spreads its shading boughs over almost 1 acre (0.4 ha). This tree is the **largest banyan in the state,** planted in April 1873 by Sheriff Bill Smith in commemoration of the Congregationalist Missions' golden anniversary. The 2023 fires damaged the tree, but it stands victorious. Check www.mauicounty.gov for updates during your trip—an official date for reopening to the public has not yet been determined.

and adventure. With the consistency of an apple but the look of an exotic poppy-seed muffin, dragon fruit is tropical and native to Central and South America, although it's most often seen in Southeast Asia. In addition to dragon fruit, various other crops are grown on this certified organic farm.

Tropical fruit-tasting walking tours ($45 adults, $35 children) take place 9am-4pm Monday-Friday. Additional adventure activities include a 450-ft-long (135-m) zip line (9am, 10:30am, noon, 2pm Mon.-Fri.; $119 adults, $99 children) and an enormous plastic "Aquaball" (9am, 10:30am, noon, 2pm Mon.-Fri.; $119 adults, $99 children) filled with water and then rolled 450 ft (135 m) downhill with you inside. Combine the farm tour, zip line, and the Aquaball for $189 adults, $169 children.

Olowalu Petroglyphs

For every 1,000 people who snorkel at Olowalu, probably only one makes it back to the ki'i pohaku, the petroglyphs behind the Olowalu General Store. Hidden 0.5 mi (0.8 km) back in the recesses of Olowalu valley, the 70 rock carvings on the face of Pu'u Kilea date to around 300 years ago, when there was no written form of the Hawaiian language. To find the petroglyphs, drive on the road

112   WEST MAUI

behind the Olowalu fruit stand at mile marker 15 and proceed on the paved segment, which runs back toward the valley. After 0.5 mi (0.8 km) are signs for the Olowalu Cultural Reserve, and when the road turns to dirt, the petroglyphs are about 200 yards (180 m) farther, on the rock face. Unfortunately, some of the petroglyphs have been vandalized, so visitors are asked to keep a respectful distance from them.

BEST BEACHES

KAPALUA, NAPILI, AND HONOKOWAI

Known to locals simply as "up north," the beaches along this stretch include tropical turquoise coves sandwiched between condos and luxurious homes. Napili and Kapalua beaches are the most popular, but past the entrance to Kapalua, the shore gets wilder and the crowds start to thin. The wind can howl in the afternoons and massive surf crashes into the coast October-April. Over the winter the shore-break often grows to 10 ft (3 m) or larger.

D. T. Fleming Beach Park

D. T. Fleming Beach Park has been named the number one beach in the United States. Fleming's is a hybrid stretch of sand where the southern half is dominated by Ritz-Carlton resort guests and the northern half is popular with locals. This is one of the best beaches on the island for bodysurfing and bodyboarding, although the surf can get rough and dangerous in the winter. Luckily, this is one of the few beaches on the West Side with lifeguards. There are restrooms and showers at the northern end.

Napili Bay and Kapalua Bay

There is a lot of debate about which beach is better: Napili Bay or Kapalua Bay. A couple of factors distinguish one from the other: Although a mere 0.25 mi (0.4 km) from each other, the shore-break at Napili Bay can be larger in the winter, whereas Kapalua is more protected. The snorkeling between the two reefs is

Napili Bay (left); D. T. Fleming Beach Park (right)

BEST BEACHES 113

TOP BEACH
KAʻANAPALI BEACH

This stunning, uninterrupted expanse of sand, lined from end to end with world-class resorts, has been named the number one beach in the United States. Pick any island beach activity—surfing, snorkeling, scuba, snuba, paddleboarding, cliff-jumping, volleyball, parasailing (summer), or whale-watching (winter)—and you'll find it on Kaʻanapali Beach. This area is also full of great restaurants, hotel bars, and snack shops.

The best snorkeling is found at Puʻu Kekaʻa (Black Rock) in front of the Sheraton at the far northern end of the beach. Most of the water sports take place at KP Point in front of the Kaʻanapali Aliʻi, and the beach volleyball court is in front of the Sheraton. For bodyboarding, the best area is between Whalers Village and Puʻu Kekaʻa. Since the beach faces directly west, it can pick up waves any time of year. Be careful on days with big shore-break, however, and use common sense. A paved pathway runs the length of the beach and is popular with joggers in the morning.

The wind can often be a factor here in the afternoon, so it's best to get your water activities in early before the trade winds start blowing. If the wind is blowing too hard by the Sheraton, you can find a pocket of calm at the southern end of the beach by the Hyatt. Also, if you plan on going for a morning swim, be alert when you're in the water in front of Kaʻanapali Beach Hotel or Whalers Village, where large catamarans come ashore to pick up passengers.

Unless you're staying at one of the resorts along the Kaʻanapali strip, parking is challenging since most free public spots are taken by 9am. There is one small public garage between the Sheraton and the Kaʻanapali Beach Hotel, a lot between Whalers Village and the Westin, a handful of beach parking stalls in the front lot of the Kaʻanapali Beach Hotel, and a small public lot on Nohea Kai Drive just before the Hyatt.

a toss-up, although Kapalua often has more fish while Napili has more sea turtles. Napili Bay is a little larger, although it can also become more crowded. If you're traveling with children, Kapalua Bay is the better bet since the water is calmer and there is easy access to beach showers and restrooms.

Oneloa Bay (Ironwoods)

Hidden from view from the road through Kapalua, Oneloa Bay is virtually always empty. This epic expanse of shore sits right along the Kapalua Coastal Trail, although since the swimming is poor and it's out of sight, it's also out of mind. Mornings on Oneloa can be calm and still, and this is a popular spot for sunset wedding photo shoots. Oneloa is a great beach for those who just want to commune with nature and need a bit of an escape. The beach is also known as Ironwoods because of the big evergreen trees plentiful in the area.

Mokulei'a Bay (Slaughterhouse)

Tucked at the base of dramatic cliffs, Mokulei'a offers some of the best snorkeling on the West Side. It's known to locals as Slaughterhouse Beach, but the name is less sinister than it sounds: A slaughterhouse was once located here but is now long gone. The bay is part of the Honolua Bay Marine Life Conservation District, so no fishing or spearfishing—or any other kind of slaughter—is allowed. This is also a popular beach for bodysurfing, although the surf can be treacherous during large winter swells. This beach is nearly always deserted in the early morning hours, but lately is packed by 11am.

★ Punalau Beach (Windmills)

Sandy, serene, and almost always empty, Punalau is little visited by tourists—but not for lack of beauty. The local name, Windmills, is derived from an old windmill that once stood here but has long since been destroyed. This is now a popular place for advanced surfers and ambitious beachcombers who scour the shore for flotsam and shells. The road down to the shore can often be rough, so unless you have a high-clearance vehicle, it's best to leave your car parked by the highway and make the five-minute trek on foot. Bring all of your valuables with you, and also pack a blanket or towel for lying in the sun and soaking up the silence. Since the reef is shallow and can be razor sharp, don't snorkel or swim here. This is also one of Maui's best spots to watch large winter surf, and the left break at the far southern end has been referred to as Maui's version of the Pipeline.

SOUTH OF LAHAINA

On the stretch of shore between Lahaina and Ma'alaea are a grand

Mokulei'a Bay (Slaughterhouse)

BEST BEACHES 115

Launiupoko Beach Park (left); Ukumehame Beach Park (right)

total of zero resorts. Paddleboards and fishing poles rule this section of coast, and even though the swimming is poor, there is one spot that offers good snorkeling. Most visitors pass these beaches without giving them another thought, but if you do decide to pull over to watch the whales, visit the beach, or photograph the sunset, don't stop in the middle of the road. If you're headed in the Lahaina direction, it's easiest to pull off on the right side of the road and wait for traffic to clear before crossing.

Launiupoko Beach Park

Located at the only stoplight between Ma'alaea and Lahaina, Launiupoko is the most family-friendly beach park on the West Side of Maui. It has a protected wading area for small keiki (children), a decent sandy beach on the south end of the park, a wide, grassy picnic area, and numerous surf breaks that cater to beginner surfers and stand-up paddle boarders. This park is so popular with the weekend barbecue crowd that local families arrive before dawn to stake their claim for a birthday party with a bounce house. There is a large parking lot as well as restrooms and showers, and since most of the parking spots are taken by 8am, there is an overflow lot on the mauka (mountain side) of the highway. The water is too shallow for swimming and the snorkeling is poor, but this is a good place to put your finger on the local pulse and strike up a good conversation.

Ukumehame Beach Park

Ukumehame Beach Park is a small yet scenic beach along the shore. Look for mile marker 12 along Honoapi'ilani Highway, where you'll find a parking lot. The beach is an ideal spot for kayak launches, snorkeling, and surfing. In fact, it's one the best places for beginning surfers thanks to its numerous surf breaks, and it earns its nickname, "Thousand Peaks." Many people bring picnic lunches or food to barbecue in the pits. While visitors have been known to spend an entire day, the best time for snorkelers to experience this park is in the morning hours when the wind is moderate.

SCENIC DRIVES

NORTHWESTERN COAST
Driving Distance: *14.8 mi (23.8 km)*
Driving Time: *45 minutes*
Start: *Kapalua*
End: *Kahakuloa*

Exploring the island's northwestern coast is one of the island's best day trips—like a miniature Road to Hana without the waterfalls, but with far better beaches and views. If you continue all the way around the back of West Maui past the town of Kahakuloa (the road isn't limited to 4WD vehicles like your car-rental map might say, but it is far narrower, curvier, and scarier than the Road to Hana), you can combine the drive with the waterfalls of Makamaka'ole Valley in Central Maui for a full-day experience. This journey is not for the timid. Most turn back toward Kapalua once they reach Kahakuloa.

BEST HIKES AND WALKS

There aren't nearly as many hiking trails on the West Side of the island as you might expect. Much of the access in West Maui is blocked by private land or lack of proper trails. Also, since much of West Maui sits in the lee of Mauna Kahalawai, there aren't any accessible waterfalls, as there are in East Maui. Nevertheless, the hiking options in West Maui offer their own sort of beauty, from stunning coastal treks to grueling ridgeline hikes.

KAPALUA, NAPILI, AND HONOKOWAI

★ Kapalua Coastal Trail
Distance: *1.75 mi (2.8 km) one-way*
Duration: *just over 1 hour*
Elevation Gain: *209 ft (63 m)*
Effort: *easy*
Trailhead: *Kapalua Bay*

Arguably the best coastal walk in Hawaii, the Kapalua Coastal Trail is bookended on each side by beaches that have each been named the number one beach in the United States: Kapalua Bay and D. T. Fleming Beach Park. It also affords grand views of both Moloka'i and Lana'i. While most walkers, joggers, and hikers begin the trail at Kapalua Bay, you can also access the trail from other junctions at the Kapalua Bay Villas, Oneloa Bay, the Ritz-Carlton, and D. T. Fleming Beach Park.

If you begin at Kapalua Bay, the trail starts as a paved walkway

Kapalua Coastal Trail

BEST HIKES AND WALKS 117

paralleling the beach and weaves its way through ultra-luxurious residences. The trail eventually switches to dirt, and a spur trail leads straight out toward **Hawea Point,** a protected reserve that is home to the island's largest colony of 'ua'u kani (wedge-tailed shearwaters). If you follow the grass trail to the left of the three-way junction, it connects with the trail to **Namalu Bay**—the rocky Mediterranean cove hidden in the craggy recesses.

Continuing along, the main Kapalua Coastal Trail leads over a short rocky section before emerging at a smooth boardwalk along **Oneloa Bay.** The boardwalk here was constructed as a means of protecting the sensitive dunes of Kapalua, and in the morning Oneloa is one of the most gloriously empty beaches you'll find on Maui. At the end of the boardwalk, the trail leads up a flight of stairs and eventually connects with **Lower Honoapi'ilani Road.** From here, take a left and follow the sidewalk as it connects with the trail running in front of the Ritz-Carlton before finishing at the water's edge at **D. T. Fleming Beach Park.** For a side trip, hike out parallel to the golf course to **Makaluapuna Point**—otherwise known as Dragon's Teeth (page 105).

Village Walking Trails

Distance: *1.25-3.6 mi (2-5.8 km) round-trip*
Duration: *2 hours*
Elevation Gain: *800 ft (243 m)*
Effort: *easy-moderate*
Trailhead: *Kapalua Village Center*
The village walking trails are the next most popular hikes in the Ritz-Carlton resort area. Weaving their way up the mountainside through the

cool and forested uplands are the 1.25-mi (2-km) **Cardio Loop** and the 3.6-mi (5.8-km) **Lake Loop,** an uphill, butt-burning workout popular with local joggers. More than just a great morning workout, sections of the trail offer sweeping views looking out toward Moloka'i and the area around Honolua Bay. To find the access point for the trails, park in the lot for the Kapalua Village Center (between Sansei restaurant and the Kapalua Golf Academy) and follow a paved cart path winding its way down toward an underpass, where you will find the trailhead for both loops.

KA'ANAPALI

Ka'anapali Beach Walk Trail

Distance: *3 mi (4.8 km) one-way*
Duration: *2-3 hours*
Elevation Gain: *29 ft (11 m)*
Effort: *easy*
Trailhead: *in front of Hyatt resort*
The southern terminus of the Ka'anapali Beach Walk Trail is in front of the Hyatt resort, and the easiest public beach parking is at Hanakao'o Beach Park along the highway between Ka'anapali and Lahaina. From here the boardwalk runs north all the way to the Sheraton, about 1.5 mi (2.4 km), although if you follow the paved walkway through the lower level of the Sheraton and through the parking lot, you will notice the trail re-forms and starts skirting the golf course. The walkway then runs through the Royal Lahaina resort and the parking lot of adjoining hotels. Following the Beach Walk signs, you eventually join another boardwalk that runs all the way down to the Honua Kai resort.

SNORKELING

Snorkeling is the most popular activity in West Maui. Hundreds of people ply the waters of the island's western shore, flipping their fins as they chase after schools of yellow and black manini (convict tang). But there is always room to find your own section of reef, and the waters of West Maui teem with everything from graceful green sea turtles to the playfully named humuhumunukunukuapua'a—the Hawaiian state fish, whose name translates as "big lips with a nose like a pig."

Mornings are the best time of day for snorkeling. Different times of year also mean different snorkeling conditions. During the winter, places such as Honolua Bay and Napili can be dangerous due to the huge surf, so summer is the best time for exploring these reefs. Similarly, snorkeling spots on the south shore such as Olowalu can be prone to large surf during summer, although with much less frequency than the northern beaches in winter. If the surf is too big or the conditions too poor, there is probably another place that is calm and beautiful just a 20-minute drive away.

SNORKELING SPOTS
Kapalua, Napili, and Honokowai
HONOLUA BAY

Honolua Bay's wide, scenic cleft in the coast is not only a biodiverse marine reserve, it's also protected from the afternoon trade winds. Honolua Bay is one of the most sacred and revered spots on the West Side of the island. The valley, bay, and shore exude a supernatural beauty. Somewhere between the lush green foliage of the valley and the shimmering turquoise waters is

snorkeling in Honolua Bay

a palpable magic unlike anywhere else.

The "beach" is more a collection of boulders. Facing the water, the right side has a much larger snorkeling area and a greater concentration of marinelife. The center of the bay has a sandy bottom and is mostly devoid of marinelife, so it's best to trace the shore and snorkel around to the right. If there aren't any charter boats tied up on the right side of the bay between 9am and noon, it means that the conditions aren't good enough to bring paying snorkelers here. Also, if you see breaking waves out toward the point and there are more than 20 surfers in the water, it means that the visibility is going to be less than stellar and conditions will be dangerous. If it isn't raining on the shore but the stream on the left side of the bay is gushing with brown water, it means that it's raining farther up the mountain and the runoff is emptying into the bay, which also makes for subpar conditions.

If, however, the sun is shining brilliantly, here's your guide to the best snorkeling area: When you enter the water from the rocky shore, swim straight out for about 20 yards (18 m) and then turn right toward the shore. You'll want to hug the shore in 5-10 ft (1.5-3 m) of water and follow it in a ring around the right side of the bay. To find Hawaiian green sea turtles, the best spot to check out is the **turtle cleaning station** on the right center of the bay. It's about 200 yards (180 m) out from the boat ramp, in line with the bend in the cliff on the right side of the bay, in about 15-20 ft (4.5-6 m) of water. Snorkeling in Honolua Bay during winter, you can dive a few feet underwater to listen for the distant song of humpback whales. Keep a keen eye out for boat traffic, as a number of catamarans make their approach through the middle of the bay.

NAMALU BAY

An out-of-the-way snorkeling experience in a rocky, almost Mediterranean cove, Namalu Bay is one of West Maui's best spots. There isn't much in the way of live coral, but you can spot green sea turtles, reef fish, and the occasional eagle or manta ray. The center of the bay is about 40 ft (12 m) deep, and the areas ringing the shore are a more manageable 5-15 ft (1.5-4.5 m). As a bonus, the rocks also make for some enjoyable cliff-jumping.

KAPALUA BAY

Kapalua Bay is a sandy cove that is a favorite for snorkeling with small children. Its relatively small size means it is easy to scour the entire bay, and you can expect to see colorful parrotfish, lots of goatfish, and even the occasional green sea turtle. Although depths rarely exceed 20 ft (6 m), the best snorkeling is found along the right side of the bay where the rocks extend out to the distant point. If you're a strong snorkeler and the conditions are calm, you can even snorkel around the northern point into neighboring Namalu Bay.

Ka'anapali

PU'U KEKA'A (BLACK ROCK)

The best snorkeling in Ka'anapali is at Pu'u Keka'a, better known as Black Rock. At the far northern end of Ka'anapali Beach in front of the Sheraton, this area offers the most consistently beautiful snorkeling conditions and a relatively easy entry. The morning hours are best, and the best chance for seeing sea turtles is during high tide, when the water comes up on the side of the rock and all the limu (seaweed) falls into the water. Since this is a favorite delicacy of the green sea turtles, occasionally three or four of them congregate in the shallow cove in only 5-10 ft (1.5-3 m) of water. Since the cliff is also a favorite place for cliff-jumping, steer clear of the immediate landing zone, and if you see the wind whipping up whitecaps out by the point, stay in the cove, protected from the wind and with gentler currents.

KA'ANAPALI POINT
On the other end of Ka'anapali Beach is the reef at Ka'anapali Point, in front of the Marriott. It's not nearly as popular as the reef at Pu'u Keka'a but covers a larger area and isn't nearly as crowded. If Pu'u Keka'a is a flotilla of fins, take a 10-minute stroll to the southern end of the beach and try your luck at this less visited spot.

Lahaina
MALA WHARF
Mala Wharf reopened with limited use after the 2023 fires. This is an ideal snorkeling site where legions of sea turtles and numerous reef sharks live under the pilings littering the ocean floor. The only time you don't want to snorkel here is when the river draining into the bay is a torrent of runoff. This typically occurs with huge downpours or consistent rains, and mostly during the winter months.

South of Lahaina
OLOWALU
The best snorkeling south of Lahaina is at Olowalu, otherwise known as mile marker 14. The reef here is a wide expanse of coral heads. The outer reef is popular with tour and dive boats, and the inside sections can teem with large parrotfish and

Hawaiian green sea turtles. Directly out from the mile marker is a sand channel that leads through the shallow reef and allows access to deeper water. If you venture out from a random spot along the coast, there is a good chance you will get trapped in a maze of shallow coral heads where the water is often murky and the snorkeling is poor. If possible, get here in the morning before the winds pick up.

BEST TOURS
Kapalua, Napili, and Honokowai
SHORELINE SNORKEL
Hanakao'o Beach Park; 808/214-4743; www.shorelinesnorkel.com; 6am-9:30pm daily
Shoreline Snorkel offers exceptional tours, including a 90-minute guided tour with snorkel instruction ($125). Its Three Beach Adventure ($299) showcases the best of West Maui and includes stops at three beaches—two for snorkeling, the third for lunch—with snorkel gear and drinks included (bring cash for lunch). A standout excursion is the Night Snorkel Adventure ($139), an opportunity to glimpse ocean life that few people experience. Enjoy the sparkling glow of bioluminescence, or spot octopuses and lobsters as a guide leads you from shore using LED lights.

Ka'anapali
TRILOGY
808/874-5649; www.sailtrilogy.com
Of the charters departing from Ka'anapali Beach, Trilogy loads in front of the Ka'anapali Beach Hotel and offers 7:30am snorkeling trips, making them the first boat to reach Honolua Bay. The tours from Ka'anapali are usually aboard the *Trilogy III*, a few feet smaller than other boats

SNORKELING 121

SNORKELING TOURS AND RENTALS

NAME	LOCATION	CONTACT INFO
KAPALUA, NAPILI, AND HONOKOWAI		
★ **Shoreline Snorkel**	Hanakao'o Beach Park	808/214-4743; www.shorelinesnorkel.com
Water Works Sports	5315 Lower Honoapi'ilani Rd.	808/298-2446; www.waterworkssportsmaui.com
Snorkel Bob's	5425 Honoapi'ilani Hwy.	808/669-9603; www.snorkelbob.com
KA'ANAPALI		
★ **Trilogy**	n/a	808/874-5649; www.sailtrilogy.com
Teralani Sailing Adventures	n/a	808/661-7245; www.teralani.com
The Snorkel Store	2580 Keka'a Dr.	808/669-1077; www.thesnorkelstore.com
LAHAINA		
Ocean Project Maui	843 Waine'e St.	808/280-0873; www.oceanprojectmaui.com
★ **Captain Woody's**	Mala Ramp	808/667-2290; www.captainwoodysmaui.com
★ **Ultimate Snorkel Adventure**	n/a	808/667-5678; www.ultimatewhalewatch.com

along the beach. The maximum capacity is about 49 people. All the food is made fresh on board. Both the Trilogy crew and the level of customer service are widely regarded as the best in the industry. Due to its slightly smaller size and its light weight, the *Trilogy III* is the fastest of the Ka'anapali sailboats. Five-hour charters are $175 for adults, include all food and equipment, and usually return to the beach around 1:30pm.

Lahaina

Most snorkeling charters depart from behind the banyan tree on Front Street; a few set out from Mala Ramp on the northern edge of town.

Snorkeling charters in Lahaina run the gamut from small inflatable rafts to massive two-tiered catamarans. It's important to find a tour company with the type of experience you want. Note that due to their bouncy nature, rafts aren't recommended for pregnant women or anyone with back problems. If you're prone to seasickness, note that the waters often become rough during the afternoon.

CAPTAIN WOODY'S
Mala Ramp; 808/667-2290; www. captainwoodysmaui.com
For private excursions, Captain Woody's operates charters of only six people and leaves from Mala

ACTIVITY	PRICE
charter/tour	$125-299 guided tours, including a night tour
rental shop	$10 per day or $30 per week
rental shop	weekly rentals ($44 adults, $30 children)
charter/tour	from $175
charter/tour	from $119
rental shop	$37 per day
charter/tour	$145 adults, $120 children
charter/tour	from $295
charter/tour	from $200

Ramp. Fishing, snorkeling, and seasonal whale-watching can all be included in these small group tours, which usually last six hours. Prices start at $295.

ULTIMATE SNORKEL ADVENTURE
808/667-5678; www. ultimatewhalewatch.com
Ultimate Snorkel Adventure is the best option of all the rafts, though it is best to call ahead to determine daily availability. It operates in north Lahaina. Group sizes are kept to 22, and this rigid inflatable is the fastest boat at speeds over 35 mph (56 km/h). Snorkeling locations are chosen off the island of Lana'i based on the best conditions, and unlike some of the other options that go ashore on Lana'i, this excursion snorkels off the raft. Due to its small size, it can navigate close to the shore of Lana'i to find blowholes or follow pods of spinner dolphins hanging out by the rocks. Six-hour snorkeling trips are $200 adults, and this is a great option for a semiprivate tour with a relaxed but professional captain and crew.

SCUBA DIVING

Scuba diving from the West Side of the island involves one of two options: departing from a West Side harbor for an excursion to Lana'i or diving along the West Maui shore. While certified divers should seek out a dive charter, there are also shore operators that offer introductory dives. For certified divers diving independently, ask at the rental shop about current conditions, and always use a dive flag. Dive spots along the northern section of the island are inaccessible during winter due to large surf. Summer is the best time for diving up north.

DIVE SITES
Kapalua, Napili, and Honokowai
HONOLUA BAY
The best shore dive in West Maui is Honolua Bay, although slogging all of your gear down to the water can be an exhausting undertaking. Diving from shore, launch from the center of the beach and hug the right side of the bay where the reef drops off into the sand channel. Maximum depth can reach about 40 ft (12 m), and you can expect to see green sea turtles and a wide variety of reef fish, and you may even have a rare encounter with spinner dolphins.

KAPALUA BAY
For a beginner-friendly introductory dive, Kapalua Bay can offer everything from a shallow dive of 25 ft (7.6 m) to a more advanced dive of 40 ft (12 m) rounding the corner toward neighboring Namalu Bay. There are showers and facilities as well as easy sandy-beach entry.

Ka'anapali
KAHEKILI BEACH PARK
The northernmost dive site in Ka'anapali and the one preferred by independent instructors is Kahekili Beach Park. The depth is shallow, rarely exceeding 35 ft (11 m), and the coral begins immediately. The reef parallels the shore, with the greatest

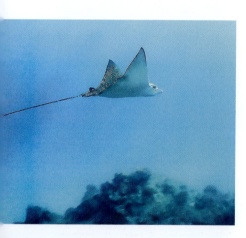

eagle ray in the waters of Ka'anapali (top); picasso triggerfish at Pu'u Keka'a (Black Rock) (bottom)

diversity of life found at 15-25 ft (4.5-7.5 m). The beach is long, and the healthiest amount of coral is found right off the beach park. It is uncrowded compared to neighboring Ka'anapali Beach, and there is easier parking for lugging gear from the car. Showers and restrooms are conveniently located in the middle of the beach park.

PU'U KEKA'A (BLACK ROCK)

The best dive in Ka'anapali is Pu'u Keka'a, also known as Black Rock. Despite the relative ease of the dive and the fairly shallow depths, the rocky promontory draws all sorts of marinelife. Although not always guaranteed, divers frequently sight sea turtles, reef fish, eels, octopuses, and rare squid or cowries. The best way to dive Pu'u Keka'a is to do a drift dive from the southern end of Kahekili Beach Park and swim around to the front of the rock, or enter the water in front of the Sheraton, swim partway around the rock, and then double back the way you came. This is a great dive for those who have just been certified. For a real treat, consider a night dive.

Lahaina

HANAKAO'O BEACH PARK

Within walking distance of southern Ka'anapali, Hanakao'o Beach Park is the northernmost beach in Lahaina and the site of many introductory dive classes. This is a good dive if you're practicing your skills over sand. The shallow area is also good for spotting turtles and colorful reef fish, and you can find turtles if you follow the rocks south toward Wahikuli Beach Park.

MALA WHARF

The best dive in Lahaina is Mala Wharf, although it's most often accessed as a boat dive. When Hurricane Iniki came storming through in 1992, the 30-ft (9-m) waves it created were strong enough to destroy the outer half of Mala Ramp. Today the collapsed pilings are still lying in 25 ft (7.5 m) of water, and the result has been decades of live coral development on what is now one of the island's best artificial reefs. The caverns of the pilings are home to numerous turtles and whitetip reef sharks, some of which can reach up to 6 ft (1.8 m). Even though the depth never exceeds 35 ft (10.5 m), this is a favorite of island dive charters due to its proximity to the harbors and wealth of marinelife.

South of Lahaina

OLOWALU

Known to some operators as Turtle Reef or Turtle Point, Olowalu is an offshore, turtle-laden area popular with charter boats on the offshore reefs. Maximum depths are about 30 ft (9 m), and on nice days the visibility is close to 100 ft (30 m). This area is also popular with independent dive operators as a confined-water area for practicing dive skills. If you are shore-diving independently, the easiest way to get to deeper water is to enter around the mile marker 14 sign and swim in a straight line until you reach depths of 20-25 ft (6-7.5 m). When navigating your way through the coral heads, it's imperative to make sure that your gear doesn't drag across the reef, and bring a dive flag with you so that boats know you're below.

SCUBA DIVING 125

DIVE OPERATORS

NAME	LOCATION	CONTACT INFO
KAPALUA, NAPILI, AND HONOKOWAI		
In 2 Scuba Diving Maui Dive Co.	65 Ala Hoku Pl.	808/264-8198; www. in2scubadivingmaui.com
KA'ANAPALI		
★Tiny Bubbles Scuba	3350 Lower Honoapi'ilani Rd.	808/870-0878; www. tinybubblesscuba.com
Maui Diving Scuba & Snorkel Center	910 Lower Honoapi'ilani Rd.	808/667-0633; www. mauidiving.com
LAHAINA		
★Extended Horizons	94 Kupuohi St.	808/667-0611; www. extendedhorizons.com
Dive Maui	1223 Front St.	808/661-7333; www. goscubadivemaui.com

BEST DIVE OPERATORS

Ka'anapali

TINY BUBBLES SCUBA

3350 Lower Honoapi'ilani Rd.; 808/870-0878; www. tinybubblesscuba.com; 8am–5pm daily

Tiny Bubbles Scuba operates shore dives along the West Maui coast. Under the lead of the vivacious and knowledgeable instructor Timmerz, all of the instructors for Tiny Bubbles have been diving the Maui shore for over a decade and are acquainted with the nuances of Maui diving. Introductory courses are $149, and certified divers can participate in a private guided beach dive for $129. Night dives ($149) and scooter dives ($149) are also offered. Depths on these shore dives rarely exceed 40 ft (12 m). All gear is included, and while the business is run out of the Ka'anapali Beach Club, the exact dive site is determined by the conditions.

Lahaina

EXTENDED HORIZONS

94 Kupuohi St.; 808/667-0611; www. extendedhorizons.com

On the north end of Lahaina at Mala Ramp, Extended Horizons is another reputable operation that offers tours to Lana'i and the west shore of Maui. Extended Horizons takes only six passengers, and it's the only charter boat on the island to run completely on biodiesel. Morning tours check in at 6:10am at the Mala boat ramp for dives along West Maui ($205). Other dive options include trips to Lana'i as well as night dives, beach dives, and certification classes.

ACTIVITY	PRICE
introductory lessons, night dives	$139–238
introductory lessons, beach dives, night dives, scooter dives	$129–149
introductory lessons	from $149
tours, night dives, beach dives, certification classes	from $205
introductory lessons, tours	$120

SURFING

Surfing is more than a hobby in West Maui—it's a way of life. In Lahaina, legions of longboarders begin each morning by watching the sunrise from the water, and flotillas of surf schools operate throughout the day. Up north, Honolua is the proving ground of the island's burgeoning surfers, and whenever "The Bay" starts breaking, a palpable buzz runs through the community. Not all breaks are suitable for beginners, and only a handful of breaks are included in this guide. Practice common etiquette, and enjoy the serenity that comes with surfing one of the most beautiful spots in the world.

SURF SPOTS

Kapalua, Napili, and Honokowai

POHAKU BEACH PARK

Pohaku Beach Park in Kahana is the epicenter of the West Side's longboard community. From the parking lot, you can see two distinct breaks. To the right is **Mushrooms,** which can be a fun wave, but it's shallow on the inside section. To the left is **S-Turns,** where you'll notice a couple of A-frame peaks a long paddle offshore. Surfing at S-Turns is as much a paddle workout as a surfing workout, and you're forgiven if you need to stop to catch your breath on the way out. Beginners stay on the inside section, while more experienced surfers favor the outer peaks. Also, there have been some shark issues at S-Turns in the past, so be wary if the water is murky and no one else is out. S-Turns starts breaking on a moderate northwest swell, and on the largest of days can reach a few feet overhead.

HONOLUA BAY

If you're an avid surfer, Honolua Bay

SURF SHOPS

NAME	LOCATION	CONTACT INFO
KAPALUA, NAPILI, AND HONOKOWAI		
★ 808 Boards	5425 Lower Honoapiʻilani Rd.	808/667-0808; www.808boards.com
KAʻANAPALI		
Island Style Adventures	n/a	808/244-6858; www.isasurfschool.com
LAHAINA		
★ Goofy Foot	505 Front St., Ste. 123	808/244-9283; www.goofyfootsurfschool.com
★ Maui Surfer Girls	n/a	808/214-0606; www.mauisurfergirls.com

needs no introduction. The wave here is truly one of the best in the world, holding almost religious significance for the locals. Honolua is for experienced surfers, but even nonsurfers should come here during a large swell to watch the island's best pull into the gaping, barreling perfection. Honolua can become crowded, and if you paddle out and nobody recognizes you, your chances of getting a wave decrease significantly. Granted, on days when the surf is only about head high and the crowd isn't too thick, there can still be enough waves for everyone—provided you know what you're doing.

WINDMILLS
Windmills is a surf break at Punalau Beach suited to experienced surfers and an epic spot for watching the island's best. The massive left tube barrels with such ferocity it has been called Maui's Pipeline. Many professional surf films have been shot here, and the best vantage point is on the side of the road about 1 mi (1.6 km) after the dirt turnoff for the bluffs at Honolua Bay.

South of Lahaina
BETWEEN PUAMANA BEACH PARK AND LAUNIUPOKO BEACH PARK
For beginning surfers and longboarders, the 1-mi (1.6-km) stretch of coast between Puamana Beach Park and Launiupoko Beach Park has numerous breaks with mellow waves for beginners. In between the two parks are peaks known as **Guardrails, Woody's,** and **Corner Pockets.** There can be small waves here most times of year, although summer sees the most consistent surf.

BEST SURF SHOPS
Kapalua, Napili, and Honokowai
808 BOARDS
5425 Lower Honoapiʻilani Rd.; 808/667-0808; www.808boards.com; 8am-5pm daily; $40 per week
Experienced surfers will get the best selection with 808 Boards, who will pick up and drop off the board at no additional charge.

ACTIVITY	PRICE
rental shop	$40 per week
lessons, rental shop	lessons $79-125, rentals $30 per hour plus $15 per additional hour
lessons	from $180
lessons	from $99

Lahaina

GOOFY FOOT

505 Front St., Ste. 123; 808/244-9283; www.goofyfootsurfschool.com; 7am-4pm Mon.-Sat.

Inside the 505 shopping center, Goofy Foot has helped over 100,000 students ride their first wave since opening in 1994. Two-hour lessons are $180 per person, and the owner, Tim, was the private surf coach for Jimmy Buffett. The lessons take place at a beach of the instructor's choosing, depending on the day; most lessons take place south of Lahaina on beaches with less tourist activity.

MAUI SURFER GIRLS

808/214-0606; www.mauisurfergirls. com

To get away from the Breakwall crowds, Maui Surfer Girls is the island's premier female-only surf camp operator, although they also offer coed group lessons for $99 per person. It costs a few dollars more than in town, and lessons take place a few miles south of town along a mellow stretch of beach. Lessons are offered at 8am and 10:30am daily. At certain times of year, all-inclusive one- and two-week classes are offered to empower teenage girls through learning surfing.

KAYAKING AND SUP

KAYAKING AREAS

Kapalua, Napili, and Honokowai

The most popular kayak trip on the upper West Side of the island is the paddle from **D. T. Fleming Beach Park to Honolua Bay.** Along this stretch of coast, you pass rugged rock formations inaccessible from the road, and you'll hug this dramatic coast past Mokulei'a Bay and into Honolua. Because of the high surf during winter, these tours are only offered in summer, and all trips depart D. T. Fleming Beach Park in the early morning hours before the

KAYAKING AND SUP TOURS, LESSONS, AND RENTALS

NAME	LOCATION	CONTACT INFO
KAPALUA, NAPILI, AND HONOKOWAI		
Water Works Sports	5315 Lower Honoapi'ilani Rd.	808/298-2446; www.waterworkssportsmaui.com
Bring Me a Kayak	n/a	800/633-3580; www.bringmeakayak.com
LAHAINA		
★ Hawaiian Paddle Sports	n/a	808/442-6436; www.hawaiianpaddlesports.com
SOUTH OF LAHAINA		
Kayak Olowalu	800 Olowalu Village Rd.	808/661-0606; www.kayakolowalu.com

afternoon trade winds pick up. Snorkeling in Honolua Bay is included in the excursions, and you are likely to encounter Hawaiian green sea turtles or potentially even Hawaiian spinner dolphins.

South of Lahaina

The main areas for kayaking south of Lahaina are **Olowalu** (mile marker 14) and **Coral Gardens,** off Papalaua Beach Park (mile marker 11), where you can paddle along the rugged sea cliffs that plunge down into the sea and see the natural reef formations. This is a popular area for kayaking in winter since the large surf on the northern shores makes kayaking there impossible, and these are fantastic coral reefs for spotting Hawaiian green sea turtles.

SUP SPOTS

Kapalua, Napili, and Honokowai

One of the best stretches of coast for paddling is the section between **Kapalua Bay and Hawea Point.** The sandy entry at Kapalua Bay makes it easy to launch a board into the water. **Napili Bay** is another popular spot for morning paddles.

Never bring a stand-up paddleboard into Honolua Bay. It's heavily frowned upon by locals and you'll likely be sent back to the beach by the surfers in the water.

stand-up paddling off Ka'anapali

ACTIVITY	PRICE
paddleboard rental	$20 per hour, $40 per day
kayak and paddleboard rental	$95 per day
SUP lessons, kayaking and canoeing tours	$189–249
kayaking tours	from $70

Ka'anapali

Sandy Ka'anapali is the perfect spot for stand-up paddling, but only during the morning hours before the wind picks up. On winter days, the water can be as smooth as glass, with dozens of whales breaching around you. Being out on the water during whale season can be an exciting adventure, but the same laws apply to stand-up paddlers as to boats: Stay 100 yards (90 m) from humpback whales—unless, of course, they swim over to you.

BEST TOURS AND LESSONS

South of Lahaina

HAWAIIAN PADDLE SPORTS
808/442-6436; www. hawaiianpaddlesports.com

For personalized service in an area that isn't as crowded, Hawaiian Paddle Sports offers lessons on beaches south of Lahaina, run by instructors who have a deep-rooted respect for the island, the environment, and Hawaiian cultural history. While they're more expensive, these tours will leave you with a deeper appreciation for the ocean. Paddling lessons are $249 for a private session and $189 per person for groups of two or more. They also offer group excursions for kayaking ($109 pp) and canoeing packages ($189 pp). The educational component and respect for culture are superior to other operations.

KAYAKING AND SUP 131

OUTRIGGER CANOES

outrigger canoes

WHAT ARE OUTRIGGER CANOES?
Outrigger canoes are traditional boats equipped with one or more lateral support floats, called outriggers, which provide stability in the water. Originating from Polynesian and other Oceanic cultures, these canoes are designed for navigating open waters and are used for fishing, transportation, and racing. The outrigger helps balance the canoe against waves, making it ideal for coastal and ocean voyaging. Today, outrigger canoe paddling is both a popular sport and a way to preserve cultural traditions, especially in places like Hawaii and the Pacific Islands.

OUTRIGGER CANOE TRIPS
Off Kahekili Beach Park in front of the Westin Villas, **Maui Paddle Sports** (2780 Keka'a Dr.; 808/283-9344; www.mauipaddlesports.com; 7am-7pm daily) offers two-hour outrigger canoe rides in a six-person outrigger ($149 pp), a memorable one-hour turtle-watching outrigger experience ($119), and a whale-watching outrigger excursion (during whale season; $149). Trips run from 7am daily. This is a convenient option if you're staying in the area off Kahekili Beach.

sunset cruise (left); a Trilogy sailboat (right)

SUNSET CRUISES

Few Maui activities are more iconic than a sunset sail off the West Maui coast. The feeling of the trade winds in your hair as you glide along is a sensation of freedom you can't experience on land. Watch as the setting sun paints the sky every shade of orange and pink. On most days you can make out a rainbow hovering over the lush valleys of Mauna Kahalawai.

A sunset sail off Ka'anapali Beach can be the most magical moment of your vacation, but there are a few things to understand to make the most of the magic. Make sure to ask when you need to check in, as departure times for sunset sails are different in summer and winter. There's also a chance that the departure will be moved to Lahaina Harbor due to large surf on the beach. Since this isn't possible to predict until the day before, it's a good idea to double-check on the morning of your sail to confirm where the boat will be loading.

While it's fun to dress up a little, remember you'll be on a boat and outfit yourself accordingly. The Ka'anapali boats are all sailing catamarans, which are boarded from the sand, and since some days can have moderate shore-break, there's a good chance you'll end up wet from the shins down. Your shoes are collected prior to boarding (to prevent sand tracking onto the boat), so don't put too much effort into matching them with your outfit. The northerly trade winds can often be chilly, so it's a good idea to bring a light jacket. And even though the vessels are wide, spray may come over the sides. If your idea of a sunset sail is a stable platform that putts along at 3 knots (5.6 km/h), the dinner cruises from Lahaina are a better bet.

TRILOGY
808/874-5649; www.sailtrilogy.com
Trilogy offers sunset sails ($115) daily that feature live music and Pacific Rim pupu. Trilogy's sail isn't marketed as a booze cruise, but three premium alcoholic beverages are included in the rates, including mixed drink cocktails like the Moloka'i Mule. Trilogy also offers a dinner cruise ($129 adults, $99 children, free for 2

WATER SPORTS TOURS AND LESSONS

NAME	LOCATION	CONTACT INFO
KA'ANAPALI		
★ **UFO Parasail**	2435 Ka'anapali Pkwy.	800/359-4836; www.ufoparasail.net
West Maui Parasail	675 Wharf St. Slip 15	808/661-4060; www.westmauiparasail.com
Maui Watersports	n/a	808/667-2001; www.mauiwatersports.com
Wake Maui	n/a	888/347-4790; www.wakemaui.com
LAHAINA		
★ **Luckey Strike**	n/a	808/661-4606; www.luckeystrike.com
★ **Maui Spearfishing Academy**	n/a	808/446-0352; www.mauispearfishing.com

and under). The power catamaran used for this charter is the nicest of the large diesel boats, and the menu includes locally sourced produce and sustainably harvested seafood. Unless the surf is high and they need to load from Lahaina Harbor, the check-in for all Trilogy tours is in front of the Ka'anapali Beach Hotel.

TERALANI SAILING ADVENTURES
808/661-7245; www.teralani.com
In front of Whalers Village, Teralani offers two different sails departing nightly year-round (departure time varies throughout the year depending on sunset time). The original sunset sail ($99 adults) includes a pupu menu as well as an open bar of beer and mixed drinks. For those who would rather dine on board, the full dinner sail ($129 adults) is 30 minutes longer.

HULA GIRL
808/665-0344; www.sailingmaui.com
The most yacht-like experience departing from the beach is on the *Hula Girl*, which not only offers the newest boat but luxurious upgrades like throw pillows, free Wi-Fi, panoramic viewing from the fly-bridge, and high-tech sailing. For a full-service dinner cruise, *Hula Girl* offers cruises on Tuesday-Sunday ($200 adults) featuring upscale Pacific Rim dining options made fresh in the onboard kitchen. Standard sunset cruises ($121) offer a kids' menu and top-shelf tropical cocktails. In many ways, it's more like a floating restaurant with a cover charge.

SAIL MAUI
808/244-2087; www.sailmaui.com
If you know what it means to "shake a reef," you'll be much happier watching the sunset aboard a small sailboat than on a large, motorized platform. The fastest sailing catamaran offering sunset sails ($95 adults) from Lahaina is Sail Maui, which provides sailing, pupu, beer, wine, and mai tais. Trips run Monday-Saturday, and maximum capacity of the cruise is just 24 people.

ACTIVITY	PRICE
parasailing tour, fishing charter	parasailing from $129, fishing from $189
parasailing tour	from $139
jet skiing	$104 for a 45-minute ride
wake surfing charter	from $799 for up to six people
fishing charter	$145 pp for up to six people
spearfishing charter	from $239 pp

WHALE-WATCHING

Any vessel that floats is going to be offering whale-watching December 15–April 15. While whale season officially lasts until May 15, whales aren't encountered with enough regularity after mid-April to guarantee sightings. The peak of the season is January–March, and simply being out on the water turns any trip into a whale-watching expedition.

Most snorkeling and sailing operators offer whale-watching during winter, with most boats carrying whale naturalists well-versed in the study of these gentle giants. Since most prices are about the same, the choice ultimately comes down to what sort of vessel best suits your comfort level.

TERALANI SAILING ADVENTURES
808/661-7245; www.teralani.com; from $120

Sailboats from Teralani Sailing Adventures offer whale-watching trips from Ka'anapali Beach, sharing the experience with other passengers. The tour guarantees whale sightings, or you are offered another classic whale watch.

whale-watching

OTHER WATER SPORTS

In addition to snorkeling, diving, surfing, and thrilling whale-watching excursions, West Maui offers a range of other water sports, with activities for all levels of adventure.

BEST TOURS AND LESSONS

Parasailing

Parasailing isn't possible December 15-May 15. During the summer and fall, however, parasailing is a peaceful adventure option for gazing at West Maui from hundreds of feet above the turquoise waters.

UFO PARASAIL

2435 Ka'anapali Pkwy.; 800/359-4836; www.ufoparasail.net; from $129 ($89 for observers)

UFO Parasail departs from Ka'anapali Beach, in front of Leilani's restaurant. The staff and captains who run these tours do hundreds of trips over the course of the season, and from a safety and efficiency standpoint, the crew has it down to a science. Taking off and landing on the boat makes for a dry entry and exit, and you will be blown away by the serenity you experience up in the air. You must weigh at least 130 pounds (59 kg) to fly alone, and trips usually start around 8am.

Fishing

LUCKEY STRIKE

808/661-4606; www.luckeystrike.com; $145

Take note of Luckey Strike, which operates on the premise that using live bait for smaller fish is better. Captain Tad Luckey has been fishing these waters for over 30 years, and like most captains in the harbor, he has an enviable and well-earned amount of local knowledge to put into every trip.

MAUI SPEARFISHING ACADEMY

808/446-0352; www.mauispearfishing.com; from $239 pp

To take snorkeling to the next level and maybe take home dinner, Maui Spearfishing Academy teaches visitors how to spearfish and eradicate invasive species, and can teach you the technique behind holding your breath to spear-dive and target the right fish.

ADVENTURE SPORTS

Even though water sports dominate the recreation options on the island's West Side, there are still a number of places where you can get a thrill on the land or over the water.

ZIP-LINING

Kapalua, Napili, and Honokowai

KAPALUA ZIPLINES

500 Office Rd.; 808/756-9147; www.kapaluaziplines.com; 7am-5pm Mon.-Fri.

All the lines of Kapalua Ziplines' seven-line course are tandem. You can zip next to your loved one and watch them grimace with glee as you soar up to 2,100 ft (640 m) across the Kapalua mountainside. You'll walk over one of Hawaii's longest suspension bridges and ride an ATV to

Skyline Hawaii zip line (left); parasailing (right)

the summit. Tours (from $179) are offered five times per day. Since the tours can sometimes be canceled due to wind, try to go early in the morning.

Ka'anapali

SKYLINE HAWAII

2580 Keka'a Dr.; 808/427-2771; www.skylinehawaii.com; 7am-6pm Mon.-Sat.; from $189

The largest zip-lining tour in West Maui is Skyline Hawaii, a company that was the first zip-line operator on Maui. Each of the eight zip lines has a historical, environmental, or cultural connection explained by the guides, and the main draw is the view toward Lana'i and Moloka'i across the royal-blue channels. These tours are so popular they run eight times a day, with the earliest starting from the Fairway Shops office at 8am daily. The benefit of an early tour is that temperatures are still cool and winds are calm, although there can sometimes be some lingering morning showers, and the dirt roads can be muddy from this moisture. Try to get on the 8am or 9am tour, although there is never a bad time to be up here zip-lining. Children must be 10 years of age for the Ka'anapali course, closed-toe shoes are required, and the maximum weight is 260 pounds (118 kg).

ATV RIDES

Lahaina

KAHOMA RANCH

808/667-1978

The best ATV ride on the West Side of the island is with Kahoma Ranch, to get dirty and rip across dirt roads on your own ATV ($214) or a shared ATV ($149). At the end, when you're all hot and sweaty, you can take a plunge down one of three different waterslides. Tour participants are awarded with views looking out at the island of Lana'i and back into Kahoma Valley. The tour area is closed to the public, so this is the only way you will see these views.

The waterslides look like little more than tarps stretched over a hole in the ground, but the speeds you can achieve are much faster than you'd expect. Tour cost for children is $82, and those as young as age five can accompany a driver of legal age. Tours take place at 7:30am, 10am, 12:30pm, and 3pm daily, although the 7:30am tour doesn't include the waterslides.

ADVENTURE SPORTS   137

GOLF

KAPALUA, NAPILI, AND HONOKOWAI

KAPALUA PLANTATION COURSE
2000 Plantation Club Dr.; 877/527-2582; www.golfatkapalua.com

For serious golfers, the name Kapalua should be synonymous with the Kapalua Plantation Course. This 7,411-yard (6,777-m), par-73 course is the island's most famous and is the site of the Hyundai Tournament of Champions. With the course's fame comes big greens fees: $369, but discounted to $339 if you are staying at the Ritz-Carlton resort. Greens fees decrease as the day wears on, as low as $219 in the late afternoon for nine holes, but expect the wind to be howling. Club rentals ($89) include two sleeves of balls, and shoe rental is $19. To find the clubhouse, travel along Honoapi'ilani Highway (Hwy. 30) for 1 mi (1.6 km) past the main entrance to Ritz-Carlton and make a right onto Plantation Club Drive. Continue up the hillside; the clubhouse is on the right.

KAPALUA BAY COURSE
300 Kapalua Dr.; 808/669-8044; www.golfatkapalua.com

The Kapalua Bay Course along the Kapalua shore is more forgiving at par 72 and 6,600 yards (6,035 m). While all of the holes offer resort-quality play, the highlight is hole 5, where the green is sandwiched between Oneloa Bay and D. T. Fleming Beach Park and you are surrounded by 270 degrees of brilliant blue ocean. The Bay Course is windy in the afternoon, so early mornings are best for calm conditions. Greens fees are $235, discounted to $224 for those staying at the Ritz-Carlton resort.

golfing in Kapalua

The fees decrease through the day, to as low as $169 for nine holes. To find the clubhouse, turn on Kapalua Drive from Lower Honoapi'ilani Road, across the street from Oneloa Bay (Ironwoods Beach). Travel up the road by the tennis center to the clubhouse on the right.

SPAS AND WELLNESS

KAPALUA, NAPILI, AND HONOKOWAI

SPA MONTAGE
1 Bay Dr.; 808/662-6600; www. montagehotels.com; 9am-6pm daily
The best spa on the northwest side is the fantastically luxurious Spa Montage, a wellness retreat unlike any other, incorporating state-of-the-art workout equipment with peaceful surroundings looking out toward Kapalua Bay. Inspired by the island's bounty, the award-winning spa offers highly personalized treatments using Maui-inspired products. Lounge poolside afterward. A 60-minute massage runs $240. For one of the island's best spa deals, purchase a day pass for $65, which gives you access to the facilities, including the fitness center, hydrotherapy circuits, and impossibly calming surroundings.

ZENSATIONS SPA
3600 Lower Honoapi'ilani Rd.; 808/669-0100; www.zensationsspa. com; 9am-5pm Mon.-Sat.
For a spa experience outside a resort, Zensations Spa, in the 5A Rent-A-Space mall in Honokowai, offers 60-minute massages for $135 as well as a full range of aromatherapy and facial and body treatment options. The spa is within walking distance of many Honokowai condos.

KA'ANAPALI
While nearly every resort in the Ka'anapali complex has a spa or beauty center, a couple stand out.

HEAVENLY SPA
2365 Ka'anapali Pkwy.; 808/661-2588; www.westinmaui.com; 9am-4pm daily
At the Westin Maui next to Whalers Village, Heavenly Spa has been lauded as one of the top spas in the United States and has 50-minute massages beginning at $189.

SPA AT BLACK ROCK
2605 Ka'anapali Pkwy.; 808/667-9577; www.blackrockspa.com; 9am-5pm daily
For slightly more affordable rates, the Spa at Black Rock offers 50-minute massages beginning at $150.

MOBILE MASSAGE
NA ALI'I MASSAGE
808/250-7170; www. mymauimassage.com
If you would rather enjoy an in-room, mobile massage, Na Ali'i Massage will meet you anywhere on the West Side and offers rates much lower than the resorts or local massage parlors. A 60-minute massage is $120, and they offer a full range of other services, such as body scrubs, reflexology, and hand and foot treatments.

hand-carved crafts (left); Whalers Village (right)

SHOPPING

KA'ANAPALI
WHALERS VILLAGE
2435 Ka'anapali Pkwy.; 808/661-4567; www.whalersvillage.com; 9am-9pm daily

Without a doubt, the undisputed epicenter of the Ka'anapali shopping scene is Whalers Village, smack in the middle of Ka'anapali Beach between the Whaler Hotel and the Westin Maui. With three levels of restaurants, clothing boutiques, jewelry galleries, and kiosks, Whalers Village is the see-and-be-seen spot for all of your island souvenir shopping. While many of the stores are name-brand outlets you're already familiar with, there are still a handful of locally run stores. Get your parking validated, since the garage rates are expensive.

If you park in the Whalers Village garage, you can't help but walk directly past **Hilo Hattie** (808/875-4545; www.hilohattie.com), a gift and clothing shop with an impressive array of offerings, including Hawaiian chocolates. They also offer free shipping.

Soul Lei (808/661-6663) is a diverse island-themed gift shop, featuring a large variety of clothing, sandals, and shoes for men, women, and children, as well as many gift items. They even have pet supplies.

FOOD

The number of dining options on the West Side is overwhelming. In most places you pay a premium for the location, so prices may seem high at ocean-view tables. That said, it's still possible to get a meal for under $10 per person outside the main visitor areas. While there is an overabundance of places on the West Side to sit and casually dine, there are only a handful of decent places for an affordable lunch on the run.

STANDOUTS
Kapalua, Napili, and Honokowai

MERRIMAN'S
1 Bay Club Pl.; 808/669-6400; www. merrimanshawaii.com; 11:30am-2pm and 5pm-8:30pm daily; $24-69

Merriman's is one of the most scenic dining spots on the island. Arrive early to enjoy a glass of wine while watching the sunset from the oceanfront fire pit, and then enjoy a menu of farm-to-table fare, where over 90 percent of the ingredients are sourced from local farmers, fishers, and ranchers. Acclaimed chef Peter Merriman is one of the founders of the Hawaiian Regional Cuisine movement, and his genius is evident in everything from the gluten-free taro cake and ahi ginger poke to the lobster, avocado, and tomato salad. For pairings, there are probably nations with constitutions shorter than the wine list, which features over 40 different varietals. Reservations are strongly recommended.

PLANTATION HOUSE
2000 Plantation Club Dr.; 808/669-6299; www.cohnrestaurants.com; 8am-8:30pm daily; $14-67

Overlooking the Plantation golf course, the Plantation House offers spectacular views with succulent food to match. Considering the luxurious venue, the more affordable breakfast and lunch menu make you feel like you're getting away with something. Breakfast is served until 2pm, and for dinner, you can pair fresh fish such as ahi and provençale with a glass from the extensive wine list.

THE GAZEBO
5315 Lower Honoapi'ilani Rd.; 808/669-5621; 7:30am-2pm daily; $12-24

The Gazebo has the island's best breakfast. This isn't a secret, however, and there is a line out the door by 6:45am. What makes this spot so popular is not only the oceanfront location, gazing out toward Moloka'i, but also the famous macadamia nut pancakes and enormously filling portions. Lunch is offered until closing at 2pm, and by then the line has shrunk. Finding parking can be challenging; try for a spot along Napili Place, or park by the Napili Bay beach access on Hui Drive and walk to the restaurant across the sand of Napili Bay.

Ka'anapali

ROY'S
2290 Ka'anapali Pkwy.; 808/669-6999; www.royshawaii.com; 11am-7pm daily; $29-64

Even though every resort in Ka'anapali has some sort of Hawaiian Regional Cuisine option, none can hold a candle to world-famous Roy's. The location, inside the golf clubhouse, would be nicer if it had an ocean view, but what the restaurant lacks in decor, it makes up for in flavor. Chef Roy Yamaguchi was one of the founders of the Hawaiian Regional Cuisine movement, and his mastery is evident in the misoyaki butterfish and honey mustard-braised short ribs. Even though there are over 30 Roy's locations around the country, every restaurant has a menu and a style unique to the venue. Dinner entrées are pricey; the lunch menu ($14-26) is more affordable. The chocolate ganache cake is a dessert favorite.

Lahaina

MALA OCEAN TAVERN
1307 Front St.; 808/667-9394; www. malatavern.com; 9am-9pm daily; $34

FOOD   141

WEST MAUI FOOD OPTIONS

NAME	LOCATION	CONTACT INFO
KAPALUA, NAPILI, AND HONOKOWAI		
★ **Merriman's**	1 Bay Club Pl.	808/669-6400; www.merrimanshawaii.com
★ **Plantation House**	2000 Plantation Club Dr.	808/669-6299; www.cohnrestaurants.com
Honokowai Okazuya & Deli	3600 Lower Honoapi'ilani Rd.	808/665-0512
Sansei	600 Office Rd.	808/669-6286; www.sanseihawaii.com
Taverna Maui	2000 Village Rd.	808/667-2426; www.tavernamaui.com
Maui Tacos	5095 Napilihau St.	808/665-0222
★ **The Gazebo**	5315 Lower Honoapi'ilani Rd.	808/669-5621
Honolua Store	502 Office Rd.	808/665-9105
KA'ANAPALI		
★ **Roy's**	2290 Ka'anapali Pkwy.	808/669-6999; www.royshawaii.com
Monkeypod Kitchen	2435 Ka'anapali Pkwy.	808/878-6763; www.monkeypodkitchen.com
Leilani's on the Beach	2435 Ka'anapali Pkwy.	808/661-4495; www.leilanis.com
Duke's	130 Kai Malina Pkwy.	808/662-2900; www.dukesmaui.com
LAHAINA		
★ **Mala Ocean Tavern**	1307 Front St.	808/667-9394; www.malatavern.com
China Bowl Asian Cuisine	2580 Keka'a Dr.	808/661-0660; www.chinabowlmaui.com
SOUTH OF LAHAINA		
★ **Leoda's Kitchen and Pie Shop**	820 Olowalu Village Rd.	808/662-3600; www.leodas.com

FOOD	HOURS	PRICE
Hawaiian Regional	11:30am-2pm and 5pm-8:30pm daily	$24-69
Hawaiian Regional	8am-8:30pm daily	$14-67
local style	11am-2:30pm and 4:30pm-8:30pm Mon.-Sat.	$11-22, cash only
Japanese	5pm-8:30pm daily	$17-32
Italian	noon-9:30pm daily	$18-40
Mexican	11am-8pm daily	$7-16
breakfast and lunch	7:30am-2pm daily	$12-24
breakfast and lunch	6:30am-7pm daily	$7-20
Hawaiian Regional	11am-7pm daily	$29-64
Hawaiian Regional	11am-10pm daily	$14-47
Hawaiian Regional	11am-10pm daily	$14-34
Hawaiian Regional	8am-9pm daily	$15-54
contemporary	9am-9pm daily	$34
Chinese	11am-9pm daily	$12-23
sandwiches	10am-6pm daily	$6-22

WEST MAUI BARS AND NIGHTLIFE

NAME	LOCATION	CONTACT INFO
KAPALUA, NAPILI, AND HONOKOWAI		
★ Masters of Slack Key	5900 Lower Honoapi'ilani Rd.	www.slackkeyshow.com
★ Sansei	600 Office Rd.	808/669-6286; www.sanseihawaii.com
Maui Brewing Company	4405 Honoapi'ilani Hwy.	808/669-3474; www.mauibrewingco.com
Dollie's Pub & Café	4310 Lower Honoapi'ilani Rd.	808/669-0266; www.dolliespizzakahana.com
KA'ANAPALI		
★ Wailele Polynesian Luau	2365 Ka'anapali Pkwy.	808/667-2525; www.westinmaui.com
★ Maui Nui Luau at Black Rock	2605 Ka'anapali Pkwy.	877/877-4852; www.sheratonmauiluau.com
Drums of the Pacific	200 Nohea Kai	808/667-4727; www.drumsofthepacificmaui.com
Myths of Maui Luau	2780 Keka'a Dr.	877/273-7494; www.mythsofmaui.com
Java Jazz & Soup Nutz	3350 Lower Honoapi'ilani Rd.	808/667-0787; www.javajazzmaui.com
LAHAINA		
★ Old Lahaina Luau	1251 Front St.	800/667-1998; www.oldlahainaluau.com

Spreading much aloha, Mala has long been a staple on the north end of Front Street, with stunning vistas and waterside tables. The attire here is "island smart casual." Expect mouthwatering delights with catches of the day, island-themed appetizers, fresh meat selections, salads, and much more.

South of Lahaina

LEODA'S KITCHEN AND PIE SHOP

820 Olowalu Village Rd.; 808/662-3600; www.leodas.com; 10am-6pm daily; $6-22

The only restaurant between Lahaina and Ma'alaea is Leoda's Kitchen and Pie Shop, in the Olowalu store

VENUE TYPE	HOURS
live music	6:30pm Wed. and Sat.
sake bar, karaoke	5pm–8:30pm daily
brewpub	11:30am-9pm daily
sports bar	11am-midnight daily
luau	Tues.-Thurs. and Sun.
luau	Mon., Wed., and Fri.
luau	Mon.-Sat.
luau	Sun.-Fri.
live music	6am-10pm daily
luau	daily

building. Using many sustainable ingredients from local farms, this sandwich and pie shop has quickly become an island favorite. The deli sandwiches, potpies, and baked goods are so good, however, that you'll often find a line stretching out the front door. Try the veggie burger for a healthy lunch, or a savory chicken potpie.

BARS AND NIGHTLIFE

West Maui is the island's entertainment hot spot, with the island's best luau and most happening bars. You can't walk more than a few paces in Lahaina without tripping over an evening drink special. More than just booze, West Maui is also home to family entertainment options ranging from free hula performances and whale lectures to evening magic performances.

Despite the happening surroundings,

WEST MAUI LODGING OPTIONS

NAME	LOCATION	CONTACT INFO
KAPALUA, NAPILI, AND HONOKOWAI		
Napili Village Hotel	5425 Lower Honoapi'ilani Rd.	808/669-6228; www.napilivillagehotel.com
Maui Kai	106 Ka'anapali Shores Pl.	808/667-3500; www.mauikai.com
★ **Napili Kai Beach Resort**	5900 Lower Honoapi'ilani Rd.	808/669-6271; www.napilikai.com
★ **Ritz-Carlton Kapalua**	1 Ritz-Carlton Dr.	808/669-6200; www.ritzcarlton.com
Montage Kapalua Bay	1 Bay Dr.	808/626-6600; www.montagehotels.com
KA'ANAPALI		
★ **Ka'anapali Beach Hotel**	2525 Ka'anapali Pkwy.	808/661-0011; www.kbhmaui.com
Royal Lahaina	2780 Keka'a Dr.	808/661-3611; www.royallahaina.com
Westin Ka'anapali Ocean Resort Villas	6 Kai Ala Dr.	808/667-3200; www.westinkaanapali.com
Hyatt Regency Maui Resort and Spa	200 Nohea Kai Dr.	808/661-1234; www.hyatt.com
Sheraton Maui Resort & Spa	2605 Ka'anapali Pkwy.	808/661-0031; www.sheraton-maui.com
SOUTH OF LAHAINA		
Camp Olowalu	800 Olowalu Village Rd.	808/661-4303
Ho'oilo House	138 Awaiku St.	808/667-6669; www.hooilohouse.com

however, if you're the clubbing type who likes to party into the wee hours of the morning, you're out of luck since most bars close by 11pm, and only a handful stay open later than 1am. Also, even though almost all of the nightlife options involve bars and pubs that have lively atmospheres, the options for dancing are woefully inadequate. For the most up-to-date info on the latest evening scene, pick up a free copy of the *Maui Time* newspaper or check out "The Grid" section on the website at www.mauitime.com.

STANDOUTS
Kapalua, Napili, and Honokowai
MASTERS OF SLACK KEY
5900 Lower Honoapi'ilani Rd.; www.slackkeyshow.com; 6:30pm Wed. and Sat.

Can't get enough of ki ho'alu (slack-key guitar)? The Masters of Slack Key

TYPE	PRICE	BEST FOR
condo	$170–224	families, couples
condo	$359–429	families, couples
condo	$394–831	families, couples
resort	$799–5,000	luxury-lovers, honeymooners
resort	$1,200–5,200	couples, families, honeymooners, luxury-lovers
hotel	$231–488	families, couples
hotel	$279–415	couples
resort	$573–772	families, couples
resort	$594–1,500	families
resort	$597–769	families, honeymooners
camping	$24–195	budget travelers
B&B	from $369	couples, honeymooners

performance at the Aloha Pavilion of the Napili Kai Beach Resort is the best show you'll find on the island. Tickets can be purchased either online or when the doors first open. Price for the show is normally $45.

SANSEI

600 Office Rd.; 808/669-6286; www. sanseihawaii.com; 5pm-8:30pm daily
The karaoke sessions at Sansei restaurant in the Ritz-Carlton resort are the most happening evenings on the northwestern side. This popular sushi and sake bar draws in a spirited crowd.

Ka'anapali

WAILELE POLYNESIAN LUAU

2365 Ka'anapali Pkwy.; 808/667-2525; www.westinmaui.com; $170-270
Of the numerous luau in Ka'anapali, the best show is the Wailele

BARS AND NIGHTLIFE 147

Polynesian Luau at the Westin Maui resort. The fire dancers are the best, and the food is above average compared to the other options. Shows take place Tuesday through Thursday evenings typically, as well as Sunday during busier times of the year, although the schedule varies. If you're driving to Kaʻanapali, the one downside of this show is that parking can be challenging. Try to find free beach parking in the lot between Whalers Village and the entrance to the Westin. If you can't find a free spot, the most economical option is to park in the Whalers Village garage and then buy an ice cream or a quick beer after the show to get your parking validated for three hours.

MAUI NUI LUAU AT BLACK ROCK
2605 Kaʻanapali Pkwy.; 877/877-4852; www.sheratonmauiluau.com; $198

Maui Nui Luau at Black Rock is Monday and Wednesday, as well as some Friday evenings, at the Sheraton resort. The crowds aren't quite as large as at other shows, and the grassy luau grounds are more spacious. While the food is fine and the dancers are entertaining, the best part is the atmosphere, looking out at Puʻu Kekaʻa and experiencing the torch-lighting ceremony. While children are welcome, it mainly caters to couples and adults.

Lahaina
OLD LAHAINA LUAU
1251 Front St.; 800/667-1998; www.oldlahainaluau.com; daily; $230 adults, $140 children

Old Lahaina Luau is hands down the best on Maui, with exceptional food and lush luau grounds. You're greeted with a lei made of fragrant fresh flowers. Hula lessons for all ages are offered, and there are lawn games. Premium bar selections are included in the rates. There is a large imu (underground oven) for the pig, although it gets insanely crowded, so hang by the imu early to get a good view of the unearthing. The private oceanfront setting provides the perfect perch for watching the sun go

hula dancers at Old Lahaina Luau

down. The live show focuses on the history of Hawaii. For seating, choose either traditional lauhala mats (closest to the stage) or tables with chairs, which still provide a good view. The only places where it's hard to see the show are the seats in the far corners. Seating preference is given to those who book first. Remarkably, shows are offered seven days a week.

LODGING

RESERVATIONS AND TIPS

Generally speaking, hotels in Ka'anapali tend to attract the most clientele, so plan far in advance. The perk to staying in any of the Ka'anapali hotels is that you have easy access to all the hotels via a walking path and proximity to Whalers Village, which features many shops and popular restaurants. Kapalua is scenic but remote; if you want to leave the hotel to explore, you will have to drive to other areas.

STANDOUTS
Kapalua, Napili, and Honokowai

NAPILI KAI BEACH RESORT
5900 Lower Honoapi'ilani Rd.; 808/669-6271; www.napilikai.com; $394-831
On the point between Napili and Kapalua Bays, the Napili Kai Beach Resort is a West Side classic that offers individually owned condos in a family-friendly resort setting. This is a great option for families who want to stay in one place and play on the beach. There is a miniature putting course, multiple swimming pools, and a weekly mai tai party. Many of the units have recently been renovated and are the nicest they've ever been.

RITZ-CARLTON KAPALUA
1 Ritz-Carlton Dr.; 808/669-6200; www.ritzcarlton.com; $799-5,000
The largest and best-known resort on the northwestern side is the Ritz-Carlton Kapalua, offering the amenities expected of a Ritz-Carlton. Also offered are several cultural and environmental programs, such as the acclaimed Ambassadors of the Environment. It can often be windy and wetter than in central Lahaina, but showers usually pass quickly.

Ka'anapali

KA'ANAPALI BEACH HOTEL
2525 Ka'anapali Pkwy.; 808/661-0011; www.kbhmaui.com; $231-488
As the slogan says, Ka'anapali Beach Hotel is Maui's "most Hawaiian hotel." A genuine feeling of aloha permeates this laid-back resort, and while it's not nearly as lavish as its neighbors, KBH occupies prime oceanfront real estate a two-minute stroll from Pu'u Keka'a (Black Rock). The open lawn is the perfect place to relax in the shade of an ulu tree, and while there is no hot tub, there is a swimming pool next to the popular tiki bar, a welcoming place for families. On the lawn is an outrigger sailing canoe crafted by employees of the resort, and free hula shows are held each night on the hotel's outdoor stage. Guests are made to feel like 'ohana (family), and the rates are much more affordable.

TRANSPORTATION

Air

Kapalua-West Maui Airport

4050 Honoapi'ilani Hwy.; 808/665-6108
Above Kahana is the small Kapalua-West Maui Airport (JHM), which is a convenient option for those staying in the area and who need to go to/from Honolulu. The interisland fares fluctuate in price weekly (often from $85 and up) and are often a little higher than at the larger Kahului Airport, but when you factor in the hour of driving you save, it's worth the few extra dollars. This small airport is used principally by Mokulele Airlines, but it's also used by small commercial tour companies. Surrounded by former pineapple fields, the single airstrip is short and used by small propeller aircraft only. The check-in counters, inspection station, boarding gate, and baggage claim are only a few steps from each other.

Mokulele Airlines (808/495-4188; www.mokuleleairlines.com) has several flights a day between Kapalua and Honolulu. The earliest flight typically departs at 7:30am, and the last flight of the day is at 5pm. Outside those times, you'll have to go to Kahului. There are also flights to Moloka'i and Lana'i, and they vary depending on the day. It's best to check with the airline and schedule ahead.

Car

Traffic in West Maui is unpredictable so plan ahead. Typically mid-mornings and late afternoons have the most traffic as people are venturing out for daily excursions or heading to dinner, if they're not staying in a hotel.

Car Rental

The largest car-rental providers on the West Side are in Honokowai, equidistant from Lahaina Harbor and Kapalua Airport. Here you'll find both **Avis** (11 Halawai Dr.; 808/661-8760; www.avis.com; 8am-2pm daily) and **Budget** (11 Halawai Dr.; 808/661-8760; www.budget.com; 9am-2pm daily). Provided you arrive at the harbor or Kapalua Airport during business hours, they have a shuttle that will pick you up.

In the Sheraton resort in Ka'anapali, **Enterprise** (2605 Ka'anapali Pkwy.; 808/661-8804; www.enterprise.com; 8am-11am Mon.-Fri.) has a service counter and will pick you up anywhere from Lahaina Harbor to Kapalua.

Taxi

In West Maui, the best taxi options include **West Maui Taxi** (808/661-1122) and **Lahaina Taxi Service** (808/661-5959). A ride from Lahaina to Ka'anapali is about $20, and from Ka'anapali to Kapalua about $30. Going rates for a cab ride to Kahului Airport from Ka'anapali hover just about $100, so you might want to think twice about taking a cab to the hotel.

Bus

The cheapest way to get around West Maui, albeit slowly, is the **Maui Bus** (808/249-2900; www.co.maui.hi.us/bus), which provides service in and between various parts of the island. There are four different routes in West Maui, and departures are once per hour. All trips cost $4 per person boarding, and you can buy a day pass for $4. The bus stations in Lahaina are in the back of the Wharf Cinema Center across the street from the banyan tree, and at the intersection of Front Street and Papalaua Street. To get from one side of Lahaina to the other, bus 23 makes various stops around town 8am-11pm daily.

Shuttle

The free **Kapalua Shuttle** (808/665-9110) runs throughout resort areas for guests on an on-demand basis 7am-11pm daily. In Ka'anapali, the **resort shuttle** offers free transportation across the resorts and runs on a set schedule 9am-9pm daily. For a shuttle to the airport, **Speedi Shuttle** (877/242-5777; www.speedishuttle.com) offers shared ride services that range from around $40 per person in Lahaina to $65 per person from Ka'anapali.

Motorcycle and Moped

If you want the wind whipping through your hair, there are a number of different motorcycle, Harley, and moped rentals scattered across the West Side.

The place with the largest selection of bikes is **Aloha Motorsports** (30 Halawai Dr.; 808/667-7000; www.aloha motorsports.com; 9am-5pm daily), in Honokowai, across the highway from the Honua Kai resort. The company offers free pickup and drop-off on the West Side. Rates for mopeds can be as low as $89 for 24 hours, and Harley rentals average around $269 for 24 hours. During slower times of the year there can be specials available.

If you don't need a full-on hog and just want a moped for the day, check out **West Maui Moped** (1036 Limahana Pl.; 808/276-5790; 9am-5pm Mon.-Sat.), in a small warehouse district and near Maui Brewing Company. Rates are $45 per day.

LEAVING WEST MAUI

South Maui (Kihei)

From Lahaina, take Keawe Street to Lahaina Bypass (Hwy. 3000) going south toward Olowalu. Lahaina Bypass turns slightly left and becomes Honoapi'ilani Highway (Hwy. 30). Turn right onto North Kihei Road and right again onto South Kihei Road. The 24.7-mi (39.7-km) drive is about 45 minutes.

Haleakalā National Park

From Lahaina, take Keawe Street to Lahaina Bypass (Hwy. 3000) going south toward Olowalu. Lahaina Bypass turns slightly left and becomes Honoapi'ilani Highway (Hwy. 30). Turn right onto Kuihelani Highway (Hwy. 380) and continue onto Mayor Elmer F. Cravalho Way. Turn right onto Hana Highway (Hwy. 36) and right again onto Haleakalā Highway (Hwy. 37) and stay on this road as it begins to ascend. This road will take you directly into Haleakalā National Park. The 51-mi (82-km) drive is about 90 minutes.

Start of the Road to Hana

From Lahaina, take Keawe Street to Lahaina Bypass (Hwy. 3000) going south toward Olowalu. Lahaina Bypass turns slightly left and becomes Honoapi'ilani Highway (Hwy. 30). Turn right onto Kuihelani Highway (Hwy. 380) and continue onto Mayor Elmer F. Cravalho Way. Turn right onto Hana Highway (Hwy. 36). Stay on this road, passing the communities of Pa'ia and Ha'iku, until you reach the Road to Hana mile marker 0 (Hwy. 360). The 39.5-mi (63.6-km) drive is about one hour.

TRANSPORTATION   151

view from Waiheʻe Ridge Trail, overlooking Kahului and Haleakalā

CENTRAL MAUI

Central Maui is industrial, urban, and—most important—real.

The site of Kahului International Airport, Central Maui is the first part of the island most visitors encounter. It's more built up than you'd expect of "paradise," but beyond the traffic lights, box stores, and increasing lanes of asphalt, Central Maui is the beating heart of the island's cultural past. It's also rich in natural beauty, with muddy trails leading deep into the mountains and miles of sandy shore. It's home to the island's widest array of multicultural cuisine. The sport of kitesurfing was invented here on the shores of Kanaha Beach Park. While there might not be any palm-lined resorts or tropical beach bars with mai tais, there's something that travelers might find much more interesting: a true sense of island community.

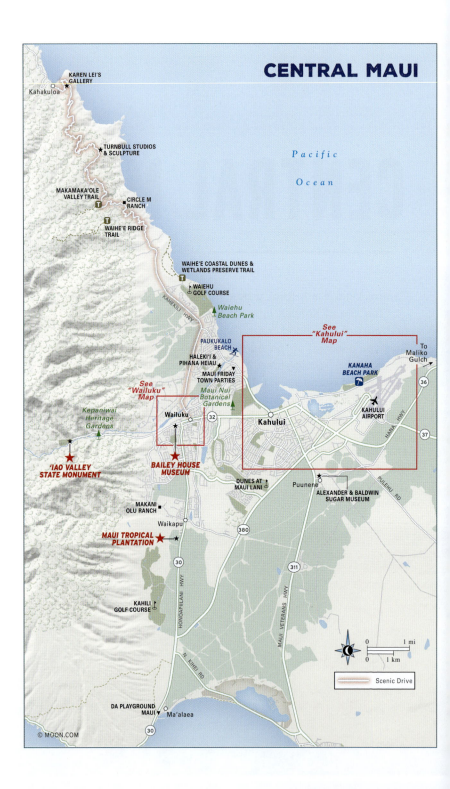

TOP 3

★ **1. BAILEY HOUSE MUSEUM:** View authentic Hawaiian artifacts, including a surfboard ridden by Duke Kahanamoku (page 163).

★ **2. ʻIAO VALLEY STATE MONUMENT:** Learn about the Battle of Kepaniwai and snap a photo of the iconic ʻIao Needle (page 165).

★ **3. MAUI TROPICAL PLANTATION:** Enjoy a tram tour, zip-lining, shopping, and a phenomenal restaurant (page 166).

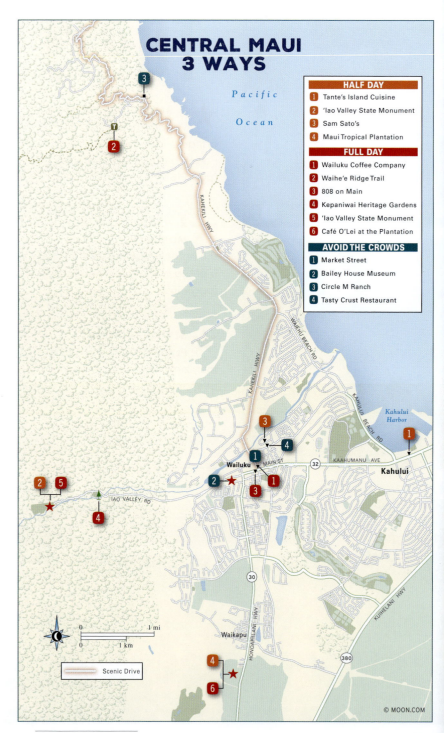

CENTRAL MAUI 3 WAYS

HALF DAY

1. Begin the morning before 9am with java along with a crab cake and avocado Benedict or island pork chops and eggs at **Tante's Island Cuisine.**

2. Enjoy breathtaking views along the 133-step walkway up to the 'Iao Needle Lookout at **'Iao Valley State Monument.**

3. Stop by **Sam Sato's** for delicious comfort food like their dry noodles or classic burgers.

4. After lunch, explore the vast gift shop and art gallery at the **Maui Tropical Plantation.** If you have more time, consider taking a tram ride or zip line through the plush emerald surroundings.

FULL DAY

1 Begin the day early with coffee and breakfast from **Wailuku Coffee Company.**

2 By 9am you'll be lacing up your boots to hike the **Waihe'e Ridge Trail,** which offers dramatic views of rugged mountain terrains, valleys, and ocean views.

3 After working up a sweat and snapping some photos, grab some lunch at **808 on Main** in Wailuku for pupu and other island and farm-fresh offerings.

4 After lunch, stop by the **Kepaniwai Heritage Gardens,** a serene waterside park with a Japanese temple. Enjoy walks through the themed gardens celebrating Hawaii's culture.

5 Drive up to **'Iao Valley State Monument,** where a walkway with 133 steps awaits you. This is one of the most scenic, lush areas of the island, and there are great walks alongside the running water and through lush gardens. Plan anywhere from an hour to three or more hours here.

6 Finish the day with a memorable dinner at **Café O'Lei at the Plantation,** and consider the miso eggplant and root vegetable bowl or slow-cooked lamb shank.

CENTRAL MAUI 3 WAYS 159

AVOID THE CROWDS

1 Stroll, shop, and eat on and around **Market Street** in downtown Wailuku, a historic town that isn't often inundated by tourists.

2 Instead of going all the way to 'Iao Valley State Monument, visit standout sites nearby, such as **Bailey House Museum,** which offers guided or self-guided tours through various rooms and outdoors areas featuring an extensive collection of artifacts dating to pre-recorded times.

3 Hold onto your saddle at **Circle M Ranch** for a leisurely 90-minute ride along a truly scenic ridge to the Maui coastline.

4 The atmosphere at **Tasty Crust Restaurant** is low-key and very diner-esque, but the comfort foods, like club sandwiches, pancakes (all day), and island-themed salads make for a good experience.

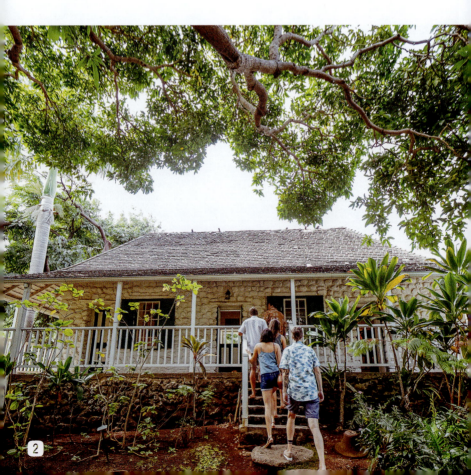

ORIENTATION AND PLANNING

ORIENTATION

Central Maui comprises two main towns just 2 mi (3.2 km) apart from each other: **Kahului** and **Wailuku.** The communities of **Waihe'e, Waikapu,** and **Waiehu** are almost completely residential and, when combined with Kahului and Wailuku, contribute to a Central Maui population of 57,000. This is Maui's most populated region. It doesn't become rural until you pass Waihe'e on **Kahekili Highway.** The airport and cruise port are both in Kahului, and the tightest cluster of shopping and restaurants is around **Market Street** in Wailuku. **'Iao Valley State Monument** is several miles just beyond downtown Wailuku.

PLANNING YOUR TIME

Most visitors experience Central Maui when they drive away from the airport or take a day trip to 'Iao Valley before rushing off someplace else. Rather than devoting an hour, however, first-time visitors with a full week in Maui should spend at least half a day experiencing Central Maui's sights, whereas returning visitors looking to see new sights could easily spend two days: one day hiking, exploring the beaches, or seeing the most popular sights, and another in museums and enjoying the abundance of food.

HIGHLIGHTS

KAHULUI
Maui Nui Botanical Gardens
150 Kanaloa Ave.; 808/249-2798; www.mnbg.org; 8am-4pm Mon.-Sat.; free

For anyone with an interest in Polynesian flora or sustainable farming techniques, the Maui Nui Botanical Gardens is an absolute must-stop. Native trees and informational placards are displayed, and small signs warn you to watch out for falling ulu, or breadfruit, which populate the treetops above. Take a self-guided walking tour, and learn the differences between endemic, indigenous, and introduced plant species. More than 70 species of dryland kalo, or taro, are successfully growing in a dry coastal dunes system. Although not as expansive as the botanical gardens in Kula, the gardens espouse the Polynesian view that humans are but stewards of the land.

Alexander and Baldwin Sugar Museum
3957 Hansen Rd.; 808/871-8058; www.sugarmuseum.com; 10am-2pm Mon.-Thurs.; $10

There's no place on the island where you can gain a better understanding of Maui's plantation heritage than at the Alexander and Baldwin Sugar Museum, a small, worndown building in Pu'unene. The $10 entrance fee gets you a yellow booklet called *Passport to the Past*, which also includes entry to the Bailey House Museum in Wailuku,

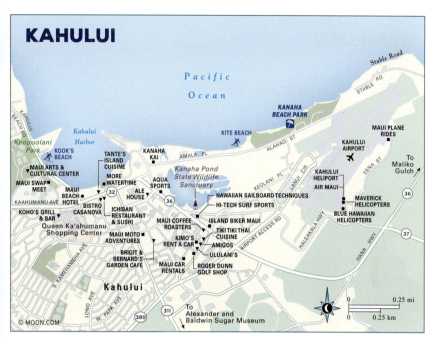

KAHULUI

as well as Lahaina's Baldwin House Museum and Wo Hing Museum. Here in the Sugar Museum, exhibits discuss everything from sugar's Polynesian roots to historical profiles of the island's first sugar barons.

WAILUKU

★ Bailey House Museum
2375-A Main St.; 808/244-3326; 10am-2pm Tues.-Fri.; $10 adults, $8 seniors, $5 ages 7-12

Regardless of whether you're a museum person, every visitor to Maui should see the Bailey House Museum, on the road to 'Iao Valley. It's listed on the National Register of Historic Places, and Duke Kahanamoku's redwood surfboard is outside on the lawn. Handcrafted in 1910 for Hawaii's "Ambassador of Aloha," the surfboard rests near a 33-ft-long (10-m) canoe that's made from a single koa log, built around 1900 and one of the last of its kind. Inside the museum, the Hawaiian Room houses artifacts of precontact Hawaii, such as wooden spears, stone tools, knives made from conch shells, and daggers made from shark's teeth. In the same room are stone ki'i, or statues, depicting the Hawaiian war god Ku; expertly crafted wooden calabashes; and an exhibit of artifacts found on

Maui Nui Botanical Gardens

HIGHLIGHTS 163

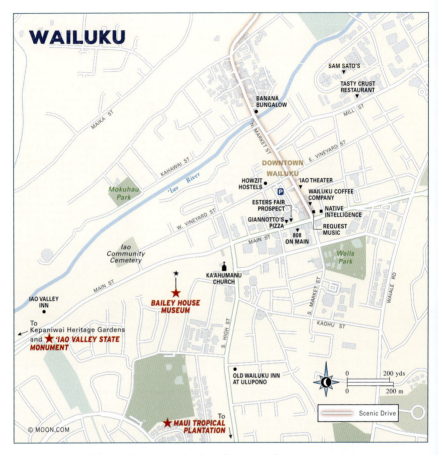

the island of Kaho'olawe from both the pre- and post-bombing eras. For a good book or to learn more about Hawaiian history and culture, the museum bookstore has the island's best selection of Hawaiian historical texts.

Ka'ahumanu Church
103 S. High St.; 808/244-5189; www.kaahumanuchurch.org

The historic Ka'ahumanu Church is surrounded by tranquil monkeypod, kukui, mango, and kou trees. As the legend goes, when Queen Ka'ahumanu, wife of King Kamehameha, visited the congregation in 1832 in its first year of existence, meetings were held in a shed. She asked that when a larger church was constructed that the congregation name it after her. The second thatched-hut structure wasn't large enough to accommodate the ballooning congregation, and the third had roofing issues. Finally, in 1876, Queen Ka'ahumanu's request was honored when the present sanctuary was built by Edward Bailey, an accomplished Hawaiian missionary and artist. Today the site is listed on the National Register of Historic Places and the Hawaii Register of Historic Places. Call for guided tours.

BEST SUNSET VIEWS

Waiehu Beach Park

One of the best sunset destinations in Central Maui is **Waiehu Beach Park** (page 169), which offers a diverse take on the experience for the sheer fact the sun sets over the West Maui Mountains behind you, spreading the sky with a vibrant array of colors.

Kepaniwai Heritage Gardens

870 'Iao Valley Rd.; 808/270-7232; 7am-5:30pm daily; free

Tucked on the banks of 'Iao Stream, this simple but informative cultural park is far more interesting than it looks, as it details Maui's "mixed plate" culture. In addition to pavilions that make great picnic spots (and double as great drinking spots for locals), the park features a small monument devoted to each of the island's plantation-era immigrant communities—Japanese, Chinese, Puerto Rican, and Portuguese, each monument with a small dwelling constructed in traditional style. Along the stream are a few places where you can swim in the shallow (and cold!) waters, although use some caution when scrambling down the bank as there aren't any official trails. Unless you're a major history buff, 30 minutes here will suffice.

★ 'Iao Valley State Monument

end of 'Iao Valley Rd.; 7am-6pm daily; $5 entrance, $10 parking

Crane your neck and look skyward toward peaks that tickle the passing clouds, and embrace the feeling you've suddenly traveled 100 years back in time. When you reach the park, rather than hastily parking, walking, and rushing to see the 'Iao Needle, take a moment to read the history of all that's happened in the park, from the gruesome and bloody Battle of Kepaniwai to how soldiers would use the valley ridgelines to spot warriors approaching from sea. When you do begin to hike the "trail,"

HIGHLIGHTS 165

Kepaniwai Heritage Gardens (top); 'Iao Needle at 'Iao Valley State Monument (middle); Maui Tropical Plantation (bottom)

a walkway with 133 steps, admire the landscape that lines the edge of the stream. Once you conquer the stairs, enjoy the view of **Kuka'emoku**—better known as **'Iao Needle**—rising 2,250 ft (685 m) above the distant shore. While most visitors tend to focus on and photograph the needle, what's more spectacular is the rugged ridgelines and isolated interior of the mountain, which is so inaccessible and untouched it's believed the bones of Hawaiian royalty are buried deep inside caves where they'll never be disturbed.

★ Maui Tropical Plantation

1670 Honoapi'ilani Hwy.; 808/244-7643; www.mauitropicalplantation.com; 10am-4pm Tues.-Sun.; free

You can easily spend up to several hours in this lush haven, which features everything from zip-line tours, a coffee shop, an ice cream stand, an art gallery, and a fresh organic farm stand. Best of all, the palate-bending **Café O'Lei at the Plantation** restaurant is on the property, and much of the food served is sourced right here on the farm. The longtime draw is the **Tropical Express Tram Tour** ($25 adults, $12.50 children), a 40-minute ride that runs seven times daily, making a loop through surrounding fields as the driver discusses the crops. While children will be excited to ride on a train (it's the island's last), adults will enjoy the informative commentary.

Haleki'i and Pihana Heiau

With its historical importance, this site is officially classified as a Hawaii state park, but the gate to the heiau (temple) is no longer open for vehicular access and its condition has fallen into disrepair. Nevertheless, it's still easy to park on the street in front of the heiau and make the five-minute walk up the hill. In ancient Hawaii these two heiau served as the religious center of the entire Wailuku ahupua'a, or land division. Many of Maui's ruling ali'i came here to either honor their deceased or commune with religious deities. It's believed that Keopuolani, the woman who would become queen, was born here at Pihana heiau, a site that is also believed to have been a luakini heiau, used for human sacrifice.

Kahakuloa village and bay

KAHAKULOA

Lonely and remote, there are few places left in Hawaii that are quite like Kahakuloa, accurately called "old Hawaii" and "a place that time has forgotten." This fishing village offers visitors a unique opportunity to glimpse Hawaiian traditions, still in practice, that managed to evade modernity.

Turnbull Studios & Sculpture

5030 Kahekili Hwy.; 808/244-0101; www.turnbullfineart.com; 10am-5pm Thurs.-Sat., 11am-3pm Sun.-Mon.

Turnbull Studios & Sculpture is an eclectic sculpture garden with handmade crafts by local Hawaiian artists. The artist has been making sculptures at this mountainside garden for over 25 years. There are only a few parking spaces, and if it's been raining heavily, think twice before going down the short but steep driveway in a low-clearance rental car.

Karen Lei's Gallery

Kahekili Hwy.; 808/244-3371; www.karenleisgallery.com; 10am-5pm daily

Inside a mountaintop home overlooking Kahakuloa Valley, this gallery features more than 120 local artists and their paintings, jewelry, and crafts, and the views from the parking lot looking up the valley make it the most scenic gallery on the island.

BEST BEACHES

The little-known beaches of Central Maui are defined by wind and water sports. You won't find any tiki bars or rows of beachfront cabanas, but you will find narrow stretches of sand where the world's best boarders hang out.

KAHULUI
Stable Road

To really get away from it all and just relax on an empty patch of sand, look for the string of beaches off Stable Road, which are a bit of a local secret. You'll find fishers

TOP BEACH
KANAHA BEACH PARK

This beach is known for its vibrant energy, particularly in the afternoon. You'll find windsurfers, kitesurfers, paddleboarders, and surfers out riding the waves, and on Sunday the park is bumping with barbecues and pickup games of beach volleyball. Go for long strolls along sandy beaches in the early mornings. In the afternoon, the cobalt waters become flecked with whitecaps and dozens of colorful sails as windsurfers and kitesurfers race across the water—particularly in summer, when it's windier. The large, grassy beach park has showers and restrooms, and there's a roped-off area for swimming to cool off or wade. Since it's only minutes from the airport, it's also a convenient place to kill time before a flight if you've already checked out of your hotel. It's worth noting that the park is a frequent hangout for some of the island's unhoused population, but people mostly keep to themselves.

To reach Kanaha from Hana Highway, make a right at the stoplight for Hobron Avenue and then another right onto Amala Place. Drive for about 1.5 mi (2.4 km). The best entrances for Kanaha Beach Park are the two at the end of the road. For a shortcut, loop through the airport, past Arrivals and Departures, and make a right onto Ka'a Street, continuing past the car-rental counters until you reach the end of the road. Turn right; the beach park is on the left.

casting rods and dropped tailgates with coolers, but if you walk a couple of yards down the beach, you can usually find your own patch of sand that's perfect for a chair and book. Afternoons are often windy—and don't expect any snorkeling—but a couple of spots are deep enough for swimming, and days with light wind are gorgeous. To reach Stable Road, drive on Hana Highway (Hwy. 36) in the direction of Pa'ia, and 1.4 mi (2.3 km) from the junction with Haleakalā Highway (Hwy. 37), make a left onto a narrow paved road. From here, travel about 0.5 mi (0.8 km) until you see sandy parking lots on the right side.

WAILUKU

Waiehu Beach Park

Sunsets on this spacious, sandy, and tranquil beach are memorable. Better yet, the stellar views of the islands of Lana'i and Moloka'i are sublime during dusk, with deepening hues and tranquil waves. This is a good beach to simply escape and spend several hours sunbathing or swimming. While it doesn't offer the best snorkeling options, it's that go-to beach, perfect for picnics and relaxation.

SCENIC DRIVES

THE ROAD TO KAHAKULOA

Driving Distance: *13.9 mi (22.3 km)*
Driving Time: *30-45 minutes*
Start: *Wailuku*
End: *Kahakuloa*

The Road to Hana is one thing. Then there's the Road to Kahakuloa. Sheer drop-offs with no guardrails and completely blind turns are part of the experience of one of the island's most thrilling road trips. Many choose to get to Kahakuloa from the West Side of the island by following the **Northwestern Coast** drive past Kapalua, Honolua Bay, and Nakalele Blowhole, but because this road is a loop, Kahakuloa can similarly be accessed from Wailuku.

While this is one of the most scenic, hair-raising car rides you can take in Hawaii, a lot of confusion surrounds the drive. Some car-rental maps show the road as for 4WD vehicles only. Others say that it's one lane. Still others say you shouldn't drive it at all. Despite the dangers, incidents are rare. The road does not require a 4WD vehicle. It's paved, although some sections can be bumpy. The road is narrow, with the narrowest section between Circle M Ranch and Kahakuloa village, and at some places only wide enough for one car. Drive carefully around corners and honk your horn on those you

the Road to Kahakuloa

SCENIC DRIVES 169

can't see around. Put the cell phone away, and turn the radio off so you can hear if anyone is honking from the other direction. All drivers on this road are experiencing pretty much the same adventurous back-road as you are, and coordination is sometimes necessary to share the road wisely.

It will take you 30-45 minutes to reach Kahakuloa from Wailuku—and there aren't any gas stations, so be sure you have at least half a tank of gas before driving along the coast.

BEST HIKES AND WALKS

Guided hiking tours of the Waihe'e area are available through **Unique Maui Tours** (844/550-6284; www.uniquemauitours.com). Prices start at $89 per person for custom group hikes with spectacular views, and the guides have lots of local knowledge and stories.

WAILUKU

Waihe'e Coastal Dunes and Wetlands Preserve Trail

Distance: *2 mi (3.2 km) one-way*
Duration: *1-1.5 hours*
Elevation Gain: *negligible*
Effort: *easy*
Trailhead: *near Waiehu Golf Course*

Wildly underrated, the 2-mi (3.2-km) trail in the Waihe'e Coastal Dunes and Wetlands Preserve runs the length of one of Maui's last undeveloped shorelines. The trail parallels the shore and passes by a couple of abandoned houses before reaching the cultural relics at the Kapoho fishing village, estimated by scholars to have been populated as early as AD 300-600. Expect the round-trip journey to take a little over an hour; add 30 minutes to explore the coast or ruins.

To reach the trailhead, make a right on Halewaiu Place off Kahekili Highway (Hwy. 340) and follow the signs for Waiehu Golf Course. When the road makes a sharp turn to the right and starts heading toward the golf course, notice an unmarked dirt road going to the left. Park here, because around the corner is a stream crossing that's unsuitable for rental cars. Traveling on foot, the trailhead will be on the left, just uphill from the stream crossing. Avoid leaving valuables in your car.

Waihe'e Ridge Trail

Distance: *5 mi (8 km) round-trip*
Duration: *3 hours*
Elevation Gain: *2,560 ft (780 m)*
Effort: *moderate-strenuous*
Trailhead: *1 mi (1.6 km) after mile marker 7*

This trail rises to 2,560 ft (780 m) elevation, the highest hiking trail west of Haleakalā, and offers sweeping views into Waihe'e and Makamaka'ole Valleys. In the distance, Makamaka'ole Falls tumbles dramatically through the forest; look the other direction, and the turquoise waters of the Waihe'e shore form a dramatic backdrop. The trail continues to Lanilili summit, where you can see the northern slope of the mountain on clear days. If you start hiking before 9am, you'll usually get clear conditions.

This 2.5-mi (4-km) trail starts on a steep concrete incline, but fear not—if you can make it up this hill, you can make it the rest of the way. Eventually the trail levels out a bit and the

170 CENTRAL MAUI

Waihe'e Coastal Dunes and Wetlands Preserve (left); Waihe'e Ridge Trail (right)

concrete changes to dirt, which can often lead to muddy conditions, particularly if it has recently rained. This trail takes some energy, so count on three hours for the 5-mi (8-km) trip. The parking area for the Waihe'e Ridge Trail is at mile marker 7 of Kahekili Highway, across from Circle M Ranch. If the gate is open, which it usually is 7am-7pm daily, continue driving for 1 mi (1.6 km) to the upper parking area.

Makamaka'ole Valley Trail

Distance: nearly 2 mi (3.2 km) round-trip
Duration: up to 2 hours
Elevation Gain: 400 ft (122 m)
Effort: moderate
Trailhead: 0.8 mi (1.3 km) past Circle M Ranch

There aren't many waterfalls in Central Maui that you can access, but one exception is at Makamaka'ole Valley, off the side of Kahekili Highway. The main trail winds its way downhill for about 10 minutes before arriving at a small swimming hole, where you'll find a rushing waterfall and a rope swing. Along the way you're rewarded with a dramatic view of Makamaka'ole Valley as it weaves toward the ocean below.

After the first swimming hole, the trail continues deeper into the valley toward a waterfall more dramatic than the first. After five minutes, the trail ends at a large banyan tree. To reach the pool below, climb down using the roots of the banyan as if descending a ladder. This maneuver requires athletic ability, so it should only be attempted by those who are agile and accepting of the risks. The reward, however, is a small swimming hole where you can bathe beneath a waterfall in a hidden tropical setting.

Approaching from Wailuku, the discreet trailhead is 0.8 mi (1.3 km) past Circle M Ranch. At this point the road has climbed in elevation and narrowed in places to a single lane. You'll pass a sharp turn in the valley, and when the road starts pointing back toward the ocean, you'll notice a small dirt pullout that can accommodate four or five vehicles. The trailhead is a very narrow but well-defined dirt pathway that heads downhill into the brush. There's also a false trailhead that departs from the same parking area but only goes for a few yards. If the trail suddenly ends, turn around and look for the other one.

BEST HIKES AND WALKS

SURFING

SURF SPOTS

The majority of surfing on this side of the island takes place October–April. Some eastward-facing locations can pick up wind swell during the summer months, but it's choppy and sloppy. No surf schools operate along this stretch of coast, and anyone opting to surf around here needs to be at least an intermediate surfer. On the biggest winter swells, teams of professional surfers have been known to tow-surf the outer reefs here, where waves can reach 70 ft (21 m). Thanks, but we'll be watching from shore.

Kahului

LOWERS

For longboarding and stand-up paddle surfing, Lowers at **Kanaha Beach Park** is a popular North Shore favorite. When standing on the sand, look for the lifeguard tower, which is where you'll paddle out. The wave at Kanaha breaks on an offshore reef and requires an arm-burning paddle, but a long paddle means a long ride, and the surf usually won't close out until the faces reach 10 ft (3 m). Mornings are best, before the wind picks up, which is usually around 11am.

Wailuku

BIG LEFTS

The most popular surf break in Wailuku is Big Lefts at **Paukukalo Beach.** This is a long left-hand wave that can get very big on north and northeasterly swells, although it's for advanced surfers only and is heavily localized.

WAIEHU BEACH PARK

For a mellow longboarding wave, there's a break in front of Waiehu Beach Park that usually has fewer people than neighboring Paukukalo. The wave quality isn't as good, but this is still a good wave in the early morning during any north swell.

SURF SHOP

HI-TECH SURF SPORTS

425 Koloa St.; 808/877-2111; www.surfmaui.com
This shop rents surfboards from $30 per day.

OTHER WATER SPORTS

WINDSURFING

Kanaha Beach Park

Maui is one of the world's top destinations for windsurfing, and at Kanaha Beach Park, the trade winds are so consistent during the summer months that they arrive like clockwork around 11am. In winter, the trade winds are a little less consistent, and waves can reach 15 ft (4.6 m) or higher. There's strictly no windsurfing before 11am, and Kanaha is split into two main launching areas conveniently named **Uppers** and **Lowers.** Many of the windsurfing schools operate by Uppers at a cove known as **Kook's Beach.** For more information on Maui windsurfing, go to www.mauiwindsurfing.net for photos, rental operators, and descriptions of the various launching sites.

KITESURFING
Kite Beach
This hallowed ground is where the sport was born. All kitesurfing schools operate here. Even if you aren't a kitesurfer, this is a fantastic spot to sit and watch as dozens of colorful kites zip through the gusty trade winds. Since Kite Beach is so close to Kanaha Beach Park, the unwritten rule is that kitesurfers are supposed to stay downwind (closer to Kahului Harbor) of the windsurfers to avoid high-speed entanglement. Even though this is one of the premier spots on the planet for kitesurfing, unless you're an experienced kitesurfer, lessons are imperative. The narrow strip of sand has multiple entrances—all with sand or dirt parking lots—and you can expect kitesurfers to start launching between 11am and noon. Learn more at www.kitesurfmaui.org. For a webcam of current wind and weather conditions, go to www.kitebeachcam.com.

BEST LESSONS
HAWAIIAN SAILBOARD TECHNIQUES
425 Koloa St.; 808/871-5423; www.hstwindsurfing.com

BIKING

BIKE ROUTES
Waiehu Beach Park to Kahakuloa
The road bike ride to Kahakuloa (12 mi/19.3 km one-way) is one of the best on the island, where cyclists are treated to quad-burning

Founder Alan Cadiz has been teaching windsurfing on Maui since 1985, making this the longest-running outfit on the island's North Shore. Cadiz was one of the first instructors to teach the sport to others, and an instructor will accompany you on a stand-up paddleboard. A 2.5-hour kitesurfing lesson is $325, and private windsurfing starts at $299. Stand-up paddle lessons begin at $299 for a 90-minute class.

windsurfing at Kanaha Beach Park (top); kitesurfing at Kanaha Beach Park (bottom)

WATER SPORTS LESSONS AND RENTALS

NAME	LOCATION	CONTACT INFO
KAHULUI		
★ **Hawaiian Sailboard Techniques**	425 Koloa St.	808/871-5423; www.hstwindsurfing.com
Action Sports Maui	n/a	808/283-7913; www.actionsportsmaui.com
Kiteboarding School of Maui	n/a	808/873-0015; www.ksmaui.com
Aqua Sports	Kite Beach	808/242-8015; www.mauikiteboardinglessons.com
Kanaha Kai	140 Hobron Ave.	808/877-7778; www.kanahakai.com

ascents, hairpin turns through the rainforest, and sweeping views of the entire North Shore. Begin at Waiehu Beach Park and ride northwest on Kahekili Highway. Sharing the road with cars can be tough, considering how narrow it gets, but most cars are traveling so slowly around the tight turns that altercations are rare.

BIKE SHOPS AND RENTALS

Kahului

ISLAND BIKER MAUI
415 Dairy Rd.; 808/877-7744; www.islandbikermaui.com; 9am-1pm Mon.-Fri., 10am-2pm Sat.
Island Biker Maui offers rentals that begin at $85 per day or $275 per week. Mountain bikes and road bikes are available.

HORSEBACK RIDING

WAILUKU

CIRCLE M RANCH
3530 Kahekili Hwy.; 808/871-5222; www.mendesranch.com; $135
The family-run Mendes Ranch, on the road toward Kahakuloa, has managed 300 head of cattle since the 1940s, when it was just a homestead. Today, aside from the sweeping ocean views and trails that run along the coast, what makes Mendes such a popular option is that rather than nose-to-tail riding, you can run the horses on a 1.5-hour authentic paniolo (cowboy) experience of life on a working ranch. Rides depart at 9am and 12:30pm Monday-Saturday.

MAKANI OLU RANCH
363 W. Waiko Rd.; 808/870-0663; www.makanioluranch.com
Rides here accommodate four people at most, and since the entire ride is at a walking pace, this is a great option for novice riders who

174 CENTRAL MAUI

ACTIVITY	PRICE
windsurfing, kitesurfing, paddleboarding lessons	windsurfing lessons from $299, kitesurfing and SUP lessons from $325
surfing, windsurfing, kiteboarding, SUP lessons	kite foilboarding lessons from $295, windsurfing lessons from $389
kiteboarding lessons	from $300
kiteboarding lessons	from $360
rental shop	stand-up paddleboards from $25 per day

just want the view from the saddle. The journey traverses Waikapu Valley and crosses Waikapu Stream, allowing you access to a part of the island you'd otherwise never see. From the lookout points, the views are back toward the central isthmus, as well as up the valley walls leading deep into the heart of the mountains. Two-hour rides are $150, and you can upgrade to a three-hour ride ($175) that includes lunch while riding through the valley. If you're nervous about getting on a horse, the Makani Olu Ranch Ride ($75) includes a one-hour lesson before heading out on the trail. The ranch is 25 minutes from Wailea and 35 minutes from Ka'anapali.

BIRD-WATCHING

KAHULUI

KANAHA POND STATE WILDLIFE SANCTUARY

Amala Pl.; www.dlnr.hawaii.gov/ wildlife/sanctuaries/kanaha; sun-rise-sunset daily Aug. 31-Mar. 31; free
Only five minutes from the Kahului Airport, this area was once a royal fishpond that was built in the 1700s and is now home to 90 species of native and migratory birds. Look for the endangered Hawaiian stilt (ae'o), a slender, 16-in (41-cm) bird with sticklike pink legs that, according to most recent population estimates, numbers around 2,000 statewide. The Hawaiian coot ('alae ke'oke'o), a gray-black duck-like bird that builds large floating nests, may also be seen here. In summer, when the sanctuary is closed for nesting season, an observation pavilion is maintained on the pond's south edge, which is open year-round.

zip line at Maui Tropical Plantation (left); Kanaha Pond State Wildlife Sanctuary (right)

ZIP-LINING

FLYIN HAWAIIAN ZIPLINE
1670 Honoapi'ilani Hwy.; 808/463-5786; www.flyinhawaiianzipline.com; 8am-3pm Mon.-Fri.; $235

For travelers who only go big or go home, the eight-line Flyin Hawaiian Zipline covers 2.5 mi (4 km) of West Maui mountainside and finishes in a different town. The most enticing reason to book this tour is the ultra-long, cheek-clenching, three-screamer zip line that runs for more than 3,600 ft (1,100 m)—the longest on the island. The lines aren't parallel, and the height off the ground isn't as high as the fifth line at Pi'iholo, but you also get a short ATV ride at the end as they shuttle you back where you started. Enjoy views toward Haleakalā during this four- to five-hour tour. Small snacks are included. Riders must be at least 10 years old and weigh 75-250 pounds (34-113 kg). Guests meet at the Maui Tropical Plantation for a 4WD ride back into Waikapu Valley, where you suit up for your midair journey across the mountain. This tour often sells out well in advance, so reservations are a must.

MAUI ZIPLINE
1670 Honoapi'ilani Hwy.; 808/633-2464; www.mauizipline.com; 9am-5pm Tues.-Sat.; $149

If you'd rather ease into it, or are traveling with children, the most beginner-friendly zip line in the central valley is Maui Zipline, on the grounds of the Maui Tropical Plantation. Children as young as five and as light as 45 pounds (20 kg) can take part in this five-line adventure; children under age 11 must be joined by an adult. Because the course caters to young children, it isn't as extreme as some others, but the guides introduce educational elements to the program, such as the weather patterns of the area and lessons on plant species, making this a great option for families. Cable lengths range 300-900 ft (90-275 m), and two cables run parallel to each other, so you can go two at a time.

176 CENTRAL MAUI

HELICOPTER AND FLIGHTSEEING TOURS

HELICOPTER RIDES

Helicopter tours are the island's best splurge. They're expensive, and some people find them scary, but they are the best way to experience Maui's beauty. The majority of the island is only accessible by helicopter, and until you've seen waterfalls powerfully plunging through hidden mist-shrouded valleys or buzzed below the world's tallest sea cliffs and seen humpback whales from the air, you'll never know the breadth of beauty that Maui really has to offer. All pilots have logged thousands of flying hours and put an emphasis on safety, and when narrating the tours, most also provide information on geology, biology, and history. Morning tours are best because they offer the clear conditions necessary for visiting spots such as 1,100-ft (335-m) **Honokohau Falls,** Maui's tallest waterfall, or peering into **Haleakalā Crater.**

All helicopter flights depart from the **Kahului Heliport** (0.5 mi/0.8 km from the junction of Hana Hwy. and Haleakalā Hwy.), and the two most popular tour options are those combining the West Maui Mountains with Moloka'i, and East Maui (Hana) with Haleakalā. Regardless of which operator you choose, inquire about getting the two front seats next to the pilot, since it's much easier to take photos. If you're really serious about photos, wear long sleeves and dark-colored clothing to avoid reflection in the window, and to get really pro, consider wearing gloves. Remember that you cannot have been scuba diving within 24 hours before the flight (although snuba is OK). All prices listed are for advance online reservations.

Honokohau Falls

AIR MAUI
108 Lelepio Pl.; 808/877-7005; www. airmaui.com

Air Maui has a perfect safety record and has options you won't find elsewhere, including the West Maui and Moloka'i tour ($330 pp), where you tour the mountains and marvel at thundering waterfalls. There are also standard West Maui-Moloka'i and Hana- Haleakalā tours ($272 pp), including one with a cliff-side landing on the back side of Haleakalā. All helicopters are the A-Star variety, which seat up to six.

BLUE HAWAIIAN HELICOPTERS
1 Lelepio Pl.; 808/871-8844; www. bluehawaiian.com

The largest operator on the island, with cheaper flights, is Blue Hawaiian Helicopters, operating both A-Star and more expensive ECO-Star helicopters, with individual bucket seats and larger viewing windows. Options include the Waterfalls of West Maui and Moloka'i ($389 pp) and Hana & Haleakalā ($389 pp). For a truly memorable experience, book the 1.5-hour Complete Island Maui ($473 pp), which combines a West Maui tour and a Hana & Haleakalā tour, including a remote landing on the slopes of Haleakalā, complete with refreshments.

FLIGHTSEEING TOURS
MAUI PLANE RIDES
90 Kuhea St.; 808/800-6394; www. mauiplanerides.com

A six-minute island journey filled with scenic views of Haleakalā and Maui's neighboring islands begins at $599 for a single-engine plane (up to three people) and $1,399 for 4-5 people. A big standout here is that it offers Maui's only fully opening camera-port window for stellar clear shots of lush emerald landscapes.

GOLF

If you don't want to pay resort prices for golf but still appreciate a course that's well cared for, the three courses in Central Maui have some of the island's best deals. All have affordable restaurants with ice-cold beer. Prices listed are summer rates; expect to pay approximately $35 more per round in winter.

KAHULUI
DUNES AT MAUI LANI
1333 Maui Lani Pkwy.; 808/873-0422; www.dunesatmauilani.com; 7am-6pm daily

This Scottish-style links course weaves through natural sand dunes. Course designer Robert Nelson utilized the natural topography of the dunes in creating this 6,841-yard (6,255-m) course, so it includes a healthy number of bunkers. On the 18th hole, which is par 5, two pot bunkers short of the green famously challenge even those with the lowest of handicaps. The afternoon trade winds can make this course difficult, and the greens fees are priced accordingly: $100 for morning rounds, $88 after noon, $60 after 3pm. Club rental is $55, and the central location makes it easy to sneak in a round before the 10-minute drive to the airport.

Kahili Golf Course

WAILUKU
KAHILI GOLF COURSE
2500 Honoapi'ilani Hwy.; 808/242-4653; www.kahiligolf.com; 6am-6pm daily

On the hillside in Waikapu, the 6,554-yard (5,993-m) Kahili Golf Course is one of the island's best golf values. Greens fees for visitors are $109, although if you tee off after 2pm, it drops to $95; club rentals are $59. The bicoastal views are better than at Maui Lani, although instead of links-style golf, the course is set on a gently sloping hillside. Kahili is a 35-minute drive from Ka'anapali, 25 minutes from Wailea.

WAIEHU GOLF COURSE
200 Halewaiu Rd.; 808/243-7400; 6:30am-5pm daily

If you just want to tee up the municipal course, Waiehu Golf Course is a 6,330-yard (5,788-m), par-72 course that's wildly popular with locals. Visitor greens fees are $65 weekdays, $72 weekends, although you can sneak in nine holes for only $32 if you tee off after 3pm. Cart rentals are $30 for 18 holes, and hand carts are only $6. Club rentals are $25, and a couple of the holes have oceanfront tee boxes and sweeping resort-quality views.

RENTAL SHOPS
ROGER DUNN GOLF SHOP
293 Dairy Rd.; 808/873-5700; 9am-6pm Mon.-Sat., 10am-5pm Sun.

Regardless of where you're golfing, you can save on rental clubs by stopping at Roger Dunn Golf Shop, just a couple of minutes from the airport. Rental rates start at $30 per day or $85 per week—far more affordable than the $65-100 you would pay daily at some resorts.

SHOPPING

KAHULUI
QUEEN KA'AHUMANU SHOPPING CENTER
275 W. Ka'ahumanu Ave.; 808/877-4325; www.queenkaahumanucenter.com; 10am-8pm daily

Kahului has the island's largest amount of shopping, though it's mainly the box-store variety. The two-story Queen Ka'ahumanu Shopping Center is Kahului's largest mall, though many of the stores are large corporate chains.

MAUI SWAP MEET
310 W. Ka'ahumanu Ave.; 808/244-3100; www.mauiexposition.com; 7am-1pm Sat.; $0.50 adults, free under age 12

For a classic Maui shopping experience, head to the Saturday Maui Swap Meet at UH Maui College, where over 200 local vendors gather to sell their foodstuffs and crafts. You can find everything from homemade jams to hand-turned koa wood bowls—often at prices much reduced from what you'd find in the stores.

WAILUKU
Sleepy Wailuku is turning into a hot shopping outpost. With a tight little cluster of shops, **Market Street** rivals Lahaina, Pa'ia, and Makawao for shopping and strolling. The difference here, however, is that many of the stores have authentic local connections—either selling products

from local vendors or traditional Hawaiian crafts.

NATIVE INTELLIGENCE
1980 Main St.; 808/249-2421; www.native-intel.com; 10am-5pm Mon.-Fri., 10am-4pm Sat.

One of the island's most culturally authentic stores, Native Intelligence is filled with traditional Hawaiian culture and values, selling everything from textbooks printed in Hawaiian to traditional lei-making supplies. You'll also find hand-carved weaponry, jewelry, and immaculate colorful feather-work, and occasional classes help introduce visitors to traditional Hawaiian culture. For anyone with an interest in traditional culture, this store is a must-visit.

REQUEST MUSIC
10 N. Market St.; 808/244-9315; 11am-5pm Mon.-Sat.

A longtime Wailuku institution, Request Music is the last holdout of true island record shops, kept alive by loyal music lovers who still want to feel the vinyl, admire the album covers, and talk with people who *really* love music. Most of the merchandise caters to the reggae and roots lifestyle, but the basement is filled with music that goes back decades.

FOOD

In addition to the restaurants in Kahului and Wailuku, Central Maui is the island's epicenter for quirky gourmet **food trucks.** A local favorite is **Like Poke?,** which you can find among a cluster of food trucks across from the Costco gas station on Haleakalā Highway. The dirt parking area across from the Maui Arts and Cultural Center is another hub for food trucks.

covered seating for food trucks

CENTRAL MAUI FOOD OPTIONS

NAME	LOCATION	CONTACT INFO
KAHULUI		
★ **Tante's Island Cuisine**	100 W. Ka'ahumanu Ave.	808/277-0300
Ichiban Restaurant & Sushi	47 W. Ka'ahumanu Ave.	808/871-6977
Tiki Tiki Thai Cuisine	395 Dairy Rd.	808/893-0026
Brigit and Bernard's Garden Café	335 Ho'ohana St.	808/877-6000; www. brigitandbernards.com
Bistro Casanova	33 Lono Ave.	808/873-3650; www. bistrocasanova.com
Amigos	333 Dairy Rd.	808/872-9525; www. amigosmaui.com
Ululani's	333 Dairy Rd.	808/877-3700; www. ululanisshaveice.com
Maui Coffee Roasters	444 Hana Hwy.	808/877-2877; www. mauicoffeeroasters.com
WAILUKU		
★ **Café O'Lei at the Plantation**	1670 Honoapi'ilani Hwy.	808/500-0533; www. cafeoleirestaurants.com
Sam Sato's	1750 Wili Pa Loop	808/244-7124
★ **808 on Main**	2051 Main St.	808/242-1111; www.808onmain.com
Giannotto's Pizza	2050 Main St.	808/244-8282; www. giannottospizza.com
★ **Tasty Crust Restaurant**	1770 Mill St.	808/244-0845; www. tastycrustrestaurant.com
Wailuku Coffee Company	26 N. Market St.	808/495-0259

STANDOUTS

Kahului

TANTE'S ISLAND CUISINE

100 W. Ka'ahumanu Ave.; 808/277-0300; 7am-2pm and 5pm-8:30pm daily; $12-23

This island institution serves island-infused meals featuring fish and island vegetables. Try the Filipino dishes, too, and be sure to check out the happy hour, one of the longest on the island, running noon-6pm.

Wailuku

CAFÉ O'LEI AT THE PLANTATION

1670 Honoapi'ilani Hwy.; 808/500-0533; www.cafeoleirestaurants.com; 11am-8pm Tues.-Sat.; $18-55

FOOD	HOURS	PRICE
local style	7am-2pm and 5-m-8:30pm daily	$12-23
Japanese	10:30am-2pm and 5pm-9pm Mon.-Fri., 5pm-9pm Sat.	$8-14
Thai	10am-10pm daily	$11-23
German	11am-2:30pm and 5pm-9pm Mon.-Fri., 5pm-9pm Sat.	$16-38
Italian	11am-2pm and 5pm-9pm Mon.-Fri., 5pm-9pm Sat.	$14-38
Mexican	9am-9pm daily	$9-12
shaved ice	10:30am-6pm daily	$7
coffee shops	7am-6pm Mon.-Fri., 7am-5pm Sat.	$9
Hawaiian Regional	11am-8pm Tues.-Sat.	$18-55
local style	7am-2pm Mon.-Sat.	$7, cash only
eclectic	10am-3pm Mon.-Sat.	$10-36
Italian	11am-8pm Mon.-Sat.	$8-18
diner	6am-8pm Wed.-Mon.	$6-24, cash only
coffee shops	7am-5pm Mon.-Sat., 7am-2pm Sun.	$5-9

Inside the Maui Tropical Plantation, Café O'Lei at the Plantation brings one of the island's most popular culinary outposts (Café O'Lei) into a tropical setting. Blending farm-to-table artistry with island favorites, standout dishes include Maui onion soup en croute ($12), slow-cooked lamb shank ($32), and a miso eggplant and root vegetable bowl ($21). Happy hour runs 3pm-5pm, when beers go for $4-5 and tossed flatbreads run an affordable $14. This is one of the most memorable dining options on the island.

808 ON MAIN
2051 Main St.; 808/242-1111; www.808onmain.com; 10am-3pm Mon.-Sat.; $10-36

FOOD 183

CENTRAL MAUI BARS AND NIGHTLIFE

NAME	LOCATION	CONTACT INFO
KAHULUI		
★ **Maui Arts and Cultural Center**	1 Cameron Way	808/242-7469; www.mauiarts.org
★ **Ale House**	355 E. Kamehameha Ave.	808/877-0001; www.kahuluialehouse.com
Koho's Grill and Bar	275 W. Ka'ahumanu Ave.	808/877-5588
WAILUKU		
★ **Maui Friday Town Parties**	Market St.	www.mauifridays.com
'Iao Theater	68 N. Market St.	www.mauionstage.com
★ **Esters Fair Prospect**	2050 Main St.	808/868-0056
Da Playground Maui	300 Ma'alaea Rd.	808/727-2571; www.daplaygroundmaui.com

Just half a block from Market Street is 808 on Main, where you can get filling paninis, sandwiches, and salads with creative culinary flare. Try the mahimahi quinoa bowl ($18) or Southern Squealer hoagie with pulled pork ($14). House favorites on the cocktail menus include a blueberry mojito and the Maui martini with Hapa Hawaiian vodka, Maui Shrub Farm ginger, and Hawaiian chili shrub. Cheers!

TASTY CRUST RESTAURANT
1770 Mill St.; 808/244-0845; 6am-8pm Wed.-Mon.; $6-24, cash only
Tasty Crust is an island institution serving traditional breakfasts, lunches, and dinners, but don't leave without experiencing island-infused meals. This place also boasts some of the best pancakes around.

BARS AND NIGHTLIFE

STANDOUTS
Kahului
MAUI ARTS AND CULTURAL CENTER
1 Cameron Way; 808/242-7469; www.mauiarts.org
It's not often you can be in paradise and have access to top-notch entertainment. In between suntanning and other island adventures, consider taking in a theatrical show or music performance at Maui Arts and Cultural Center. The 1,200-seat Castle Theater inside has three levels of seating, and the acoustics are designed in such a way that an

VENUE TYPE	HOURS
live music and cultural center	varies
bar and music venue	11am-9pm Mon.-Wed., 11am-10pm Thurs.-Sun.
restaurant and bar	11am-9pm Mon.-Wed., 11am-9:30pm Thurs.-Sat., 7am-9pm Sun.
street festival	5:30pm-9pm the first Friday of every month
theater	varies
cocktail bar	noon-midnight Wed.-Fri., 3pm-midnight Sat. and Mon.-Tues.
live music and bar	7pm-midnight Wed.-Sun.

unamplified guitar can be heard from each seat. The 250-seat McCoy Studio is a black-box theater that hosts smaller plays and theatrical events, while the 5,000-seat A&B amphitheater has drawn some of the world's biggest musical talent, from Elton John to The Eagles. Multiple shows often happen on the same evening. Check the website for a list of upcoming events.

ALE HOUSE
355 E. Kamehameha Ave.; 808/877-0001; www.kahuluialehouse.com; 11am-9pm Mon.-Wed, 11am-10pm Thurs.-Sun.
The best bar in Kahului is Ale House, which has live music every night and 24 beers on draft. There are 40 TVs for watching the game, as well as ice-cold beer, surprisingly good sushi, and happy hour 3pm-6pm.

Wailuku
MAUI FRIDAY TOWN PARTIES
@estersmaui
Market Street is closed to vehicular traffic 5:30pm-9pm the first Friday of every month, and the area becomes a festive pedestrian thoroughfare. Enjoy live music in Banyan Tree Park,

Friday Town Party

CENTRAL MAUI LODGING OPTIONS

NAME	LOCATION	CONTACT INFO
KAHULUI		
Maui Beach Hotel	170 Ka'ahumanu Ave.	808/877-0051; www.mauibeachhotel.com
WAILUKU		
Banana Bungalow	310 N. Market St.	808/244-5090; www.mauihostel.com
Howzit Hostels	2080 W. Vineyard St.	808/868-0023
★ **Old Wailuku Inn at Ulupono**	2199 Kaho'okele St.	808/244-5897; www.mauiinn.com
★ **Iao Valley Inn**	80 'Iao Valley Rd.	808/633-6028; www.iaovalleyinn.com

street performers, food concessions from local restaurants, activities for children, and a beer garden for the adults. This is the most popular of the Maui Friday Town Parties, free events that rotate weekly from town to town.

ESTERS FAIR PROSPECT
2050 Main St.; 808/868-0056; noon-midnight Wed.-Fri., 3pm-midnight Sat. and Mon.-Tues.

Esters Fair Prospect is a great go-to. Inventive tropical cocktails abound here, like the Knickerbocker a la Monsieur, which pairs rum with fresh raspberry, curaçao, and lemon, or the Stirred Down Wailuku Town, which features whiskey, cocoa, sherry, and coconut oil. There are lovely views out on the patio, and the venue typically offers $3 deals for a great glass of wine.

LODGING

RESERVATIONS AND TIPS

This area of the island has the most affordable accommodations. If you stay here, car rentals or ride share services are vital. The winds tend to be more frequent on this side of the island, too, so if you're hoping for consistently calm beach days, consider driving to South Maui.

STANDOUTS
Wailuku
OLD WAILUKU INN AT ULUPONO
2199 Kaho'okele St.; 808/244-5897; www.mauiinn.com; $192-325, 2-night minimum

The nicest place to stay in historic Wailuku is the Old Wailuku Inn at Ulupono, built in 1924 and listed on the Hawaii Register of Historic Places. The 10 rooms are filled with period furniture that evokes the feeling of Grandma's house. Although it sounds

TYPE	PRICE	BEST FOR
hotel	$269-359	budget travelers
hostel	$50-159	budget travelers
hostel	from $60	budget travelers
B&B	$192-325, 2-night minimum	couples
B&B	$279-439	couples

like marketing, this really is Maui's most Hawaiian bed-and-breakfast. Wi-Fi is included, and each room has a private bath. A filling gourmet breakfast is served at 8am daily. Most rooms are set up for double occupancy.

IAO VALLEY INN
80 'Iao Valley Rd.; 808/633-6028; www.iaovalleyinn.com; $279-439

For peace and serenity in 'Iao Valley, the Iao Valley Inn is a spectacular B&B on 37 lush acres (15 ha), a true sanctuary that's just minutes outside Wailuku. There are two guest rooms and a separate cottage that can sleep up to four.

TRANSPORTATION

Air

The island's main airport, **Kahului Airport** (OGG; Keolani Pl.; 808/872-3830; www. airports.hawaii.gov/ogg), is in this neck of the woods. Exiting the airport, take Highway 32 or Highway 380 to your destination.

Car

Traffic in this area can be lighter than in other areas of the island. There tends to be more traffic heading toward Maui Ocean Center, on the way to West Maui, so expect delays heading into that area, especially in the mid-morning and throughout the afternoon.

Car Rental

Most of the major car rental companies have rental desks at the airport. Other options in Kahului, which are often cheaper, include **Maui Car Rentals** (190 Papa Pl.; 800/567-4659; www.mauicarrentals.net) and **Kimo's Rent A Car** (440 Alamaha St.; 808/280-6327; www.kimosrentacar.com). Most local car-rental companies offer free transportation to the airport if arranged ahead of time.

Parking

Parking on this side of the island is plentiful, with big lots at beach parks and easy street parking around restaurants and shops.

Taxi

R&L Taxi (808/339-5348) is reliable and a perfect choice for taxi service on this side of the island.

Bus

The Queen Ka'ahumanu Shopping Center in Kahului is the central hub of the **Maui Bus,** and if you are connecting from one bus to another, there is a good chance that you'll end up making a stop at the mall. All segments on the bus cost $4 per person, and this is the terminus and starting point for routes heading upcountry as well as to Kihei and Lahaina.

To just get across town, buses on the Wailuku Loop (bus 1) make various stops around Wailuku and run hourly 6:30am-9:30pm daily. Similarly, buses on the Kahului Loop (bus 5) make various stops around Kahului and run hourly 6:30am-9pm daily. From Queen Kaʻahumanu to the Kahului Airport, you have to get on the Upcountry Islander bus (bus 40), which runs every 90 minutes 6:10am-9:10pm daily. For more information, a full schedule, and to see routes to other parts of the island, visit www.mauicounty.gov and navigate to "For Residents" and then "Maui Bus."

Motorcycle and Moped

If the idea of zipping ocean-side on a groovy Yamaha is your preferred method of getting from A to B, **Maui Moto Adventures** (60 E. Wakea Ave.; 808/269-9515; www.mauimotorcyclerentalsandtours.com; open 24 hours daily) offers rentals from the Kahului shop just minutes from Kahului Airport.

LEAVING CENTRAL MAUI

South Maui (Kihei)

From Kahului, head south on Maui Veterans Highway (Hwy. 311). Continue onto Piʻilani Highway (Hwy. 31) to Kihei. The 11.9-mi (19.1-km) drive is 25 minutes.

West Maui (Lahaina)

From Kahului, take Puʻunene Avenue to Kuihelani Highway (Hwy. 380) toward Maʻalaea. Continue on this highway until it merges with Honoapiʻilani Highway (Hwy. 30) and follow it along the scenic coastline directly into Lahaina. The 23.3-mi (37.4-km) drive is 45 minutes.

Haleakalā National Park

From Kahului, take Hana Highway (Hwy. 36) eastbound. Turn right onto Haleakalā Highway (Hwy. 37) and follow the road as it ascends. Continue on this road as it turns into Crater Road (Hwy. 378), which will lead you directly into Haleakalā National Park. The 40-mi (64.3-km) drive takes about 90 minutes.

Start of the Road to Hana

From Kahului, take Hana Highway (Hwy. 36) eastbound. Stay on this road, passing the communities of Paʻia and Haʻiku, until you reach the Road to Hana mile marker 0 (Hwy. 360). The 17-mi (27.4-km) drive is about 30 minutes.

Haleakalā National Park

HALEAKALĀ AND UPCOUNTRY

Upcountry is Maui's little secret that's just now starting to get out. Here's a place where the smell of eucalyptus replaces the rustle of palms, and truck-driving farmers with scuffed boots replace the pool boys with towels.

Upcountry is where you throw on a flannel shirt and go for a morning drive, perhaps stopping to relax on the porch of a small family-run coffeehouse. It's a place to go hiking through forests of pine trees or sip on Maui-made wine and watch the day begin or end over Haleakalā Crater. It's seeing a Sunday polo game and wandering through Makawao's galleries and buying vegetables straight from the source at a stand on the side of the road. It's eating doughnuts at a family bakery that's been serving them for over a century or settling in for a colorful sunset over bicoastal views each night. Most of all, it's slowing down and taking time to breathe the mountain air and trading the glamour of beachfront resorts for the charm of a small town.

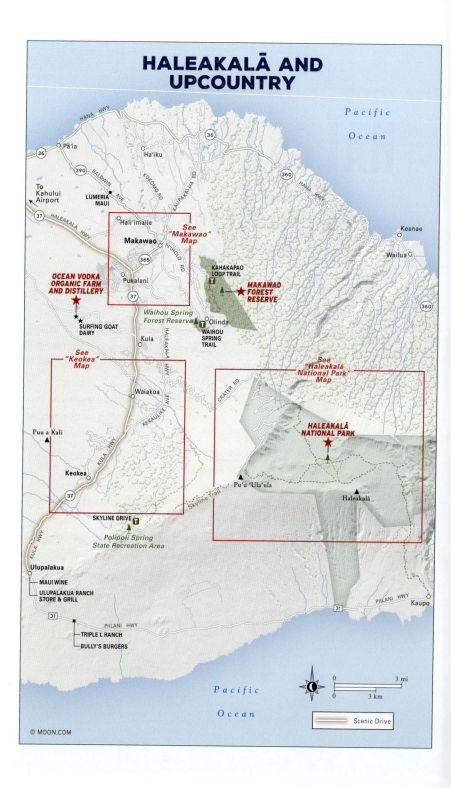

TOP 3

★ **1. HALEAKALĀ NATIONAL PARK:** Experience sunrise or sunset at Haleakalā and hike across the crater floor (page 199).

★ **2. OCEAN VODKA ORGANIC FARM AND DISTILLERY:** Tour the distillery and top it off with samplings of Maui's celebrated organic vodka (page 207).

★ **3. MAKAWAO FOREST RESERVE:** Hike or bike through a majestic reserve filled with fragrant eucalyptus trees (page 215).

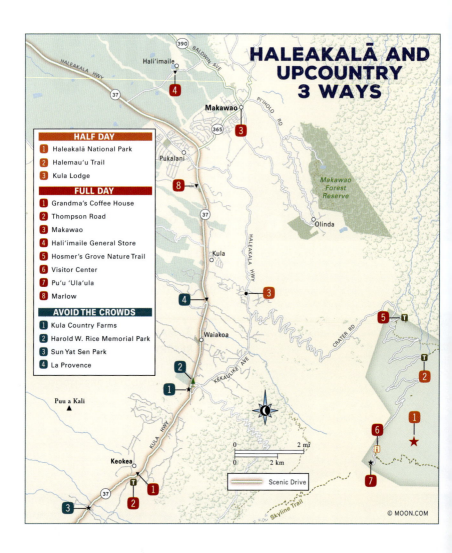

HALEAKALĀ AND UPCOUNTRY 3 WAYS

HALF DAY

1 Experience the sunrise at **Haleakalā National Park.** Book ahead for entry.

2 When you're ready, make your way to the trailhead for **Halemau'u Trail** (Switchback Trail) between mile marker 14 and 15 on Haleakalā Highway. Take this exciting path down to the floor of Haleakalā crater.

3 Reward yourself with a hearty post-hike lunch at **Kula Lodge.** Consider the wagyu burger or mochiko chicken and waffles.

FULL DAY

1 Begin the day in Keokea with breakfast at **Grandma's Coffee House.**

2 Walk off breakfast with a 30-minute stroll on neighboring **Thompson Road.**

3 Drive to **Makawao** to explore the historic town and shop for eclectic clothing, gifts, souvenirs, and artwork.

4 Grab a bite from **Hali'imaile General Store** before making your way to Haleakalā National Park in the afternoon.

5 Just past the Haleakalā National Park gate entrance, stop to explore **Hosmer's Grove Nature Trail.**

6 Hop back in your car and continue leisurely driving toward the summit. There are various scenic overlooks, and near the end of the road toward the summit is the **visitor center,** where maps, books, and gifts are available.

7 You'll know you've topped out when you reach the glass-sided observation area at **Pu'u 'Ula'ula** (Red Hill), where you can stake out a seat 45-60 minutes before sundown. The sunset experience is less crowded than the sunrise, and the westward view offers a stunning look at Moloka'i, Lana'i, and West Maui.

8 For dinner, head to **Marlow** back in Makawao for exceptional wood-fired sourdough pizzas.

HALEAKALĀ AND UPCOUNTRY 3 WAYS   197

AVOID THE CROWDS

1️⃣ Plant yourself at **Kula Country Farms,** where you can peruse the grounds, enjoy scenic views of the ocean, and shop the local store. Not too many crowds in this open space.

2️⃣ Bring a picnic lunch to **Harold W. Rice Memorial Park** and enjoy the stunning ocean views.

3️⃣ In the afternoon, head to **Sun Yat Sen Park,** a stellar historical and cultural park that offers quaint walks through ornamental gardens, statues, and sculptures.

4️⃣ Enjoy the spaciousness of **La Provence,** a hidden gem in Kula featuring bistro classics for dinner.

ORIENTATION AND PLANNING

ORIENTATION

Generally speaking, Upcountry comprises Makawao, Pukalani, Kula, Keokea, and Ulupalakua. **Makawao** has the greatest selection of restaurants and shops, as well as a defined center, whereas **Kula,** which is up the highway several miles away from and higher in elevation than Makawao, is a patchwork of houses, farms, and restaurants that are fairly spread out. Tiny **Keokea** is the gateway between Kula to the east and the winery in **Ulupalakua,** where the road continues all the way around to Kaupo and the "back way" to Hana. The drive from Makawao to Ulupalakua takes 35 minutes, versus 10 minutes to the beach in Pa'ia near the start of the Road to Hana or 15 minutes to Kahului Airport.

At an elevation of 1,500-4,000 ft (460-1,220 m), Upcountry is also home to the 10,023-ft (3,055-m) summit of **Haleakalā Crater.** From sea level, the 38-mi (61-km) drive to the summit is the shortest climb to 10,000 ft (3,050 m) of any paved road in the world. From Makawao or Kula, reaching the summit of Haleakalā Crater is about an hour's drive, and from Ka'anapali or Wailea takes a little over two hours.

PLANNING YOUR TIME

While it's possible to experience Upcountry's highlights in a single day, try to spend two full days seeing the area—one day at Haleakalā Crater either watching the sunrise and exploring Upcountry on the way back down, or gradually visiting Upcountry sights before heading to Haleakalā for sunset. On the second day, start with horseback riding or zip-lining, and then see the sights you didn't get to see the day before. While many people drive to Upcountry from the beach, there are numerous lodges and bed-and-breakfasts where you can base yourself on the hill. It's also possible to visit Upcountry when driving the "back road" from Hana, but by the time you get here after a full day in Hana, there's really only time for the winery.

HIGHLIGHTS

★ HALEAKALĀ NATIONAL PARK

www.nps.gov/hale; $30 per car
"Hale-a-ka-la," House of the Sun. Few places are more aptly named than this 10,023-ft (3,055-m) volcano. Believed to have been dormant since 1790 (the summit area has been inactive for 600 years), Haleakalā is 30,000 ft (9,145 m) tall when measured from the seafloor—surpassed only by the peaks on the Big Island as the tallest mountain on earth.

Given its size and spellbinding nature, it's little wonder the mountain is considered sacred to indigenous Hawaiians. This is where the powerful volcano goddess, Pele, crafted her colorful cinder cones, and it's a *wahi pana,* or sacred place,

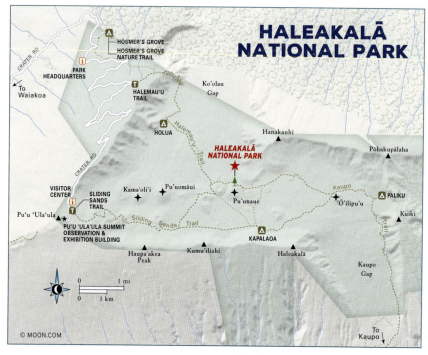

inhabited only by the gods. It's where the demigod Maui lassoed the sun to slow its path across the sky so his people could have time to grow their crops and dry their cloth in the sun. It's also a fragile ecological treasure, with more endangered species than any other national park.

Today, the most popular activity for visitors to Maui is visiting Haleakalā for sunrise—but there's far more to this national park than simply the light of dawn. Over 30 mi (48 km) of hiking trails crisscross the crater, where backcountry cabins and campgrounds provide a classic wilderness experience. The sunsets and stargazing are as spectacular as viewing the crater at sunrise, and even the drive leading up to the park—where the road gains 10,000 vertical ft (3,050 m) in only 38 mi (61 km)—is part of the magical, mystical experience of standing atop Haleakalā.

Visiting the Park
WHEN TO VISIT

The biggest question surrounding Haleakalā is not if you should visit, but when.

- **Sunrise** is the most popular option, and everyone should experience a Haleakalā sunrise at least once. Reservations are required and can be made online at www.recreation.gov up to 60 days in advance (for questions, call 877/444-6777); visitors are allowed to purchase only one sunrise reservation per three-day period. Sunrise is crowded, it's tough to find parking, it requires waking up around 2am-3am, and it's often near or below freezing.

- **Sunset** is a display nearly as colorful but without all the crowds (and no reservations required). You don't get the benefit of watching the sun emerge from the horizon, but there are often only 40 people instead of 400, and it isn't as cold.

If you want to hike the crater floor, arrive at the summit in the middle of the day and time your exit for sunset. Sunrise and sunset are always the most populated times here, and oftentimes parking can be challenging. Plan ahead to make sure you arrive at least 90 minutes prior to sunrise or sunset.

WEATHER

Please note it is about 30 degrees cooler here than at sea level, and the weather, unfortunately, can be unpredictable. Rain and even snow can fall at any time of year, but summer typically has better conditions. Statistically, on 85 percent of mornings, it's clear enough to see the sunrise. For sunset, a good rule of thumb is that if you can't see the mountain from below, you probably shouldn't bother. On the other hand, if you can see the mountain, but not the top, the sunset will seem to float on a colorful sea of clouds. To take the guesswork out of the equation, call the National Weather Service **Hotline for Haleakalā Summit** (808/944-5025, ext. 4) for an up-to-date weather forecast. You can also check out the University of Hawaii astronomy website (www.ifa.hawaii.edu/haleakalanew/weather.shtml) for up-to-the-minute weather data, including windchill, visibility, and rainfall, before heading to the summit.

ADMISSION

Admission ($30 per car) to Haleakalā National Park is good for three days and includes the Kipahulu section past Hana, home to the Pools of ʻOheʻo.

VISITOR CENTERS

Just past the park entrance, you'll soon arrive at **park headquarters** (808/572-4400; 8am-4pm daily) at an elevation of 6,800 ft (2,075 m). Stop for information, camping permits, gifts, toilets, and a pay phone. There are some ʻahinahina (silversword) plants outside, and sometimes nene (Hawaiian geese) frequent the area.

Near the end of the road toward the summit is the **visitor center,** at 9,740 ft (2,969 m). It's about 10 mi (16 km) up the mountain from headquarters, about a 30-minute drive. This is where all of the bike tour companies bring you for sunrise, as it's the best view looking down into the crater. It's open sunrise-3pm daily and contains clear and concise displays on the geology of Haleakalā. Maps and books are available, and a 30-minute ranger-guided walk takes place most days at 10am and 11am.

Puʻu ʻUlaʻula (Red Hill) Summit Observation and Exhibition Building

On the road toward the summit, **Leleiwi** is an overlook that's a great alternative at sunrise. **Kalahaku,** on the other side, is another overlook that's popular at sunrise but can only be accessed when traveling downhill.

If you want to top out above 10,000 ft (3,050 m) and officially summit Haleakalā, **Puʻu ʻUlaʻula** (Red Hill) is the highest point on Maui at 10,023 ft (3,055 m). Here you'll find a glass-sided observation area that's open

HALEAKALĀ AT SUNSET

There's big buzz about experiencing mighty Haleakalā at sunrise, but one of the lesser-known facts is how dynamic it is during sunset. Locals know this well, often declaring the sunset experience to be just as stellar—if not more so—than what you'll experience during the early morning hours. Here are some reasons to consider catching a sunset rather than sunrise:

sunset at Haleakalā

- **Crowds:** Sunrise at Haleakalā has been heavily promoted in so many travel magazines and websites that hundreds of tourists flock here for it. This has resulted in the park system requiring reservations for sunrise (which can be made online up to 60 days in advance). Not so for sunset, when crowds are considerably smaller in size—nearly 60 percent less—and views from the observation deck less obstructed.

- **Timing and parking:** To arrive in time for sunrise, you'll need to arrive before 4:30am to find a much-coveted parking spot. Depending on where you're staying on the island, this may mean setting your alarm between 2am and 3am. For sunset, it's much easier to find a parking spot; you'll just need to arrive about 45-60 minutes prior to catch the best colors.

- **Position of the sun:** Watching the sun set into the ocean is particularly striking, offering a sublime color palette. Depending on cloud coverage, this time of day also offers rare and extraordinary panoramic views of Maui's south and west sides, which are in shadow around dawn.

- **Stargazing options:** If you visit Haleakalā for sunset, you can stay and do some stargazing, possibly catching some shooting stars as a finale. Orion's Belt and the planets Mars and Venus will compete for attention with the Milky Way. While the stars are also visible before sunrise, with the scrambling required to find a parking space and jostling for a viewing spot, you won't be able to focus on the dark sky.

24 hours daily. The view of the Big Island and coast of Maui is better than at the visitor center below. The lava rock ridge just in front of the parking area is the best place to watch the sunset. For perspective, it's 100 mi (160 km) from the top of Haleakalā to Mauna Loa in the distance.

Close to the summit is the **Maui Space Surveillance Complex** (www.ifa.hawaii.edu/haleakala), a.k.a. Science City. It's closed to the public and highly controversial, with occasional protests over the construction of a telescope on culturally sacred land.

Camping and Cabins

To really appreciate Haleakalā's beauty, you need to stay overnight. The most accessible campground is at **Hosmer's Grove,** where you don't even need a permit. There are a handful of tent sites, a few barbecue grills, a pit toilet, and running water. You can drive up to the campsites, which makes it an easy option. The campground is at 6,800 ft (2,070 m), so nights can get close to freezing. It also makes a great staging ground for driving to the summit for sunrise.

For a rugged overnight backpacking experience, there are wilderness campsites inside the crater at both **Holua** (elevation 6,940 ft/2,115 m) and **Paliku** (6,380 ft/1,945 m). Camping in the crater requires a permit, which can be picked up for free from the park headquarters. Both campsites have pit toilets and nonpotable water, and although the sites are first-come, first-served, they can accommodate up to 25 people and are rarely full. Maximum stay is three nights in a 30-day period, and no more than two nights in a row at the same site. Holua is accessible by a 3.7-mi (6-km) hike down **Halemau'u Trail** (page 214) and is set in a field of subalpine scrub brush looking toward the Ko'olau Gap. Paliku, on the other hand, requires hiking 9.2 mi (14.8 km) from the **Sliding Sands Trail** (page 214) at the summit (or a 10.3-mi/16.6-km hike on Halemau'u Trail) and is wet, lush, surrounded by foliage, and a good place for spotting nene. This is also the preferred area for those opting to hike the **Kaupo Gap** (page 215).

In addition to campgrounds, **backcountry cabins** ($75 and up) are available at **Kapalaoa** (7,250 ft/2,210 m), as well as Holua and Paliku. Due to their popularity, however, securing reservations can be difficult. Reservations can be made up to 180 days in advance by creating a profile on www.recreation.gov and searching for Haleakalā National Park (Cabin Permits). Cabins are often booked four months in advance, so if you want to include this on your trip to Maui, plan ahead and be flexible. Cabins include 12 padded berths, a wood-burning stove, and basic kitchen utilities. Bed linens are not provided, so please bring your own, or a sleeping bag. Pit toilets and nonpotable water are available, and all trash must be packed out.

MAUI VACATION EQUIPMENT RENTALS

59 Ho'okele St., Kahului; 808/909-2211; www.mauivacationequipment.com; 9am-4pm daily; $6-7.50 linens, $5 sleeping bag, $9 portable camping stoves

One of the best things about this company is that it coordinates island-wide free delivery service directly to clients, their vacation rental manager, or a hotel for orders over $150. Small tents, lanterns, compact chairs, coolers, and more are available.

MAKAWAO
Hali'imaile Distillery
883 Hali'imaile Rd.; 808/758-5154; www.haliimailedistilling.com; tours 4-5 times daily beginning as early as 10am; $15

When was the last time you tried vodka made from pineapples? Hali'imaile Distillery is the only place in the world you'll find the sugary spirit. The team in this Quonset hut is completely redefining cocktails, from the world's only vodka aged in French oak to Kona coffee-flavored whiskey and chocolate macadamia nut vodka. Master distiller Mark Nigbur helped pioneer the process of distilling with glass, instead of copper or steel, and he's partnered with Sammy Hagar, his wild blond doppelgänger, to create Sammy's Beach Bar Rum. Tours last 45 minutes and pass through the distillery, which is sandwiched between Hawaii's only sugar plantation and America's only pineapple plantation. Notable brands are Pau Maui Vodka and Paniolo Whiskey, and the tour is capped off by three-quarter-ounce (22-ml) pours for visitors over age 21.

Hui No'eau Visual Arts Center
2841 Baldwin Ave.; 808/572-6560; www.huinoeau.com; 9am-4pm Wed.-Sat.; $4 donation

About 1 mi (1.6 km) downhill from Makawao is the Hui No'eau Visual Arts Center, on a gorgeous 10-acre (4-ha) estate owned by the Baldwin family. The centerpiece is the neo-Spanish mansion built in 1917 and transformed in 1934 into a spectacular center for the arts. Touring the grounds is free, as is perusing the gallery, which hosts the work of local artists and has rotating exhibitions. You can pick up a self-guided tour ($6) of the property or take an hour-long guided tour ($12). History buffs should head directly to the room full of old black-and-white photographs that show what it was like to live on the estate 100 years ago.

Makawao History Museum
3643 Baldwin Ave.; 808/572-2482; 10am-5pm daily; donation

If you're curious how Portugal's Azores Islands are tied to Makawao's pastures, or wonder what it was like to live on a ranch in 19th-century Maui, a short visit to the Makawao History Museum is an easy way to find out. In historic Makawao town amid art galleries and boutiques, the small museum has won awards for historic preservation. Look at old black-and-white photos of early Makawao ranches and read profiles of community members who helped shape the town. The museum is completely volunteer-run and supported in part by donations. Pick up a cookbook of family recipes from Makawao's original families.

Upcountry Farmers Market
55 Kiopa'a St.; www.upcountryfarmersmarket.com; 7am-11am Sat.

Ideally, arrive between 8am and 10am before things sell out at the popular Upcountry Farmers Market, located in Kulamalu Town Center, across from Longs Drugs. You can pick up picnic items on the way from Makawao to Upcountry sights like the Surfing Goat Dairy, Ocean Vodka Organic Farm and Distillery, and the Ali'i Kula Lavender Farm. Organic farmers, bakers, fishers, artists, and other colorful locals converge weekly to showcase and sell

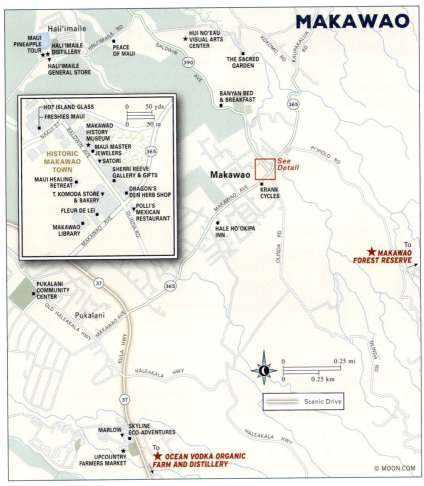

their products and socialize; it's a quintessential people-watching hot spot. Fetch some fresh produce, artisanal breads, homemade jellies, pastries, and other locally made products, including woodcrafts and jewelry that make a nice Maui-made souvenir. Sample various treats like freshly baked banana bread, raw nut cheeses, locally made kombucha, fresh-pressed juices, pineapples, coconuts, and much more. It's very pet-friendly.

KULA

On the slopes of Haleakalā between 2,000 and 4,000 ft (610-1,220 m) elevation, Kula is the hub of Maui's rural and agricultural life. Tractors drive on two-lane roads where stands sell local produce, and flannel-clad farmers lament how deer are getting into their cabbage. For visitors, the bicoastal views are reason enough to drive here, but so are the farm tours, the winery, the shops, and the laid-back small-town vibes.

Harold W. Rice Memorial Park

Lower Kula Rd., across from Kula Country Farms

Harold W. Rice Memorial Park is a great spot for both sunset-watching and stargazing. About nine picnic tables are spread across the nearly four-acre park in this lush Upcountry region. It's one of the best spots to visit for a sweeping westward view of the ocean, capturing the islands of Lana'i and Moloka'i in the distance. Some grills are available, and there's ample parking. It's a great locale and just off the main highway. Nighttime stargazing is mesmerizing here.

Surfing Goat Dairy

3651 Omaopio Rd.; 808/878-2870; www.surfinggoatdairy.com; 9am-5pm Tues.-Sat.

While it's a bit out of the way, eccentric Surfing Goat Dairy is a must-see. Where else are you going to get the chance to hand-milk a goat and then feast on gourmet cheese? Three miles (4.8 km) down Omaopio Road off Kula Highway (Hwy. 37), a line of enormous palms provides what's probably the most regal entrance to a goat dairy anywhere. There are 30-plus flavors of gourmet goat cheese and over 25 types of goat cheese truffles. The best reason to visit is the "casual" tours ($15-21), which typically run every 30 minutes 10am-3pm daily. Adventurers may want to consider lending a hand to the farmers during the one-hour Evening Chore and Milking Tour ($25-28) or the Kid Goat Interaction Experience ($20-25), where you play and snuggle with baby goats.

Hali'imaile Distillery (top); Hui No'eau Visual Arts Center (middle); Harold W. Rice Memorial Park (bottom)

BEST SUNSET VIEWS

sunset along the Kula Highway

Some of the best sunsets in the world can be experienced on Maui, and in Kula—given the area's elevation—they are particularly radiant.

- Expect nothing short of glorious at **Harold W. Rice Memorial Park** (page 206). Park and find a picnic table, or bring a blanket and sit on the lawn as you relish panoramic ocean views as well as the landscapes of West and South Maui.
- **Keokea Park** (page 209) is a family-friendly spot, complete with a small playground. Its elevation—approximately 2,800 ft (854 m)—means the rays of the setting sun off Maui's south side are particularly dramatic.
- Across the street from Keokea Park is **St. John's Episcopal Church** (page 209), a small and picturesque church with a lawn overlooking all of South Maui, the West Maui Mountains, and the glorious Pacific Ocean.
- Up the highway, between mile markers 18 and 19, is **Sun Yat Sen Park** (page 209), which is filled with ornamental statues and sculptures. Sunsets at this elevation—some 2,400 ft (730 m) above sea level—feel somewhat mystical, with occasional layers of clouds reflecting the sunset colors.

★ Ocean Vodka Organic Farm and Distillery

4051 Omaopio Rd.; 808/877-0009; www.oceanvodka.com; 10:30am-7pm daily

It isn't a vacation until you're sipping vodka by noon. Next door to Surfing Goat Dairy, Ocean Vodka Organic Farm and Distillery offers 10 tours daily ($17) of its fully sustainable farm, beginning at noon. The facility's energy is provided by 240 solar panels, and 30 types of Polynesian sugarcane provide the juice for the

HIGHLIGHTS 207

Ali'i Kula Lavender Farm (left); Kula Botanical Garden (right)

vodka and rum that's distilled and bottled here. The cane is hand-harvested, bottles are labeled by hand, and leftovers are used as organic mulch, while chickens take care of the pests.

At the outdoor thatched-roof tasting room, amid fields of waving sugarcane and in view of the panoramic foothills of Haleakalā, sip on samples of vodka and rum sourced from different types of sugar. Some have flavors of banana and coconut despite not containing them. Even stranger, the water that's used in distilling the spirits is sourced from 3,000 ft (915 m) below sea level, where heavy mineral-laden water has spent 2,000 years drifting from Greenland to the coast of the Big Island (really). Tours run every 30 minutes until 5pm.

The open-air café (open until 7pm daily) offers stunning views and a locally inspired menu. Signature cocktails made with the farm's own Ocean Vodka, Kula Rum, Fy Gin, and Brum spirits are available. It's a great place to visit later in the day; the sunset views are extraordinary.

Kula Country Farms

6240 Kula Hwy.; 808/878-8381; www.kulacountryfarmsmaui.com; 9am-4pm Mon.-Sat.

Surfing Goat Dairy (left); Ocean Vodka Organic Farm and Distillery (right)

Kula Country Farms perfectly captures Kula's agricultural spirit. Stop in for affordable produce where colors explode off the shelves. Buy a healthy snack to enjoy with the ocean view. In October the farm gets festive and features a corn maze and an 8-acre (3.2-ha) pumpkin patch, although the main reason to visit is to support local farmers.

Kula Botanical Garden
638 Kekaulike Ave.; 808/878-1715; www.kulabotanicalgarden.com; 9am-4pm daily; $10 adults, $3 children

By Waipoli Road, the Kula Botanical Garden is a 19-acre (7.7-ha) private garden with 2,500 species of plants. There are over 90 varieties of protea alone, and the self-guided walking tour takes 45 minutes. If you're on your way down from Haleakalā and didn't get to see a nene goose, the botanical garden has two, which means you can at least get photos. You'll also find a chameleon exhibit, a Christmas tree farm, three carved wooden tiki gods, and coffee that's grown on the farm.

Ali'i Kula Lavender Farm
1100 Waipoli Rd.; 808/878-3004; www.aliikulalavender.com; 10am-4pm Fri.-Mon.; $3, $5 pp for group tours

If you've ever wanted lavender tea, lavender sunscreen, lavender body butter, or lavender scones, Ali'i Kula Lavender Farm is worth a stop. At the top of Waipoli Road on the way up toward Polipoli, the views at 4,000 ft (1,220 m) elevation stretch all the way to the ocean. The air is crisp for walking around the farm, and the shrill calls of ring-necked pheasants echo above the pastures. The farm itself is 13.5 acres (5.5 ha), and guided walking tours ($15) are offered daily.

A small café serves scones and tea. The view, the serenity, and a warm cup of tea make this a relaxing stop.

KEOKEA AND ULUPALAKUA

Keokea Park
218 Lower Kula Rd.; 808/572-8122; 7am-7pm daily

You'll know you've reached the community of Keokea when you see Keokea Park on the left, a small field that also has a playground and public restrooms; it's a great spot for sunset watching and stargazing.

St. John's Episcopal Church
8992 Kula Hwy.; 808/878-1485; www.stjohnsmaui.org; 10am-4pm Mon.-Wed. and Fri., 7:30am-10:30am Sun.

Picturesque St. John's Episcopal Church is just across the highway from Keokea Park, and also a perfect perch for panoramic views of the island and ocean at sunset.

Sun Yat Sen Park
13434 Kula Hwy.; 7am-7pm daily; free

By mile marker 18, on the way to Ulupalakua, is the small Sun Yat Sen Park, named for the revolutionary

St. John's Episcopal Church

KEOKEA

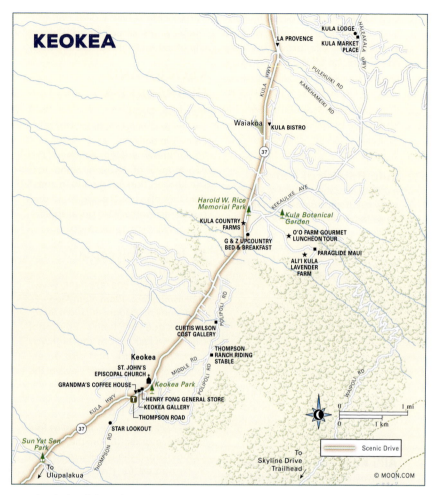

who helped found modern China. After parking, follow the paved concrete trail, which winds through a scenic setting featuring ornamental statues, sculptures of historic figures, and lush gardens. There are some benches to sit on if you'd like to bring along a book and unwind for an hour.

Maui Wine

14815 Pi'ilani Hwy.; 808/878-6058; www.mauiwine.com; 11am-5pm Tues.-Sun.

Once considered an island novelty that only served pineapple wine, Maui Wine, like a fine wine, is getting better by the year. There are three varieties of pineapple wine, but there's also grenache, malbec, syrah, viognier, and chenin blanc. Aside from the wine and complimentary tastings, what makes the winery a must-see is its history and beauty. The tasting room bar is 18 ft (5.5 m) long and made from a single mango tree. The guest cottage where King Kalakaua stayed when he visited the ranch in 1874 is now the tasting room. A small room attached to the tasting area details the history of the ranch (allegedly Kalakaua had too much cheer and wagered Molokini while gambling), and free tours trace the ranch's progression from potatoes to sugarcane to wine.

TOURS
Makawao
MAUI PINEAPPLE TOUR
883 Hali'imaile Rd.; 808/665-5491; www.mauipineappletours.com; 9am-4pm Mon.-Fri.; $65-75
If you think pineapples grow underground or on trees, you should probably spend a couple of hours on the Maui Pineapple Tour, which visits several farms. Learn why Maui's pineapples are sweet and taste like golden candy. Everyone gets a free pineapple, and you can eat Maui gold in the fields until your gums tingle. Bring a camera for the sweeping views, and don't forget the sunscreen. Check the website for tour times and availability. The minimum age is five, and the pineapple tour conveniently aligns with distillery tours next door.

Kula
O'O FARM GOURMET LUNCHEON TOUR
651 Waipoli Rd.; 808/667-4341; www.oofarm.mybigcommerce.com; 10:30am-1:30pm Mon.-Fri.; $150 adults, $75 children
For a romantic Maui farm luncheon, where you can sip wine beneath a vine-covered trellis and dine on fish or chicken prepared by a chef in an outdoor kitchen, check out the O'o Farm Gourmet Luncheon Tour, where visitors take a tour around the 8-acre (3.2-ha) farm and choose from 60 different crops while picking a salad in the fields. The air up here is misty and cool, at least when the clouds roll in, and there's nothing like a cup of French-pressed coffee. The first hour is spent touring the farm and meeting the on-site chef, who arrives at the farm at sunrise to source ingredients from the fields. Much of the produce used travels a total of 400 ft (120 m). Instead of a farm-to-table restaurant, the table has been brought to the farm. The wine is BYOB, and there's also a **Coffee & Brunch Tour** with coffee grown on the farm (8:30am-11:30am Mon.-Fri.; $135 adults, $67 children).

MAUI STARGAZING
808/298-8254; www.mauistargazing. com; reservations required; $235-250
Limited to 11 people, this unforgettable sunset and stargazing tour lasts six hours. The tour meets at Kula Lodge (15200 Haleakalā Hwy.), where you'll set out for the Haleakalā summit. Following sunset viewing, you'll be treated to an educational laser-guided survey of the constellations, visible planets, nebulae, star clusters, the Milky Way, and more, plus 1-1.5 hours of guided telescope time through the largest portable telescope on Haleakalā. The tour provides winter jackets and snowboard pants; it gets cold 10,000 ft (3,050 m) up at night! Note that no scuba diving is allowed within 24 hours of your tour to avoid decompression sickness.

STARGAZING IN UPCOUNTRY

stars above Haleakalā National Park

Come nightfall, the sky in Upcountry is so luminous and the Milky Way so valiantly on display—thanks to the lack of light pollution and elevation—that you may feel like you're in outer space. The best time for stargazing is during the new moon or before the moon rises.

STARGAZING SPOTS
Locals and visitors in the know often drive up and down the lightly trafficked rural Kula Highway at night, which has several safe pullouts for brief stops to stargaze, as well as other exceptional locales that allow you to linger longer. **Harold W. Rice Memorial Park** (page 206), across from Kula Country Farms on Lower Kula Road, is an ideal place to bring a blanket, lie down, and witness the star show. Farther up Kula Highway at **Keokea Park** (page 209), you'll find an open field to lie on—prime stargazing real estate with a broader sky view, perfect for spotting shooting stars. Both are also prime sunset-watching spots, so come early with a picnic dinner and stay for nightfall.

If you don't want to venture too far up in elevation, stay in Makawao and visit the grounds at **Lumeria Maui** (page 222), a wellness retreat with grounds that are open to the public. Find space near the giant Buddha statue on the central lawn for a near-spiritual experience.

GUIDED TOUR
If you'd like a guided tour of the night sky in Upcountry, you can book the impressive six-hour stargazing tour that includes sunset on Haleakalā offered by **Maui Stargazing** (page 211), which also includes access to the largest portable telescope on Haleakalā.

SCENIC DRIVES

KULA HIGHWAY
Driving Distance: *25 mi (40 km)*
Driving Time: *45 minutes*
Start: *Kahului Airport*
End: *Maui Wine*

Kula Highway (Hwy. 37) heading to Upcountry from the airport is one of the best scenic drives on the island. As the elevation grows, the landscape shifts, featuring rolling hills, vibrant forests, and scenic ocean views. Travel all the way up to Maui Wine, stopping occasionally at the turnouts along the highway, and you'll be treated to panoramic island vistas. If you're here during spring, the jacaranda trees lining the road are stunning.

BEST HIKES AND WALKS

HALEAKALĀ NATIONAL PARK

Thanks to the colorful cinder cones and trails that crunch underfoot, anyone who hikes across Haleakalā Crater will swear they could be on the moon. Covering a total of 19 sq mi (49 sq km), the crater basin is a vast wilderness with 30 mi (48 km) of trails. It's a place of adventure, mythology, and silence—and home to Maui's best hiking. If you love the outdoors, no trip to Maui is complete without spending a day on the crater floor.

Hikers need to be prepared, however, as temperatures can range 30–80°F (–1–27°C) over the course of a single day. The hiking is at high elevation, 7,000–10,000 ft (2,135–3,050 m), and hiking back up generally takes twice as long as the hike down. **Hike Maui** (808/201-3485; www.hikemaui.com; $220) is the only company that offers commercially guided hiking tours, which typically run seven hours. Should you go on your own, here's a rundown of the most popular hikes, listed from shortest to longest.

Hosmer's Grove Nature Trail (left); jacaranda trees along the Kula Highway (bottom)

Hosmer's Grove Nature Trail

Distance: *0.5 mi (0.8 km) round-trip*
Duration: *30 minutes*
Elevation Gain: *175 ft (53 m)*
Effort: *easy*
Trailhead: *less than 0.25 mi (0.4 km) from Haleakalā National Park gate entrance*

Unlike other trails in the park, the Hosmer's Grove Nature Trail is at the park's lower boundary just after you enter the park. The short trail loops through a dense grove of trees, planted in 1910 as part of an unsuccessful experiment to test the viability of the lumber industry. Surrounded by sweet-smelling pine and fir, grab a fleece and go for a stroll through the 20-plus species of trees, listening for forest birds that flit around in the treetops. To reach the trailhead, make a left on the road pointing toward the campground immediately after entering the park. The walk, over mostly level ground, should take 30 minutes. To extend the trip, hike the **Supply Trail** for 2.3 mi (3.7 km) to where it meets with the crater rim.

Halemau'u Trail (Switchback Trail)

Distance: *7.5 mi (12 km) round-trip*
Duration: *4.5 hours*
Elevation Gain: *1,850 ft (563 m)*
Effort: *strenuous*
Trailhead: *between mile marker 14 and 15 on Haleakalā Highway*

Beginning from an altitude of only 7,990 ft (2,435 m), the first 1.1 mi (1.8 km) of this trail meander through scrub brush before bringing you to the edge of a 1,000-ft (300-m) cliff. The view down into the Ko'olau Gap is better here than from the summit, and although the trail is well defined, the drop-offs can be a bit disconcerting. After 3.7 mi (6 km)—and a 1,000-ft (300-m) drop—the trail passes Holua Cabin, where you can turn around. Tack on another mile (1.6 km) by continuing to Silversword Loop, a section of the crater known for its numerous 'ahinahina, or endangered silversword plants.

Sliding Sands Trail

Distance: *12.2 mi (19.6 km) one-way*
Duration: *6 hours*
Elevation Gain: *3,000 ft (914 m)*
Effort: *very strenuous*

Haleakalā volcano crater as seen from the Sliding Sands Trail (top); ariel view of Kaupo Gap (bottom)

Trailhead: *bulletin board by the entrance to Haleakalā Visitor Center parking lot*

If you're in good shape and have a full day to devote to exploring the crater, this is hands-down the best day hike in the summit area. Park at the Halemau'u trailhead, and from there you'll hike down to the crater floor on the Sliding Sands Trail. Follow the signs toward Holua Cabin and the Halemau'u Trail, where a leg-burning, switchbacking, 1,000-ft (300-m) climb leads back to the car.

If you really want an island adventure that you'll never forget, consider hiking the trail at night in the light of a full moon. For this night hike, bring a backpack of extra clothing, carry extra water and a flashlight, and dress for windchill that can drop below freezing any time of year.

Kaupo Gap

Distance: *17.5 mi (28 km) one-way*
Duration: *2 days*
Elevation Gain: *7,000 ft (2,133 m)*
Effort: *very strenuous*
Trailhead: *access from Halemau'u or Sliding Sands Trail*

Of all the hikes in Haleakalā Crater, none are more legendary, or more extreme, than "shooting" the Kaupo Gap, a two-day trip, with a stay at Paliku campground, that drops 9,500 vertical ft (2,900 m) over 17.5 mi (28 km). Permits are required for camping at Paliku, in the crater's remotest corner, 9.2 mi (14.8 km) from the Sliding Sands trailhead.

On the second day of the hike, you'll descend from Paliku outside the national park boundary, and legally continue across private land until you reach Kaupo Store. Along the trail, keep an eye out for goats and deer that roam the windswept grasslands. When you finally finish the hike in Kaupo, it's best if you've

prearranged a ride. If not, you may have to convince the rare passerby to shuttle your sweaty body all the way to the other side of the island. Despite the logistical challenges and the grueling backcountry terrain, this is a unique and memorable hike.

MAKAWAO
★ Makawao Forest Reserve

It's Oregon meets Maui in the Makawao Forest Reserve. Lush and green and perched 2,500 ft (760 m) above sea level, this magical hamlet with flowering ginger plants and fragrant eucalyptus trees encompasses nearly 2,100 stunning acres (850 ha). It's one of Upcountry's most prominent destinations, ideal for sightseeing or more adventurous outings, thanks to miles of crisscrossing trails to entice hikers and bikers. There are phenomenal views of the island and ocean, and the reserve is a perfect place to take a break from the sun and warmer temperatures at sea level. Trails can be wet from occasional rain, so plan accordingly with proper footwear. A trail directory and trail maps are available on-site.

KAHAKAPAO LOOP TRAIL

Distance: *5.7 mi (9.2 km) round-trip*
Duration: *3 hours*
Elevation Gain: *975 ft (297 m)*
Effort: *moderate*
Trailhead: *2 mi (3.2 km) down Kahakapao Road (4.3 mi/ 6.9 km from Makawao)*

In the heart of the reserve, the Kahakapao Loop Trail is popular with families walking their dogs and mountain bikers. This verdant, easy-to-follow 5.7-mi (9.2-km) loop weaves through eucalyptus, pines, ferns, and wild ginger, and the air

BEST HIKES AND WALKS 215

is cool at just over 3,000 ft (915 m) elevation.

To reach the trailhead from Makawao, follow Makawao Avenue toward Ha'iku for 0.3 mi (0.5 km) before turning right on Pi'iholo Road. After 1.5 mi (2.4 km), just past the Pi'iholo zip-line tours, take a left at the fork in the road and follow it for 0.5 mi (0.8 km). Here you'll make a right onto Kahakapao Road and drive 1.5 mi (2.4 km) on a narrow uphill until you reach a metal gate (open 7am-7pm daily). From the gate, a steep asphalt road continues for another 0.5 mi (0.8 km) to a gravel parking lot.

Waihou Spring Forest Reserve

WAIHOU SPRING TRAIL

Distance: *2 mi (3.2 km) round-trip*
Duration: *1.5 hours*
Elevation Gain: *850 ft (259 m)*
Effort: *moderate*
Trailhead: *5 mi (8 km) from Makawao on Olinda Road*

If you don't feel like dealing with throngs of bikers, head to the Waihou Spring Trail, toward the top of Olinda Road. This 2-mi (3.2-km) trail is open to hikers only and doesn't have as steep an elevation gain as at Kahakapao. It's uniquely situated among an experimental planting of pine trees, and while the wooded trail is nice enough for walking, the treat is at the end, where a steep switchback leads to a hidden gulch. Here you'll find a 30-ft (9-m) vertical rock face with tunnels bored through, and if you have a flashlight, you can climb in the tunnels and follow them for a short distance. To reach the trailhead for Waihou Spring, go to Makawao's only intersection and follow very curvy Olinda Road uphill for 5 mi (8 km).

KULA

Polipoli Spring State Recreation Area

For a place to escape and commune with the serenity of nature, channel your inner Emerson or Thoreau, and meditate up in the mists, get a 4WD vehicle and head to Polipoli Spring State Recreation Area, an out-of-the-way forested spot with some of the island's best hiking. Trails pass through old-growth redwoods, eucalyptus, ash, and pines. Be sure to wear bright colors, since hunters are frequently in the area.

SKYLINE DRIVE

Distance: *6.8 mi (10.9 km) round-trip*
Duration: *3-5 hours*
Elevation Gain: *3,000 ft (915 m)*
Effort: *strenuous*
Trailhead: *The Ballpark*

It's possible to hike all the way from Polipoli to the summit of Haleakalā. Follow the 6.8-mi (10.9-km) dirt road, known as Skyline Drive, a "back entrance" to Haleakalā National Park. If it has snowed recently atop Haleakalā and the rangers have closed the road, this is an alternative way to hike into the park and be the only person there. Even on regular days, however, Skyline is a strenuous hike providing panoramic views down the mountain's southwest rift zone. Though Haleakalā has been dormant for more than 220 years, volcanologists claim that when the mountain erupts again, magma will cover the barren landscape that's visible from this trail. To reach the trailhead for Skyline Drive, turn left at the fork that leads down to the campground from the main dirt road. From here, the road continues climbing and begins to double back toward the north. Eventually you'll reach a locked gate at an area

POLIPOLI: THE LAST FRONTIER

While no official statistics are kept, there's a good chance that **Polipoli Spring State Recreation Area** is Maui's least visited corner. Even a place as desolate as Kaupo sees more people. High above the protea farms, the lavender farm, the disc golf course, and even the paragliding school, Polipoli is almost an afterthought, so far removed from the rest of the island that most visitors don't even know it's there.

This isolation makes Polipoli an enchanting place, set between 5,300 and 7,100 ft (1,615-2,165 m) elevation. There are sweeping views down to the shore as well as trails completely enveloped in trees and thick mists. Bathed in the scent of redwood and pine (yes, there are redwoods on Maui), it's a magical, spooky, and refreshing place.

This 10-acre (4-ha) recreational area of the Kula Forest Reserve was extensively logged during the 1930s by the Civilian Conservation Corps (CCC). A large clearing at 7,000 ft (2,135 m) is nicknamed "The Ballpark," where corps members would gather on their lunch break to play high-altitude baseball. Today Polipoli is frequented by hikers and hunters looking for wild boars, goats, and pheasants. This is also the island's premier mountain biking destination, where a forested woodland of downhill and single-track provides a ride akin to Oregon or Northern California.

Mornings offer the clearest views for hiking in Polipoli, and for anyone wanting to hit the trails early, there's a small campground ($12) and a rustic cabin ($90) that can accommodate up to 10 people (no electricity). Both are reachable along the steep, switchbacking Waipoli Road, 9.7 mi (15.6 km) uphill from Kekaulike Highway (Hwy. 377). The last 4 mi (6.4 km) are unpaved and require a 4WD vehicle. For cabin reservations, contact the **Division of State Parks** (54 S. High St., Ste. 101, Wailuku; 808/984-8109; 8am-3:30pm Mon.-Fri.). Make campground reservations online at www.hawaiistateparks.org.

known as The Ballpark (7,000 ft/2,135 m). From here it's a 3,000-vertical-ft (915-m) switchbacking trail to the summit. Pack plenty of water and warm clothing, and be aware of the challenges of hiking at altitude.

KEOKEA AND ULUPALAKUA

Thompson Road

Distance: *nearly a mile (1.6 km) round-trip*
Duration: *25 minutes*
Elevation Gain: *200 ft (61 m)*
Effort: *easy*
Trailhead: *across from Grandma's Coffee House*

Across from Grandma's Coffee House is the turnoff for Thompson Road, a one-lane pasture-lined country road that offers one of the island's best views and a leisurely spot for a stroll. The ocean views are breathtaking from here, with higher elevation looks at the island of Lana'i and Moloka'i.

BIKING

HALEAKALĀ

You've seen the brochures, you've heard the hype; here's the deal with cycling down Haleakalā Volcano.

It's imperative to be confident and competent on a bicycle. It is marketed as beginner-friendly, but in reality, dozens of people are seriously injured each year. In almost all cases it's because they took their eyes off the road or were riding too fast.

That said, watching the day begin from Haleakalā Crater and then weaving through cow-speckled pastures with the crisp air in your face is magical. A wide range of operators have different options, and the key to an enjoyable trip is choosing carefully. Decide whether you want to include sunrise at Haleakalā Crater. This means waking up early, with pickups at 2am. After watching the sunrise, it's back in the van for the drive down to 6,500 ft (1,980 m), where all the tours begin the cycling portion, outside the national park. If you opt for a tour that doesn't include sunrise, you'll be driven to this spot, usually arriving about 10am. The next option is whether to ride with a guide. The benefit is safety, but it means you have to follow the pace of the group. For independent-minded travelers, it's probably best to choose a company that lets you ride on your own.

The third factor to consider is where the tour ends: in Upper Kula with a zip-line combo, or all the way down at Baldwin Beach. It's possible to ride from the summit to the beach with your own car and bike. **Krank Cycles** and **Bike Maui** offer independent rentals, although **Maui Sunriders Bike Co.** is the most convenient, as their shop is near the beach.

UPCOUNTRY
Mountain Biking

The mountain biking on Maui is really good. The two main areas in Upcountry are the Makawao Forest Reserve, about 15 minutes above Makawao, and Polipoli, above Kula.

MAKAWAO FOREST RESERVE

Thanks to the team at Krank Cycles, the Makawao Forest Reserve has undergone over $500,000 in trail work, which means Makawao has some of the best trails in Hawaii. With 16 mi (26 km) of trail in total, there are terrain parks, single-track, 2-mi (3.2-km) climbs, and even a 30-ft (9-m) banked wooden wall you'd expect to find in a place like Whistler. The "Pineapple Express" is 2 mi (3.2 km) of downhill, and the west loop on the Kahakapao Trail is the most popular trail for climbing.

POLIPOLI

Polipoli, on the other hand, offers rugged downhill mountain biking, with a network of trails that switchback through redwoods, lava flows, and wide-open plains. You'll need a 4WD vehicle to reach some trailheads, and forget about visiting after a rain, since you'll get stuck in the mud. For a classic climb and single-track descent, park where the **Mamane Trail** meets the road toward the campground. Start by riding in the direction of the campground and turn uphill at the fork,

TIPS FOR BIKING THE VOLCANO

- If you go with a tour, you can't ride from the summit. To **bike from the summit,** you have to provide your own bicycle and transportation.

- **Seeing the sunrise isn't guaranteed:** 15 percent of the time the crater is clouded in. Variations in the weather aren't seasonal, so all you can do is hope for the best.

- If you want to spend more than 15 minutes at Haleakalā after sunrise, **save sunrise for a separate trip** and book a midmorning bike ride. The trip will be cheaper, and you'll be able to hike and explore the crater without having to rush back to the van.

biking Haleakalā

- Be prepared to wake up *really* early for a **sunrise tour.** Companies collect guests from the farthest hotels first, so if you're staying in Makena or Kapalua, expect to meet your driver as early as 1:45am. Try to book this excursion early in your trip, when you're still jet-lagged and waking up early.

- If you're on a **budget,** opt for a **midmorning tour.** It isn't as cold, you don't have to wake up as early, it isn't as crowded, and the trips are substantially cheaper. Companies charge more for the sunrise tours because they're popular.

- Remember that you're **sharing the road** with cars. There are no bike lanes, so be sure to keep your eyes on the road at all times.

- Pack **closed-toe shoes, long pants,** a **rain jacket,** and **warm clothing.** Early morning temperatures often dip below freezing at the summit. Although many tour companies provide rain gear, the more protection you have against the elements, the better.

- Don't expect to get any **sleep** in the van ride up. The road switchbacks incessantly, and drivers entertain the riders with island history and jokes.

- If you're skittish, go with a **guided group.** To go it alone, choose an independent company so you can ride without a guide.

- Don't schedule your bike ride for the day after scuba diving; **decompression sickness** can kill.

where you'll climb along the spine of the mountain before the 2-mi (3.2-km) Mamane Trail drop.

SKYLINE DRIVE

For the island's longest off-road descent, the chance to bike from 10,000 ft (3,050 m), have someone drive you to Haleakalā for the start of Skyline Drive. The unpaved road begins by Science City and switchbacks its way across desolate cinder that looks like the surface of the moon. Watch for wild goats and hunters, and definitely wear bright clothing. After 6 mi (9.7 km), turn down the Mamane Trail for 2 fast miles (3.2 km) of single-track. For a full 7,000-ft (2,135-m) vertical descent, continue riding all the way down to Highway 37, then turn left for the 2-mi (3.2-km) ride on pavement to **Grandma's Coffee House.** Arrange to have your ride pick you up here.

TOURS AND RENTALS

MAUI EASY RIDERS

808/344-9489; www.mauieasyriders. com; $185

Maui Easy Riders is a small operation run by two brothers, both named Billy (really). Group size is small, only eight people, and tours begin at 8:30am in the parking lot of Pa'ia Bay. The ride begins at 6,600 ft (2,010 m) up Haleakalā Volcano, just above where other companies begin, and the 25-mi (40-km) ride to the beach is longer than any other company's. This guided tour makes a stop in Makawao for 30 minutes of exploring on foot, and at the end you can literally jump off your bike and into the waves.

KRANK CYCLES

1120 Makawao Ave.; 808/572-2299; www.krankmaui.com; 10am-5pm daily

For Upcountry bike rentals, Krank Cycles is in Makawao and offers daily rentals ($65-89). One day is plenty of time for the Makawao trails, but not for all of the Polipoli trails, so plan accordingly. Krank is Maui's most dedicated mountain bike shop; check out their website for current trail conditions.

HORSEBACK RIDING

Upcountry is horse country, and in the rolling Upcountry pasturelands, horseback riding is a slice of authentic Upcountry life. All of Upcountry's horseback options are on working ranches, which means you're dealing with real paniolo who still ranch, wrangle, and ride.

KULA

THOMPSON RANCH RIDING STABLE

1311 Waianu Rd.; 808/878-1910; www. thompsonranchmaui.net; $200-225, cash only

For a small-scale, intimate experience in the most beautiful pastures on Maui, Thompson Ranch Riding Stable offers guided trail rides on their Keokea ranch. This is a family-run working cattle ranch that's far from touristy, and the ranch owners love their horses. The view here is unforgettable, with green pastures rolling down to the blue Pacific. The climb is steep, and the maximum weight for riders is 200 pounds (90 kg). All rides/tours are by advanced reservation only.

TRIPLE L RANCH
15900 Pi'ilani Hwy.; 808/280-7070; www.triplelranchmaui.com; 8am-6pm daily

For a ranch adventure unlike any other, book the half-day lunch tour (3.5 hours; $300) with the crew at Triple L Ranch. Located 4 mi (6.4 km) past Maui Wine on the back road toward Hana, the ranch is set in windswept Kanaio, the youngest part of Maui. The cattle are all free range and roam the mountain without fences. There's no denying the magic of riding a horse to an isolated beach, even though it's rocky and lacking sand. Kanaio is laden with archaeological sites and abandoned lava-rock fishing villages. Maximum weight is 220 pounds (100 kg), and minimum age is 12. Group size is limited to two or three.

BIRD-WATCHING

HALEAKALĀ NATIONAL PARK

If you're an avid bird-watcher, just get in the car, drive uphill, and don't stop until you reach the entrance of Haleakalā National Park. Given Hawaii's extreme isolation, 71 different species of birds were once endemic to the islands. Of those species, 23 have gone extinct, and dozens more are critically endangered due to mongooses, feral cats, and the gradual loss of habitat. Endangered species such as 'akohekohe find themselves clinging to a fragile existence on Haleakalā's slopes.

Moving higher up toward the summit, bird-watchers should look for two endangered species: the 'u'au (Hawaiian petrel), which burrows in areas near the summit visitors center, and the nene (Hawaiian goose), which can be spotted along park roadways and the valley floor. The nene is Hawaii's state bird, and one of the best places to spot them is in grasslands surrounding Paliku Cabin.

One of the best bird-watching places is at **Hosmer's Grove** on the moderate 0.5-mi (0.8-km) loop trail. Even if you don't see native honeycreepers (birds whose bills have adapted to extract nectar from native plant species), the treetops chirp with birdsong different from anywhere else on the planet.

MAKAWAO

WAIKAMOI PRESERVE
808/572-4400; 9am Mon., Wed., and Fri.

While casual hikers might spot an 'i'wi or 'apapane (scarlet Hawaiian honeycreeper), the best way to spot rare species is to take the three-hour ranger-led **guided walks** into the neighboring privately owned

nene in Paliku Cabin area, Haleakalā

Waikamoi Preserve. Reservations are required. On a less frequent basis, hikes into the preserve are arranged by the **Maui Forest Bird Recovery Project** (808/573-0280; www.maui forestbirds.org).

ADVENTURE SPORTS

PARAGLIDING

PARAGLIDE MAUI

1100 Waipoli Rd., Kula; 808/874-5433; www.paraglidemaui.com; 6am-7pm daily

When was the last time you ran off a hill and experienced total silence? Paraglide Maui is Hawaii's only paragliding school. The launch and landing sites are perfect for learning, and nearly every flight takes place in the morning before the clouds fill in. The most popular booking is The Top Gun flight ($395), which takes off at the upper "Ferns" at 6,500 ft and descends 3,000 ft (915 m) to the landing zone, lasting approximately 12 minutes. Tandem flights drop 1,000 ft (300 m) for $115 or 3,000 ft (915 m) for $220 over the Polipoli treetops. This unforgettable island experience is highly recommended.

ZIP-LINING

SKYLINE ECO-ADVENTURES

12 Kiopa'a Pl., Kula; 808/518-2860; www.skylinehawaii.com; 7am-7pm daily

Believe it or not, Upcountry is where zip-lining was born in the United States. In 2002 Skyline Eco-Adventures opened in Kula's misty uplands, the first in the country. Today, Skyline offers a five-line course best for beginners, since the length of the lines and vertical drops aren't dramatic. There's also the option to combine a zip line with a sunrise Haleakalā bike tour, although the bike ride only descends 2,500 ft (760 m), so the combo is best for people who just want a sample of both activities. The course is on the road toward Haleakalā at approximately 4,000 ft (1,220 m) elevation, and the lines run through misty, cloud-shrouded groves of eucalyptus and koa. Once you unhook from the final line, which is the longest and easily the most thrilling, stroll through the neighboring lavender farm with a warm drink from the café.

SPAS AND WELLNESS

MAKAWAO

LUMERIA MAUI

1813 Baldwin Ave.; 808/579-8877; www.lumeriamaui.com

Lumeria Maui is a spa, retreat center, and lodging, with beautifully landscaped grounds overlooking Maui's North Shore. The main building is the oldest wooden structure on Maui, and in its first incarnation was the original home of Fred C. Baldwin, the famous sugarcane titan. More than half of the wellness treatments offered are designed with the teachings of the islands in mind. The spa menu changes each season. Explore the website and plan ahead.

THE SACRED GARDEN
460 Kaluanui Rd.; 808/573-7700; www.sacredgardenmaui.com; 9am-5pm daily; donation

The Sacred Garden is several miles from downtown Makawao, alongside a rushing creek in a lush rainforest. Owner Eve Hogan infuses her popular nursery and retreat center with charm and good intentions. This is a tranquil place where you can peruse tropical plants and birds, a spiritual and self-help library, a gift shop, creative gardens, and three outdoor meditation spaces. The centerpiece is a stunning medieval labyrinth (not to be confused with a maze), set in the rainforest behind the main nursery, which guests are encouraged to wander. There's also a smaller labyrinth within the nursery. One of the most popular events is Hogan's monthly full-moon labyrinth walks amid tiki torches in the forest.

MAUI HEALING RETREAT
3660 Baldwin Ave.; 808/870-3711; www.mauihealingretreat.com; 8am-8pm daily

Maui Healing Retreat offers customized wellness sessions ranging from acupuncture to massage to more avant-garde fare like a Magical Holistic Facial and Sound Healing Therapy. Prices typically run $240 and up for a 1.5-hour session. Book ahead for day visits. The center's location is definitely a draw, sitting on a peaceful 9 acres (3.6 ha) of agricultural land.

SHOPPING

MAKAWAO

Makawao has often been called "the biggest little town" in the area. Once a thriving rodeo town known for its Hawaiian cowboys (or paniolo), it has since the late 19th century become a charming hot spot for shopping, dining, and strolling down historical Baldwin Avenue. It's a great area for an afternoon excursion and dinner.

Art Galleries

MAUI MASTER JEWELERS
3655 Baldwin Ave.; 808/573-5400; www.mauimasterjewelers.com; 10am-3pm Tues.-Fri., 10am-2pm Sat.

For Polynesian jewelry, visit Maui Master Jewelers, where works by over 30 local artists are on display. They are the island's leading source for New Zealand bone and jade carvings and also offer Tahitian pearl jewelry.

SHERRI REEVE GALLERY & GIFTS
3669 Baldwin Ave.; 808/572-8931; www.sreeve.com; 9am-4pm Mon.-Sat., 10am-3pm Sun.

Sherri Reeve Gallery & Gifts showcases this ebullient Makawao artist whose distinctive floral designs grace shirts, cards, paintings, and prints. This is a worthwhile stop among the large number of galleries in town.

HOT ISLAND GLASS
3620 Baldwin Ave.; 808/572-4527; www.hotislandglass.com; 9am-5pm daily

Hot Island Glass is the island's best-known glass studio, where you can watch artists blow glass; call ahead to check the demonstration schedule.

SHOPPING   223

Clothing and Gifts

FLEUR DE LEI

1169 Makawao Ave.; 808/269-8855; https://fleurdelei.com; 10:30am-5:30pm daily

Fleur de Lei is an eco-boutique with clothing items made from organic cotton, as well as "sail bags" made from recycled windsurfing and kite-surfing sails. The store promotes fair trade and sustainable practices, and if you aren't familiar with vegan leather, stop in and ask.

DRAGON'S DEN HERB SHOP

3681 Baldwin Ave.; 808/572-2424; https://dragonsdenhawaii.com; 10am-6pm Mon.-Sat., 11am-4pm Sun.

Dragon's Den has been a staple in town since 1982. The popular shop features a large variety of herbs, alternative and natural medicines, and gifts.

KULA

Art Galleries

CURTIS WILSON COST GALLERY

808 Polipoli Rd.; 808/878-6544; www.costgallery.com; 2pm-5pm daily

There's only one artist on the island who really nails Upcountry. Driving past the Kula Lodge to Haleakalā, make a stop at the Curtis Wilson Cost Gallery, tucked neatly beneath the restaurant. The vibe is like a fine wine cellar filled with exceptional art. Having painted the island's rural corners for over 40 years, Cost now has the longest-running one-man gallery in Hawaii. Art can be ordered with custom koa frames or individually commissioned, and the work of his daughter, Julia Cost, is also displayed.

Gifts

KULA MARKET PLACE

15200 Haleakalā Hwy.; 808/878-2135; www.kulamarketplace.com; 8am-5pm daily

Down the driveway from Kula Lodge is the exceptional Kula Market Place, an oasis of gifts from over 200 local artists, including jams, honey, coffee, music, and clothing. It's a great place to wander while digesting breakfast from neighboring Kula Lodge.

KEOKEA AND ULUPALAKUA

Art Gallery and Fine Furniture

KEOKEA GALLERY

9230 Kula Hwy.; 808/283-7925; 9am-3pm Tues.-Sat., 10am-2pm Sun.-Mon.

Next to Grandma's Coffee House, tiny little Keokea Gallery has linocut collages, handmade frames, and a collection of painted surfboards. The affable artist in residence, Sheldon, is always up for a chat, and the works here are surprisingly good considering the rural location.

Clothing and Gifts

ULUPALAKUA RANCH STORE AND GRILL

14800 Pi'ilani Hwy.; 808/878-2561; 10am-5pm daily

All the way out here in "deep Upcountry," the only real place for clothing and gifts is the Ulupalakua Ranch Store and Grill, open for 150 years. The store features products from a dozen local vendors, and since it is on a working ranch, you'll find Wranglers and belts rather than aloha shirts and sunscreen. Consider buying a hat or shirt to help the ranch stay afloat, which helps keep the open spaces and paniolo heritage alive.

HENRY FONG GENERAL STORE
9226 Kula Hwy.; 808/878-1525; 8am-5pm daily
Family-business Fong Store is a fascinating time portal, where oversize cigarette boxes still serve as decor. Mrs. Fong will be quick to point out that this store is in the "new" location, since 1932; the original store opened in Keokea in 1908.

FOOD

STANDOUTS
Makawao
HALI'IMAILE GENERAL STORE
900 Hali'imaile Rd.; 808/572-2666; www.hgsmaui.com; lunch 11am-2:30pm Tues.-Fri., dinner 5pm-8pm Tues.-Sat.; $21-48
The Hali'imaile General Store, which serves gourmet food in an old-school roadhouse that was once a general store, is easily the island's most unlikely location for food of this caliber. Master chef Beverly Gannon—frequently voted Maui's top chef and a founder of the Hawaiian Regional Cuisine movement—crafts appetizers such as sashimi Napoleon and famous crab pizza. Entrées include paniolo barbecue ribs and coconut seafood curry. Portions are plentiful.

MARLOW
30 Kupaoa St.; 808/868-3366; www.restaurantmarlow.com; 7am-2pm Mon.-Sat., 8am-2pm Sun., 4:30pm-9pm daily; $17-34
Marlow has become an Upcountry hot spot, thanks to the wood-fired creations from chef Jeff Scheer. His dishes are inspired by Italy's best ingredients. The wood-oven sourdough pizzas are sublime, and toppings include locally sourced meats and vegetables. Enjoy an unforgettable—and fun—dining experience in this sleek, modern location just on the outskirts of Makawao.

Kula
KULA BISTRO
4566 Lower Kula Rd.; 808/871-2960; www.kulabistro.com; 11am-8pm daily; $13-34

Grandma's Coffee House (left); Baldwin Avenue in historic Makawao (right)

UPCOUNTRY FOOD OPTIONS

NAME	LOCATION	CONTACT INFO
MAKAWAO		
★ **Hali'imaile General Store**	900 Hali'imaile Rd.	808/572-2666; www.hgsmaui.com
★ **Marlow**	30 Kupaoa St.	808/868-3366; www.restaurantmarlow.com
Satori	3655 Baldwin Ave.	808/727-9638
Polli's Mexican Restaurant	1202 Makawao Ave.	808/572-7808; www.pollismexicanrestaurant.com
Freshies Maui	3620 Baldwin Ave.	808/868-2350; www.freshiesmaui.com
T. Komoda Store & Bakery	3674 Baldwin Ave.	808/572-7261
KULA		
La Provence	3158 Lower Kula Rd.	808/878-1313; www.laprovencemaui.com
★ **Kula Bistro**	4566 Lower Kula Rd.	808/871-2960; www.kulabistro.com
Kula Lodge	15200 Haleakalā Hwy.	808/878-1535; www.kulalodge.com
KEOKEA AND ULUPALAKUA		
Ulupalakua Ranch Store	14800 Pi'ilani Hwy.	808/878-2561; www.ulupalakuaranch.com
Bully's Burgers	15900 Pi'ilani Hwy.	808/878-1362; www.bullysburgersmauistore.com
★ **Grandma's Coffee House**	9232 Kula Hwy.	808/878-2140; www.grandmascoffee.com

For Italian food paired with local favorites, Kula Bistro surpasses all others. Tasting the pesto chicken flatbread or jumbo lobster ravioli, it's obvious that owner Luciano Zanon has been perfecting this cuisine since his childhood in Venice. Maui-grown coffee is served at breakfast, and lunch has kalua pork paninis and filling hamburger steak. Most ingredients are sourced locally, the desserts are baked fresh daily, and there's no corkage fee. To pick up some booze for the BYOB, Morihara Store across the street has a decent selection.

FOOD	HOURS	PRICE
Hawaiian Regional	lunch 11am-2:30pm Tues.-Fri., dinner 5pm-8pm Tues.-Sat.	$21-48
Italian	7am-2pm Mon.-Sat., 8am-2pm Sun., 4:30pm-9pm daily	$17-34
Japanese	noon-7pm daily	$8-23
Mexican	11am-9pm daily	$11-30
breakfast and lunch	7am-3pm Tues.-Sat., 7am-noon Sun.	$7-17
bakeries	7am-1pm Mon.-Tues. and Thurs.-Sat.	$5-12
French	8am-2pm and 5pm-8pm Wed.-Sun.	$14-22, cash only
Italian	11am-8pm daily	$13-34
breakfast and lunch	7am-3:30pm daily	$14-36
burgers	10am-4pm Tues.-Sun.	$9-18
burgers	noon-6:30pm Wed.-Mon.	$8-15
coffee shops	7am-2pm daily	$5-12

Keokea and Ulupalakua

GRANDMA'S COFFEE HOUSE

9232 Kula Hwy.; 808/878-2140; www. grandmascoffee.com; 7am-2pm daily; $5-12

While it doesn't look like much from the outside, there's a simple romance to Grandma's Coffee House that makes it Maui's best coffee shop.

"Grandma" started brewing her own coffee back in 1918, and locally grown beans are roasted in the kitchen using her 100-year-old roaster. The beans are still harvested and processed by four generations of her family. For breakfast, order the French toast made with homemade cinnamon bread ($10) and enjoy it out on the

FOOD   227

UPCOUNTRY LODGING OPTIONS

NAME	LOCATION	CONTACT INFO
MAKAWAO		
★ **Hale Hoʻokipa Inn**	32 Pakani Pl.	808/572-6698; www.maui-bed-and-breakfast.com
★ **Peace of Maui**	1290 Haliʻimaile Rd.	808/572-5045; www.peaceofmaui.com
Banyan Bed and Breakfast	3265 Baldwin Ave.	808/866-6225; www.bed-breakfast-maui.com
The Sacred Garden	560 Kaluanui Rd.	808/573-7700; www.sacredgardenmaui.com
Lumeria Maui	1813 Baldwin Ave.	808/579-8877; www.lumeriamaui.com
KULA		
Polipoli Spring State Recreation Area	9.7 mi (15.6 km) upland from Kula on Waipoli Rd. off Kekaulike Ave. (Hwy. 377); 4WD vehicle required	permits 808/984-8109 or www.dlnr.hawaii.gov
G and Z Upcountry Bed and Breakfast	60 Kekaulike Ave.	808/224-6824; www.gandzmaui.com
★ **Kula Lodge**	15200 Haleakalā Hwy.	808/878-1535; www.kulalodge.com
KEOKEA AND ULUPALAKUA		
★ **Star Lookout**	622 Thompson Rd.	907/250-2364; www.starlookout.com

porch, where slack-key musicians periodically offer live music on weekend mornings. Or grab a cup of coffee to go and enjoy a stroll on Thompson Road, across the street. The only downside is that the restrooms are located at Keokea Park, a five-minute walk.

LODGING

RESERVATIONS AND TIPS

The Upcountry region is rustic. As always, plan and make reservations ahead. During the winter months, nighttime temperatures are cooler, so if you're traveling during this time, pack a sweater or jacket. This region is also a bit damper than beach communities because the forest trees keep things shaded.

TYPE	PRICE	BEST FOR
B&B	$145–195	couples
inn	$148–250	budget travelers
B&B	$200–300	couples
retreat	from $250	solo travelers, small groups, couples
retreat	from $559	solo travelers, couples, groups
camping	$18–100	budget travelers, adventure travelers
B&B	$149	budget travelers, couples
cottage	$384–494	couples, hikers
cottage	$300, 2-night minimum	couples

STANDOUTS
Makawao
HALE HO'OKIPA INN
32 Pakani Pl.; 808/572-6698; www.maui-bed-and-breakfast.com; $145-195

Built in 1924 and used by a Portuguese family to raise 13 children, the five-bedroom plantation house Hale Ho'okipa Inn has been turned into a lovely B&B with bedrooms ($145-168) and a two-bedroom suite ($195) within walking distance of Makawao town. While improvements have been made, it still has the feel of an old-fashioned country home, and the accommodating owners provide tips and insight into Maui life. Organic fruits from the garden are served.

PEACE OF MAUI
1290 Hali'imaile Rd.; 808/572-5045; www.peaceofmaui.com; $148-250

Down near the intersection of Hali'imaile Road and Baldwin Avenue is the guesthouse Peace of Maui, centrally located between Makawao and Pa'ia. Peace of Maui overlooks the pineapple fields, and while the rooms aren't extravagant, they are clean and affordable. Rooms in the

Kula Lodge

main lodge share a kitchen and baths. For a private bath, rent the two-bedroom cottage, which also provides access to the jetted tub.

Kula

KULA LODGE
15200 Haleakalā Hwy.; 808/878-1535; www.kulalodge.com; $384-494
The Kula Lodge is Upcountry's most popular option. On Highway 377 at 3,200 ft (975 m) elevation, the air is crisp, cool, and more comfortable than on the coast. There are five detached chalets, and all feature private lanais and electric fireplaces. The rustic yet comfortable setting makes a perfect base for visiting Haleakalā Crater, and the lodge's **restaurant** offers a filling breakfast or lunch stop on your way up or down the peak.

Keokea and Ulupalakua

STAR LOOKOUT
622 Thompson Rd.; 907/250-2364; www.starlookout.com; $300, 2-night minimum
For rural tranquility in a cool Upcountry setting, the Star Lookout is on Thompson Road just minutes from Grandma's Coffee House. This single cottage is a ranch-style retreat with views over the Keokea pastureland to the South Maui shore. From the "Star Bed," fall asleep gazing out at the stars through the enormous picture window. Advance reservations are required—it's Upcountry's most desirable spot.

TRANSPORTATION

Car

With the exception of central Makawao, where it's possible to walk between shops, Upcountry can only be visited by car. There aren't any rental agencies for cars or mopeds, and parking is free. The main road that leads to Upcountry is Highway 37, with Highway 377 forming a loop through Kula. Haleakalā National Park is up Highway 378. There aren't any gas stations in Upper Kula or on Highway 378. From Kula, expect it to take about an hour to drive to the summit of Haleakalā, and from Ulupalakua over to Makawao, the drive is about 30 minutes.

Bus

Some parts of Upcountry are served by **Maui Bus** (808/871-4838; www.co.maui.hi.us/bus), with the Upcountry Islander (bus 40) connecting Upcountry with downtown Makawao, and the Kula Islander (bus 39) connecting all the way to Kula. For the Upcountry Islander, bus stops are in front of the Pukalani Community Center, the Makawao Library, and in the center of Hali'imaile. Rates are $4 per person, and the bus makes stops at the Kahului Airport as well as at Queen Ka'ahumanu Mall, where you can link up with other lines. The earliest bus leaves from Keokea at 5:56am daily and heads all the way to Kahului.

LEAVING HALEAKALĀ AND UPCOUNTRY

South Maui (Kihei)

From Makawao, take Haleakalā Highway (Hwy. 37) to Hansen Road in Kahului. Turn left onto Hansen Road and left again onto Maui Veterans Highway (Hwy. 311). Continue onto Pi'ilani Highway (Hwy. 31) to Kihei. The 21.4-mi (34.4 km) drive is 30 minutes.

West Maui (Lahaina)

From Makawao, take Haleakalā Highway (Hwy. 37) for 7.2 mi (11.6 km). Turn left onto Hana Highway (Hwy. 36) and left again onto Mayor Elmer F. Cravalho Way. Continue onto Kuihelani Highway (Hwy. 380) toward Ma'alaea. Stay on this highway until it merges with Honoapi'ilani Highway (Hwy. 30) and follow it along the scenic coastline directly into Lahaina. The 35.2-mi (56.6 km) drive is 55 minutes.

Kahului Airport

From Makawao, take Haleakalā Highway (Hwy. 37) for 7.2 mi (11.6 km). Turn left onto Hana Highway (Hwy. 36) and right onto Mayor Elmer F. Cravalho Way at Kahului Airport. The 11.5-mi (18.5-km) drive is 20 minutes.

Start of the Road to Hana

From Makawao, head northeast on Makawao Avenue toward Baldwin Avenue. Continue onto Kaupakalua Road for 5.4 mi (8.7 km). Turn right onto Hana Highway (Hwy. 360) for the start of the Road to Hana. The 6.5-mi (10.5-km) drive is 15 minutes.

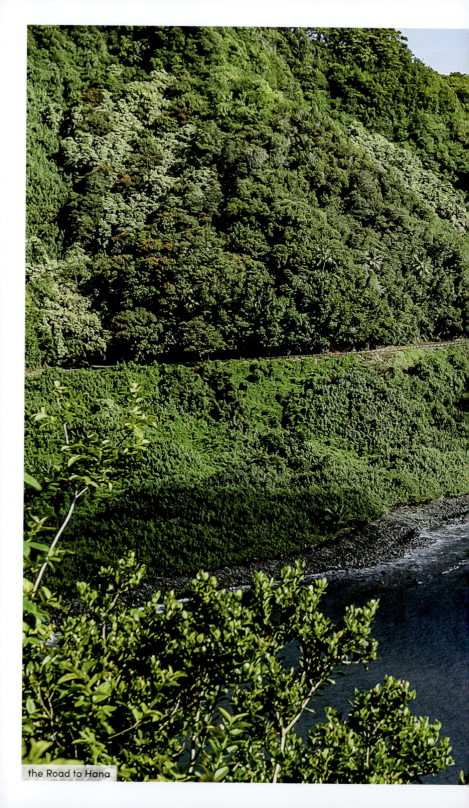
the Road to Hana

THE ROAD TO HANA AND EAST MAUI

East Maui is more than a destination. It's a different mindset.

Lush, tropical, and riddled with waterfalls, East Maui is the location of the famous Road to Hana and where Maui locals come to escape for a few days. From the windswept taro patches of the Ke'anae Peninsula to the empty pastures of Kaupo, time in East Maui ticks by at a slower place. By no means, however, does that make East Maui lazy. It's the island's adventure center, where an average day could consist of trekking to remote waterfalls, cliff-jumping in a bamboo forest, spelunking hidden caves on a black-sand beach, or bodysurfing off sandy shores.

Many who reach the end of the legendary Road to Hana ask, "This is it?" and "Where is the rest of town?" Hana is not a destination—it's famous for what it isn't more than for what it is, a sleepy little fishing hamlet. Neighbors still talk to each other and wave as they pass on the street, fishing nets hang in front yards, and the fish end up on the table. You don't come to Hana to reach something; you come out here to leave everything else behind.

East Maui is also home to Pa'ia (pa-EE-ah), a trendy, funky, and sexy town nominated by *Coastal Living* magazine as one of the "happiest seaside towns in America." Laid-back and worry-free, Pa'ia skanks to the beat of its own bongo. It also has the island's best shopping and food—even better than Lahaina—and the beaches are undeveloped and unheralded sanctuaries of calm.

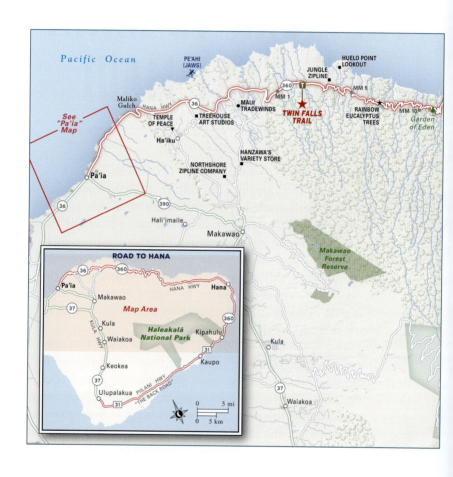

234 THE ROAD TO HANA AND EAST MAUI

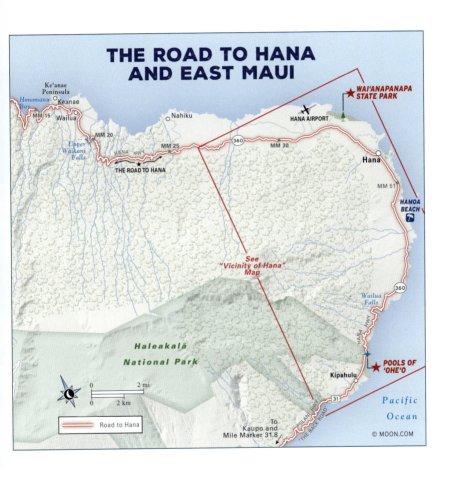

TOP 3

★ **1. WAI'ANAPANAPA STATE PARK:** Bask on the shores of a black-sand beach, swim inside hidden caves, and walk in the footsteps of kings (page 250).

★ **2. POOLS OF 'OHE'O:** Swim beneath waterfalls that tumble down to the ocean (page 254).

★ **3. TWIN FALLS TRAIL:** Take an easy hike to the first series of waterfalls on the Road to Hana (page 261).

THE ROAD TO HANA AND EAST MAUI 3 WAYS

HALF DAY

1 In Ha'iku, hit up **Colleen's,** a longtime local favorite, for breakfast.

2 Spend the morning hiking and exploring **Twin Falls,** which offers several walking trails and a stunning lagoon at the base of two sublime waterfalls.

3 After hiking, make your way to the **Garden of Eden,** where you can enjoy a picnic lunch in the lush rainforest haven.

FULL DAY

1 Get a good night's sleep, because this is going to be a long day. Grab breakfast on the go from **Paia Bay Coffee & Bar.**

2 Embark on the famous **Road to Hana,** and remember to stop often to hike, swim, and drink in the beauty of the coast.

3 Stop by **Kahanu Garden** and consider booking a 90-minute Kahanu Garden tour, where you can explore the grounds and admire the lush landscape.

4 Your next stop is **Wai'anapanapa State Park** for a look at the black-sand beach, taking time for a short dip in the underground freshwater pools.

240   THE ROAD TO HANA AND EAST MAUI

5 Continue to Hana for food at **Braddah Hutts BBQ Grill,** and try the kalua pork tacos, barbecue chicken plate, or fish tacos.

6 Make a stop at **Hamoa Beach** for a quick splash in the waves.

7 Continue on to the **Pools of 'Ohe'o** at Haleakalā National Park. Spend an hour or more here, hiking self-guided trails through a bamboo forest. The Pipiwai Trail, an island favorite, heads to the stunning 400-ft (122-m) Waimoku Falls.

8 You'll want to leave by 4:30pm to drive **the back road** around the mountain, which offers stunning southeastern views, lava formations, and gradual inclines toward lush Upcountry and Kula.

THE ROAD TO HANA AND EAST MAUI 3 WAYS 241

Pools of 'Ohe'o

AVOID THE CROWDS

1 Start with a leisurely stroll on **Baldwin Beach,** which offers brilliant views of the ocean and the West Maui Mountains. Perfect for those Instagram and TikTok posts.

2 Follow your beach walk with a visit to **Island Fresh Café,** which serves traditional island breakfasts, such as eggs served with Portuguese sausage or bacon, aloha buttermilk pancakes, a variety of fruit-based acai bowls, and much more.

3 Spend the afternoon exploring galleries and gift stores in **Haʻiku.**

4 Grab a light meal at **Nuka,** where you can choose from small plates, sushi rolls, specialty rolls, and sashimi prepared with fresh, local, and seasonal ingredients.

ORIENTATION AND PLANNING

ORIENTATION
East Maui comprises Pa'ia, Ha'iku, and the famous Road to Hana. **Pa'ia** is a bohemian-chic surfer town, and **Ha'iku** is mostly residential, with the exception of some restaurants and B&Bs. The **Road to Hana** stretches 45 mi (72 km) from Pa'ia to the center of **Hana,** but it continues another 37 mi (60 km) around the island's back. Pa'ia is only 10 minutes from Kahului Airport, although reaching Hana takes at least a couple of hours—or 20 minutes by plane. The Hana region is spread out over 22 mi (35 km) from **Nahiku** to **Kipahulu,** over an hour's drive. If you're staying overnight in Hana, be sure to check exactly how far the lodging is from the center of town.

PLANNING YOUR TIME
The biggest mistake you can make on Maui is skimping on your time in East Maui. Ideally, the region is worth three full days. Choosing to spend a couple of nights in Hana town allows more time for exploring. If you only have a day, devote the entirety to driving the Road to Hana so you can see it without feeling rushed. Pa'ia is a nice place for breakfast on the way. If you have the time, visit Pa'ia separately from Hana; it's worthy of at least half a day to spend shopping, strolling, or catching a bite to eat at Paia Fishmarket or other fabulous restaurants here.

HIGHLIGHTS AND SCENIC DRIVES

THE ROAD TO HANA
Driving Distance: *45 mi (72 km)*
Driving Time: *2 hours without stopping*
Start: *Pa'ia*
End: *Hana town*
Ah, yes, the Road to Hana—the most loved and loathed section of the

rainbow eucalyptus trees (top); Twin Falls (bottom)

BEST SUNSET VIEWS

For a truly memorable sunset experience, with the West Maui Mountains as a backdrop and sublime thin cloud cover producing epic colors, consider heading to **Ho'okipa Beach Park** (page 258) just east of Pa'ia. Another great option is to book a dinner at the popular **Mama's Fish House** in Pa'ia (page 272).

island divides visitors into two camps: those who swear it's heaven on earth and those who swear never to drive it again. Most people who don't enjoy the trip didn't know what they were getting themselves into. Three words will make or break your trip: Don't rush Hana.

Devote a full day to the experience at minimum. You're visiting one of the most beautiful places on earth; two or three days are even better. Don't expect to breeze through and see it quickly, and don't expect to be back on the other side of the island to make dinner reservations. Staying in Ka'anapali or Wailea, it will take you 3.5 hours just to reach the **Pools of 'Ohe'o** (a.k.a. the Seven Sacred Pools). That's not including stops, and the stops are what make the journey worthwhile.

Twin Falls

When you round the hill by mile marker 2 (remember that the mileage markers started over at the junction of Kaupakalua Rd.), you'll be amazed at the large gravel parking lot on the right side of the road packed with cars. Twin Falls is the first set of waterfalls you encounter on the Road to Hana, and thus is the closest to many hotels. The 20-minute **hike** to the falls is relatively easy (page 261). Parking is limited and costs $10.

Rainbow Eucalyptus Trees

At mile marker 6.7 is a grove of rainbow eucalyptus trees, silently rising from the green pasturelands. One of the most photographed sights on the Road to Hana, these trees have bark that drips with pastel red, pink, orange, green, and gray, the strokes running the length of each narrow tree.

Unlike trees with cork-like bark, rainbow eucalyptus has a smooth, hard exterior constantly in regrowth. As a section of tree undergoes exfoliation and sheds a section of bark, the young exposed wood has a deep green hue. As the new bark ages in the sun, the wood changes from green to blue to purple to orange, eventually dying again to reveal the green growth below, starting the cycle anew.

Garden of Eden

808/572-9899; www. mauigardenofeden.com; 8am-4pm daily; $20 adults, $10 children

At mile marker 10.5 is the enticing Garden of Eden, an ornately manicured 26-acre (10.5-ha) rainforest utopia with trails winding through the property. The Garden of Eden has more than 600 individually labeled plants, and visitors are often welcomed by a flock of ducks or a muster of peacocks. Walk down to the farthest reaches of the arboretum

HIGHLIGHTS AND SCENIC DRIVES 245

Garden of Eden (top); Honomanu Bay (middle); Ke'anae Peninsula (bottom)

toward the unique overlooks—several raised and covered wooden platforms, flanked by 'ohi'a trees—which offer dazzling ocean views as well as views of the **Upper and Lower Puohokamoa Falls,** the latter of which cascades dramatically over a 200-ft (60-m) cliff below the Road to Hana. The garden also collaborates with **Rappel Maui** to offer visitors opportunities to rappel the falls.

This makes a great picnic spot; bring a packed lunch and nosh at the picnic tables overlooking the falls or Keopuka Rock, also known as Jurassic Rock for its appearance in the opening sequence of the 1993 film *Jurassic Park*.

Honomanu Bay

At mile marker 14, Honomanu Bay is a gorgeous gray-sand beach in a valley that's accessible by 4WD. If you have a low-clearance vehicle, find a parking space at the top of the road and visit the beach on foot. It's a rocky beach, so bring proper footwear. Swimming is subpar—wading in the water is fine—but the area attracts fishers, a small local surf crowd, and spectators. Honomanu Bay doesn't have any facilities, but it warrants a picnic lunch or visit if only to capture postcard snapshots of the bay itself and vibrant vegetation surrounding it.

Ke'anae Peninsula

When you turn off the highway at mile marker 16.6, you pass through a portal to a way of life that many forgot once existed. The peninsula is a mosaic of green taro fields, vital to the livelihood of Ke'anae. Taro, also known as kalo, isn't just a crop; it's a representation of indigenous Hawaiian heritage. In Hawaiian mythology, a child named Haloa was stillborn

TIPS FOR DRIVING THE ROAD TO HANA

One of the most beautiful activities on Maui is driving the Road to Hana. Weaving 45 mi (72 km) around 600 curves and 56 one-lane bridges, it's the most loved and loathed stretch of road on the island. Here's how to plan a visit to Hana that will leave you poring over a photo album instead of searching for a divorce lawyer.

1. **Hana is not a destination, but a journey.** Visitors who race to the sleepy village of Hana are left saying, "This is it?" With a population of around 1,200, Hana is a place to get away from it all.

2. **The Road to Hana doesn't end at Hana.** The famous Road to Hana is the 45-mi (72-km) stretch between Pa'ia and the town of Hana, but many of the natural treasures are in the 10 mi (16 km) beyond Hana town. Hamoa Beach, consistently voted one of the top beaches in the country, is a few miles past Hana, as is Waioka Pond, a hidden pool on the rocky coast. Thirty minutes beyond Hana town are the Pools of 'Ohe'o (the Seven Sacred Pools), with a series of cascading waterfalls falling directly into the Pacific.

3. **Stop early and stop often.** Take a break for a morning stroll or for breakfast at a tucked-away café. Pick up some snacks and watch the waves. Stop and swim in waterfalls, hike through bamboo forests, and pull off at roadside stands for banana bread or locally grown fruit. If the car behind you is on your tail, pull over and let it pass—there isn't any rush.

4. **Bring a bathing suit and hiking shoes.** Hana is a land of adventure: Pack the necessary wardrobe and equipment for your activity of choice.

5. **Don't drive back the way you came.** Car-rental contracts may tell you the road around the back of the island is for 4WD vehicles only, but that's not true. Parts are bumpy, and a few miles are dirt road, but unless there's torrential rain, the road is passable with a regular vehicle. Following the back road all the way around the island grants new views as the surroundings change from lush tropical rainforest to arid windswept lava flows.

6. **Don't make dinner reservations.** Too many people try to squeeze Hana into half a day or end up feeling rushed. Hana is a place to escape the rush, not add to it. If you're planning a day trip to Hana, block off the entire day, leave early (7am), and see where the day takes you.

7. **If you see a sign that says Kapu (Keep Out), respect it.** Move along and enjoy a spot more accessible to the public.

8. **Don't drive home in the dark**—especially going the back way. Driving on narrow one-lane roads with precipitous drop-offs is difficult enough in daylight. Leave by 4pm to ensure a well-lit journey home.

and, upon being buried, turned into a taro plant. Haloa's brother became the ancestor of the Hawaiian people.

Indigenous Hawaiians thus have a blood relationship to the plant that provides them with sustenance. It's a staple of the Aloha 'Aina movement currently sweeping the state, that we humans are but stewards of the land, placed on this earth to protect

HIGHLIGHTS AND SCENIC DRIVES 247

Upper Waikani Falls (Three Bears)

it—ensuring its health as we would our own family's, and protecting it for future generations.

In addition to the taro fields, you can watch the powerful surf crash onto the rugged volcanic shore. There aren't any beaches on the Ke'anae Peninsula, and you'll often encounter locals fishing.

Upper Waikani Falls (Three Bears)

Also called Three Bears Falls, this is a great place for a photo op or a swim. Around mile marker 19.6, there is a narrow rough trail, about 150 yards (137 m), on the Hana side of the bridge. Most people stop, take snapshots, and move on, but if you want to linger a while longer, drive about 0.1 mi (160 m) beyond the falls, turn left, park in the designated parking area, and then walk back in the direction you came. The trail starts with a slightly sharp drop-off from the bridge, but you can breathe more freely after those first few precarious steps because it gets flatter. The scene at the falls is downright dreamlike, with water cascading into a swimming hole with remarkably clear water, ideal for a dip.

Ka'eleku Caverns

205 'Ula'ino Rd.; 808/248-7308; www.mauicave.com; 10:30am-4pm daily; $15 pp

At mile marker 31 you'll see the signs for Ka'eleku Caverns, also known as the Hana Lava Tubes. Turn down 'Ula'ino Road to visit this 2-mi (3.2-km) subterranean network of lava tubes, the 18th largest in the world and the only lava tubes on Maui that are navigable and open to the public. Cave explorers are given a flashlight to examine the stalactite-encrusted surroundings. On your

Kahanu Garden (top); Hana Farms Roadside Stand (middle); freshwater caves at Wai'anapanapa State Park (bottom)

HIGHLIGHTS AND SCENIC DRIVES

way out, navigate through the maze of red ti leaves that create the only such maze anywhere on the planet. Walking the caverns at an average pace will take about 30 minutes. There are no garbage cans or restrooms, so pack out your trash.

Kahanu Garden

650 'Ula'ino Rd.; 808/240-1301; www. ntbg.org; 9am-3pm Mon.-Fri.; $16, free under age 12

On 'Ula'ino Road, the pavement gradually gives way to a potholed dirt road leading to Kahanu Garden. This 464-acre (188-ha) property is in Honoma'ele, an area ceded in 1848 to Chief Kahanu by King Kamehameha III. The land has remained largely unchanged since the days of ancient Hawaii. The sprawling gardens focus on species integral to Polynesian culture. You're greeted by a massive grove of ulu (breadfruit), and there are groves of bananas, coconuts, taro, sweet potato, sugarcane, and 'awa. A self-guided tour details the history of the plants and the uses they had for Polynesians.

Kahanu Garden is home to towering **Pi'ilanihale Heiau,** a massive multitiered stone structure. It's the largest remaining heiau (temple) in Hawaii. The walls stretch 50 ft (15 m) high in some places, and the stone platforms are the size of two football fields. Multiple archaeological surveys have determined that the temple was most likely built in stages and dates as far back as the 14th century. To learn about the heiau and the property, you can arrange ahead of time for an hour-long guided tour ($25 pp). To get really involved, lend a hand by volunteering (call for times and details)—you could end up pulling taro with locals at neighboring Mahele Farms.

Hana Farms Roadside Stand

808-248-7371; 8am-7pm daily

Up the road 0.2 mi (0.3 km) from the turnoff for Ka'eleku Caverns and Kahanu Garden, and only a few miles before the town of Hana, the legendary Hana Farms Roadside Stand features six different types of banana bread as well as a full range of fruits, coffee, sauces, and flavorings. There will be more fruit stands between Hana and Kipahulu, but none are like this. Stop for a coffee, banana bread (get a loaf with chocolate chips), and advice on your Hana adventure.

★ Wai'anapanapa State Park

At mile marker 32, rugged Wai'anapanapa State Park is also known as "black-sand beach." At the beach overlook is one of the most iconic vistas on the drive to Hana. Take it slow on the 0.5-mi (0.8-km) road down to the park; there are often small children playing. Once you reach the park, turn left at the parking lot and follow the road to the end, where you can access the black sand of **Pa'iloa Beach** and its freshwater caves.

Made of crushed black lava rock, the sand is as black as Hana's night sky. Lush green foliage clings to the surrounding coast, and dramatic sea arches and volcanic promontories jut into the frothy sea. Since it faces almost directly east, this is a popular venue for sunrise weddings, and if you spend the night in Hana, I highly recommend getting up early to come here for sunrise.

On the main paved trail by the parking lot overlook, you'll see a trail that runs in the opposite direction of the beach; this is the beginning of

250 THE ROAD TO HANA AND EAST MAUI

BEST SUNRISE VIEWS

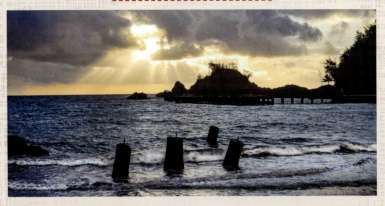

sunrise at Hana Bay Beach Park

Prepare to be dazzled. One of the best places to catch the sunrise on this side of the island is **Hana Bay Beach Park** (page 261). Arrive 20-30 minutes prior to sunrise and enjoy this waterfront park with its stunning black sand beach.

a popular **coastal hike.** One of the more popular stops along this trail is a blowhole that erupts on days with large surf. Maintain a safe distance; people have been swept into the ocean here.

The other main draw of Wai'anapanapa is the system of **freshwater caves** hidden in a grotto not far from the parking area. Following the cave trail from the parking lot, you'll see a sign that details the legend of the caves. Go left at the sign and travel downhill on a short loop trail. After a three-minute walk you'll reach the cave entrance. The clear water is crisp and cold, and if you swim back in either direction, you'll find some hidden caves. Bring a waterproof light, and don't go so far that you can't find your way back!

Reservations are required to enter the park. There is a $10 parking fee in addition to a $5 entrance fee (Hawaii residents can access the park for free). For more information reservation requirements, visit https://gostateparks.hawaii.gov/waianapanapa.

HANA

Before the arrival of Western explorers, Hana was a stronghold that was conquered and reconquered by the kings of Maui and the Big Island. The most strategic and historically rich spot is **Ka'uiki Hill,** the remnant of a cinder cone that dominates Hana Bay. It's said that the demigod Maui transformed his daughter's lover into Ka'uiki Hill and turned her into the gentle rains that bathe it to this day.

Hana was already a plantation town in 1849 when sea captain

George Wilfong started producing sugar here on 60 acres (24 ha). After sugar production faded in the 1940s, San Francisco industrialist Paul Fagan bought 14,000 acres (5,670 ha) of what was to become the **Hana Ranch.** Today, Hana's population of 1,200 continues to be predominantly Hawaiian. There are far more sights in the Hana area than you can see in a single day.

Fagan Memorial

Once you finally roll in to Hana town, one of the most prominent sights is a massive cross above the village. Set on the 545-ft (166-m) summit of Pu'u O Kahaula (Lyon's Hill), the Fagan Memorial was constructed to honor the town's modern founder, Paul Fagan, after he died in 1960. Fagan is credited with the creation of modern Hana when he started Hana Ranch and opened the Ka'uiki Inn, which in 1946 was the island's first resort, today called the Hana-Maui Resort.

The memorial is accessible by following a steep walking path from the parking lot of the Hana-Maui Resort. Atop the summit you're treated to the best view in Hana, with a panoramic vista over Hana Bay and 'Alau Island in the distance.

Hana Cultural Center

4974 Uakea Rd.; 808/248-8622; www.hanaculturalcenter.org; hours vary; $5

While it might not look like much from the outside, the humble yet informative Hana Cultural Center provides the historical backbone for the town. Over the course of Maui's history, Hana has been a unique eastern outpost. See ancient Hawaiian artifacts excavated from the Hana region, such as stone adzes and hand-woven fishnets, and walk

Fagan Memorial (top); Waioka Pond (Venus Pool) (middle); Wailua Falls (bottom)

HIGHLIGHTS AND SCENIC DRIVES 253

around the **Hana Courthouse,** listed on the National Register of Historic Places. The one-room courthouse still hosts proceedings the first Tuesday of each month, and in a testament to the island's multicultural heritage, they can take place in 24 different languages. When court isn't in session, the courthouse serves as a somber museum where Hana residents recount the morning of the 1946 tsunami, which devastated the eastern end of the island.

HANA TO KIPAHULU
Mile Marker 51
After Hana town (mile marker 34), the miles count down in the opposite direction, starting at mile marker 51 and decreasing toward Kipahulu.

Waioka Pond (Venus Pool)
Hidden at mile marker 48, Waioka Pond, or Venus Pool, is a local favorite. You have to cross a private pasture to get to the oceanfront pool, and because it's such a popular spot, the landowners haven't yet restricted access.

The first challenge is finding a legal parking spot. Because the mauka side of the road is lined with residential homes, the only parking is along a fence on the makai (ocean side) of the road. In order for you to park legally—facing the correct direction—you have to cross the bridge past the mile marker 48 sign, pull off the road, do a U-turn, and drive back toward Hana town. Once you're facing the right way, park along the grass bordering the thin metal fence.

Once you've parked, follow the fence line toward the bridge, where you'll notice an opening in the fence. Walk through and then follow the thin dirt trail down toward the shore.

Make a right through the trees at the concrete structure and you'll emerge at a cliff face looking out over a large pool. This first overlook is a popular cliff-diving spot among locals. To reach the pool without jumping, clamber down the rocks to the right. The pool is fed by both a stream and saltwater washing in from the ocean. There's a small island in the middle of the pool; swim over for a view of the rocky shore.

Wailua Falls
This 80-ft (24-m) cascade at mile marker 44.8 may be the most photographed on Maui. The best way to experience it is to take the short trail down to the base and take a dip in the swimming pools, away from the crowds.

★ Pools of 'Ohe'o (Seven Sacred Pools)
808/572-4400; www.nps.gov/hale; $30 per vehicle
The fabled Pools of 'Ohe'o, inside **Haleakalā National Park,** are one of the island's most popular attractions. The name Seven Sacred Pools is the largest misnomer on the island. There are far more than seven, and there's no record in history of them having been sacred. The name likely began as a marketing ploy by hoteliers in the 1940s. The name stuck and is used to this day. The real name is 'Ohe'o (pronounced oh-HEY-oh); locals will appreciate you using it.

This part of the island is truly stunning and a highlight of visiting Maui. The first taste you'll get of the park is crossing over 'Ohe'o Gulch on a bridge at mile marker 42.1, but try not to linger too long as you'll stop traffic. The entrance to the park is 0.4 mi (0.6 km) down the road, and if you have visited Haleakalā National

UNDERSTANDING "THE BACK ROAD"

The back road from Hana, **Highway 31,** is unlike any other stretch of road on the island. On this windswept plain, it feels like you've journeyed to the edge of the earth. Panoramic views stretch to the horizon, and the back of Haleakalā opens up as it plunges from summit to sea.

TERRAIN AND ACCESS

At the beginning of the drive, past Ono Organic Farms, the terrain changes from a lush paradise laden with waterfalls to grasslands. Past Kaupo Store the road straightens, and the last half of the drive, between Manawainui and Kanaio, is one of the nicest stretches of pavement on the island. You may like this section of road better than the famous front section.

The biggest misconception about the Road to Hana is that the back road around Kaupo is only accessible with a 4WD vehicle, and you'll be told that driving this section of road violates your car-rental policy. Neither of these common opinions is accurate, and on almost every day of the year, the back road is passable in any vehicle, including a regular passenger car. The road is unpaved but well-graded dirt for 5 mi (8 km), and at some points it is only one lane wide and has precipitous drop-offs, but at no point is 4WD essential. The only time you would need 4WD is during a torrential rainstorm—and in that situation, you should stay off the road altogether. Your car-rental company won't penalize you because you drove out here, but if something goes wrong, they aren't going to come out and help you either. Luckily, island locals are some of the friendliest people you'll meet, and if you have problems, you won't have any trouble flagging someone down for help.

PREPARATION

Preparation is key to enjoying a drive around the back side of Maui. Make sure that you have plenty of gas—at least half a tank when leaving Hana. Driving this road at night can be dangerous, and is pointless since you miss the expansive views. Keep an eye out for free-range cattle on the road. Other than Kaupo Store, there isn't anywhere to get food or water. If you're not a confident driver, the narrow sections and steep drop-offs may be too much. The road periodically closes due to construction, landslides, or flooding, so call the **Road Closure Advisory Line** (808/986-1200, ext. 2) for the latest information. Finally, no matter what your cell phone or GPS map says, there's no road from Ulupalakua back down to Kihei or Wailea.

Park within the last three days, your receipt will still gain you entry.

Once inside the park you'll notice a large parking lot next to an informative visitor center. It's the best place on this side of the island to gain an understanding of the history, culture, and unique environment of the Kipahulu region. Rangers here are the best source of information on current trail and waterfall conditions in the park.

HIGHLIGHTS AND SCENIC DRIVES   255

The visitor center is also where you begin the **Kuloa Point Loop Trail** leading down to the famous pools. Along the 10-minute walk, you'll go through groves of hala trees and past a number of historic sites. Eventually the trail emerges at a staircase down to the pools and one of the most iconic vistas in Hawaii, showcasing Haleakalā to the east and the tranquil blue Pacific Ocean to the west.

The three main pools are open most days for exploring and swimming, although they're closed during heavy rains and flash floods. Reaching the uppermost pools requires some rock scaling; it's worth the effort, but be careful on the slippery rocks.

Ono Organic Farms
41319 Hana Hwy.; 808/344-6700; www.onofarms.com; 10am-5pm daily
There are numerous organic farms in Kipahulu, but the granddaddy of them all is 50-acre (20-ha) Ono Organic Farms, 0.5 mi (0.8 km) past the entrance to Haleakalā National Park. You'll be blown away by the selection of exotic produce. In addition to producing 3,000 pounds (1,360 kg) of bananas *every week,* Ono also grows durians, cacao, coffee, tea, star fruit, Surinam cherries, and 60 other tropical and exotic fruits. Private tours ($375) last two hours.

The tour offers a culinary journey in certified organic and GMO-free produce directly from the land. A genuine spirit of aloha permeates the farm. It's easiest to take the tour if you're staying overnight in Hana. The driveway up to the farm is part of the adventure.

Mile Marker 39
The road begins to deteriorate and becomes narrow, with precipitous drop-offs. This is where you should turn around if you don't want to drive around the back of the island. As a point of reference, from this point it's 50 mi (81 km) to Kahului Airport via the back road, which takes about two hours without stops. If you return the way you came, it's nearly

the Pools of 'Ohe'o (Seven Sacred Pools)

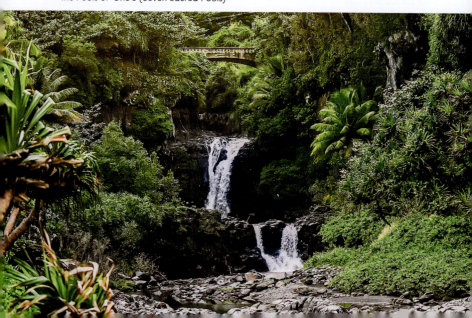

60 mi (97 km), about 2.5 hours without stops. While bumpier, the back road is much straighter and has less traffic.

Mile Marker 31.8

If you decide to drive the back road, or even just go a little farther before turning back, your reward at mile marker 31.8 is the most amazing view of Haleakalā you will see. If you thought the stretch between Kipahulu and Kaupo was desolate, you're in for a treat. The southeastern flank of Haleakalā opens up into the dramatic panorama—a pristine expanse of wide-open country where visitors gawk at the desolate beauty.

There are several places to pull over on the highway. As always, proceed with caution as this is a two-lane roadway, and some pullouts are smaller than others.

BEST BEACHES

Beaches in East Maui are blissfully undeveloped, though due to the trade winds there isn't much snorkeling, and the water can be rough and choppy. Mornings offer the calmest conditions for a jog, a quick dip, or to commune with nature.

PA'IA

Baldwin Beach

The long, wide, and mostly empty Baldwin Beach is a popular local bodysurfing spot, although the waves can get large during winter. During the afternoon, if the wind is howling, the cove on the far eastern end of Baldwin is sheltered and offers calm swimming most of the year. It's flanked by **Baby Beach,** which families with small children will love for its protected cove, and **Secret Beach,** which draws hippies and nudists.

Pa'ia Bay

The closest beach to the center of town, Pa'ia Bay is as active as Baldwin is calm, with a basketball court in a small park area and overflow parking for the town. The skate park at the Pa'ia Youth Center teems with area youth. Bodyboarders and surfers flock here for the waves, and a

Pa'ia Bay (left); Ho'okipa Beach Park (right)

number of downhill bike companies finish tours here after descending the mountainside. There are restrooms, a beach shower, and an ever-changing cast of entertaining and colorful characters.

Kuau Cove

This beach is the scenic backdrop for **Mama's Fish House** where many take a sunset photo. This small cove has a smattering of sand and an intriguing system of tide pools great for exploring with small children. The beach shrinks at high tide, so low tide is best for poring over the rocks to see all the slippery critters. There are a few parking spots near Mama's Fish House; the spaces with blue cones are designated as beach parking.

Hoʻokipa Beach Park

Hoʻokipa is the global epicenter of the windsurfing world as well as the go-to spot for surfers on the island's North Shore. It also has a thin, sandy beach pleasant for tanning and strolling (not so much swimming), offering ideal opportunities to appreciate and photograph Maui's rocky North Shore as well as witness the athletic skills of the surfers and windsurfers. A fringing reef creates a small pond nice for small children, and a wide range of people can usually be found hanging out on

258   THE ROAD TO HANA AND EAST MAUI

shore. Mornings are usually calm at Ho'okipa, and when the surf isn't too high, it's possible to snorkel in front of the rocks and find numerous honu (sea turtles). Every night in the hour before sunset, anywhere from half a dozen to 50 of them haul out on shore in front of the pavilions; this is quite a scene and attracts many onlookers. Remember that sea turtles are protected, and it's illegal to touch them. Note also that parking can be tight here—especially when the surf is up.

THE ROAD TO HANA
Pa'iloa Beach (Black-Sand Beach)

Just a few miles before the sleepy center of Hana and just past the turnoff for Hana Airport, Pa'iloa Beach, the black-sand beach at Wai'anapanapa State Park, is the most popular beach in Hana. Dense foliage and black lava rock abut the crashing blue surf. The water along the shore is often rough, particularly in the afternoon. The beach is formed of crushed black lava rock, the result of the tumultuous wave erosion. The color of the sand is as black as the night sky. To reach the shore, walk down a paved path from the parking lot of the state park. When you reach the bottom, you'll notice some sea caves you can explore at low tide. Since the sand is formed from lava rock, it isn't very comfortable; bring a blanket or a towel if you plan to hang out.

Reservations are required to enter Wai'anapanapa State Park; visit https://gostateparks.hawaii.gov/waianapanapa for more information.

HANA
Kaihalulu Beach (Red Sand Beach)

Before visiting Kaihalulu, be aware that Red Sand Beach is a nude beach. It can also be dangerous to access, as there are rockslides, slippery scree slopes, and sheer drop-offs. This is one of the coast's most famously scenic spots. This cavernous cove hidden in the mountainside offers decent swimming inside the rocks,

Pa'iloa Beach (Black-Sand Beach) (top); Kaihalulu Beach (Red Sand Beach) (bottom)

BEST BEACHES

TOP BEACH
HAMOA BEACH

A popular beach all around, this pristine haven can be found along Haneo'o Road, paralleling the ocean south of Hana town. Public restrooms and foot-washing stations are a perk at Hamoa Beach, but it's the ocean views and opportunities to swim in tranquil waters that are the biggest draws. You can catch the snowcapped peak of Mauna Kea on the Big Island, especially during the winter months. At low tide you can also see the remnants of the ancient **Haneo'o Fishpond,** although access is via private land. As the road rounds back to the right, you'll finally catch glimpses of Hamoa Beach, which Mark Twain considered one of the most beautiful in the world.

Parking is tight. Park only on the right side of the road so that traffic flows smoothly on the left. You might have to drive past the beach before you find a space. Access to the beach is down the stone stairway. The park area at the bottom of the stairs is property of the Hana-Maui Resort, but the sandy beach is public property.

This is the best spot in Hana for a relaxing day at the beach. On the calmest of days, it's possible to snorkel along the rocky coast, though most prefer to bodysurf the consistent playful shore-break. This can also be one of the best surf breaks in the area. This is an exceptional remote locale, away from hotels and restaurants. You truly feel at one with the islands here.

and the red sand gets its color from the cinder cone.

To find the trail for Red Sand Beach, find a legal parking area on Uakea Road by the ballpark (don't park facing the wrong direction), and walk toward an open grass field where the road dead-ends by the community center. Walk across the grass field, keeping an eye on the bushes on your right for a couple of narrow trails.

Wading for a minute through waist-high grass, you'll eventually emerge at a small dirt trail that snakes down the roots of a tree. The footing can be slippery, so bare feet or closed-toe shoes are better than rubber slippers. The thin trail continues to the left up and over a bluff, where landslides can leave a lot of scree on the trail. Once at the top of the bluff, you'll be greeted with your first photo op of the stunning cove. From here it's a one-minute walk along a cliff until you emerge on the red shore.

Hana Bay Beach Park

This popular bayside park wins points for its sublime black-sand beach and beautiful eastward ocean views. It's a community beach park, so expect children splashing around in the water and picnickers enjoying the scenic rocky beach. Musicians and croquet players frequent the beach, too. Picnic tables, grills, and restrooms are available.

BEST HIKES AND WALKS

THE ROAD TO HANA

★ Twin Falls Trail

Distance: *1.3 mi (2 km) round-trip*
Duration: *1-2 hours*
Elevation Gain: *328 ft (100 m)*
Effort: *easy*
Trailhead: *Twin Falls parking lot, mile marker 2*

At mile marker 2, 11.4 mi (18.3 km) past Pa'ia, Twin Falls is one of the easiest and shortest waterfall hikes in East Maui. Most of the "trail" is a gravel road that is wide and easy to stroll. Parking is limited and on a first-come, first-serve basis and costs $10. Plan your visit by bringing a sense of adventure—and mosquito repellent.

Myriad waterfalls await, but two main ones are the most accessible. From the parking lot, walk through a small gate and into a lush and forested orchard. There are portable toilets on the right side of the trail, and visitors are encouraged to leave a donation for their maintenance and upkeep. After 10 minutes of walking, you'll come to a stream crossing that can flood during heavy rain. If the trail is closed, it will be

Twin Falls Trail

here. Five minutes past the stream crossing is a three-way fork in the road; go straight. After five more minutes is another fork, where the trail to the left has a wooden plank crossing a small stream. Go straight, and after two minutes of clambering around an irrigation flume, you'll find a waterfall that has a small pool for swimming. While this waterfall is nice enough, there's a second waterfall, known as Caveman, that is far more dramatic, although it can be more difficult to reach.

To get to Caveman, turn around and go back to the fork in the trail with the wooden plank. Cross the wooden plank, ascend a small hill, take the fork to the left, and then take a right 50 yards (46 m) later. You'll be walking downhill, and a few minutes later you'll reach a concrete irrigation structure with steps leading up and over it. From here you'll begin to see the waterfall in the distance. To reach the base of the falls, wade across a stream that is usually about knee-deep. If the stream is manageable, a short scramble past it will bring you to a cavernous waterfall begging you to take your photo behind it. Since the water isn't clear enough to see the bottom, don't even think about jumping off the top. Adjacent to the pool at Caveman is a thin trail that switchbacks up the hill, leading to more pools and waterfalls, although since it's easy to get lost back here, it's best to have a guide to venture any farther.

HANA

King's Highway Coastal Trail
Distance: *3 mi (4.8 km) one-way*
Duration: *90 minutes*
Elevation Gain: *88 ft (27 m)*
Effort: *moderate*

Trailhead: *main parking lot, Wai'anapanapa State Park*
One of the few hiking options in East Maui that doesn't involve a waterfall, the 3-mi (4.8-km) King's Highway Coastal Trail between Wai'anapanapa State Park and the northern tip of Hana Bay is one of the few navigable remnants of the ancient King's Highway that once circled the island. Today, only scarce bits of this ancient trail are evident, but the most prominent section is here on the coast south of Wai'anapanapa. Parking for the trailhead is in the main lot of the state park. Along the course of this trail, you'll weave around azure bays flanked by black sand, pass beneath dense groves of dry lauhala trees, and gaze upon lava rock arches carved from the coast by the tumultuous sea.

Wear hiking boots, as the jagged 'a'a lava can rip rubber slippers to pieces. Carry plenty of water—there are no facilities along the trail. As you get closer to Hana Bay, the trail becomes a little more treacherous. Most people start from the Wai'anapanapa trailhead and hike about halfway before turning back.

Reservations are required to enter Wai'anapanapa State Park; visit https://gostateparks.hawaii.gov/waianapanapa for more information.

KIPAHULU AND BEYOND

Pipiwai Trail
Distance: *4 mi (6.4 km) round-trip*
Duration: *2.5-5 hours*
Elevation Gain: *650 ft (198 m)*
Effort: *moderate*
Trailhead: *Kipahulu section of Haleakalā National Park*
This is one of the best trails on Maui and the undisputed highlight of

the Kipahulu section of Haleakalā National Park. At 4 mi (6.4 km), plan for a 2.5-hour expedition on this moderate trail, unless you indulge and camp overnight at the Kipahulu campground.

To find the trailhead, drive 30-40 minutes past the town of Hana to mile marker 41.7, where you enter the Kipahulu section of Haleakalā National Park. Parking for the trailhead is within the park boundaries. You'll have to pay the $30 park entry fee. Walk back to the road and 100 yards (90 m) toward Hana, where you'll see signs for the trailhead on the left. Much of the Pipiwai Trail parallels **'Ohe'o Gulch,** and you can hear the rush of the water as you make your way uphill toward the falls. It's not safe to access the pools or waterfalls in the river. After 10 minutes on the trail you'll reach the lookout for **Makahiku Falls,** a 200-ft (60-m) plunge that can be anything from a trickle during drier months to a violent torrent. Past the falls, the trail begins gaining elevation for another five minutes before emerging in the shade of a beautiful banyan tree. The section between the tree and the first bridge has multiple spur trails that lead to waterfall overlooks offering views of the canyons and pools.

Ten minutes past the tree is the first of two bridges that zigzag across the stream. This is a great place to snap pictures of the waterfalls and the first bamboo forest. After crossing the second bridge, when the trail turns into stairs that climb steeply toward the bamboo, there's an opening in the railing on the left side where a path leads down to a rocky streambed. This is the **Palikea Stream,** and if you rock-hop up the riverbed for about 15 minutes, you'll emerge at a waterfall that is less dramatic—but also less visited—than neighboring Waimoku Falls. Back on the main trail, continuing up the stairs, a boardwalk leads through the densest bamboo on the island. As you

bamboo forest along the Pipiwai Trail

emerge from the creaking cavern, five more minutes of rock-hopping brings you to the pièce de résistance, 400-ft (120-m) **Waimoku Falls.** This is one of the most beautiful corners of the island.

HIKING TOURS
HIKE MAUI
808/879-5270; www.hikemaui.com; $159-279
While many private adventure tours will take you hiking as part of the experience, one group that focuses specifically on hiking is Hike Maui, with knowledgeable guides who will take you hiking in a private area hidden behind Twin Falls. Group sizes are usually small. What makes these hikes worthwhile is not only being taken directly to the trailhead but also learning about the island's flora, fauna, history, and mythology from guides who love what they do.

SURFING

Surfing in East Maui is for intermediate and advanced surfers. Ho'okipa Beach Park and Hamoa Bay can see surf at any time of year, and this stretch of coast roars to life October-April with North Pacific swells. This is some of the largest, heaviest surf on the planet. Even watching from the shore, you can feel the rush of waves large enough to shake the ground beneath you.

SURF SPOTS
Pa'ia
HO'OKIPA BEACH PARK
The epicenter for surf on the island's North Shore will forever be Ho'okipa Beach Park, 3 mi (4.8 km) past the town of Pa'ia, a legendary wind-swept cove. For surfers, Ho'okipa has four sections: Pavilions (Pavils), Middles, The Point, and Lanes. Seen from the beach, **Pavilions** is the break that's the farthest to the right and can pick up wrapping wind swell even during the summer. Since it's the most consistent, it can also be the most localized, so beginners should be wary.

In the center of the beach, **Middles** is a big A-frame that breaks in deep water and can get

windsurfers at Ho'okipa (left); paddleboarding (right)

264 THE ROAD TO HANA AND EAST MAUI

SURF ALERT: JAWS

a surfer riding a giant wave at Jaws

Pe'ahi, also called **Jaws,** can see 70-ft (21-m) waves, but only a few days a year October-April. The waves are created by massive storms in the North Pacific that churn between the Aleutian Islands and Japan. Since the North Pacific is calm during summer, it's only in winter that you stand a chance of seeing the large surf at Jaws.

Thanks to the wonders of surf forecasting, the massive waves can be predicted up to a week ahead of time. If Jaws is "going off," a high surf warning will be issued. The warning requires wave heights of 25 ft (7.6 m) or greater on the island's North Shore. This differs from a high surf advisory, issued when waves are 15 ft (4.5 m) or greater. If a high surf advisory is issued, there aren't going to be 70-ft (21-m) waves at Jaws.

If a high surf warning has been posted, ask a local what they've heard about the waves at Jaws—your concierge, a surf shop staffer, or any boat crew. Since island surfers watch the surf forecast like a trader watches stock futures, they'll be in the know. If Jaws is going to be breaking, get there in the morning. By the time the wind comes up in the afternoon, most of the surfers have left.

board-shatteringly heavy during the winter. The wave can accommodate a larger crowd than Pavils, although you should still be skilled to paddle out. On the left side of the beach is **The Point,** a heavy right that's popular with windsurfers. Finally, **Lanes** is a left-hand wave that breaks in the cove to the west of Ho'okipa, but it's a long paddle.

Ho'okipa Beach Park is also the North Shore's destination for **windsurfing,** though note that windsurfing is prohibited before 11am.

SURFING 265

Haʻiku

PEʻAHI (JAWS)
Peʻahi, also called Jaws, is quite possibly the most famous surf break on the planet. If Jaws is breaking, there will be dozens of cars parked along the side of the highway. The best thing to do is park near the highway and hitch a ride to the bottom of the hill. The viewing area is from a coastal bluff at the bottom of a 4WD road, and the chances of hitching a ride increase tenfold if you barter a six-pack of beer.

Hana

There are no lifeguards at either beach in Hana.

KOKI BEACH
One of the main Hana surf breaks frequented by visitors is Koki Beach on Haneoʻo Road, 1.5 mi (2.4 km) past the town of Hana. Because of its easterly location, Hana gets waves any time of the year. Since the waves are often the result of easterly wind swell, conditions can be rougher than elsewhere on the island. The steepness of the wave here is better suited for shortboards than longboards. Koki is where many of Hana's keiki (children) first learn how to pop up and ride.

HAMOA BEACH
Around the corner from Koki Beach, also on Haneoʻo Road, is Hamoa Beach, a protected bay that offers a respite from the trade winds. Koki breaks fairly close to shore, but the wave at Hamoa breaks farther out over a combination of sand, reef, and rocks. On moderate days, this is a good place for riding a longboard or a stand-up board, since the wave isn't as steep, but the largest waves are for experts.

LESSONS AND RENTAL SHOPS

Paʻia

ZACK HOWARD SURF
488 Kahua Pl.; 808/214-7766; www.zackhowardsurf.com
Given the advanced surf conditions of the island's North Shore, there aren't as many surf schools in East Maui as in Lahaina or Kihei. Professional longboarder Zack Howard is one of the few instructors who offers lessons ($220 private, $260 for two, and $100 pp for six or more) to surf on Maui's North Shore. While most of his lessons are conducted at locations on the south shore on the road to Lahaina, advanced surfers can paddle out on the North Shore if the conditions are right.

HI-TECH MAUI
58 Baldwin Ave.; 808/579-9297; www.surfmaui.com; 9am-6pm daily
Hi-Tech Maui offers casual board rentals ($30 per day) and has a full range of longboards, shortboards, and fun boards. It's an affordable option for playing in the waves of Paʻia Bay or on a multiday safari to Hana.

SIMMER HAWAII
99 Hana Hwy.; 808/579-8484; www.simmerhawaii.com; 10am-6pm daily
Although most of the windsurfing rental shops are in Kahului, Simmer Hawaii is the closest shop to Hoʻokipa and the best spot on the North Shore for windsurfing rentals and supplies.

STAND-UP PADDLEBOARDING

THE MALIKO RUN

There's no stretch of water more legendary and hallowed than the 9-mi-long (14.5-km) Maliko Run. It's the spot where downwind racing was born, and the place where the world's best train for the professional tour. In the Maliko Run, paddlers begin at **Maliko Gulch** to the east of Ho'okipa Beach Park and paddle downwind to either Kahului Harbor or the beach at Kanaha Beach Park in Central Maui. On a typical day, paddlers will be up to a mile (1.6 km) offshore and in winds of 30 mph (48 km/h), riding on ocean swells that can range from knee-high to a couple of feet overhead. Average paddlers complete the 9-mi (14.5-km) run between Maliko and the harbor in a little under two hours, whereas the world's top paddlers can finish the course in a little over an hour—a seven-minute mile pace.

Maliko Runs are a favorite weekend activity of the island's water sports enthusiasts, and over 200 racers gather each year for the professional races, with one of the largest being the OluKai race at the end of April. A Maliko Run isn't an activity for anyone who isn't an avid stand-up paddler, but for stand-up paddling enthusiasts, this is the Holy Grail.

If you're a competent paddler and have lots of experience in the ocean, **More Watertime** (www.malikoshuttle.com) has a shuttle service ($15-18 pp; cash is preferred and exact change is encouraged) with daily runs to Maliko that leave from Kanaha and Kahului Harbor. For boards, an increasing number of Kahului shops are now renting race boards, and a couple of schools will even provide lessons where an experienced instructor can accompany you.

BIKING

BIKE ROUTES
ROAD TO HANA BIKE RIDE

The Road to Hana Bike Ride (90 mi/144 km round-trip) is a must for avid cyclists, but any cyclist can take it on. It's a curve-happy experience that requires much concentration because you are sharing the road with vehicles. There are occasionally specified bike lanes; however, the roadway, which features some areas to allow drivers to pass, is mostly a two-lane experience, so proceed with care. Plan ahead and begin early. Give your back a respite at **Hana Farms Roadside Stand,** a popular hangout in the unofficial "town square" area. Or, have friends meet you there for a one-way trip experience (45 mi/72 km), which is just as invigorating. Bring water and snacks. This is a workout and will take up to three hours one way.

BIKING 267

BIKE TOURS AND SHOPS

Pa'ia

MAUI CYCLERY

99 Hana Hwy.; 808/579-9009; www.gocyclingmaui.com; 10am-5pm Mon.-Sat.

One of the most comprehensive cycling experiences on Maui is at Maui Cyclery, a small but thorough shop in the heart of Pa'ia. In addition to offering rentals (from $85 per day), parts, services, and sales, the staff offers guided tours for some of the island's best rides.

Ha'iku

BIKE MAUI

810 Ha'iku Rd., Ste. 120; 808/575-9575; www.bikemaui.com; 8am-9pm daily

In the Ha'iku Cannery, Bike Maui specializes in group tours making the ride down Haleakalā Volcano. You can rent a bike (from $40 per day), and if you arrange your own transportation to the top, you'll be able to ride from the summit of the volcano.

ADVENTURE SPORTS

ZIP-LINING

Ha'iku

NORTHSHORE ZIPLINE COMPANY

2065 Kauhikoa Rd.; 808/269-0671; www.nszipline.com; 8am-5pm Mon.-Sat.; $147 pp

Most adventure sports along Maui's North Shore are in the water, but NorthShore Zipline Company has seven zip lines that run through the trees of rural Ha'iku in a onetime military base. The course is family-friendly and caters mainly to first-time zippers. Children as young as five can participate as long as they're accompanied by an adult. Don't think that you won't still get a rush, however, as you can hit speeds of up to 40 mph (65 km/h) on the last line of the course, and the viewing platforms provide a unique vantage over the rural mountainside.

JUNGLE ZIPLINE

50 E. Waipio Rd.; 808/628-4947; www.junglezip.com; 8am-4pm daily; $128-148

If you're short on time and want to combine a zip-line adventure with a day trip to Hana, Jungle Zipline, on the Road to Hana, is a great way to take a break from the car. The full course ($148) is eight lines and takes two hours. To merge this with driving the Road to Hana, opt instead for a morning tour on the abbreviated five-line course ($128). It takes about one hour, so you still have time to reach Hana. The minimum age is eight, and maximum weight is 250 pounds (113 kg).

RAPPELLING

RAPPEL MAUI

808/270-1500; www.rappelmaui.com; 7am-5pm daily; from $230

To get all Navy SEAL on your Maui vacation, Rappel Maui will teach you how to strap on a harness and walk down waterfalls. The company has exclusive access to waterfalls behind the Garden of Eden, and while the first descent is a dry run on a dirt hillside, eventually you're leaning backward over a waterfall

Rappel Maui

ADVENTURE SPORTS 269

with a 60-ft (18-m) drop. The guides are professional and completely committed to your safety. You could end up getting the best photo of your vacation. Weight limits are 70-250 pounds (32-113 kg). Don't look down!

HANG GLIDING

HANG GLIDING MAUI

808/264-3287; www. hangglidingmaui.com; 9am-6pm Sun.-Fri., 9am-6:30pm Sat.; from $260 pp

This is the way to see the Hana coast. All flights are private, since the hang glider only has two seats, and the instructor teaches you the basics of steering the glider as well as lift, wind speed, and direction. This ultralight trike has wheels and a motor, so you take off down the Hana runway as you would in a regular plane, but when you reach a cruising altitude of 2,000-3,000 ft (600-900 m), you cut the engine and hang-glide back down, listening only to the wind. The view from here is life-changing, and there aren't even windows like a helicopter—just you, the instructor, and the sky. Lessons are 30-minute ($260), 45-minute ($320), or one-hour ($400) flights and are offered Monday-Tuesday and Thursday-Friday.

SKYDIVING

Hana

MAUI SKYDIVING

700 Alalele Rd.; 808/379-7455; www. mauiskydiving.info; from $299 pp

Love the thrill of jumping out of a plane? Maui Skydiving is the island's first commercial skydive operation. The minimum age is 18, and maximum weight is 240 pounds (109 kg), with a $2 per pound ($4.40 per kg) surcharge for those over 200 pounds (91 kg).

HELICOPTER TOURS

MAVERICK HELICOPTERS

Lelepio Pl., Kahului; 808/893-7999; www.maverickhelicopter.com

Don't just drive the Road to Hana; fly above it. Maverick Helicopters is one of the few operators that offer a Hana-specific tour. The superb 75-minute Hana Rainforest Experience ($339 pp) traces Maui's North Shore with rare shoreline views of the towns of Pa'ia, Ha'iku, and Hana. The tour's grand opus is descending and landing in the Hana rainforest, where guests disembark and explore the grounds of a former taro plantation in the Wailua Valley. Your pilot explains the finer nuances of this remote landscape, which few people ever visit.

AIR MAUI

1 Keolani Pl., Hangar 110, Kahului; 808/877-7005; www.airmaui.com

Air Maui covers two of Maui's most popular sights on its Hana- Haleakalā tour ($272 pp), which lasts an impressive four hours and includes a cliff-side landing on the back side of Haleakalā, followed by a charted route over Hana's rainforest, remote valleys, and waterfalls. All helicopters seat up to six. Tours are offered twice daily, at 8am and noon.

SPAS AND WELLNESS

TEMPLE OF PEACE
575 Ha'iku Rd.; 808/575-5220; www. templeofpeacemaui.com; 9am-5pm Mon.-Fri., 10am-2pm Sun.

No trip to Maui is complete without at least one visit to Temple of Peace. Dubbed "Maui's Healing Sanctuary," the very boho Buddhist temple has been operating for decades. Check the website for special events. You can book a quasi-spa day here and fill it with meditation and relaxing. For a real kick, Sunday morning services are lively and filled with music and singing.

SHOPPING

PA'IA

Once known for hippies, surf culture, and sugarcane, Pa'ia now features some of the island's trendiest boutiques and arguably the island's best shopping, with beachwear boutiques and craft galleries populating the one-stoplight town.

Art Galleries
MAUI HANDS
84 Hana Hwy.; 808/579-9245; www. mauihands.com; 10am-6pm daily

Maui Hands has stunning works of art from local creators and well-known artists. Many pieces reflect island culture.

Clothing and Swimwear
HONOLUA SURF COMPANY
115 Hana Hwy.; 808/579-9593; noon-6pm daily

For surf, skate, or even snowboard wear, you can find some of the finest apparel here in America's happiest surf town.

Jewelry and Gifts
STUDIO 22K
161 Hana Hwy.; 808/579-8167; www. studio22k.com; noon-6pm Tues.-Sat.

While Pa'ia doesn't have as many jewelry stores as Lahaina, Studio 22K, on the far Hana side of town, is a small studio that specializes in handmade 22-karat-gold items with metal malleable enough to morph into all sorts of twisting shapes and designs.

HA'IKU
Art Galleries
TREEHOUSE ART STUDIOS
375 W. Kuiaha Rd.; www. treehouseartstudios.com; hours vary, check website

Treehouse Art Studios is a festive enclave where the creations of local artists are on display. It is conveniently located in the Pauwela Cannery.

HA'IKU STYLE GALLERY
810 Ha'iku Rd.; 808/283-1706; 10am-6pm Tues.-Sat.

A great place to stop for both art and souvenirs is Ha'iku Style Gallery. There's a tremendous trove of artwork from local artists, and you'll always find something unique.

SHOPPING 271

THE ROAD TO HANA
Gifts and Souvenirs
NAHIKU TI GALLERY
mile marker 28.7; 808/248-8800; hours vary, usually 10am-5pm daily

The best place for real shopping along the Road to Hana is at Nahiku Ti Gallery, a small gallery within the Nahiku Marketplace. This curious strip mall in the rainforest is already strange in that it offers legitimate food options in the middle of nowhere, and the art gallery rivals those in Ka'anapali and Wailea. While nowhere near as large as the south shore shopping venues, the gallery has a varied selection of jewelry, crafts, paintings, and pottery, and a surprising collection of art.

HANA
Art Galleries
HANA COAST GALLERY
5031 Hana Hwy.; 808/248-8636; www.hanacoast.com; 9am-5pm daily

By far the most comprehensive gallery in Hana, the Hana Coast Gallery might be the nicest art gallery on the island. A freestanding building within the Hana-Maui Resort, the Hana Coast Gallery features fine works by Hawaiian artists. Oil paintings, ceramics, and wooden sculptures are on display in this sophisticated space, and the depth of knowledge of the staff on the intricacies of individual pieces provides an educational component to this fine-art experience.

FOOD

STANDOUTS
Pa'ia
MAMA'S FISH HOUSE
799 Poho Pl.; 808/579-8488; www.mamasfishhouse.com; 11am-8:30pm daily; $26-65

Mama's Fish House is synonymous with Maui fine dining. Its cult-like followers claim that if you haven't been to Mama's, you've never been to Maui. The oceanfront location and romantic ambience are unbeatable, and the fish is so fresh that the menu tells you it was caught that morning and who caught it. Call well in advance for reservations, timing your meal for sunset if possible. Lunch is an affordable alternative.

PAIA FISHMARKET
100 Baldwin Ave.; 808/579-8030; https://paiafishmarket.com; 11am-9:30pm daily; $12-24

While your hotel concierge will recommend Mama's, local surfers will point you to Paia Fishmarket, on the corner of the only stoplight in town. Lines stretch out the door for the popular ono and mahimahi burgers. My personal favorite is the ahi burger, paired with a Hefeweizen on draft. The fish tacos and seafood pasta are shockingly good as well.

Paia Fishmarket

CAFÉ DES AMIS
42 Baldwin Ave.; 808/579-6323; www.cdamaui.com; 11am-8:30pm Mon.-Fri., 9am-8:30pm Sat.-Sun.; $12-24

The most relaxing place for a meal in Pa'ia is at Café des Amis, where you can sit in a tucked-away outdoor courtyard with Italian coffee and crepes. Lunch has exceptional Indian curries, in addition to savory crepes, and happy hour is 4pm-6pm daily.

Hana
THAI FOOD BY PRANEE
5050 Uakea Rd.; 808/264-9942; 11am-5pm Fri.-Tues.; $10-15

Thai Food by Pranee is a culinary gem in the humblest of locations. Little more than a glorified food truck across from the Hana Ballpark, this open-air restaurant gets packed for lunch—especially since it's open on weekends. The filling portions of pad thai and green curry are worth the wait, and if the food is too spicy, you can ask them for coconut milk to bring the heat down. Parking is along Uakea Road, and be sure to park facing the correct direction, since violators are often ticketed.

LODGING

RESERVATIONS AND TIPS

While the majority of hotel stays are in Hana itself, you can book Airbnbs in the area. Additionally, if you're venturing out later in the day and want to spend the night somewhere, several retreat centers just past Twin Falls, such as **Hale Akua Retreat Center** (808/572-9300; https://hale-akua.org), may be a good option. As always, plan ahead and make reservations.

Pa'ia Inn

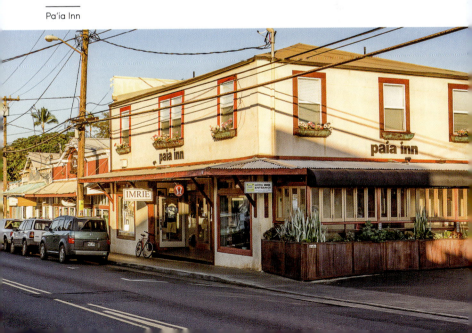

EAST MAUI FOOD OPTIONS

NAME	LOCATION	CONTACT INFO
PA'IA		
★ **Mama's Fish House**	799 Poho Pl.	808/579-8488; www.mamasfishhouse.com
★ **Paia Fishmarket**	100 Baldwin Ave.	808/579-8030; https://paiafishmarket.com
Flatbread Company	89 Hana Hwy.	808/579-8989; www.flatbreadcompany.com
★ **Café des Amis**	42 Baldwin Ave.	808/579-6323; www.cdamaui.com
Milagros	3 Baldwin Ave.	808/579-8755; www.milagrosfoodcompany.com
Paia Bay Coffee & Bar	115 Hana Hwy.	808/579-3111; www.paiabaycoffeeandbar.com
Island Fresh Café	381 Baldwin Ave.	808/495-3133
HA'IKU		
Nuka	780 Ha'iku Rd.	808/575-2939; www.nukamaui.com
Colleen's	810 Ha'iku Rd.	808/575-9211; www.colleensinhaiku.com
Wailuku Coffee Company	810 Kokomo Rd.	808/868-3229; www.wailukucoffeeco.com
HANA		
★ **Thai Food by Pranee**	5050 Uakea Rd.	808/264-9942
Hasegawa General Store	5165 Hana Hwy.	808/248-7079
Braddah Hutts BBQ Grill	5305 Hana Hwy.	808/264-5582

STANDOUTS

Pa'ia

PA'IA INN

93 Hana Hwy.; 808/579-6000; www.paiainn.com; $299-1,875

In the center of town, the Pa'ia Inn is a trendy and chic boutique hotel steps from the beaches of Pa'ia. The decor has a dark-wood Balinese tone, and each individually designed room offers a luxurious private getaway in the middle of Pa'ia's bustle.

THE INN AT MAMA'S FISH HOUSE

799 Poho Pl.; 800/860-4852; www.mamasfishhouse.com; adults only; $375-1,050

Right on Kuau Cove, The Inn at

FOOD	HOURS	PRICE
seafood	11am-8:30pm daily	$26-65
seafood	11am-9:30pm daily	$12-24
Italian	11am-9pm daily	$16-28
Mediterranean	11am-8:30pm Mon.-Fri., 9am-8:30pm Sat.-Sun.	$12-24
Mexican	11am-9pm daily	$12-25
coffee shops	7:30am-10pm Tues.-Sat., 7:30am-6pm Sun.	$5-16
health food, organic meals	7:30am-4pm daily	$7-18
Japanese	10:30am-2:30pm Mon.-Fri. and 4:30pm-10pm daily	$7-34
diners	7am-9:30pm daily	$9-28
coffee shops	7am-5pm daily	$4-13
Thai	11am-5pm Fri.-Tues.	$10-15
general stores	9:30am-6pm daily	$4-12
food trucks	11am-2:30pm Mon.-Fri.	$8-14

Mama's Fish House is an impossibly romantic boutique hotel in one of the North Shore's best settings. The suites, studios, and cottages feature amenities such as full kitchens, maid service, and 15 percent off at the restaurant.

The Road to Hana

HUELO POINT LOOKOUT
222 Door of Faith Rd.; 800/871-8645; www.maui-vacationrentals.com; $285-545
In Huelo you'll find the Huelo Point Lookout, a collection of five vacation

EAST MAUI LODGING OPTIONS

NAME	LOCATION	CONTACT INFO
PA'IA		
Aloha Surf Hostel	221 Baldwin Ave.	808/868-0117; www. alohasurfhostel.com
★ **Pa'ia Inn**	93 Hana Hwy.	808/579-6000; www. paiainn.com
★ **The Inn at Mama's Fish House**	799 Poho Pl.	800/860-4852; www. mamasfishhouse.com
HA'IKU		
Maui Tradewinds	4320 Une Pl.	www.mauitradewinds. com
THE ROAD TO HANA		
★ **Huelo Point Lookout**	222 Door of Faith Rd.	800/463-7042; www. maui-vacationrentals. com
HANA		
Hana Inn	4870 Uakea Rd.	808/248-7033; www. hanainn.com
★ **Bamboo Inn**	4869 Uakea Rd.	808/248-7718; www. bambooinn.com
Hana Retreat Ala Kukui	4224 Hana Hwy.	808/248-7841; www. alakukui.org
★ **Hana-Maui Resort**	5031 Hana Hwy.	808/400-1234; www.hyatt.com
KIPAHULU AND BEYOND		
Kipahulu Campground	Haleakalā National Park, Hana Hwy., mile marker 41	877/444-6777; www. recreation.gov

rentals in a lush and heavenly section of the island, not for the resort-loving crowd. These five separate vacation rentals provide sweeping views of the Huelo coast and are a place to escape from it all. There is no beach outside your door, but there is a blanket of stars every night and outdoor hot tubs from which to enjoy them. Those traveling with a group could also book the entire Lookout House, which features a large kitchen and an outdoor hot tub.

Hana

BAMBOO INN

4869 Uakea Rd.; 808/248-7718; www. bambooinn.com; $285-395
The funky, ultra-relaxing Bamboo Inn offers three oceanfront rooms that look out over the water toward Waikoloa Beach. A thatched-roof hut serves as the centerpiece for the property. The owner, John, is a wealth of information on Hana history and culture, and this is a modern,

TYPE	PRICE	BEST FOR
hostel	$56–194	budget travelers
inn	$299–1,875	couples
inn	$375–1,050	couples, honeymooners
B&B	from $275	couples, honeymooners
vacation rental	$285–545	couples
inn	$169–242	budget travelers
B&B	$285–395	couples
retreat	$365–1,545	solo travelers, groups
hotel	$595–1,275	couples, families
camping	$8–25	budget travelers

soothing place to fall asleep to the crash of the waves. Wi-Fi is available in the courtyard, and breakfast is included.

HANA-MAUI RESORT
5031 Hana Hwy.; 808/400-1234; www.hyatt.com; $595-1,275
Hana-Maui Resort, the nicest place in Hana, is a luxurious compound featuring dynamic ocean views from many of its rooms. It's right in the center of town and was the island's first resort hotel when it opened in 1946. Since that time it has continued as the island's best resort in various iterations. Amenities include tennis courts, a swimming pool, a fitness center, spa, several restaurants, and meeting rooms. The resort has Wi-Fi but no TVs, as you're supposed to unwind, relax, untether, and breathe.

TRANSPORTATION

Air

At the small **Hana Airport** (HNM; 700 Alalele Pl.; 808/872-3808; www.airports. hawaii.gov/hnm), you can swap the nausea-inducing three-hour drive for the convenience of a 20-minute flight. Of course, you'll miss out on all the sights along the Road to Hana, but if your focus is on getting to Hana and relaxing at the resort, **Mokulele Airlines** (808/495-4188; www.mokulele airlines.com) operates flights twice daily between Kahului Airport and the landing strip in Hana. Often the **Hana-Maui Resort** runs specials with the airfare included with a stay of three nights or more. If you fly to Hana, however, remember that there aren't any car-rental agencies there, so you'll have to arrange your own transportation from the airport before you get on the flight.

Car

There aren't any car-rental operators in East Maui, so plan on driving here yourself or taking a guided tour.

Gas

- Pa'ia: There are two gas stations within walking distance of each other in Pa'ia. Be sure you have close to a full tank for the long, winding journey out to Hana. Neither of the stations has a public restroom; the closest ones are at Pa'ia Bay.

- Ha'iku: Tucked away on a back road that visitors only end up on if they're lost, the only gas station in Ha'iku can be found at **Hanzawa's Variety Store** (1833 Kaupakalua Rd.; 808/298-0407; 9:30am-6pm daily), about halfway between Hana Highway and the town of Makawao.

- Hana: In all of Hana there is only one gas station. **Texaco** (5200 Hana Hwy.; 808/270-5299; 7am-8pm daily) is across from Hasegawa General Store. It has a few auto supplies, snacks, and a telephone, although for a public restroom you're better off going down to the Hana Ballpark. Gas in Hana is expensive: $0.50 or more per gallon higher than elsewhere on the island. Fill up before leaving town, because the nearest gas station west is in Pa'ia; going south around the bottom of the island, the closest is in Keokea in Upcountry, and it isn't open in the evening.

Guided Tours

Despite how much fun it is to craft your own Hana adventure, you can visit Hana as part of a private tour.

The best option is **Valley Isle Excursions** (808/871-5224; www.tour maui.com; $264 adults, $244 children), the only guided Hana tour that's part of the Hawaii Ecotourism Association. Guides are professional, knowledgeable, and funny, and the company has gone to exceptional lengths to eliminate waste from their tours. Book online and save $10.

Temptation Tours (808/877-8888; www.temptationtours.com; from $174) offers small group tours in "limo vans" and has a number of different options for visiting Hana with a picnic lunch. One of the tours explores the recesses of Ka'eleku Caverns, and a Hana picnic tour has a similar itinerary but much nicer vans. The top choice, however, is the Hana Sky Trek ($449 pp), driving the Road to Hana and then hopping aboard a helicopter at the Hana Airport for the ride back to Kahului. During the flight you'll zip by towering waterfalls you would never see from the road and buzz over the multihued cinder cones of Haleakalā Crater.

Bus

The **Maui Bus** provides regular service between Pa'ia, Ha'iku, the Kahului Airport, and Queen Ka'ahumanu Center in Kahului, where you can connect with buses to anywhere else on the island. The rate is $4 per boarding or $4 for a day pass, and pickups begin in Pa'ia at 5:53am daily headed toward Ha'iku and 6:29am daily headed toward Kahului. The route also makes stops at the Ha'iku Marketplace and Ha'iku Community Center, with the final bus going from Ha'iku to Kahului departing the Ha'iku Marketplace at 9:11pm daily.

LEAVING THE ROAD TO HANA AND EAST MAUI

South Maui (Kihei)

From Hana, head north on Hana Highway (Hwy. 360) for 34.3 mi (55.2 km). Continue onto Highway 36 for 13.8 mi (22.2 km) and turn left on Hansen Road. Turn left onto Maui Veterans Highway (Hwy. 311) and continue onto Pi'ilani Highway (Hwy. 31) to Kihei. The 60-mi (96-km) drive is 2 hours 15 minutes.

West Maui (Lahaina)

From Hana, head north on Hana Highway (Hwy. 360) for 34.3 mi (55.2 km). Continue onto Highway 36 for 15 mi (24.1 km) and turn left on Mayor Elmer F. Cravalho Way. Continue onto Kuihelani Highway (Hwy. 380) and turn left onto Honoapi'ilani Highway (Hwy. 30). Continue onto Lahaina Bypass (Hwy. 3000) and take the Keawe Street exit. The 74-mi (119-km) drive is 2 hours 30 minutes.

Kahului Airport

From Hana, head north on Hana Highway (Hwy. 360) for 34.3 mi (55.2 km). Continue onto Highway 36 for 15 mi (24.1 km) and turn right on Mayor Elmer F. Cravalho Way to Kahului Airport. The 50-mi (80-km) drive is 1 hour 50 minutes.

Lana'i sea cliffs

LANA'I

It's hard to find an outdoor playground more stunning than Lana'i, home to a mere 3,500 residents and crisscrossed by just 30 mi (48 km) of paved roads.

The late 1980s saw this island's cash crop transition from the world's largest pineapple plantation to high-end tourism. With the construction of the luxurious Four Seasons Resort, the island instantly became one of Hawaii's most exclusive getaways. In 2012, Oracle CEO Larry Ellison purchased 98 percent of the island, and while projects ranging from a winery to a college to a tennis center have been discussed for the tiny island, as of yet the largest change has been the spectacular renovations of the Four Seasons Resort, comprising two hotels, one on the Manele waterfront and one inland called Sensei Lana'i.

Resort life aside, visitors come to enjoy the snorkeling at Hulopo'e Beach Park and the plantation-era charm of cozy Lana'i City—the island's only town. Choose to explore a little deeper, however, with morning hikes on pine-shrouded mountain trails, off-roading through otherworldly moonscapes, and surfing empty waves along an empty beach.

Lana'i is an island of unparalleled luxury, but it's also about 4WD trucks with deer skulls mounted to the bumper, aging Filipino plantation workers "talking story" in Dole Park, and petroglyphs scattered across rock faces that predate any of the island's modern history. It's a tight-knit community where townsfolk greet each other with first names and a smile.

TOP 3

★ **1. LANA'I CULTURE AND HERITAGE CENTER:** View everything from wooden spears used in ancient battles to old photographs of Lana'i's plantation days (page 294).

★ **2. KEAHIAKAWELO:** Take in an otherworldly landscape dotted with red boulders that appear to have fallen from the sky (page 296).

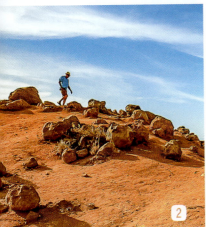

★ **3. POLIHUA BEACH:** Escape to what feels like the end of the earth at this secluded beach on the island's northern coast (page 300).

LANA'I 3 WAYS

HALF DAY

If you're visiting Lana'i as a day trip from Maui, get an early start by taking the 6:30am ferry from Ma'alaea Harbor. Make ferry reservations beforehand.

1 Have breakfast at **Blue Ginger Café,** with heaping loco moco plates of fried eggs, hamburger meat, rice, and gravy.

2 Carve out an hour and hike the **Kapiha'a Fisherman's Trail,** a moderate to challenging 1.5-mi (2.4-km) round-trip trail near Lana'i City. This is a great experience, and often you'll find other travelers enjoying the walk and views.

3 Enjoy a delicious lunch at **Pele's Other Garden,** where an assortment of fresh salads, sandwiches, and pizza awaits.

4 Spend what time you have after lunch at **Hulopo'e Beach Park** before catching the 1pm ferry back to Maui.

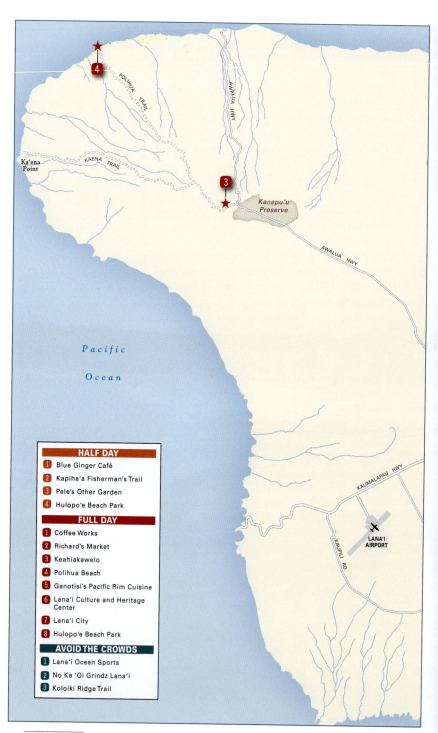

288 LANA'I

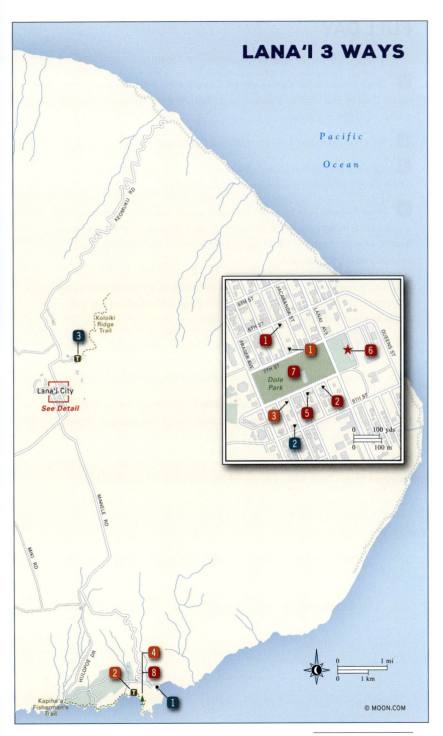

FULL DAY

You'll need a 4WD vehicle to use on Lana'i for the day.

1 Grab breakfast at **Coffee Works.** Consider the fresh omelet of the day or the Shuffle Dat Waffle, a delicious Belgian waffle that arrives with a scoop of vanilla ice cream.

2 Pick up water and snacks at **Richard's Market.**

3 On your way to the island's west side, stop by **Keahiakawelo** (Garden of the Gods) to take in the otherworldly landscape.

4 Here's where your Jeep will be put to good use. From Keahiakawelo, it's about 25 minutes down a switchbacking, rutted dirt track to **Polihua Beach,** where a tranquil white-sand beach perfect for strolling and sunbathing is your reward.

5 Once you've left your footprints in the sand, drive for an hour back to Lana'i City for a late lunch at **Ganotisi's Pacific Rim Cuisine.** Try the cheeseburger or butter garlic shrimp plate.

6 After lunch, spend an hour at **Lana'i Culture and Heritage Center,** where you can explore natural habitats and museum exhibits, and learn more about the unique heritage and culture of the island.

7 Spend 30 minutes strolling **Lana'i City** to check out the local shops, where you can pick up shirts, caps, hoodies, island-themed Christmas ornaments, specialty candles, and more.

8 Return your Jeep to Manele Harbor, and people-watch at the nearby **Hulopo'e Beach Park** while you await the 5:30pm ferry back to Maui.

LANA'I 3 WAYS 291

AVOID THE CROWDS

1 If you're staying at one of the Four Seasons properties on the island, book a one-of-a-kind experience with **Lanaʻi Ocean Sports.** These private charted services offer the perfect opportunity for you and your loved ones to experience the island's glorious offshore beauty.

2 Enjoy a stellar lunch at **No Ka ʻOi Grindz Lanaʻi.**

3 In the afternoon, hike **Koloiki Ridge Trail,** a scenic 5-mi (8-km) round-trip trail that is moderate and not often heavily trafficked.

ORIENTATION AND PLANNING

ORIENTATION

The island's only town, **Lana'i City,** is in the middle of the island at about 1,700 ft (520 m) elevation, 20 minutes north of **Manele Harbor** and the **Four Seasons Resort Lana'i** and about 10 minutes east of the **Lana'i Airport.** The inland wellness resort **Sensei Lana'i,** located less than 1 mi (1.6 km) northeast of Lana'i City, is also about 10 minutes from the airport. **Hulopo'e Beach Park** is a 10-minute walk west from the harbor, and with the exception of the restaurants and shops at the Four Seasons Resort Lana'i, all of the island's stores and facilities are in Lana'i City. The rest of the island is a network of dirt roads perfect for off-road exploring, with many sights 45 minutes to an hour outside Lana'i City.

PLANNING YOUR TIME

Most people visit Lana'i as a day trip from Maui. If you take the 6:30am ferry from Ma'alaea Harbor, you have 8-10 hours to explore the island before catching the ferry back. You'll have enough time to visit Hulopo'e Beach and do some snorkeling, hiking, and sunbathing, as well as time to rent a Jeep and explore the island's east shore. (Book the Jeep about two months prior to your stay.) If you spend a couple of nights on Lana'i, you'll have enough time to explore the island's remote and isolated spots and still be able to relax and enjoy the island's slow pace.

HIGHLIGHTS

LANA'I CITY

★ Lana'i Culture and Heritage Center

730 Lana'i Ave.; 808/565-7177; www. lanaichc.org; hours vary, check website; free

There's no better place to learn about the history of Lana'i than at the Lana'i Culture and Heritage Center. In a building adjacent to the Hotel Lana'i, the exceptionally informative little museum features displays pertaining to the days of ancient Hawaii through the end of the Dole plantation. Black-and-white photos from Lana'i's ranching days are joined by stone adzes, poi pounders, and a 10-ft (3-m) 'ihe pololu (wooden spear) used as a weapon similar to a jousting lance. More than just a collection of historical photos and artifacts, the center also highlights how the culture of Lana'i has been influenced by historic events.

Luahiwa Petroglyphs

The good thing about the Luahiwa Petroglyphs is they are only 10 minutes north from Lana'i City and accessible with a regular car. The bad part is they have been permanently scarred by modern graffiti, and they no longer resemble the

294   LANA'I

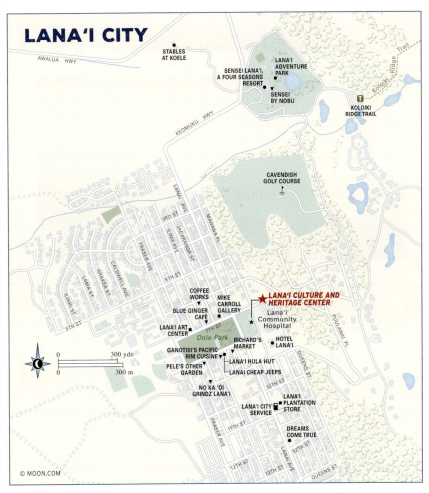

rock art they once were. There are nearly 1,000 drawings at Luahiwa, and stepping from one rock to another reveals different tales emblazoned on the out-of-place boulder formations. While 95 percent of the drawings date before Western contact, some etchings, such as those featuring horses, suggest that the petroglyphs are a multigenerational canvas that records Lana'i's varied history. From Lana'i City, take Keomuku Highway to Luahiwa.

NORTHWEST LANA'I
Kanepu'u Preserve

Six mi (9.7 km) down Polihua Road, just before reaching Keahiakawelo (Garden of the Gods), Kanepu'u Preserve is the only remaining dryland forest of its kind in Hawaii. Thanks to a fence erected in 1918 by Lana'i Ranch manager George Munro, this 590-acre (240-ha) preserve is home to 48 species of native Hawaiian plants that covered most of the island prior to the arrival of the invasive kiawe (mesquite) tree

HIGHLIGHTS 295

BEST SUNSET VIEWS

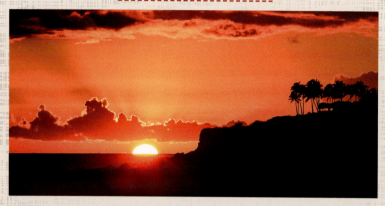

Lana'i sunset

Between its striking tide pools, curved shoreline, and stunning ocean views, **Hulopo'e Beach Park** (page 299) is the best place to experience a sunset for people staying on the island. The beach is in front of the Four Seasons Resort, so access is relatively easy. Arrive 30 minutes or more before sunset and experience something sublime.

and root-destroying goats and sheep. Managed by The Nature Conservancy, the preserve features a short, self-guided trail where visitors can see native hardwoods such as lama (Hawaiian ebony) and olopua (Hawaiian olive). The trail only takes about 15 minutes to walk, and it makes a nice stop before exploring the Garden of the Gods.

★ Keahiakawelo (Garden of the Gods)

Although we've successfully put a rover on Mars, Keahiakawelo is the closest most of us will ever get to walking on the red planet. Despite being only 7 mi (11.3 km) from the pine-lined streets of Lana'i City, the Garden of the Gods looks like a moonscape. Erosion created ravines and rock spires in deep reds, purples, and sulfuric yellows. The best time to visit this dry, dusty, and often windswept area is at sunset, when the rich palette of color is enhanced by the afternoon light.

Keahiakawelo is almost completely devoid of vegetation, but the strangest part of the panorama is the expanse of boulders that tumble over the barren hillside. It's unclear how they got here, but the ancient Hawaiians had a number of theories. According to legend, the rocks were dropped by gods as they tended their heavenly gardens, providing the site's English name, Garden of the Gods.

Keahiakawelo remains a must-see for its consuming sense of seclusion. The road here can be rutted and rough, and a 4WD vehicle is needed if you're visiting after a heavy rain.

Ka'ena Iki Heiau

On the dusty stretch of road between Keahiakawelo and Polihua Beach, a side road branches off to the left and leads to the island's westernmost promontory, **Ka'ena Point.** The deep waters off Ka'ena make this a favorite among islanders for fishing. The main reason to venture down Ka'ena Trail, however, is to see Ka'ena Iki Heiau, a large stone platform constructed in the 17th century and the largest remaining heiau (temple) on Lana'i. It doesn't take long to explore the area around the heiau, but it makes a nice side trip.

SOUTHWEST LANA'I

Lana'i Cat Sanctuary

1 Kaupili Rd.; 808/215-9066; www.lanaianimalrescue.org; 10am-3pm daily; free

Known as the "Little Lions" of Lana'i, all of the felines at the quirky Lana'i Cat Sanctuary are rescues that were once feral. Today they exchange petting for purr-filled moments at their comfortable outdoor sanctuary. Volunteers are encouraged to drop by and help pet and play with the cats.

TOURS

LOST ON LANA'I

888/716-6336; www.lostonlanai.com

To visit the top tourist spots on the island, Lost on Lana'i can arrange a half-day tour ($260) of the island for visitors staying on Lana'i or those coming from Maui, creating an itinerary around your schedule. Convenient hotel or airport pickups on Lana'i or at the harbor if you take

Keahiakawelo (Garden of the Gods) (top); Luahiwa Petroglyphs (middle); Lana'i Cat Sanctuary (bottom)

the ferry from Maui are a perk. The experience includes a visit to the cat sanctuary, Lana'i Culture and Heritage Center, and Lana'i City, and might also include other island hot spots, such as the Garden of the Gods and Shipwreck Beach on the north shore.

BEST BEACHES

Unless you have a 4WD or high-clearance vehicle, Lana'i only has one accessible beach, which is also the only one with any facilities. If you procure a Jeep or a local's truck, there are a number of undeveloped beaches where you can run around naked with no one there to care.

NORTHEAST LANA'I
Kaiolohia (Shipwreck Beach)

The most popular beach among island visitors after Hulopo'e is Kaiolohia, also called Shipwreck Beach. Traditionally this area was known as Kaiolohia. The current moniker originates with the unnamed World War II Liberty ship that was intentionally grounded on the fringing reef. Numerous vessels have met their demise on this shallow stretch of coral, but this concrete oil tanker has deteriorated more slowly than most. Stoic in its haunted appearance, the ship remains firmly lodged in the reef as a warning to passing vessels of the danger.

Because of the persistent northeasterly trade winds, Kaiolohia is rarely suitable for snorkeling or swimming. Your time is better spent combing the beach for flotsam: Japanese glass balls used as fishing floats are the beachcomber's ultimate reward. To reach the Liberty ship is about a mile's walk (1.6 km) along the sandy shore, although numerous rocks interrupt the thin strip of sand to give the appearance of multiple beaches.

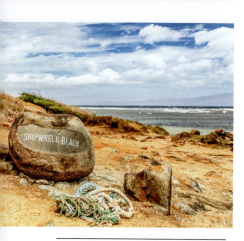

Polihua Beach (top); Kaiolohia (Shipwreck Beach) (bottom)

TOP BEACH
HULOPO'E BEACH PARK

To make your friends back home jealous, snap a picture of this beach. Hulopo'e Beach Park is the undisputed favorite hangout for islanders and has been named the country's best beach. Within walking distance of the Manele Harbor, Hulopo'e is the only beach on the island with restrooms and showers. Despite being the island's most popular, it's far from crowded. The right side of the beach is used by guests of the Four Seasons Resort Lana'i and Sensei Lana'i, who have access to the white umbrellas and lounge chairs. Similarly, guests of Trilogy Excursions' snorkel tour from Maui inhabit the left-hand side of the beach Monday-Friday, leaving the middle section of the beach for visitors to relax in the shade or bake in the sun.

Hulopo'e Bay is a marine reserve and home to one of the few reefs in Maui County that isn't in decline. The reef extends over the left side of the bay, where colorful parrotfish the size of your forearm can easily be spotted and heard nibbling on the vibrant corals. Hulopo'e is also famous for the Hawaiian spinner dolphins that regularly enter the bay. In an effort to protect the natural sleep cycles of the dolphins, swimmers are asked not to approach them. If dolphins happen to swim toward you, consider yourself lucky.

In addition to the sugary sand and perfectly placed palm trees, there are nature trails on each side of the beach. The **Kapiha'a Fisherman's Trail** departs from the right side of the bay, and the **Pu'u Pehe Overlook Trail** starts from the left side. A fantastic system of tide pools stretches around the left point of the bay, and one is even deep enough to teach young children to snorkel. The easiest way to get to the tide pools is to use the stairway on the trail to Pu'u Pehe Overlook.

BEST BEACHES   299

NORTHWEST LANA'I

★ Polihua Beach

Polihua is so remote that even Lana'i residents consider it "out there." A vast, windswept, and often completely empty stretch of sand, Polihua is utterly unrivaled in its seclusion. If you've ever fantasized about placing the only set of footprints on a deserted beach, this is the place to do it. The name Polihua derives from a Hawaiian term for "eggs in the bosom," a reference to the green sea turtles that haul out on the sand to bury eggs on the isolated shore.

The strong currents at Polihua make the water unsafe for swimming, and oftentimes the afternoon trade winds turn the entire beach into a curtain of blowing sand. The morning hours are best for a relaxing stroll through the sand dunes, and by sunset the winds have usually died down enough to watch the sun sink behind the northwest horizon. With views that stretch across the Kalohi Channel toward Moloka'i, this is one of the last beaches in Hawaii where it's still possible to feel alone.

A 4WD vehicle is imperative to reach Polihua. Travel 7 mi (11.3 km) from Lana'i City on Polihua Road to Keahiakawelo. Continue on the same road for another 25 minutes as it switchbacks down the rutted dirt track before reaching its terminus a few yards short of the beach. There are no services, so if you visit Polihua, remember to bring water and food, and to pack out everything you brought with you.

BEST HIKES AND WALKS

LANA'I CITY

Munro Trail

Distance: *11 mi (17.8 km) round-trip*
Duration: *up to 7 hours*
Elevation Gain: *1,538 ft (468 m)*
Effort: *moderate-strenuous*
Trailhead: *just north of Lana'i City; entry is past the stables of the Four Seasons Resort Lana'i*

Munro Trail doesn't look like anywhere else on Lana'i, or in Hawaii. This 11-mi (17.8-km) dirt road is more like the Pacific Northwest than the tropics. Wandering around the stands of Cook pines is one of Lana'i's most iconic adventures. Get up early, throw on a light jacket, and head into the uplands, where the smell of eucalyptus wafts through an understory of ironwoods and pines. For clear skies and dry conditions, it's best to hike Munro Trail in the morning hours before enveloping clouds blow in on the trades.

To reach Munro Trail, travel past the Sensei Lana'i resort on Keomoku Highway until you reach a sign for Cemetery Road, where you make a right just before the first mile marker. On Cemetery Road, the pavement turns to dirt and then branches off to the left, bringing you to the start of the trail. Park at the trailhead and make the 5.5-mi (8.9-km) hike to the summit, stopping at lookouts along the way.

The first lookout is **Koloiki Ridge**, about 2.5 mi (4 km) into the trail. A small red-and-white sign on the left side of the trail points the way

300 LANA'I

to the ridge, and after a brief 0.25-mi (0.4-km) jaunt, you are rewarded with grandiose views back into Maunalei Gulch and out to the islands of Maui and Moloka'i. This lookout is also accessible as part of the **Koloiki Ridge Trail,** which starts behind the Sensei Lana'i resort.

Back on the main trail, continue for a couple of miles beneath a shroud of forest until you pass some communication towers. Finally, after you've climbed an uphill section of trail, 5.5 mi (8.9 km) from the end of Cemetery Road, you'll find the 3,370-ft (1,027-m) summit of **Lana'ihale,** or The Hale, as it's known to locals. This is the only point in Hawaii where it's possible to see five other islands on the clearest days, and during winter even the snowcapped peaks of Mauna Kea and Mauna Loa on the Big Island can be seen, over 100 mi (161 km) southeast.

Koloiki Ridge Trail

Distance: *5 mi (8 km) round-trip*
Duration: *2-3 hours*
Elevation Gain: *700 ft (213 m)*
Effort: *moderate*
Trailhead: *behind the Sensei Lana'i resort*

An offshoot of the **Munro Trail,** the Koloiki Ridge Trail is a 5-mi (8-km) out-and-back hike that begins directly behind the Sensei Lana'i resort. On a nice day, this is the perfect way to spend two or three hours. Walking the trail is like taking a historical tour through Lana'i's past.

To reach the trailhead, go to the main entrance of the Sensei Lana'i resort and then follow the service road toward the golf clubhouse. Once you reach the main clubhouse, another paved service road running behind the fairway ultimately leads to the trailhead. Along the initial paved section of trail, you'll encounter white-and-red signs on the trail as part of an interpretive map available at the hotel's concierge desk.

Once the dirt trail begins, you'll find yourself walking beneath a canopy of ironwood trees and Cook pines that predate the luxury hotels. Planted in 1912 by the botanist George Munro, the pines were used as a means of securing water by trapping moisture from the passing clouds, and even today they still

Munro Trail (top); Koloiki Ridge Trail (bottom)

BEST HIKES AND WALKS 301

play a major role in providing water for the island's residents.

Making a right at the red-and-white sign marked "10" places you directly on the Munro Trail. About 0.5 mi (0.8 km) down Munro Trail at sign number 17, an arrow points the way down to the dramatic **Koloiki Ridge.** Once out from beneath the canopy of trees, you'll notice that the ridge is flanked on both sides by dramatic gulches. From this often windy vantage point at the end of the trail, the islands of Moloka'i and Maui appear on the horizon beyond the deep blue Pailolo Channel. When facing the islands, on the left side of the ridge is **Naio Gulch,** a dry rock-strewn canyon where you can occasionally catch a glimpse of the island's elusive mouflon sheep. On the right is **Maunalei Gulch,** a deep cleft in the island that once had the island's only free-flowing stream. If you look closely on the valley floor, you can still see an old service road leading to a pump house. Water from Maunalei once fed the island's sugar plantation.

AROUND HULOPO'E BEACH

Pu'u Pehe Overlook Trail

Distance: *0.9 mi (1.6 km) round-trip*
Duration: *25 minutes*
Elevation Gain: *134 ft (40 m)*
Effort: *moderate*
Trailhead: *13 mi (21 km) south of Lana'i City at Hulopo'e Beach Park*

This often photographed sea stack is an iconic symbol of Lana'i and one of the most scenic places on the island. It's not possible to climb onto Pu'u Pehe (also known as Sweetheart Rock), but the Pu'u Pehe Overlook Trail offers hikers a sweeping panorama of the rock and the surrounding coast. To reach the trailhead, walk along the dirt road at the south end of Hulopo'e Beach Park (the side opposite the resort) for 100 yards (90 m) until it reaches a set of stairs leading down to the tide pools. From here the road becomes

Pu'u Pehe Overlook Trail

a trail that wraps left across the headland before reaching a hidden sandy cove popular with bodyboarders and nudist sunbathers. To get down to this sandy cove, known as Shark's Bay, requires a scramble through a chute in the rocky cliff that involves some risk.

To reach the overlook, carefully follow the edge of the cliff until it reaches a promontory about 100 ft (30 m) above the shimmering reef below. Aside from the sweeping vista, it's also possible to get a good view from here of the heiau that stands atop Pu'u Pehe, an archaeological site that is a mystery given that it's nearly impossible to access the top of the rock.

Kapiha'a Fisherman's Trail
Distance: *1.5 mi (2.4 km) round-trip*
Duration: *1 hour*
Elevation Gain: *negligible*
Effort: *moderate*

Trailhead: *Hulopo'e Beach in front of the Four Seasons Resort Lana'i*

The Kapiha'a Fisherman's Trail begins on the side of Hulopo'e Beach in front of the Four Seasons Resort Lana'i and meanders past the mega-mansions on the point. Well-marked by a natural stone walkway, this 1.5-mi (2.4-km) trail hugs the rocky coast as it weaves its way through the ancient village of Kapiha'a. Little remains of the village today, but various historical markers point out the location of heiau still visible in the area.

Even though this trail catches the coastal breezes off the surrounding water, there is little shade. Given the rugged nature of the path, wear closed-toe shoes. After the trail reaches a dramatic terminus atop sea cliffs on the back nine of the golf course, an easier return route is to follow the cart path back to the golf clubhouse.

snorkeling at Manele Bay

SNORKELING AND DIVING

There isn't anywhere on Lana'i to rent equipment for the day, so your best bet is to bring your own. The snorkeling equipment at Hulopo'e Beach is only for Trilogy's day guests who come from Maui, and the gear at the Four Seasons beach kiosk is exclusively for guests of the Four Seasons Resort Lana'i and Sensei Lana'i.

SNORKELING SPOTS

Hulopo'e Beach Park

When it comes to snorkeling, Hulopo'e Beach Park easily trumps any other place on the island for the health of the reef, clarity of the water, and variety of fish. Thanks to its protected status as a marine preserve, the reef is in better shape than other places on the island, and snorkelers will revel in the large schools of manini (convict tang) and vibrant uhu (parrotfish) that flit around the shallow reef. The best snorkeling in the bay is on the left side of the beach. Since Hulopo'e faces south, it can be prone to large surf and shore-break April-October. The shore-break can make entry and exit to the water a little challenging, and the visibility won't be as good as on days that are calmer.

Nevertheless, even a mediocre day at Hulopo'e is better than a good day at many other places. The reef never gets deeper than 25 ft (7.6 m). Occasionally Hawaiian spinner dolphins venture into the bay, although they usually hang out over the sand on the right, closer to the hotel.

Manele Bay

Not far from Hulopo'e but equally as gorgeous is the vibrant reef at Manele Bay. Don't confuse this with snorkeling in Manele Harbor; that would be disgusting. The reef at Manele Bay is on the opposite side of the breakwall between the harbor and the cliffs. Entry from shore can be tricky, since you have to come off the rocks, but if you follow the driveway of the harbor all the way to the far end, there is a little opening in the rocks where it's possible to make a graceful entry. Schools of tropical reef fish gather in abundance, and the spinner dolphins sometimes hang out in this area as well. Although Manele Bay is 0.25 mi (0.4 km) from Hulopo'e Beach, it's still part of the marine preserve, so the same rules apply: Don't stand on the coral, and don't feed the fish. It's best not to touch anything at all.

DIVE SITES

Lana'i has some of the best diving in the state, with 14 named dive sites along the southwestern coast. The most famous are First and Second Cathedrals. Trilogy Excursions is also the island's only dive operator, offering private charters with high prices, mainly as an amenity for guests of the Four Seasons Resort Lana'i and Sensei Lana'i. Check with dive operators in Lahaina about the best way to dive off Lana'i.

First Cathedral

At First Cathedral, just offshore from Manele Harbor, the cavern entrance

304 LANA'I

is at 58 ft (18 m). Inside, beams of sunlight filter down through the ceiling like light passing through a stained-glass window. There have even been a few underwater weddings here.

The best way to exit the cathedral is via a hole in the wall known locally as The Shotgun, where divers place their hands on the sides of the cathedral and allow the current to wash through a narrow opening. In addition to the main cathedral, there are other swimthroughs and arches where you can catch a glimpse of spiny lobsters, frogfish, colorful parrotfish, and, if you're lucky, a pod of spinner dolphins passing overhead.

Second Cathedral

Down the coast at Second Cathedral, the underwater dome is about the same size but intersected by so many openings it looks like Swiss cheese. Divers can pass in and out of the cathedral from a variety of different entry points. The highlight is a rare black coral tree that dangles from the cathedral ceiling. Large schools of ta'ape (blue-striped snapper) congregate on the back side of the cathedral, and you can swim through a school that numbers in the hundreds. Visibility at both of these sites regularly reaches 80-120 ft (24-37 m), and the water can be so clear that you see most of the dive site standing on the pontoon of the boat.

CHARTERS AND TOURS

TRILOGY EXCURSIONS

808/661-4743; www.sailtrilogy.com; 6:30am-6pm; $289 pp
To explore the island's remoter reefs, only accessible by boat, Trilogy Excursions provides snorkel charters operating on Lana'i. Consider the 3.5-hour snorkeling and sailing excursion, which heads around the southwestern coast to the towering sea cliffs of Kaunolu, also known as Shark Fin Cove due to the dorsal fin-shaped rock in the middle of the bay. Given that Kaunolu is exposed to the deeper waters offshore, snorkelers intermittently see pelagic species such as spinner dolphins, bottlenose dolphins, eagle rays, manta rays, and whale sharks. Since bookings are sporadic due to the low numbers on Lana'i, call the Maui office ahead of time to inquire about a charter. Another popular tour is an eight-hour, all-day excursion, **Discover Lanai,** which includes swimming and snorkeling at Hulopo'e Beach and a plantation-style barbecue picnic. It operates out of both Lahaina and Ma'alaea Harbors. Trilogy Excursions also offers high-priced private dive charters.

LANA'I OCEAN SPORTS

Manele Harbor; 808/866-8256; www. lanaioceansports.com
Lana'i Ocean Sports offers the Lana'i Snorkel Experience daily (noon; $189-225) for Four Seasons Resort Lana'i and Sensei Lana'i guests only and departs from the Manele Harbor. Shuttle service is offered from the Four Seasons. The snorkeling tour lasts 2-3 hours and heads to Kaunolu. Guides provide information on the marinelife, which includes spinner dolphins, sea turtles, and a plethora of colorful fish. The tour includes a picnic lunch and refreshments on the way back to the harbor.

SNORKELING AND DIVING **305**

SURFING

There currently isn't anywhere to rent a board on Lana'i. You can either bring your own on the ferry or call the Lana'i Ambassador desk (808/565-2388) at the Four Seasons Resort Lana'i to inquire.

SURF SPOTS
Hulopo'e Beach Park
Hulopo'e Beach is the island's most popular surf spot. Since it faces south, it's exposed to southerly swells, which means April-October is the best season for finding surf. This left point break can be challenging, however, and it's not for beginners. The wave breaks over a shallow coral reef and the takeoff can be steep, although when Hulopo'e is firing, it can be one of the best summer waves in Maui County. The long lefthander will hold its size 2-12 ft (0.6-3.7 m). Be careful of the inside section, which can carry you straight into the shore-break.

Lopa
Lopa is the island's preeminent beginner wave, and just because it's user-friendly doesn't mean that it can't be a great ride. A beach break with multiple peaks, the waves at Lopa aren't usually as steep and are better suited for longboards and nose-riding. Winter months can be flat, but on summer days there's almost always something to ride. You'll have to bring your own board and provide your own transportation. To reach Lopa, take Keomoku Highway to where the paved road ends, then take a right and proceed for 9 mi (14.5 km).

BIKING

Your best bets for biking on the island are through guided tours with trained professionals who know the landscape.

BIKE ROUTES
Relish the striking views of the islands of Moloka'i and Maui on these bike routes, which also take you into the rich tropical landscapes of the island.

Koloiki Ridge Trail
Between its scenic ocean vistas and views of the island's hilly landscapes, the Koloiki Ridge Trail is one of the more popular rides on the island. Start at Lana'i Adventure Park behind the Sensei Lana'i resort. Mountain bikes are ideal.

Keahiakawelo Rock Garden Ride
This rugged, windy, bike ride through the Keahiakawelo rock garden (7 mi/11.3 km one-way) includes short uphill pushes and dips. Rinse and repeat. Scenic all around, the amazing rock towers, spires, and formations found here were formed by centuries of erosion. Expect a thoroughly engaging—and breezy—ride. Start at Lana'i Adventure Park behind the Sensei Lana'i resort. Mountain bikes are required.

306 LANA'I

BIKE TOURS

LANA'I ADVENTURE PARK
808/563-0096; www.lanai adventurepark.com; $120 pp

Unless you brought your own bicycle over on the ferry, the best option for biking on Lana'i is with Lana'i Adventure Park, which offers unique two-hour bike tours on electric mountain bikes. Beginning at the base of Kaiholena Gulch, the tours go on one of four scenic trails and are accompanied by candid guides, who share the history and stories of the island.

HORSEBACK RIDING

STABLES AT KOELE
1 Keomoku Hwy.; 808/565-2000; $150 pp

Lana'i is steeped in its ranching heritage. The island was once a huge sheep and cattle ranch where paniolo roamed the terrain on horseback. Cattle no longer roam, but the island's ranching heritage lives on at the Stables at Koele, where local guides who are authentic paniolo offer guided trail rides (1.5 hours) through the Lana'i City hinterlands. Keep an eye out for axis deer or mouflon sheep as you ride at your own pace on excursions geared to your skill level. The knowledgeable guides fortify the excursion with tales of the island's history.

biking with Lana'i Adventure Park

LANA'I NIGHTLIFE

Don't visit Lana'i for the nightlife. Evening is that inconvenient stretch of darkness that brings outdoor adventure to a halt. There are no nightclubs or dinner shows, and aside from the hotels, there is only one place you can even get a beer (Pele's Other Garden). Nevertheless, there is still a semblance of activity on certain nights of the week—just don't expect it to stretch past 10pm. On Wednesday, the party is at **Pele's Other Garden** (811 Houston St.; 808/565-9628; www.pelesothergarden.com), with live music rocking the bistro in the evening. On Friday, head to **Ganotisi's Pacific Rim Cuisine** (page 312), where the live jazz band provides the best entertainment in town.

GOLF

MANELE GOLF COURSE
1 Challenge Dr.; 808/565-4000; 8am-6pm daily; $375 guests, $525 nonguests

Unless you're a guest of the Four Seasons Resort Lana'i or Sensei Lana'i or have a Hawaii ID, you can't golf at the famous Jack Nicklaus-designed Manele Golf Course. If you are able to play, prepare for a round with sweeping ocean views and tee shots over the water. Finish at the 19th-hole clubhouse where you can often see dolphins splashing in the bay.

CAVENDISH GOLF COURSE
1 Keomoku Hwy.; 808/565-3000; 8am-7pm daily; free

Another course on Lana'i is open to everyone. More of the no-shirt, no-shoes, beer-a-hole type of course, the nine-hole Cavendish Golf Course is suited for recreational golfers who want a quick practice round. Best of all, the course is free. Constructed in 1947

horseback riding on Lana'i (left); golf on Lana'i (right)

shopping in Lana'i

LANA'I FOOD OPTIONS

NAME	LOCATION	CONTACT INFO
LANA'I CITY		
★ **Ganotisi's Pacific Rim Cuisine**	831B Houston St.	808/565-7120
★ **Blue Ginger Café**	409 7th St.	808/565-6363; www.bluegingercafelanai.com
No Ka 'Oi Grindz Lana'i	335 9th St.	808/565-9413
Pele's Other Garden	811 Houston St.	808/565-9628; www.pelesothergarden.com
Sensei by Nobu	Sensei Lana'i, 1 Keomoku Hwy.	808/565-4500; www.fourseasons.com/sensei
Coffee Works	604 Ilima Ave.	808/565-6962; www.coffeeworkshawaii.com
Richard's Market	434 8th St.	808/565-3781
AROUND HULOPO'E BEACH		
Nobu Lana'i	Four Seasons Resort Lana'i, 1 Manele Bay Rd.	808/565-2832; www.fourseasons.com/lanai
★ **One Forty**	Four Seasons Resort Lana'i, 1 Manele Bay Rd.	808/565-2000; www.fourseasons.com/lanai

as a recreational option for island pineapple workers, the Cavendish still operates as a place for islanders to practice their game and casually unwind. Although the fairways and tee boxes can be speckled with crabgrass and patches of dirt, the greens are still properly maintained. There are no carts or cart paths, so you get a workout walking the course's moderate elevation changes. You'll have to supply your own clubs, balls, tees, and beer.

SHOPPING

Lana'i is the only Hawaiian Island where you could visit every store on the island without having to move the car. With the exception of the small stores within the Four Seasons Resort Lana'i, every shop is within walking distance of the parking area around Dole Park in Lana'i City.

LANA'I CITY
Clothing and Souvenirs
LANA'I PLANTATION STORE
1036 Lana'i Ave.; 808/565-7227; 6am-10pm daily
The only gas station on the island, the Lana'i Plantation Store offers a great selection of island souvenirs

FOOD	HOURS	PRICE
Hawaiian/Pacific Rim	8am–8pm daily	$11–34
local style	6am–8pm Thurs.–Mon., 6am–2pm Tues.–Wed.	$6–18, cash only
local style	10:30am–1pm daily	$6–11
bistro	breakfast and lunch 11am–2pm Mon.–Fri., dinner 4:30pm–8pm Mon.–Sat.	$9–22
resort restaurant	6am–11am, noon–5pm, and 6pm–10pm daily	$16–70
coffee shops	hours vary, typically 7am–3pm daily	$2–10
markets	6am–9pm daily	$5–20
resort restaurant	5:30pm–9pm daily	$15–50
resort restaurant	6:30am–11am and 5:30pm–9:30pm daily	$29–76

and clothing along with the usual snacks and beverages.

LANA'I HULA HUT
418 8th St.; 808/565-9170; 10am-6pm Mon.-Sat.
By Dole Park, the Lana'i Hula Hut sells everything from hand-painted ceramic ornaments to women's jewelry and wind chimes. The Balinese woodwork gives an exotic feel to the interior.

Art and Jewelry

MIKE CARROLL GALLERY
443 7th St.; 808/565-7122; www. mikecarrollgallery.com; 10am-5pm daily
The most prominent gallery on the island is Mike Carroll Gallery, between Canoes restaurant and the Lana'i City theater. There's a good

chance that you'll find Mike painting right in the store. Many of his pieces focus on the simple yet captivating beauty of Lana'i. He is an in-demand artist who is constantly crafting original works. The gallery will occasionally feature visiting artists who come to relax and hone their craft in this charming plantation-style studio.

LANA'I ART CENTER
339 7th St.; 808/565-7503; www. lanaiart.org; 10am-4pm Mon.-Sat.
For a look at local artwork, visit the Lana'i Art Center to see just how much talent exists on an island of only 3,500 people. Fine photography and handmade jewelry accompany paintings and woodwork. A portion of this nonprofit's proceeds fund local art programs for Lana'i's youth.

LANA'I LODGING OPTIONS

NAME	LOCATION	CONTACT INFO
LANA'I CITY		
Dreams Come True	1168 Lana'i Ave.	808/565-6961; www.dreamscometruelanai.com
★ **Hotel Lana'i**	828 Lana'i Ave.	808/565-7211; www.hotellanai.com
Sensei Lana'i, A Four Seasons Resort	1 Keomoku Hwy.	808/565-4500; www.fourseasons.com/sensei
AROUND HULOPO'E BEACH		
★ **Four Seasons Resort Lana'i**	1 Manele Bay Rd.	808/565-2000; www.fourseasons.com/lanai
Hulopo'e Beach Park	n/a	reservations: info@lanaibeachpark.com

This gallery is a worthwhile stop after the Saturday farmers market or while walking off a Blue Ginger cheeseburger.

FOOD

STANDOUTS

Lana'i City

GANOTISI'S PACIFIC RIM CUISINE

831B Houston St.; 808/565-7120; 8am-8pm daily; $11-34

The fanciest meal in Lana'i City is at Ganotisi's Pacific Rim Cuisine. The fare is more expensive than at hole-in-the-wall plate-lunch stands, but when the waiter serves a plate of miso-marinated sea bass with mushroom potato hash, cost seems less important. Ganotisi's has the island's most comprehensive wine list. Reservations are strongly recommended, particularly on Friday evenings, when the live jazz band performs.

BLUE GINGER CAFÉ

409 7th St.; 808/565-6363; www.bluegingercafelanai.com; 6am-8pm Thurs.-Mon., 6am-2pm Tues.-Wed.; $6-18, cash only

While the exterior might not look like much, at Blue Ginger Café the swinging screen door and funky plantation-style appearance are all part of the hole-in-the-wall charm. Breakfast is heaping loco moco plates of fried eggs, hamburger meat, rice, and gravy, and the homemade hamburger patties are the lunchtime draw that has kept patrons coming in from Dole Park since 1991. It's a true local hideout.

TYPE	PRICE	BEST FOR
B&B	$185	couples, budget travelers
hotel	from $355	couples
resort	from $1,093	health-conscious travelers
resort	from $2,393	couples, honeymooners, luxury-lovers
campground	$80 per night	budget travelers, groups, families

Around Hulopo'e Beach

ONE FORTY

808/565-2000; www.fourseasons.com/lanai; 6:30am-11am and 5:30pm-9:30pm daily; $29-76

One Forty has exceptional plates of Hawaiian Regional Cuisine. The ahi poke appetizer served with dinner can compete with the best in the islands, and the hand-cut steaks and plates of fresh fish are the best that you'll find on Lana'i. For breakfast, start your day with morning tacos filled with local venison ($25).

Four Seasons Resort Lana'i (left); Hotel Lana'i (right)

FOOD 313

LODGING

While Lana'i is home to two of the most luxurious resorts in the state, there are a handful of more affordable options if you want to stay in the town. Lately, almost every vacation rental option on Lana'i has gone on **VRBO** (www.vrbo.com), the first place to check to find a little plantation home on the hill. There are still a few you can book directly by phone or through their own sites.

STANDOUTS

Lana'i

HOTEL LANA'I

828 Lana'i Ave.; 808/565-7211; www.hotellanai.com; from $355

Small and historic Hotel Lana'i is in the center of tranquil Lana'i City. This was the island's first hotel, built in 1923 for visiting guests of the ruling Dole Pineapple Company. While you won't find the same amenities as at the resorts, the 10 rooms of this plantation-style building retain a historical feel without sacrificing comfort. The best rooms are those with their own private lanai, and there is also a cottage removed from the main building. Wi-Fi and breakfast are both complimentary, and shuttle service to the harbor ($15 pp) is available, as are complimentary shuttles from the airport.

Around Hulopo'e Beach

FOUR SEASONS RESORT LANA'I

1 Manele Bay Rd.; 808/565-2000; www.fourseasons.com/lanai; from $2,393

Lavish, luxurious, and delightfully over the top, the Four Seasons Resort Lana'i is one of Hawaii's most exclusive. Owner Larry Ellison devoted millions of dollars to major renovations when he took over from David Murdock, and the Asian decor that once dominated has been replaced by Hawaiian designs. The massive tech infusion, such as futuristic Toto toilets, makes every part of staying at the Manele resort an experience unto itself. Sit beachfront by the pool and sip on a cocktail while gazing at Hulopo'e Bay as spinner dolphins splash in the distance and pool staff clean your sunglasses. You'll feel like a celebrity.

TRANSPORTATION

Air

Flying to **Lana'i Airport** (LNY; Lana'i Ave.; 808/565-7942; www.airports.hawaii.gov/lny) requires a jump from neighboring Honolulu. **Hawaiian Airlines** (800/367-5320; www.hawaiianairlines.com) operates turboprop planes with 25-minute flights from Honolulu (HNL) that run a couple of times per day.

Shuttle

If you're staying at the Four Seasons Resort Lana'i or Sensei Lana'i, there is complimentary shuttle service to Lana'i City, the airport, and the harbor. If you're staying at Hotel Lana'i, there's a complimentary shuttle from the airport and a shuttle to the harbor for $15. If you're staying elsewhere or visiting for the day, you'll have to rent a vehicle or take a cab.

Ferry

In light of the Old Town Lahaina fire tragedy in 2023, ferries are only operating from Ma'alaea Harbor (808/661-3756; www.go-lanai.com; one-way $30 adults, $20 children), traveling to Manele Harbor and back. Travel time is usually about an hour, and during whale season (Dec.-Apr.), you can frequently spot humpback whales from the outdoor seating of the upper deck. Although you can buy tickets at the harbor kiosk the morning of your journey, make reservations ahead of time, particularly for the early morning trip. Don't be late; this is one ferry that doesn't wait around. Restrooms are on the ferry and some snack items are available.

Ferry Schedule

- Ma'alaea (Maui) departures: 6:30am, 11am, 3:30pm
- Manele Harbor (Lana'i) departures: 8:30am, 1pm, 5:30pm

Car

There are two main go-to agencies for car rentals on the island. It is imperative you plan ahead to make reservations, even up to a year in advance. You can take your chances and walk into a rental place, but I don't recommend it.

Lanai Cheap Jeeps (418 8th St.; 808/489-2296; www.lanaicheapjeeps.com; 7am-7pm daily) in Lana'i City has four-door Jeep and truck rentals from $225 per day. All models are automatic transmission. The establishment offers free maps. Inquire about guided tours, which offer more freedom in exploring some of Lana'i's scenic spots.

Rental company **808 Day Trip** (10 Manele Rd.; 808/649-0664; www.808daytrip.com; 6am-11pm daily) offers economy cars and SUVs, and even provides delivery. Rates fluctuate but typically begin at $145 per day. The establishment will deliver the vehicle to the harbor per prearranged reservations or to your hotel.

Gas

There is only one station on the entire island: **Lana'i City Service** (1036 Lana'i Ave.; 808/565-7227; 6am-9pm daily) supplies fuel for all 3,500 residents. Don't worry about the price; you're better off just not looking, as it's often $1.50 more per gallon than on Maui. Then again, with only 30 mi (48 km) of paved roads, it isn't uncommon for a tank of gas to last a month or more.

Taxi

The island's only taxi service is **Rabaca's Limousine Service** (808/559-0230), which connects the airport, harbor, and Lana'i City ($15 pp).

Moloka'i sea cliffs

MOLOKAʻI

Visitors often mistake Molokaʻi's lack of typical resort activities for a lack of things to do.

But the protected vibe is incomparably relaxed and epitomizes "old Hawaii," where you find yourself talking to strangers as you would with an old friend. Molokaʻi is a step back to simpler times when life was slower. That doesn't mean it's boring. Imagine surfing perfect waves off an empty white-sand beach, hiking through rainforests to thundering falls in Hawaii's original settlement, or tattooing the sand with a string of footprints on a sunset stroll.

Molokaʻi is Hawaii's most "Hawaiian" island in that it has the highest percentage of ethnic Hawaiians and is one of the last places you might hear Hawaiian spoken on the street. It's a place where culture and ancient tradition are preferred over modern progress.

MOLOKA'I

TOP 3

★ **1. MOLOKAʻI FOREST RESERVE:** Visit one of the few places in the state with an ecosystem identical to what the Polynesians first found over 1,500 years ago (page 331).

★ **2. KALAUPAPA PENINSULA:** See the former leper colony on an air tour for a juxtaposition of Molokaʻi's darkest moments with its most dramatic surroundings (page 332).

★ **3. HALAWA VALLEY FALLS CULTURAL HIKE:** Travel to the roots of Hawaiian culture and swim at the base of a waterfall (page 340).

MOLOKA'I 3 WAYS

ONE DAY

1 Take a morning stroll along the 3-mi-long (4.8-km) and virtually deserted **Papohaku Beach.**

2 Grab a delicious meal for lunch at **Moloka'i Pizza Café.** Consider ordering a chef salad or the O'ahu Pizza, which includes pepperoni with hints of island flavors.

3 Visit the **Moloka'i Museum and Cultural Center,** and experience everything from cultural talks to photo exhibits, and a bevy of other information related to Moloka'i history and culture.

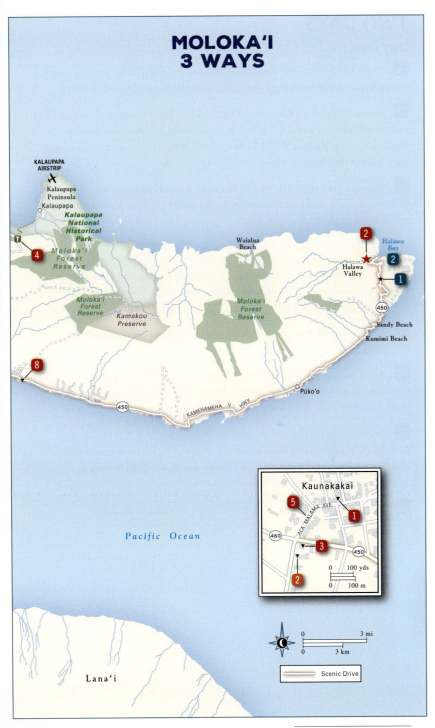

TWO DAYS

Day One

1 Grab breakfast from **Kanemitsu Bakery & Coffee Shop.** Bakery goods abound, but daily soups and specialty sandwiches are bound to entice.

2 Head to Moloka'i Forest Reserve, an ideal haven to feel more connected with nature. The lush and scenic area is home to a must-do experience, the **Halawa Valley Falls Cultural Hike.** Feel free to bring along light snacks and bottled water for this experience.

3 Reward yourself post-hike at **Moloka'i Burger.** Island-themed burgers, salads, and island side dishes are great comfort food and there's great patio seating.

Day Two

4 Enjoy a morning hike on the extraordinary **Kalaupapa Trail**, which offers unique switchbacks and stunning views of epic sea cliffs, considered to be among the tallest in the world.

5 Grab a snack and peruse shops along **Ala Malama Avenue** in Kaunakakai.

6 Stroll through the wonderful outdoor market at **Kumu Farms.** Purchase island souvenirs or sample fresh fruits. Take home homemade jams or island nuts. A wonderful social gathering ground.

7 Sunsets are extraordinary anywhere on the island, but **Papohaku Beach** has it all—from its vast white-sand beach to sublime ocean views, which not only capture the vibrant sunsets but illuminates the sky in a lovely array of colors when it's partly cloudy.

8 Cap off the night with a delicious meal at **Hiro's Ohana Grill.**

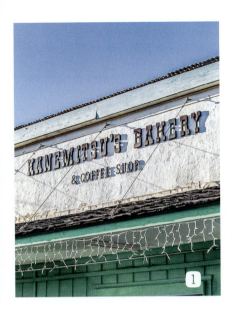

MOLOKA'I 3 WAYS   327

AVOID THE CROWDS

1 An overnight stay at **Pu'u O Hoku Ranch** is unforgettable. The 14,000-acre (5,665-ha) working ranch and farm dominates the eastern tip of the island and is a great opportunity to see a treasured region and learn more about its history.

2 If you're staying in the region and just want some time for you, it's easy to walk to nearby beaches and stroll, or simply sit down and take in the ocean views.

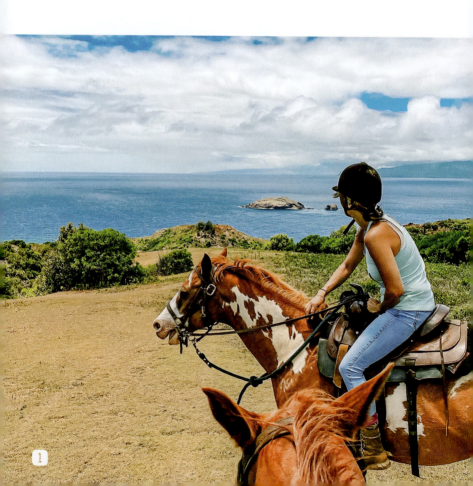

ORIENTATION AND PLANNING

ORIENTATION

The island is roughly 37 mi long (60 km) and 10 (16 km) mi wide. Its unique bean-like shape is due to the separate volcanoes that created the island. **Kamakou,** in the east, is the tallest with an elevation of 4,970 ft (1,813 m). In the west, there's **Maunaloa** at just 1,381 ft (503 m). Though the airport is in **Ho'olehua** toward the center of the island, **Kaunakakai,** located at the center of the southern coast, is the island's main town and the hub of everyday life. It's the location of the island's only gas stations and the bulk of the restaurants, and also the Hotel Moloka'i, the island's largest. The western shore is about 30 minutes away and is best for beaches and sunsets. Eastern Moloka'i has oceanfront cottages and lush **Halawa Valley.** Central Moloka'i, near **Kualapu'u,** has a handful of sights and a restaurant, and it's on the way to the misty uplands and **Kalaupapa Trail.** Moloka'i's north coast, facing the ocean with stunning sea cliffs, is commonly known as the **Topside.**

PLANNING YOUR TIME

In general, 4-5 days is plenty of time to properly visit the island, though you can visit most of the island's highlights in a very efficient two days. (In the past, a day trip to the island from Maui via ferry may have sufficed; however, ferry service to Moloka'i has been suspended indefinitely.) When scheduling your trip, plan on one day for Halawa Valley and East Moloka'i, and a second day for Kalaupapa. A third day could be spent at the west-end beaches, and fourth and fifth days provide nice buffers if activities are canceled by rain.

To visit Moloka'i in two days, head to the west end to catch the sunset after a morning in Kalaupapa, and the next day go hiking in Halawa Valley before dinner at Hiro's Ohana Grill. By staying in the vicinity of Kaunakakai, most places are within a 30-minute drive, and it's an hour to Halawa Valley.

HIGHLIGHTS

KAUNAKAKAI

Moloka'i Plumerias

1342 Mauna Loa Hwy.; 808/553-3391; www.molokaiplumerias.com; 8am-noon Mon.-Fri.; $25

Have you ever wanted to make your own lei and be surrounded by the scent of plumeria? Just west of town on Highway 460, as the road starts heading uphill, is Moloka'i Plumerias, where you can tour the property, pick your own flowers, and make a plumeria lei. Tours require advance reservations.

HIGHLIGHTS **329**

HO'OLEHUA

Purdy's Na Hua O Ka 'Aina Farm (Macadamia Nut Farm)

808/567-6601; www.molokai-aloha.com/macnuts; 9:30am-3:30pm Mon.-Fri., 10am-2pm Sat., Sun. and holidays by appointment

A popular visitor stop is Purdy's Na Hua O Ka 'Aina Farm behind the public high school on Lihi Pali Avenue. This is the island's only macadamia nut farm, where you'll learn everything you wanted to know about macadamias. An informal tour led by the jovial owner teaches you how to crack open the hard nut, how the nuts are grown, and how to pick out the good ones. There are no pesticides, herbicides, or other chemicals used in this 50-tree grove. While samples are included with the free tour, a small gift shop sells everything from macadamia-nut honey to mac nut-themed clothing.

Kumu Farms

551 Hua Ai Rd.; 808/351-3326; www.kumufarms.com; 9am-4pm Tues.-Fri.; free

The place for the island's best healthy organic produce is Kumu Farms. Despite the recent explosion of farm-to-table cuisine, this working farm has been growing crops since 1981 and is the best place on the island to pick up fresh veggies straight from the kumu, or source.

Visitors can peruse the outdoor market for certified organic and non-GMO produce and glean some expert culinary advice from recipes and cookbooks around the shop. Five minutes west of the airport on Hua Ai Road, an easy turn from Highway 460, this rapidly expanding farm now produces over 20,000 pounds (9,070 kg) of papaya every week. Pick up a bag of frozen basil and macadamia-nut pesto for a homemade pasta dinner.

Ho'olehua Post-A-Nut

69-2 Pu'u Pila Ave.; 808/567-6144; 8:30am-noon and 12:30pm-4pm Mon.-Fri.

Never have kids loved going to the post office more than in Ho'olehua. A simple one-room building on arid homesteading land, the Ho'olehua Post Office is home to the popular Post-A-Nut, where you can decorate

plumeria (top); Kumu Farms (bottom)

a coconut and ship it anywhere in the world. Postmaster Gary has shipped coconuts to Kathmandu, Namibia, Kyrgyzstan, and Antarctica (twice). Rates to the US mainland run $10-15.

Moloka'i Museum and Cultural Center

1795 Kalae Hwy.; 808/567-6436; www.kalaupapaohana.org/molokai-museum; 10am-1pm Mon.-Fri., 10am-2pm Sat.; $5 adults, $1 students
Two mi (3.2 km) north of Kualapu'u, off Highway 470, is the Moloka'i Museum and Cultural Center, a simple museum focused on the history of Kalaupapa. There's a small exhibit on Hawaiian artifacts as well as a basic gift shop, but most informative are the documentary videos and old newspaper articles about life on the Kalaupapa Peninsula. On the same grounds, behind the museum, is the **R. W. Meyer Sugar Mill**, constructed in 1878 during the island's short-lived sugar era.

TOPSIDE

★ Moloka'i Forest Reserve

As you head west from Kaunakakai, slowly gaining elevation, the turn-off for the Moloka'i Forest Reserve is just before mile marker 4. Turn right before the bridge, and after a few hundred yards you'll pass the Homelani Cemetery, where red-dirt Maunahui Road winds its way into the mountains. Your car-rental agency will tell you that this road is impassable except in a 4WD vehicle, and that's true if it has rained recently. The road is rough even when it's dry and requires at least a high-clearance truck or Jeep. Follow the rutted road up into the hills into a deep forest of 'ohi'a, pine, eucalyptus, and giant ferns planted in the early 1900s. The cool, pleasant air carries the rich earthy smells of the forest. At 5.5 mi (8.9 km) you enter the Moloka'i Forest Reserve, where nearly 98 percent of the plant species are indigenous to Moloka'i.

After 9 mi (14.5 km) is the **Sandalwood Measuring Pit,** a depression in the ground in the shape of a ship's hull. Now bordered by a green pipe fence, it's not worth the drive out here in itself. Hawaiian chiefs had the pit dug to measure the amount of sandalwood necessary to fill the hold of a ship, and traded the aromatic wood to Yankee captains for whiskey, guns, and tools. The traders carried the wood to China, where they made huge profits. The

Pala'au State Park (left); Kalaupapa Peninsula (right)

trade was so lucrative that the male populations of entire villages were forced into the hills to collect it. It took only a few years to denude the mountains of their copious stands of sandalwood, which is even more incredible when you consider that all the work was done by hand.

One mi (1.6 km) after the Sandalwood Pit is the **Waikolu Overlook,** a precipitous 3,700-ft (1,130-m) drop that's frequently lined with waterfalls. Waikolu Overlook is as far as most vehicles can go. The road is so bad that the only way forward is to park at Waikolu and walk.

Pala'au State Park

Above the residential town of Kala'e and past the mule barn, Highway 470 eventually dead-ends in the parking lot of Pala'au State Park. The park offers decent camping, and there are public restrooms at the parking lot, but no potable water and only basic facilities. The air is noticeably cooler than at the shore, and by midmorning the northeasterly trade winds are usually blowing.

To reach **Kalaupapa Overlook,** follow the paved path at the edge of the parking lot until it reaches a terminus at a low rock wall at the edge of a cliff. From this vantage point are unobstructed views of the town of Kalaupapa, the former leper settlement that still houses a handful of patients. Unless you obtained a permit to hike down, this is the closest to Kalaupapa that you can get.

Back at the parking lot, an unpaved trail leads 200 yards (180 m) through a cool canopy of trees before emerging at a sacred spot named **Ka Ule O Nanahoa,** also called **Phallic Rock** for reasons that are immediately apparent. According to legend, Nanahoa, the male god of fertility, once lived nearby in the forests surrounding Pala'au. One day, when Nanahoa sat to admire a beautiful young woman looking at her reflection in a pool, Kawahua, Nanahoa's wife, became so jealous that she attacked the young woman by yanking on her hair. Nanahoa was outraged in turn and struck his wife, who rolled over a nearby cliff before turning to stone. Nanahoa also turned to stone, in the shape of an erect penis, and sits here today.

★ KALAUPAPA PENINSULA

This isolated peninsula is where people with leprosy were sent to die. The story goes deeper than that, and touring the Kalaupapa Peninsula, now the **Kalaupapa National Historical Park,** is one of the most powerful and scenic adventures you can experience in Hawaii.

The peninsula is currently only accessible via aircraft. The Pali Trail to Kalaupapa was closed indefinitely in 2018 due to a landslide, so hiking isn't possible, and the once-popular mule ride down has been suspended indefinitely. **Mokulele Airlines** (808/495-4188; www.mokuleleairlines.com) offers air tours from the Moloka'i airport to the Kalaupapa airstrip (prices vary), providing historical background information; check with the airline as tour times shift seasonally.

Be sure to check the **National Park Service website** (www.nps. gov) or **Kalaupapa Rare Adventure/ Kekaula Tours** (808/567-6088; www. muleride.com), which had offered land tours (from $209) in the past, for updates. Land tours require a permit and guide. Guides share Kalaupapa's history and discuss its uncertain future, and take you to sights like the

BEST SUNSET VIEWS

the ocean at sunset

The sunsets at **Kepuhi Beach** (page 336) are a marvel. Find the beach at the western end of Kepuhi Place, the best road to use to get there. Parking is provided. This isn't a swimming beach—the undertow is a force here—but strolls along the beach offer great opportunities to snap photos during sunset. Bring a blanket, settle in, and witness the phenomenal sunset. There's something about this spot, and its position, that makes the sky appear even more picturesque.

Kalawao lookout and St. Philomena Church.

EAST MOLOKA'I

Since the arrival of the Polynesians, eastern Moloka'i has supported most of the island's population. The mountains provide the water, farmland, and pigs, and the ocean provides fish that have been sustainably managed for over 1,000 years. Many of the residents maintain this subsistence-based lifestyle, where the people are stewards of the land that nourishes them.

Many of the historic sites in this area have limited access because they are on private land. Sites that landowners have not opened to visitors, such as 'Ili'iliopae, the largest heiau (temple) on the island, are not included here. Nevertheless, a day trip to the east end of the island is easily Moloka'i's best road trip, with views toward Maui and humble historical sites. The white-sand beaches are nice for a picnic or a quick dip to cool off, and the road to Halawa rivals Maui's Road to Hana when it comes to magnificent views.

Ali'i Fishpond

Driving east from Kaunakakai, you'll come to Ali'i Fishpond at mile marker 3, just before One Ali'i Beach Park. It's an illuminating glimpse into early aquaculture. The 35-acre (14-ha) fishpond was originally constructed

HIGHLIGHTS 333

with lava rocks carried by hand 10 mi (16 km) over the adjacent mountain. The rocks were erected in a semicircle, creating a protective seawater fishpond. At the time of use, a gate would open to allow fish to swim into the pond until they grew too big and could not swim out. Having fallen into disrepair, the Ali'i Fishpond has been painstakingly brought back to life by Ka Honua Momona (www.kahonuamomona.org), a non-profit organization dedicated to sustainable land practices on Moloka'i. If you pull in to the parking lot and staff members are working on the property, they will happily show you around. Workers are usually here in the morning before the wind picks up, and if no one is around, it's best to admire the fishpond from a distance.

Kawela Plantation

Since the coastal road doesn't have great views, drive up to the Kawela Plantation to get a panoramic photo of the fringing reef and coast. Just a few minutes east of One Ali'i Beach Park, turn mauka (toward the mountain) into the Kawela Plantation I development, drive past rows of plumeria trees, and make the first left. From here, follow the steep hill until it dead-ends in a cul-de-sac. This is the best view of the southern coast until mile marker 20.

Pu'u O Hoku Ranch

808/558-8109; www.puuohoku.com
Past mile marker 20 and Waialua and Murphy's Beaches, the road narrows and runs near the sea. Honk your horn as you come around tight corners, and if you feel queasy from the drive, there's a sandy cove past mile marker 21 where you can rest. This far out on the island is very rural, and often you'll encounter groups of residents just hanging out and fishing. Be sure you have more than a quarter tank of gas if you plan to venture farther, as there are no facilities as you continue east.

Once Highway 450 starts gaining in elevation, the sweeping pasturelands of Pu'u O Hoku Ranch come into view. This 14,000-acre (5,670-ha) working ranch and farm dominates the eastern tip of the island. You've driven so far north and east that it's possible to see Maui's

Ali'i Fishpond (top); looking out at Halawa Valley (bottom)

northern coast. A basic store at the ranch headquarters sells their own products, such as organic honey, dried banana fingers, kale, chard, eggplant, cherry tomatoes, and sweet apple bananas. The ranch is also one of the few places that produce and sell 'awa, a traditional Polynesian medicinal and painkilling drink, and it also sells ranch-raised beef and venison. Driving through the ranch, watch for nene geese in the pastures and on the road. The ranch also has lodging options to get away from it all.

Halawa Valley

At the end of Highway 450, after utopian plantation homes, single-lane turns, and the ranchland's wind-swept bluffs, Halawa Valley suddenly appears when you reach a hairpin turn. At the lookout, you can snap a shot of Moa'ula Falls, toward the back of the valley. This is the best possible view of the falls unless you take a Halawa Valley Falls Cultural Hike (page 340).

Halawa is believed to be Hawaii's first settlement, circa AD 650, with some evidence suggesting settlement as early as AD 300. This is the "old Hawaii," where mythology, nature, and residents commune in a way not found in modern society. The handful of residents who still inhabit this valley live a subsistence lifestyle that parallels that of their ancestors. Electricity is scarce, there's no cell phone reception, and taro lo'i (fields) weave their way up the verdant valley floor. Aside from swimming at the sandy beach or joining the guided hike, there is little to do in Halawa but snap photos and enjoy the beauty.

TOURS

MOLOKA'I OUTDOORS

1300 Kamehameha V Hwy.; 808/553-4477; www.molokaioutdoors.com; prices vary

Moloka'i Outdoors offers Island Tour packages from Halawa Lookout all the way to Papohaku Beach. Operating three times per week, these tours cover the island in an air-conditioned van and usually carry a small group of only 4-8. They also occasionally rent SUVs for stays of three days or longer.

MOLOKA'I DAY TOURS

808/895-1673; www.molokaidaytours.com; 9am-5pm daily; $125 pp

Moloka'i Day Tours offers an impressive day-long tour that begins at the Moloka'i Museum and Cultural Center and includes guided stops at some of the island's most iconic spots, including Purdy's Macadamia Nut Farm. Lunch is included.

BEST BEACHES

If having a beach to yourself seems like your kind of afternoon, then pack a beach chair and a good book. Moloka'i's beaches are meant for sunbathing rather than snorkeling or swimming, as northwesterly swells bring large surf in winter and a reef lines the southern coast. You won't find beachside tiki bars or activity agents—in Moloka'i it's just you, the sand, the vast blue Pacific, and a fiery sunset each night.

BEST BEACHES   335

Kepuhi Beach (top); Papohaku Beach (middle); Halawa Bay (bottom)

KAUNAKAKAI

Kiowea Beach Park

Several miles west of Kaunakakai on Highway 450, Kiowea Beach Park is located next to a well-known coconut grove. Take note: This is a narrow and rugged beach. The ocean bottom is rocky and shallow, and not the best for swimming. However, it's downright scenic and fine for sunbathing and/or a picnic excursion.

WEST MOLOKA'I

The west end of Moloka'i has the island's best beaches, usually spared the relentless trade winds that buffet the eastern coast. Summer months are best for swimming, with the exception of Papohaku, which is always dangerous. In winter, surf turns the western coast into a cauldron of white water. The empty shores are always good for sunbathing, and the sunsets are the best on the island.

Kepuhi Beach

Kepuhi Beach fronts the Kaluakoi Villas and the abandoned Sheraton resort. It's an ideal beach for swimming during the summer, and the sunset each night is the kind that ends up on your Christmas card.

EAST MOLOKA'I

The eastern beaches are the most popular among residents, and morning hours offer the calmest conditions before the trade winds arrive. Like a South Pacific postcard, white-sand coves ringed by lazy palms are dotted by colorful fishing boats, and more than anywhere else on the island, there's a sense of enveloping calm. The swimming and snorkeling are best at high tide, the beachcombing and sunbathing are

TOP BEACH
PAPOHAKU BEACH

At 3 mi (4.8 km) long and nearly 100 yards (90 m) wide, Papohaku Beach is easily Moloka'i's most scenic and popular. Six people is considered a crowd, and while parts of the beach are dotted with homes, the majority of Papohaku is undeveloped with empty sand for strolling. Swimming is a terrible idea, as the rip currents and undertow are overwhelming year-round. Instead, take a morning jog or watch the sun set over the lights of Honolulu, 32 mi (52 km) away.

To get here from Kaunakakai, follow Highway 460 west toward the town of Maunaloa and take a right on Kaluakoi Road. Follow Kaluakoi to sea level until it wraps around to the left. The beach park has multiple entrances on the right side of the road. For extended stays, camping is possible at Papohaku if you obtain a permit from the County Parks Department (808/553-3204).

BEST BEACHES   337

better at low tide, and everything is better before the afternoon wind.

Waialua Beach

Waialua Beach is a narrow ribbon of sand 18.5 mi (30 km) east of Kaunakakai, with some of the island's best swimming. As at other beaches in the area, the wind gains in strength throughout the day, and at high tide the sand almost disappears completely. Be sure to watch for coral heads exposed at low tide.

Kumimi Beach

Also known as Twenty-Mile Beach or Murphy's Beach, Kumimi Beach is by mile marker 20 on Highway 450 and is the last stretch of sand before the road narrows to one lane. This is arguably East Moloka'i's most popular beach and has sweeping, spectacular views. It also has wide sand and is a nice spot for snorkeling, and in the afternoon hours you might see kitesurfers running laps down the coast.

Sandy Beach

Simple and small, Sandy Beach is past mile marker 21 on the winding drive along Highway 450 toward Halawa. You'll have just enough room to put down a towel, but the beach stands out on the island for its deeper ocean bottom, allowing for easier movement without having to walk over rocks or reefs. Protected from the surf by an offshore reef, this is one of the best swimming beaches on Moloka'i. Waters are crystal clear, unlike the murkier waters of many other beaches on the island, making this a fun snorkeling spot. You might share space here with kids wading in the shallows or locals selling bananas out of the back of a truck.

Halawa Bay

After you weave 10 mi (16 km) over the rocky coast and down through the lush eastern valleys, the two beaches that form Halawa Bay are like gold at the end of a rainbow. At the terminus of Highway 450, **Kama'alaea Bay** is the more protected beach on the far side of the stream. This is the best option for swimming and escaping the wind. **Kawili Beach,** at the bottom of the cliff, is more exposed to the currents and the trade winds. It's a surreal feeling to hang out on the shores of a place considered one of the oldest settlements in Hawaii. The only facilities are two portable toilets and a single trash can by the pavilion at the end of the road.

SCENIC DRIVES

KAUNAKAKAI TO HALAWA VALLEY

Driving Distance: *27 mi (43 km)*
Driving Time: *1 hour*
Start: *Kaunakakai*
End: *Halawa Valley*

The drive from Kaunakakai to Halawa Valley is a scenic journey through the heart of the island.

Starting in the main town of Kaunakakai, you'll travel east along Kamehameha V Highway, passing by ancient Hawaiian fishponds and serene coastline. As you continue, the road winds through lush greenery, offering glimpses of the ocean and the dramatic cliffs that define Moloka'i's shoreline. The final stretch into

Halawa Valley takes you through a narrow, winding road surrounded by dense tropical vegetation, eventually opening up to the valley's stunning vistas, with waterfalls and a rich cultural history waiting at the end.

BEST HIKES AND WALKS

Even for Maui residents, Moloka'i's hiking trails are shrouded in mystery. Often the trails require a 4WD vehicle to access or permission from private landowners, although there are still a number that are accessible to the public.

TOPSIDE

Bathed in the scent of eucalyptus and pine, the "topside" of central Moloka'i feels like the mountains. With trails ranging 1,500-4,000 ft (460-1,220 m) in elevation, the air is cooler, and once you enter the **Kamakou Preserve,** the weather turns wetter and the surroundings more lush. Songs of native i'iwi birds ring from the treetops while mist hangs in the silence of deeply carved valleys.

Pala'au State Park

KALAUPAPA OVERLOOK TRAIL
Distance: 0.7 mi (1.1 km) round-trip
Duration: 25-30 minutes
Elevation Gain: 173 ft (53 m)
Effort: easy-moderate
Trailhead: end of the road in Pala'au State Park

The easiest walk is the paved walkway to the Kalaupapa Overlook, which starts at the end of the road in Pala'au State Park. Take Highway 470 all the way until it dead-ends in a parking lot. There are basic restrooms here but no potable water. Be prepared for high winds that can blow your hat off, and get your camera ready for the best views of the Kalaupapa Peninsula.

KALAUPAPA TRAIL
Distance: 3.2 mi (5.2 km) round-trip
Duration: 3.5 hours
Elevation Gain: 1,700 ft (520 m)
Effort: moderate-strenuous

the winding road into Halawa (top); Kalaupapa Overlook (bottom)

BEST HIKES AND WALKS 339

Trailhead: *end of the road in Pala'au State Park*

For good reason, the Kalaupapa Trail (Mon.-Sat.) is the most popular hike on Moloka'i. It descends 1,700 vertical feet (520 m) over the course of 3.2 mi (5.2 km) and 26 switch-backs. There are photo-worthy views of the sea cliffs and the gorgeous, empty white-sand beach at the bottom. This trail was hand-cut into the mountain in 1886 by Portuguese immigrant Manuel Farinha to establish a land connection with the residents living topside. Remember that everything that goes down must come back up: Expect the hike down to take 1.5 hours, and close to 2 hours for the return.

EAST MOLOKA'I

★ HALAWA VALLEY FALLS CULTURAL HIKE

Distance: *5.5 mi (8.8 km) round-trip*
Duration: *5-6 hours*
Elevation Gain: *712 ft (217 m)*
Effort: *moderate-strenuous*
Trailhead: *26 mi (42 km) east on Kamehameha V Hwy.*

You heard it here first: The Halawa Valley Falls Cultural Hike is the best activity in Hawaii for those interested in Hawaiian culture. This hike is about more than walking through a rainforest to a beautiful waterfall; it's an educational experience and a journey back in time, where you are welcomed into one of Hawaii's most sacred valleys.

You'll pass numerous heiau, the temples that have sat here silently for centuries, and crush kukui nuts straight from the trees to feel the healing oils. Depending on the season, your guide might pick liliko'i (passion fruit) or guava from the trees to share as a snack on the trail, and if it begins to rain back in the valley, just grab an enormous elephant ear leaf as a natural umbrella. You'll learn about taro and how it's cultivated, learn how residents hunt pigs with knives, and hear stories of the 1946 tsunami from the last surviving resident. At the end of the hike is **Moa'ula Falls,** a multitiered 250-ft (76-m) waterfall that spills toward a plunge pool, where the rocks are dotted with ancient petroglyphs. This is the real Hawaii, and if you schedule the hike, bring along a ho'okupu, or offering—pieces of fruit or items you'd use around the house.

To book the trip, contact **Halawa Valley Falls Cultural Hike** (808/542-1855; www.halawavalleymolokai.com; $70, $45 under age 12). You can also book through the **Moloka'i Outdoors** desk (808/553-4477; www.molokai-outdoors.com) in Hotel Moloka'i or through **Moloka'i Fish and Dive** (53 Ala Malama Ave.; 808/553-5926; www.molokaifishanddive.com; 6am-7:30pm Mon.-Thurs., 6am-8pm Fri.-Sat., 6am-7pm Sun.). You can also just show up around 9am at the pavilion at the end of the road and hope for a last-minute spot. Be sure to pack mosquito repellent, water, snacks, and clothes that can get wet and muddy.

Moloka'i's sea cliffs in Pala'au State Park

BEST HIKES AND WALKS 341

SNORKELING AND DIVING

SNORKELING AND DIVING SPOTS

Don't tell anybody, but Moloka'i has some of the best snorkeling and diving in Hawaii. With the exception of a few protected areas, Moloka'i's dive and snorkel spots can only be accessed by boat. **Dixie Maru Beach** on the west shore and **Kumimi Beach** on the east shore usually have calm conditions and are the only two bays to snorkel from shore. The island's southern shore is home to Hawaii's longest fringing reef, and dive outfitters have 40 named spots along its outer edge. **Moku Ho'oniki,** off the eastern tip, is known for hammerhead sharks and occasionally some larger pelagic species, from tiger sharks to whales.

CHARTERS AND TOURS

Kaunakakai

MOLOKA'I FISH AND DIVE

53 Ala Malama Ave.; 808/553-5926; www.molokaifishanddive.com; hours vary, usually 6am-7:30pm

Mon.-Thurs., 6am-8pm Fri.-Sat., 6am-7pm Sun.

With an office right on a corner on Kaunakakai's main thoroughfare, literally inside the gas station, Moloka'i Fish and Dive offers three-hour snorkeling trips ($119 pp) and scuba trips ($219) to the reef. This shop is the only Professional Association of Diving Instructors (PADI) operation on the island and can accommodate a variety of snorkel and dive excursions. Prices and open hours can vary, so call for rates and availability.

MOLOKA'I OCEAN TOURS

40 Ala Malama Ave., Ste. 107; 808/298-3055; www.molokaioceantours.com; hours vary, typically 9am-6pm Mon.-Sat., 9am-noon Sun.

For whale-watching from December through late March, Moloka'i Ocean Tours offers a stellar deal at $105 per passenger on its 40-ft (12-m) catamaran. If the Moloka'i Ocean Tours office is closed, check upstairs at its sister shop, **Something for Everybody,** for rentals and more info.

SURFING

SURF SPOTS

Kaunakakai

KAUNAKAKAI WHARF

Since Kaunakakai faces directly south, the best waves are May-September. Despite the fact that the area boasts miles of shoreline, the majority is blocked by the fringing reef, which makes paddling out virtually impossible. Nevertheless, locals still flock to Kaunakakai Wharf during the big swells of summer. Expect a long paddle, since you have to get out past the reef to get to the waves, but the long paddle is rewarded by Moloka'i's best summer wave. Expect a very local crowd, as well as lots of "spongers" (bodyboarders).

West Moloka'i

Remote and empty, West Moloka'i is best in winter when the swells that send waves to O'ahu come crashing onto this coast. The difference is that there aren't 200 people vying for the same wave, and traffic on the highway is nonexistent. While the quality isn't as good as O'ahu's, the surf in western Moloka'i can be heavy, and only experienced surfers should paddle out on big-wave days.

SHERATON'S

The best-known and consequently most crowded spot on this end of the island is Sheraton's at Kepuhi Beach, named after the defunct resort that fronts the beach. Access is sandy and easy, but be wary of occasional shallow boulders while paddling out. The wave is on the left side of the beach, and on better days can be an A-frame that holds to 10 ft (3 m). Sheraton's is a decent spot for intermediate surfers if it's small, and only for experts if it's pumping.

HALE O LONO

On the southern end of the island, the beaches around Hale O Lono harbor are able to pick up swells any time of year and can often be heavy in winter. The wind can be fierce in the afternoon, and the murky conditions conjure fears of toothy predators, but there's a 95 percent chance you'll have the waves to yourself. If the wind is down, the waves are up, and the water is clear, the beaches off Hale O Lono can offer some of the most adventurous surf on Moloka'i. Follow the 7-mi (11-km) dirt road from Maunaloa town straight downhill to the shore. A 4WD vehicle is recommended.

RENTAL SHOPS

Kaunakakai

MOLOKA'I OCEAN TOURS

40 Ala Malama Ave., Ste. 107; 808/298-3055; www.molokaioceantours.com; hours vary, typically 9am-6pm Mon.-Sat., 9am-noon Sun.

If you don't bring a board from Maui (airlines only allow boards up to 6 ft/1.8 m), the best place to rent is Moloka'i Ocean Tours. Prices begin from $30 per day, with weekly specials.

KAYAKING AND SUP

KAUNAKAKAI

MOLOKA'I OUTDOORS

1300 Kamehameha V Hwy.; 808/553-4477; www.molokaioutdoors.com; hours vary, typically 8am-10am and 3pm-5pm daily

Inside Hotel Moloka'i, the desk staff for Moloka'i Outdoors can line you up with stand-up paddleboard or kayak tours (beginning at 10am Mon. and Wed.-Fri.); tours begin at $60 and meet at Hotel Moloka'i. Tours of the island's southeastern coast that range 5-8 mi (8-13 km) are memorable, with visits to the island's fringing reef—the longest of its kind in the United States. You'll paddle by fishponds, oceanfront homesteads, and colorful sections of reef, and gain fascinating insight on sustainable practices and Moloka'i's rural way of life.

BIKING

BIKE ROUTES
Moloka'i Forest Reserve
Experienced riders will enjoy the network of trails winding through Moloka'i Forest Reserve. These trails offer a challenging mountain biking experience through the island's lush topside. The best biking options here are with seasoned guides and tour companies who know the terrain and region well; check with the pros at Moloka'i Bicycle.

Kaunakakai to Halawa Valley
The ride east from Kaunakakai to Halawa Valley (27 mi/43 km one-way) is comparable to Maui's ride to Kahakuloa. Both are rugged and share the road, which is narrow at some points, with vehicles. Scenic views are a mix of ocean vistas and green hilly landscapes set against vibrant blue skies. Begin your ride from Kaunakakai Harbor.

BIKE SHOPS AND RENTALS
Kaunakakai
MOLOKA'I BICYCLE
80 Mohala St.; 808/553-3931; www. mauimolokaibicycle.com; 2pm-5pm Wed., 9am-2pm Sat.
In central Kaunakakai, Moloka'i Bicycle caters to every bike need and prices are still affordable: rentals (one-day $35 plus $20 per day thereafter, $135 per week), parts, and advice on good rides. They can arrange free pickups and drop-offs from a number of Moloka'i hotels, and $25-30 pickups from the airport and hotels such as Wavecrest.

BIRD-WATCHING

Many of Hawaii's original bird species are extinct, but rare species cling to existence on Moloka'i. The last known sightings of the oloma'o (Moloka'i thrush), for example, as well as the kakawahie (Moloka'i creeper), were both in the forests of **Kamakou Preserve,** a rugged and wet mountain area that requires a 4WD vehicle to access. During the fall and winter, it's common to see kolea (Pacific golden plover) scuttling across the shore and grassy areas of the island. These birds migrate to the Arctic Circle during summer before returning to Hawaii for the winter. Once the kolea are seen in the islands, locals know that the humpback whales aren't far behind.

The Nature Conservancy (808/553-5236; www.nature.org) leads trips into the preserve once per month March-October.

344 MOLOKA'I

FISHING

Fish are central to Moloka'i's culture, and it's the only island where fishing is sustainably managed around the Hawaiian lunar calendar. Fishing is a way of life on the island, and aside from the fishponds along the southern coast, many houses have traditional fishing nets hanging and drying in the yard. Offshore, the Penguin Banks between Moloka'i and O'ahu are some of Hawaii's best fishing grounds, although fishing near shore is good as well. As a general rule, the earlier you depart, the better your chances for success.

CHARTERS AND TOURS

MOLOKA'I FISH AND DIVE

53 Ala Malama Ave.; 808/553-5926; www.molokaifishanddive.com; *6am-7:30pm Mon.-Thurs., 6am-8pm Fri.-Sat., 6am-7pm Sun.; $795-895*
Moloka'i Fish and Dive operates several trips on the 38-ft (12-m) Delta cruiser *The Coral Queen*. It's also the best place in Kaunakakai for buying fishing accessories.

MOLOKA'I OCEAN TOURS

40 Ala Malama Ave., Ste. 107; 808/553-3290; www.molokaioceantours.com; hours vary, from $650
For a unique Moloka'i shore-based adventure, Moloka'i Ocean Tours offers several memorable tours aboard *Alele*—from snorkeling in sparkling blue waters (with visibility to the bottom of the ocean) and majestic sunset cruises to whale-watching December-March. You can also book standard deep-sea charters.

SHOPPING

If your idea of vacation is spending time at the mall, you won't find the experience here. Most shops on Moloka'i are utilitarian general stores, some with worthy souvenirs.

KAUNAKAKAI

Shopping in Kaunakakai, you don't have to go very far: All the stores are on the same street. You can park on **Ala Malama Avenue** and walk to every shop in town.

MOLOKA'I ART FROM THE HEART

64 Ala Malama Ave.; 877/305-1750; www.molokaigallery.com; 10am-5pm Mon.-Fri., 9am-2pm Sat.

Moloka'i Art from the Heart is a consignment boutique where 136 local artists are able to showcase and sell their products. Find anything from sarongs to CDs to original paintings. It's a great stop to support the local community.

SOMETHING FOR EVERYBODY

40 Ala Malama Ave.; 808/553-3332; www.allthingsmolokai.com; 10am-5pm Mon.-Fri., 9am-5pm Sat.
Something for Everybody is where you'll find na mea Moloka'i, "all things Moloka'i," from clothing and stickers to custom-made hats as well as fantastic advice about the island.

MOLOKA'I FOOD OPTIONS

NAME	LOCATION	CONTACT INFO
KAUNAKAKAI		
★ Hiro's Ohana Grill	1300 Kamehameha V Hwy.	808/658-1757; www.hotelmolokai.com
★ Kanemitsu Bakery & Coffee Shop	79 Ala Malama Ave.	808/553-5855
★ Paddler's Restaurant and Bar	10 Mohala St.	808/553-3300; www.paddlersrestaurant.com
Moloka'i Pizza Café	15 Kaunakakai Pl.	808/553-3288
Moloka'i Burger	20 Kamehameha V Hwy.	808/553-3533
Friendly Market	90 Ala Malama Ave.	808/553-5595
TOPSIDE		
Coffees of Hawaii	1630 Farrington Ave.	808/567-9490
EAST MOLOKA'I		
★ Mana'e Goods & Grindz	Hwy. 450, mile marker 16	808/558-8498

WEST MOLOKA'I

BIG WIND KITE FACTORY

120 Maunaloa Hwy.; 808/553-2364; www.bigwindkites.com; 10am-5pm Mon.-Sat., 10am-2pm Sun.

A Maunaloa staple since 1980, the Big Wind Kite Factory is an eclectic hodgepodge of handmade kites and woodwork from Bali. As the only store left in the town, it's worth a look. The owner, Jonathan, will give free factory tours of where the kites are made, help you fly a kite in the park, or even make a kite for any children you may have with you. The store has the largest collection of books found on the island. It's possible to visit repeatedly and still find something new. Look for the rainbow stairs in what is left of central Maunaloa.

FOOD

Food on Moloka'i is mostly "local style," meaning stick-to-the-ribs plate lunches, but recent years have seen a welcome increase in culinary diversity. The options are sparse outside Kaunakakai, so be sure you have a plan for food if you venture away from town.

FOOD	HOURS	PRICE
Hawaiian Regional	11:30am-2pm and 5:30pm-8:30pm daily	$10-40
local style	6am-2pm Sat.-Tues., 6am-noon Wed.-Fri.	$6-10, cash only
local style	11am-8pm Tues.-Sat.	$12-24
Italian	10am-9:30pm daily	$12-26, cash only
burgers	7am-8:30pm Mon.-Sat.	$8-22
markets	8am-6pm Mon.-Sat.	$2-20
coffee shops	7am-3pm Mon.-Fri.	$2-7
Hawaiian Regional	8am-3pm Thurs.-Tues.	$6-15

STANDOUTS
Kaunakakai
HIRO'S OHANA GRILL

1300 Kamehameha V Hwy.; 808/658-1757; www.hotelmolokai.com; 11:30am-2pm and 5:30pm-8:30pm daily; $10-40

The island's only restaurant to serve resort-quality food is Hiro's Ohana Grill, which also has Moloka'i's only restaurant tables with an oceanfront view. The restaurant's star attraction is chef Woody's fresh poke and a rotating menu of seasonal fresh seafood, surf and turf, and boneless short ribs. Another menu favorite is crab-stuffed mushrooms. For lunch, feast on a fresh fish burger or a hamburger steak plate. Since it's the island's only spot with a hotel liquor license, you can order a cocktail from the oceanfront bar.

KANEMITSU BAKERY & COFFEE SHOP

79 Ala Malama Ave.; 808/553-5855; 6am-2pm Sat.-Tues., 6am-noon Wed.-Fri.; $6-10, cash only

Kanemitsu Bakery & Coffee Shop isn't just a restaurant; it's a Moloka'i institution that has served baked goods and bread since 1922. Breakfast and lunch are plate-lunch fare, but what catapults the bakery to legendary status is **Hot Bread Lane** (hours vary so call ahead), where their famous hot bread is served from a window in a dingy, dimly lit alley out back. The experience feels illicit, trading cash for gargantuan loaves of cream cheese- and strawberry-filled bread. Other flavors include cinnamon and butter, or a blueberry with cream cheese. Loaves ($7-8) are big enough for two or three people.

MOLOKA'I LODGING OPTIONS

NAME	LOCATION	CONTACT INFO
KAUNAKAKAI		
★ **Moloka'i Shores Resort**	1000 Kamehameha V Hwy.	808/533-5954; www.castleresorts.com
★ **Hotel Moloka'i**	1300 Kamehameha V Hwy.	877/553-5347; www.hotelmolokai.com
WEST MOLOKA'I		
Papohaku Campground	Papohaku Beach	808/553-3204
★ **Paniolo Hale**	100 Lio Pl.	800/552-2631; www.paniolohale.org
TOPSIDE		
Pala'au Campground	Pala'au State Park	808/984-8109
EAST MOLOKA'I		
Ka Hale Mala	35 Kamakana Pl.	808/553-9009; www.bnbmolokai.com
Wavecrest Resort	7148 Kamehameha V Hwy.	855/201-4087
Dunbar Beachfront Cottages	9916 Kamehameha V Hwy.	808/336-0761; www.molokaibeachfrontcottages.com
★ **Pu'u O Hoku Ranch**	mile marker 25, Kaunakakai	808/558-8109; www.puuohoku.com

PADDLER'S RESTAURANT AND BAR

10 Mohala St.; 808/553-3300; www.paddlersrestaurant.com; 11am-8pm Tues.-Sat.; $12-24

Paddler's Restaurant and Bar has some of the best burgers, plate lunches, and pasta dishes on the island. In summer, it's the place to be for the canoe races. Paddler's is also the closest thing to a sports bar on the island, with multiple TVs, ice-cold beer on tap, and a happy hour (2pm-5pm daily), plus $3 Rolling Rocks all day. Order from the window inside, then grab a seat on the patio.

East Moloka'i

MANA'E GOODS & GRINDZ

mile marker 16, Hwy. 450; 808/558-8498; 8am-3pm Thurs.-Tues.; $6-15

The only restaurant on the east end is Mana'e Goods & Grindz, where a takeout window serves everything from chicken katsu to freshly made fruit smoothies. If the banana pancakes happen to be on the menu, don't even hesitate—just order them.

TYPE	PRICE	BEST FOR
hotel	$149–395	couples, families
hotel	$269–459	couples, families
campground	$10 pp Mon.–Thurs., $20 pp Fri.–Sun.	budget travelers
condo	$165–305	couples, families
campground	$18	budget travelers
B&B	$80–90	budget travelers, couples, solo travelers
condo	$225–430	couples, families
vacation rental	$270, cash only	couples
cottages	from $295	couples, honeymooners, families

LODGING

Moloka'i is gloriously free of resorts, and no building on the island is taller than a palm tree. The closest thing you'll find to a resort is laid-back Hotel Moloka'i, which has a concierge, an oceanfront restaurant, a bar, and daily maid service. Most of the island's accommodations are condos, and both **Moloka'i Vacation Properties** (800/658-1717; www.realestateonmolokai.net) and **Friendly Isle Realty** (808/553-3666; www.alohamolokairealty.com) have a wide selection of options.

Like elsewhere in the islands, check **VRBO** (www.vrbo.com) for deals on privately owned condos.

STANDOUTS
Kaunakakai
MOLOKA'I SHORES RESORT
1000 Kamehameha V Hwy.; 808/533-5954; www.castleresorts.com; $149–395
This condo-like setting has all the amenities you could ask for—from pools to lovely ocean views. Think of

Hotel Moloka'i

it as a second home as rooms come with refrigerators and microwaves. The resort also has nice walking areas, and its stellar location makes it easy to get to various parts of the island.

HOTEL MOLOKA'I
1300 Kamehameha V Hwy.; 877/553-5347; www.hotelmolokai.com; $269-459

Hotel Moloka'i is on the water and offers A-frame rooms in a resort-style setting, with a swimming pool, activities desk, included Wi-Fi, and live entertainment every night. The rooms, refurbished numerous times, have fridges and microwaves. This is a convenient, comfortable, and relaxing option. Rates vary by room size and season, and the hotel is home to the island's only oceanfront restaurant and bar.

West Moloka'i
PANIOLO HALE
100 Lio Pl.; 800/552-2631; www.paniolohale.org; $165-305

Staying in West Moloka'i means you're really far from everything—except beaches and sunsets. The Paniolo Hale is steps from the shore with sublime views. A two- to three-night minimum stay is required, and some units have longer minimum stays.

East Moloka'i
PU'U O HOKU RANCH
mile marker 25, Kaunakakai; 808/558-8109; www.puuohoku.com; from $295

At the far eastern end of the island high on the eastern hillside is 14,000-acre (5,670-ha) Pu'u O Hoku Ranch. The lodge and three cottages are some of the best and remotest on the island. This is a working ranch that's minutes away from the shore at Halawa Bay. Wi-Fi is available in a few spots, but most accommodations are "unplugged." Check in at the ranch office along the highway at mile marker 25, where a small sundries store sells basic food and gift items. The two-bedroom Sunrise Cottage has a full kitchen and a covered lanai and sleeps up to four. The larger, four-bedroom Grove Cottage (call for rates) can sleep up to eight. From this cottage there are ocean views to Maui with amazing whale-watching in winter. Five mi (8 km) closer to Kaunakakai along the main highway, the one-bedroom Sugar Mill cottage sleeps four, has a full kitchen, and is walking distance from one of the island's nicest beaches.

TRANSPORTATION

Air

Moloka'i Airport

3980 Airport Loop; 808/567-9660

The Moloka'i Airport (MKK) at Ho'olehua is a small open-air facility where you still walk out on the runway to board your plane. When flying to Moloka'i, don't expect a big plane or a smooth ride. The small aircraft are vulnerable to the brisk trade winds, although the flights are scenic. Flights from Maui, which take 30 minutes, often provide views of Moloka'i's dramatic northern sea cliffs as well as aerial views of the Kalaupapa Peninsula. From Maui, sit on the left side of the aircraft for the best chance of waterfall and coastal views.

The largest planes are with **Hawaiian Airlines** (877/426-4537; www.hawaiianairlines.com), with 37-seat aircraft and multiple flights per day from both Kahului and Honolulu. **Mokulele Airlines** (808/495-4188 or 866/260-7070; www.mokuleleairlines.com) offers direct flights from Honolulu and Kahului; any other city will require a connecting flight. Be sure to check the baggage restrictions, since there isn't much space on the planes.

Car

Car Rental

The only car-rental agency with a booth at the airport is **Alamo** (Molokai Airport, Bldg. 2, Airport Loop; 808/567-6381; www.alamo.com; 7am-7pm daily), which has a large fleet of cars and 4WD Jeeps. If you rent from Alamo, don't lose your key—they don't have extras.

For an affordable cruiser, check out **Molokai Car Rental** (3980 Airport Loop; 808/553-3299; www.molokaicars.com), a casual locally owned company that can deliver the car to the airport. They don't have 4WD vehicles, but ask about their room-and-car package at Hotel Moloka'i.

Gas

There are only two gas stations on the island, right next to each other in Kaunakakai. Be sure you have at least half a tank of fuel before heading out on a day trip to Halawa or Papohaku. **Texaco Kaunakakai** (20 Mauna Loa Hwy.; 5:30am-7pm Mon.-Sat., 7am-7pm Sun.) has longer hours and more supplies, though it costs at least $1.50 or more per gallon than on Maui.

Taxi

The best option for taxis on Moloka'i is **Hele Mai Taxi** (808/336-0967; www.molokaitaxi.com), also offering private tours of the island. Expect to pay about $45 from the airport to Hotel Moloka'i to Kalaupapa Trail.

Shuttle

On a budget, the **MEO public shuttle bus** (www.meoinc.org) operates three routes across the island—but you need to be flexible with your schedule, and there's no service on weekends. Shuttle stops include Hotel Moloka'i and in front of Misaki's Market in central Kaunakakai. The Maunaloa shuttle stops at the airport, and the shuttle typically runs six times Monday-Friday to Maunaloa, and eight times Monday-Friday to Puko'o in East Moloka'i. Along the routes the driver will usually let you get off wherever you want. Although it's free, donations to keep the shuttle going are accepted. For schedules visit the website.

Haleakalā landscape

GEOGRAPHY AND LANDSCAPES

Maui is 727 sq mi (1,885 sq km), making it the second-largest island in Hawaii. There are 120 mi (195 km) of coastline. At its widest point, the island is 26 mi (42 km) from north to south and 48 mi (77 km) from east to west.

Known as the "Valley Isle," Maui is the product of two volcanoes—Haleakalā and the older Mauna Kahalawai—that merged together into a central isthmus to form the island we know today. At 10,023 ft (3,055 m) above sea level, Haleakalā is estimated to be about 750,000 years old, making it half as old as Mauna Kahalawai, otherwise known as the West Maui Mountains, which have stood for 1.5 million years. In looking at the two mountains, it's evident that Mauna Kahalawai—with its deeply eroded valleys and dramatically carved peaks—has been exposed to the forces of nature longer than smooth Haleakalā. Haleakalā's aging is visible in the ravines of Kipahulu, the Kaupo Gap, and the cleft in the mountainside towering above Ke'anae.

Although the islands of Maui, Lana'i, Moloka'i, and Kaho'olawe are four separate landmasses today, all were once connected in an island known as Maui Nui (Great Maui). This massive island was larger than the modern-day Big Island, and it's estimated that the islands were joined until as recently as 20,000 years ago, when sea levels were lower as a result of an ice age.

CRATERS

These remarkable bowl-, funnel-, and arch-shaped depressions are a direct result of volcanic action. When magma rises to the surface, it encounters a reduction in pressure, causing gases within the magma to expand and erupt violently. This explosion blows away the top part of the volcano, leaving behind a circular or oval depression known as a crater. Over time, further eruptions or collapses can modify the shape and size of the crater. Some craters are also formed when the summit of the volcano collapses inward after the magma chamber below is partially emptied. The last time Maui had volcanic activity was more than 400 years ago, so exploring the craters is like a trip back in time.

Where to See Them

- Molokini Crater (page 68)
- Haleakalā Crater (page 199)

LAVA FLOWS

Exploring volcanic areas on Maui allows you to witness up close the fascinating geological features created by lava flows. Take note: Sunlight heats up the volcanic surfaces, which are mostly black and charcoal in color. Stay hydrated along these excursions.

Where to See Them

- Hoapili Trail and La Perouse Bay (page 66)
- Dragon's Teeth (page 105)

BLACK-SAND BEACHES

Thanks to its own volcanic activity, Maui boasts several unique sand beaches. Black-sand beaches are usually composed of tiny fragments of volcanic minerals and rocks, primarily basalt, which is formed from lava that cools rapidly. Over time, wave action and erosion contribute to the formation of these unique beaches.

Where to See Them

- Oneuli Beach (page 81)
- Pa'iloa Beach (page 259)

RED-SAND BEACHES

The distinctive reddish hue of these beaches typically comes from high concentrations of iron-rich minerals, such as hematite, found in the surrounding rocks and soils. When these iron-bearing rocks erode over time due to weathering and wave action, they break down into sand-sized particles that give the beach its red appearance.

Where to See Them

- Kaihalulu Beach (page 259)

TIDE POOLS

Tide pools are shallow, rocky basins found along the shoreline, formed by the ebb and flow of the tides. These

Molokini Crater

natural habitats are filled with seawater and are home to a diverse array of marinelife, including colorful fish, sea urchins, starfish, crabs, and various types of seaweed. As the tide recedes, water becomes trapped in the depressions among the rocks, creating these miniature ecosystems.

Where to See Them

- Kamaole Beach Parks (page 58)
- Olivine Pools (page 107)
- Kuau Cove (page 258)

CORAL REEFS

Reefs are formed of colonies of coral polyps, which are held together by calcium carbonate. The majority of coral reefs are created from stony corals, whose polyps cluster in groups. The setting is a haven for unique sealife.

Where to See Them

- Molokini Crater (page 68)
- Olowalu (page 125)

WATERFALLS

Waterfalls cascade from steep cliffs and mountains, fed by abundant rainfall that nourishes the island's dense rainforests. Found throughout Maui, particularly along the lush, tropical landscapes of the Road to Hana, some of Hawaii's most iconic waterfalls include Wailua Falls, which plunges dramatically into a pool below, and Twin Falls, a popular spot for swimming and exploring.

Where to See Them

- The Road to Hana (page 244)
- Halawa Valley Falls Cultural Hike (page 340)

Pa'iloa Beach (Black Sand Beach) (top); Kaihalulu Beach (Red Sand Beach) (middle); turtle swimming through coral (bottom)

GEOGRAPHY AND LANDSCAPES 355

waterfall in a Hana rainforest

RAINFORESTS

Maui's tropical rainforests are a fascinating moist broadleaf forest ecoregion. They cover much of the island's eastern side, particularly along the slopes of the Haleakalā volcano and the region surrounding the Road to Hana. These rainforests are characterized by their dense vegetation, towering trees, and a rich diversity of plant and animal life. Frequent rainfall nourishes the landscape, creating an environment where ferns, bamboo groves, and tropical flowers thrive. Wear appropriate walking or hiking shoes along rainforest trails, as some paths are wet or muddy, and be especially careful on any slopes, which can be slick, depending on the last rainfall.

Where to See Them

- Upper Waikani Falls (Three Bears) (page 249)
- Pipiwai Trail (page 262)

WETLANDS

Maui's wetlands are vital ecosystems that serve as a unique habitat for a variety of plant and animal species, particularly native and migratory birds. These areas are typically found in low-lying regions near the coast. The wetlands are characterized by shallow water, marshy terrain, and an abundance of grasses, reeds, and other aquatic plants. These environments play a crucial role in filtering water, controlling floods, and providing breeding grounds for wildlife. Visitors to these areas can enjoy bird-watching, particularly during migration seasons, and learn about the importance of wetlands in maintaining Maui's ecological health.

Where to See Them

- Kealia Pond National Wildlife Refuge (page 54)
- Kanaha Pond State Wildlife Sanctuary (page 175)

GEOGRAPHY AND LANDSCAPES **357**

monk seal on Lana'i

PLANTS AND WILDLIFE

Anyone who loves a mystery will be intrigued by the speculation about how plants and animals first came to Hawaii. More than 2,000 mi (3,220 km) from any continent, Hawaii is isolated from the normal ecological spread of plants and animals. Even the most tenacious flora and fauna would have trouble crossing the mighty Pacific. Those that made it by chance would find a totally foreign ecosystem where they had to adapt or perish. Survivors evolved quickly, and many plants and birds became so specialized that they were limited not only to specific islands in the chain but to habitats that frequently consisted of a single isolated valley. After traveling so far and adapting to a niche, they didn't budge again.

Before settlement, Hawaii had no fruits, vegetables, coconut palms, edible land animals, conifers, mangroves, or banyans. The early Polynesians brought 27 varieties of plants they needed for food and other purposes. About 90 percent of the plants on the Hawaiian Islands today were introduced after Captain Cook first set foot here. Tropical flowers, wild and vibrant as we know them today, were relatively few. In a land where thousands of orchids now brighten every corner, there were only four native varieties, the fewest in any of the 50 states. Today, the indigenous plants and animals have the highest rate of extinction anywhere on earth. By the beginning of the 21st century, native plants growing below 1,500 ft (460 m) in elevation were almost completely extinct or totally displaced by introduced species. The land and its life have been greatly transformed by humans and agriculture.

PLANTS

The majority of flora considered exotic was introduced either by the original Polynesians or by later settlers of European origin. The Polynesians who colonized Hawaii brought foodstuffs, including coconuts, bananas, taro, breadfruit, sweet potatoes, yams, and sugarcane. Non-Hawaiian settlers brought mangoes, papayas, passion fruit, pineapples, and the other tropical fruits and vegetables. The flowers, including protea, plumeria, anthuriums, orchids, heliconia, ginger, and most hibiscus species, have come from every continent on earth.

KOA

The koa, a form of acacia, is Hawaii's finest native tree. It can grow to more than 70 ft (21 m) and has a strong, straight trunk that can measure more than 10 ft (3 m) in circumference. The Hawaiians used koa as the main log for their dugout canoes, and elaborate ceremonies were performed when a log was cut and dragged to a canoe shed. Koa wood was also preferred for paddles, spears, and surfboards, and today, fine Hawaiian galleries across the islands sell koa wood bowls and crafts.

Where to See Them

- Maui Nui Botanical Gardens (page 162)
- Ukumehame Beach Park (page 116)

'OHI'A

The 'ohi'a is a survivor and therefore the most abundant of all the native Hawaiian trees—though an outbreak of 'ohi'a disease is currently ravaging the forests. The 'ohi'a produces a tuft-like flower—usually red, but occasionally orange, yellow, or white, the latter being rare and elusive—that resembles a pompom. The strong, hard wood was used to make canoes, poi bowls, and temple images. 'Ohi'a logs were also used as railroad ties and shipped to the mainland from Pahoa on the Big Island. It's believed that the golden spike finally linking the rail lines spanning the US East and West Coasts in Ogden, Utah, was driven into a Puna 'ohi'a log.

Where to See Them

- 'Iao Valley State Monument (page 165)

BANYAN TREES

The banyan trees on Maui are renowned for their sprawling canopies and intricate network of aerial roots that form a stunning natural maze. Planted in 1873, Lahaina's banyan tree has grown into one of the largest in the U.S., spanning an entire city block.

Where to See Them

- Lahaina Front Street (page 110)
- Makamaka'ole Valley Trail (page 171)
- Pipiwai Trail (page 262)

JACARANDA TREES

These stunning violet wonders bloom during spring. For miles and miles, jacaranda trees beautify Kula Highway in Upcountry. It is believed that Portuguese ranchers first introduced this royal-looking tree, as jacarandas originated in Brazil. The trees have an affinity for warmer regions and relish tropical climes. They handle the changing temperatures in Upcountry just fine. Legend has it that King Kamehameha often trekked ceremoniously through the area when the trees were in full bloom.

Where to See Them
- Kula Highway (page 213)

COOK PINES

There's nothing more noble than these regal trees. Cook pines are, in fact, the most common species of the Araucaria genus in Hawaii. They can rise to nearly 200 ft (60 m). Their horizontal branches are mostly short and upright, while the trunk itself tends to lean. The branches are lined with cord-like branches, and the new leaves are needle-like, while adult leaves are triangular and scaled.

Where to See Them
- Munro Trail (page 300)

'AHINAHINA (SILVERSWORD)

Found on the high alpine slopes of Haleakalā above the 6,000-ft (1,830-m) level, the 'ahinahina plant is an iconic symbol for the beauty of Haleakalā Crater. The plant may live for only a few years or for nearly a century, but each ends its life by sprouting a gorgeous stalk of hundreds of purplish-red flowers before withering from a majestic 6-ft (1.8-m) plant to a flat, gray skeleton. 'Ahinahina bloom mostly in July and August, but they can bloom as early as May and as late as November. An endangered species, 'ahinahina are completely protected.

koa (top); 'ohi'a (middle); 'ahinahina (silversword) (bottom)

PLANTS 361

protea (left); lokelani flower (right)

Where to See Them

- Haleakalā National Park (page 199)

PROTEA

The slopes of leeward Haleakalā between 2,000 and 4,000 ft (610-1,220 m) elevation have perfect growing conditions for protea. The days are warm, the nights are cool, and the well-drained volcanic soil has the right minerals. Protea make excellent gifts that can be shipped anywhere, and although they are beautiful as freshly cut flowers, they have the extra benefit of drying superbly: Just hang them in a dark, dry, well-ventilated area. You can see protea, along with other botanical specialties, at the gardens, flower farms, and gift shops in Kula.

Where to See Them

- Kula Botanical Garden (page 209)

LOKELANI FLOWER

Lokelani, the official flower of Maui, is pink and fragrant and originates from Asia. Brought to the islands in the early 1800s by the Spanish, it's the only nonnative flower recognized as an island flower. Lokelani are often used in lei making, found in gardens, and used in ceremonies.

Where to See Them

- Kula Botanical Garden (page 209)
- Garden of Eden (page 245)

BIRDS

One of the great tragedies of natural history is the continuing demise of Hawaiian birdlife. Perhaps only 15 original species of birds remain of the more than 70 indigenous species that thrived before the coming of humans. Since the 1778 arrival of Captain Cook, 23 species have gone extinct, with 31 more in danger. Hawaii's endangered birds account for 40 percent of those officially listed as endangered or threatened by the US Fish and Wildlife Service. In the last 200 years, more than four times as many birds have become extinct in Hawaii as in all of North America.

While visitors aren't likely to encounter many of the island's forest birds, those interested in these fragile species should contact the Maui Forest Bird Recovery Project (www.mauiforestbirds.org) for more information and ways to volunteer.

'AKOHEKOHE

Also known as honeycreepers, these stunning creatures measure more than 7 in (18 cm) and typically are dark with silver flecks.

Where to See Them

- Hosmer's Grove at Haleakalā National Park (page 214)
- East Moloka'i (page 344)

'I'IWI

These striking blood-orange birds have pronounced beaks and several bluish feathers.

Where to See Them

- Polipoli Spring State Recreation Area (page 216)

'AMAKIHI

This small, generalist Hawaiian honeycreeper stands out for its vivid golden-yellow color.

Where to See Them

- Kealia Pond National Wildlife Refuge (page 54)
- Hosmer's Grove at Haleakalā National Park (page 214)

HAWAIIAN STILT (AE'O)

The Hawaiian stilt is about 16 in (40 cm) tall, with a black body, white belly, and distinctively pink legs.

'i'iwi (top); 'amakihi (middle); Hawaiian stilt (ae'o) (bottom)

nene geese (left); monk seal (right)

Where to See Them
- Kealia Pond National Wildlife Refuge (page 54)
- Kanaha Pond State Wildlife Sanctuary (page 175)

HAWAIIAN COOT ('ALAE KE'OKE'O)
Ranging in length 13-16 in (33-41 cm) and weighing nearly 2 pounds (0.9 kg), the Hawaiian coot is most noteworthy for its black plumage and a prominent white frontal shield.

Where to See Them
- Kealia Pond National Wildlife Refuge (page 54)
- Kanaha Pond State Wildlife Sanctuary (page 175)

NENE GOOSE
The nene goose—the Hawaiian state bird—is a close cousin of the Canada goose.

Where to See Them
- Paliku campsites and cabins (page 221)

MARINELIFE

Hawaii's only two indigenous land mammals are the Hawaiian monk seal and the hoary bat; all other mammals have been introduced.

MONK SEALS
These earless seals are adorable yet weigh 375-450 pounds (170-205 kg) and span nearly 7.5 ft (2.3 m) in length.

Where to See Them
- Little Beach (page 61)
- Ho'okipa Beach Park (page 258)

HUMPBACK WHALES
These acrobatic, aerial cetaceans are a delight for winter visitors, and there are few things like the thrill of a 45-ton animal erupting out of the water before your eyes. Humpbacks migrate to the islands

November-May to mate, give birth, and care for their young, and during the course of their four-month stay, they don't eat anything at all.

Where to See Them

- West Maui (page 135)
- Ferry to Lana'i (page 315)

DOLPHINS

While whales are only observed during the winter, dolphins are year-round residents and a common sight around the islands. There are three distinct pods of Hawaiian spinner dolphins residing along West Maui, South Maui, and the southwestern coast of Lana'i. The acrobatic spinners can complete up to seven full rotations in the air before splashing back down into the water. Larger bottlenose dolphins are also occasionally seen, while pan-tropical spotted dolphins are confined to deeper waters.

Where to See Them

- Molokini Crater (page 70)
- Honolua Bay (page 124)
- Hulopo'e Bay (page 299)

humpback whale

Moloka'i sea cliffs from the beach

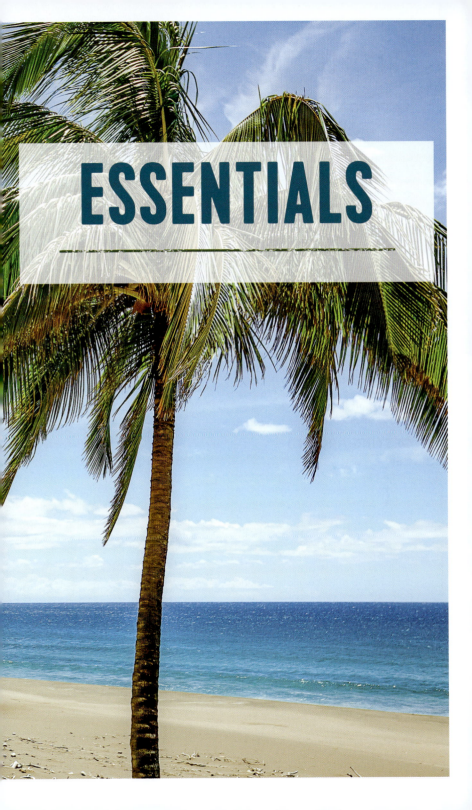
ESSENTIALS

TRANSPORTATION

GETTING THERE
Air
You'll likely land at the **Kahului Airport** (OGG; 1 Keolani Pl.; 808/872-3830; www.airports.hawaii.gov/ogg), which is 30-45 minutes by car from the resort areas of Wailea and Ka'anapali. Kahului has direct flights to a host of mainland cities and a handful of international destinations, and most major carriers serve it.

Other than Kahului, there are two small airstrips, in Kapalua and in Hana. They have no direct flights to the mainland, but there are seven flights per day from the **Kapalua Airport** (JHM; 4050 Honoapi'ilani Hwy.; 808/665-6108; www.hawaii.gov/jhm) to Honolulu on neighboring O'ahu, which can be convenient if you're hopping between islands and have a connection in Honolulu. The **Hana Airport** (HNM) has an afternoon flight that's just 20 minutes back to Kahului.

GETTING AROUND
Car
Rental cars are the easiest way to get around and explore the island. One of the airport's massive reconstruction projects relocated most major car rentals on-site. However, there are also locally owned companies that can provide better rates and more "authentic"-looking cars. A shiny new rental car is nice to drive around in, but the downside is that rentals are car thieves' preferred targets. Having a car that looks like a local's can potentially save you the cost of a break-in.

At the Kahului Airport, **Alamo** (844/913-0747), **Avis** (808/871-7575), **Budget** (808/871-8811), **Enterprise** (844/914-1547), **Hertz** (808/893-5200), and **Thrifty** (808/893-5200) all offer the standard corporate options for island car rentals. Care to splurge? **SIXT Rent-a-Car Maui** (888/749-8227)

offers long-term rentals and discounts midweek.

Most local car-rental companies offer free transportation to the airport if arranged ahead of time. Check **Maui Windsurfing Vans** (180 E. Waikea Ave.; 808/877-0090; www.mauivans.com), **Kimo's Rent a Car** (440 Alamaha St.; 808/280-6327; www.kimosrentacar.com), **Kihei Rent a Car** (96 Kio Loop; 808/879-7257; www.kiheirentacar.com), and **Manaloha Rent a Car** (200 Waiehu Beach Rd.; 808/283-8779; www.manaloharentacar.net).

Don't get a 4WD vehicle—you won't need it. The only time you need 4WD on Maui is for Skyline Drive in Polipoli, or for peace of mind on the back road to Hana. Many visitors spend a lot of money on 4WD, often double the price of a regular car, and never end up using it. Rent a 4WD vehicle just for the day if you need it.

Book far ahead if you're traveling during the peak season, and know that drivers who are under 25 will often incur extra fees.

Taxi
If you only plan to stay in the resort areas, consider using taxis instead of renting a car. With resort parking fees and fuel for the car, it can sometimes be cheaper to take taxis. If there's a specific place you want to visit that requires a car, you can rent one for 24 hours and drop it off when you're done.

More than two dozen taxi companies operate island-wide service on Maui, and besides providing normal taxi service, they will also run tours all over the island. Taxis are expensive and metered by the distance traveled. From Kahului Airport, the fare to Lahaina should be roughly $70, and $85-90 to Ka'anapali, $100-125 to Kapalua, and $60-65 to Wailea. Expect $5-10 in and around Kahului, and about $15 to the

DRIVE WITH ALOHA

Local customs come into play behind the wheel. You'll notice that even on highways, drivers cruise along slowly. The maximum speed limit anywhere on Maui is 55 mph (89 km/h), and in many places it's 30-45 mph (48-72 km/h). It's essential to go slow in residential neighborhoods or on side streets. Going fast can result in an angry fist shaken at your car or a call for you to slow down. Aside from speed, car horns are only used in an emergency (or when your friend walks by), aggressive driving is severely frowned upon, and it's common courtesy to stop and allow waiting cars into traffic. Drivers are known to wave or throw shakas at each other, and there's a good chance you'll see at least one "Slow Down! This Ain't the Mainland!" bumper sticker during your drive around the island. You're probably here to relax, so leave earlier and take time to enjoy the ride.

hostels in Wailuku. Any taxi may drop off at the airport, but only those with permits may pick up there.

Those in need of a taxi can call **West Maui Taxi** (808/661-1122; www.westmauitaxi.com), **Kihei Taxi** (808/298-1877; www.kiheitaxi.com), or **Taxi of Wailea** (808/797-3950; www.wailea-taxi.com).

Bus

The **Maui Bus** system (808/270-7511; www.mauicounty.gov) has 13 routes for an inexpensive way to get around to the major towns. Fares are $2 per boarding or $4 for a day pass, and monthly passes are also available. Although the bus does run to the airport, riders are not allowed to board with luggage that can't fit under their seat. For a full listing of island bus schedules, refer to the timetables on the website.

Shuttle

Robert's Hawaii (866/539-9400; www.robertshawaii.com) connects the Kahului Airport to virtually anywhere on the island and operates daily during flight arrival and departure times. With this door-to-door service, pickup can be either from the airport or from any hotel or condo if you're going to the airport. **Executive Airport Transportation**

(808/669-2300) offers virtually the same service to and from the airport and to points around the island for marginally better rates, which average $60-65 per person from Kahului to Ka'anapali. Although these companies will pick you up as soon as they can, they prefer several hours' or even 24 hours' notice if possible.

Bicycle

Maui is a great island for both serious road cyclists and those who prefer to just cruise around town. Towns such as Lahaina and Kihei are easily navigable by bicycle, although often cyclists are forced to share the road with similarly slow-moving traffic. Rental shops can be found in Kahului, Pa'ia, Kihei, and Lahaina, and all will have island maps detailing the best rides.

Scooter

Scooters are great for running around town. Most rental operators will ask for a cash or credit card deposit. You must be at least 18 years old, have a valid driver's license, and often stay within a certain distance from your rental office. Legally, mopeds can have only one rider.

On the West Side of the island, you can get scooters from **Aloha**

TRANSPORTATION **369**

MAUI FOR FREE

Maui can be expensive, but it doesn't have to be. A number of Maui activities don't cost a thing:

- A morning stroll on the Kapalua Coastal Trail or Baldwin Beach
- Bodysurfing at D. T. Fleming Beach Park
- Watching the sunset at Haleakalā and staying to watch the stars come out
- Hiking in Polipoli, Makena, or Hana
- Any ocean swim or even swimming beneath a waterfall on the Road to Hana
- Free evening entertainment at Whalers Village
- Watching the surfers at Lahaina or Honolua Bay or windsurfers at Kanaha Beach Park or Ho'okipa Beach Park
- Whale-watching from the Pali Lookout between Ma'alaea and Lahaina
- Attending a Maui Friday Town Party, a free event that rotates weekly from town to town

Motorsports (30 Halawai Dr.; 808/667-7000; www.alohamotorsports.com), among other providers. In Kihei, **Maui Scooter Shack** (1794 S. Kihei Rd.; 808/891-0837; www.mauiscooter-shack.com) offers scooter rentals and guided tours.

Tours

For customized private tours of the island, **Open Eye Tours** (808/280-5299; www.openeyetours.com) offers extensive, memorable full-day tours that emphasize Hawaiian culture, beginning at $1,025 per person.

TRAVEL TIPS

ACCESS FOR TRAVELERS WITH DISABILITIES

A person with a disability can have a wonderful time in Hawaii; all that's needed is a little planning. Make as many arrangements ahead of time as possible: Tell the transportation companies and hotels the nature of your disability so they can make pre-arrangements to accommodate you. Bring your medical records and notify medical establishments of your arrival if you'll need their services. Travel with a friend or make arrangements for an aide upon arrival. Bring your own wheelchair if possible and let airlines know if it is battery-powered. Boarding interisland carriers sometimes requires steps. Wheelchairs are boarded early on special lifts, but they must know in advance that you're coming. Most hotels and restaurants easily accommodate people with disabilities, but call ahead to make sure.

Information

The state Commission on Persons with Disabilities was designed to aid disabled people. It is an invaluable source of information and distributes self-help booklets, published jointly by the Disability and Communication Access Board and the Hawaii Centers for Independent Living. Any person with disabilities heading to Hawaii should write first or visit the office of the **Hawaii Centers for Independent Living** (414 Kuwili St., Ste. 102, Honolulu, HI 96817; 808/522-5400). Additional information is available on the **Disability and Communication Access Board website** (www.hawaii. gov/health).

TRAVELING WITH CHILDREN

Traveling with children on Maui can be a memorable experience. Consider the kind of trip you want and book activities accordingly. Other than the beach, one of the best sites on the island for kids is the **Maui Ocean Center,** full of hands-on activities and educational experiences. To sneak away for a romantic dinner, the best service on the island for a short-term sitter is **The Nanny Connection** (808/875-4777; www.thenannyconnection.com), where professional sitting staff will meet you at your hotel and take care of children in your absence.

LGBTQ TRAVELERS

Gay and lesbian travelers are welcome throughout Hawaii. While acceptance is part of the general state of mind, Maui has a smaller gay and lesbian community in terms of nightclubs, bars, and other gathering places than O'ahu does, for example. In 2011, Hawaii was the seventh state to legalize civil unions for same-sex couples, well before national marriage equality was established.

The first Sunday of the month, LGBTQ locals and visitors converge at **Nalu's South Shore Grill** (10:30am) in Kihei for brunch and socializing. On the second Saturday of the month, LGBTQ hikers—although everyone is welcome—head into nature; check out the **Maui LGBT Hiking Group** on Facebook for details. **Aloha Maui Pride** (www.alohamauipride.org) offers a concise calendar of upcoming events, including the annual **Pride festival** in early October, as well as general LGBTQ information.

Pride Guide Hawaii (www.gogayhawaii.com) has detailed listings of dining, nightlife, and lodging options. Another source is the **International Gay and Lesbian Travel Association** (954/630-1637; www.iglta.org), which can connect you with gay-friendly organizations and tours.

PEOPLE OF COLOR

Like the rest of Hawaii, Maui has a diverse population. Of the nearly 168,000 Maui County residents, 34.9 percent identify as white (30.1 percent non-Hispanic white), 29 percent Asian, 24.2 percent two or more races, 11.6 percent Hispanic, 10.6 percent Hawaiian or Pacific Islander, 0.8 percent Black or African American, and 0.6 percent American Indian or Alaskan Native. In 2020, there were four crimes related to race in the entire state, with one anti-white crime reported on Maui.

The **African Americans on Maui Association** (www.africanamericansonmaui.com) offers unique resources for the local population and presents cultural exhibits, arts, and programs related to the African American experience. Similarly, the **African American Heritage Foundation of Maui** strives to increase awareness of African American culture and contributions; check its Facebook page (www.facebook.com/AAHFMAUI) for information and events.

Tune into 88.5 FM at noon on Friday for *The Latino Connection,* hosted by a Maui local. The program's intention is to connect Maui's Spanish-speaking community and often includes a roundup of local events.

The **Japanese Cultural Society of Maui** (www.jcsmaui.org) seeks to perpetuate Japanese culture on the island

and offers listings of a variety of cultural events.

CLOTHING-OPTIONAL BEACHES

Little Beach in Makena in South Maui is one of the most popular clothing-optional beaches and attracts a decent-size crowd. Access it by parking in Lot 1 of Makena State Beach and heading right once you get to the main beach. It's a modest 0.5-mi (0.8-km) hike to get here, but worth the effort.

Secret Beach on the North Shore is relatively secluded, situated between Pa'ia Bay and Baldwin Beach. Access this tranquil haven by parking at Pa'ia Bay and walking through a small wooded area on the west end.

OPPORTUNITIES FOR VOLUNTEER WORK

West Maui: Honokowai Valley

Spend a Saturday with **Maui Cultural Lands** (808/276-5593; www.mauiculturallands.org) in the magical Honokowai Valley for one of the best volunteering experiences on the island. Away from the highway in a valley forgotten by time, the remains of an ancient Hawaiian village are slowly being brought back to life. The structures, including rock walls and lo'i, are over 600 years old. The village was abandoned in the 1800s when the water was diverted to grow sugarcane. Today, spending a morning volunteering in Honokowai Valley is one of the most culturally authentic and meaningful experiences you can have in West Maui. In most cases, groups meet at 9:15am Saturday at the bottom of Pu'ukoli Road across from Kahekili Beach Park.

Central Maui

Volunteer for the **Hawaii Land Trust** (808/744-2462; www.hilt.org/protected-lands/maui) and you can join a trusted guide for the day in exotic places such as the Waihe'e Coastal Dunes and Wetlands Preserve. Expect an informative day that begins early in the morning and includes planting hala trees or supporting coastal cleanup by gathering easy-to-pick-up runaway nets and more.

Upcountry: Haleakalā

For the chance to stay in a wilderness cabin inside Haleakalā Crater, volunteer with **Friends of Haleakala** (www.fhnp. org) on one of their monthly service trips. The majority of these backpacking trips are free, and a few cost $15. During the three-day trip you'll clean the cabins and remove invasive species. You'll need to pack your own sleeping bag as well as food, water, and supplies, and participants are required to be physically fit and comfortable hiking at altitude. Space is limited, so check the website for trip dates and ways you can volunteer.

HEALTH AND SAFETY

Every year Hawaii ranks among the healthiest states. People here live longer than those anywhere else in the country, with an average life span of about 80 years. Lifestyle, heredity, and diet help with these figures, but Hawaii is still an oasis in the middle of the ocean, and germs just have a tougher time getting here. There are no cases of malaria, cholera, or yellow fever, and because of strict quarantine laws, rabies is nonexistent.

Due to the perfect weather, the soothing negative ionization from the sea, and the carefree lifestyle, everyone seems to feel better in the islands. Hawaii is just what the doctor ordered: a beautiful, natural health spa. The food and water are perfectly safe, and the air quality is the best in the country.

On the other hand, tooth decay is 30 percent above the national average, perhaps because of the wide use of sugar and the enzymes present in certain tropical fruits. Obesity and related heart problems, as well as hard-drug use—especially crystal meth, or "ice"—are prevalent among native Hawaiians.

RESPECT NATURE

Many visitors' injuries are a direct result of failing to respect the power of nature. Waves are stronger than in other parts of the world, and flash floods, high winds, rough seas, and slippery rocks all claim lives annually. Heed the warning signs. "If in doubt, don't go out."

WATER SAFETY

Hawaii has a sad claim to fame: More people drown here than anywhere else in the world. Moreover, there are dozens of scuba, snorkeling, and boarding accidents yearly, with broken necks and backs or other injuries. These statistics shouldn't keep you out of the water. The best remedy is to avoid situations you can't handle, and ask lifeguards or beach attendants about conditions and follow their advice. If local people refuse to go in, there's a good reason. Even experts can get in trouble in Hawaiian waters, and while some beaches are calm and gentle, others can be frothing giants.

While beachcombing and especially when walking out on rocks, never turn your back to the ocean. Always be aware of what is going on with the water. Undertows (the water drawing back into the sea) can knock you off your feet and pull you into the shore-break. Observe the water carefully before you go in. Study it for rocks, breakers, and reefs. Look for ocean currents, especially those within reefs that can cause riptides when the water washes out a channel. Note where others are swimming or snorkeling, and go there. Don't swim alone, if possible, and obey all warning signs. When snorkeling, come ashore before you get tired.

When the wind comes up, get out. Stay out of the water during periods of high surf. High surf often creates riptides, powerful currents that can drag you out to sea. Mostly they peter out not far from shore, and you can often see their choppy waters on the surface. If you get caught in a "rip," don't fight by swimming directly against it; you'll only exhaust yourself. Swim diagonally across it, while letting it carry you, and try to stay parallel to the shore until you are out of the strong pull.

When bodysurfing, never ride straight in with your hands out in front you. This is the number one cause of broken necks in Hawaii. Instead, ride the wave at a 45-degree angle, and try to kick out the back of the wave instead of letting it slam you into the sand. Remember, waves come in sets, and little ones can be followed by giants, so watch for a while before jumping in. Standard procedure is to duck under a breaking wave. You can survive even thunderous oceans using this technique. Don't try to swim through a heavy froth, and never turn your back and let it smash you.

Sharks and Marinelife

Some visitors fear that the moment their feet can no longer touch the sand they will be immediately attacked by **sharks.** The reality is that the chances of even seeing a large shark are remarkably slim, and since Hawaiian sharks have plenty of fish, they don't usually bother with unsavory humans. Still, try to avoid the mouths of rivers, murky water, and swimming around dawn and dusk.

Portuguese men-of-war and other jellyfish put out long, floating tentacles that sting if they touch you. It seems that many floating jellyfish are blown into shore by winds on the 8th, 9th, and 10th days after the full moon. Don't wash a sting off with freshwater—this will only aggravate it. Hot saltwater will take away the sting, as will alcohol, aftershave lotion, or meat tenderizer. After rinsing, soak with a wet towel. Antihistamines may also bring relief. Expect to start to feel better in about half an hour.

Coral can give you a nasty cut and is known for causing infections because it's a living organism. Wash the cut immediately and apply an antiseptic.

HEALTH AND SAFETY 373

Keep it clean and covered, and watch for infection. With coral cuts, it's best to have a professional look at it.

Poisonous **sea urchins** found in tide pools and shallow reefs can be beautiful creatures, but if you step on them, their spines will enter your foot, break off, and burn like blazes. This is known to locals as wana (vah-na). Soaking a couple of times in vinegar for half an hour or so should stop the burning, or if that's not possible, the Hawaiian solution is urine. It might seem gross, but it should put the fire out. Don't worry—the spines will die in a few days, and there are generally no long-term effects.

Hawaiian reefs also have their share of **moray eels.** These creatures are ferocious in appearance but will never initiate an attack. You'll have to poke around in their holes while snorkeling or scuba diving to provoke them. Sometimes this is inadvertent on the diver's part, so be careful where you stick your hands while underwater.

Present in streams, ponds, and muddy soil, **leptospirosis** is a freshwater-borne bacteria, deposited by the urine of infected animals. From 2 to 20 days after the bacteria enter the body, there will be a sudden onset of fever accompanied by chills, sweats, headache, and sometimes vomiting and diarrhea. Preventive measures include staying out of freshwater sources and mud where cattle and other animals wade and drink, not swimming in freshwater if you have an open cut, and not drinking stream water. Leptospirosis may be fatal in some cases if left untreated.

SAFETY IN THE OUTDOORS

Hiking

Other than bodysurfing and swimming, the most common way that visitors end up hurt or in trouble is taking unnecessary risks while hiking. Remember that wet rocks are slippery, and that stream crossings can be dangerous since flash floods can occur without warning. Stay away from the tops of waterfalls, where something as unpredictable as a gust of wind can send you one step farther than you had originally planned. If you are doing any cliff-jumping, be sure you've scouted the landing zone for rocks and that it's been verified as safe by someone in the know. When hiking along the sea, remember that large surf can unpredictably crash onto the shore, so keep a safe distance from turbid seas and slippery rocks.

While elastic bandages and disinfectants are great for cuts and scrapes, the most important thing to pack with you before heading out on an adventure is a dose of common sense; don't go out in conditions with which you're unfamiliar, and never push yourself outside your comfort zone when wandering off on your own. As the motto says, "If in doubt, don't go out." Remember that the moment you set foot on a trail—in the mountains, the rainforest, or along the shore—every action is a direct result of choices you made. It isn't the fault of the landowner that wet rocks on the property are slippery, so be prepared to accept personal responsibility for keeping yourself safe while exploring.

Sun

Many can't wait to strip down and lie on the sand, but the tropical sun will burn you to a crisp if you aren't diligent about sunscreen. Burning rays come through more easily in Hawaii because of the sun's angle, and you don't feel them as much because there's always a cool breeze. The worst part of the day is 11am to 3pm. Even though Maui is at about 21 degrees north latitude, not even close to the equator, it's still hundreds of miles south of sunny Southern California.

While spray-on sunscreens might be convenient, they stain the decks of boats, end up in your neighbor's mouth, and can ignite your skin if you stand next to an open flame (yikes!). The best, albeit most expensive, option is a sunscreen

374 ESSENTIALS

NO LAND PREDATORS

Maui can be a hiker's dream, and not just because of the scenery. Unlike other parts of the world, where bears, mountain lions, and snakes are a concern, Maui has no land predators. Remote sections of the island are home to wild boars, axis deer, and mountain goats, although all flee at the sound of human footsteps. There are centipedes and a small number of scorpions, but unless you're hiking through a compost pile, you're not likely to encounter them. When you set off on a hike, there is nothing to worry about in the way of natural predators.

that isn't petroleum-based so that the chemicals don't wash off in the water and damage the coral. The best local sunscreen is **Doc Martin's,** developed by a local dermatologist and surfer to be highly water-resistant and great for covering your face.

Be aware of dehydration. The sun and wind sap your energy and your store of liquid. Bottled water in various sizes is readily available in all parts of Hawaii, or better yet, carry a reusable water bottle.

INSECTS

While Hawaii isn't infested with a wide variety of bugs, it does have its share. **Mosquitoes** are a particular nuisance in the rainforests. Be prepared, and bring a natural repellent such as citronella oil, available in most health food stores on the islands, or a commercial product available in grocery and drugstores. Campers will be happy to have mosquito coils to burn at night.

Bees and **wasps** tend to be found on the drier parts of the island—South Maui, West Maui, and even Haleakalā. **Cockroaches** are a common sight in Hawaii and are nothing to worry about.

While you aren't likely to encounter too many **spiders** while on vacation, brown spindly cane spiders can grow to be about the size of your hand, although their bite isn't dangerous. Also considered harmless is the yellow garden spider, which you might see in a captivating web. Two known venomous spiders on the island are the female western black widow and brown violin, but the chances of getting bitten are slim; if it does happen, wash the area thoroughly. Symptoms vary but typically result in inflammation or a rash.

Perhaps the most dangerous island critters are the fearsome-looking **centipedes,** which wiggle their way into dark places, particularly after the grass is mowed or the neighboring field harvested. Centipedes can deliver a nasty bite, causing inflammation, soreness, and some redness; juveniles pack more venom than adults. The best way to deal with them is with the old rubber slipper. If you get stung, meat tenderizer has been known to ease the discomfort.

HAOLE ROT

A peculiar skin condition caused by the sun and damp towels is referred to locally as haole rot because it supposedly affects only people of European descent, but you'll notice some dark-skinned folks with the same condition. Basically, the skin becomes mottled with white spots that refuse to tan. You get a blotchy effect, mostly on the shoulders and back. Dermatologists have a name for it, and they'll give you a prescription with a high price tag to cure it. It's common knowledge throughout the islands, however, that Selsun Blue shampoo has an ingredient that stops the white mottling effect. Just rub the

HEALTH AND SAFETY 375

lather over the affected areas, and it should clear up.

CRIME

Crime isn't overt on Maui; however, like in most places, it does exist. Rental cars can be broken into, so plan ahead and park where other cars are parked, rather than a lone spot away from the tourist hubs, and take your belongings with you.

MEDICAL SERVICES

Hospitals

Between central Kahului and central Wailuku, **Maui Memorial Medical Center** (221 Mahalani St.; 808/244-9056) is the only full-service hospital on the island.

Medical Clinics

Several clinics dot the island. In South Maui, visit **Minit Medical Urgent Care Clinic** (808/667-6161) in any of its three locations (270 Dairy Rd., Ste. 239, Kahului; 1325 S. Kihei Rd., Ste. 103, Kihei; 305 Keawe St., Ste. 507, Lahaina) or **Kihei-Wailea Medical Center** (808/874-8100) in the Pi'ilani Village Shopping Center. **Kaiser Permanente** has clinics in Lahaina (910 Waine'e; 808/243-6800), Wailuku (80 Mahalani St.; 808/243-6800), and Kihei (1279 S. Kihei Rd.; 808/243-6000). In West Maui, **Urgent Care West Maui** (808/667-9721; www.westmauidoctors.com; 8am-6pm Mon.-Sat., 8am-1pm Sun.) is in the Ka'anapali Fairway Shops, and in Hana, **Hana Health** (808/248-8294) is along the highway as you enter town.

INFORMATION AND SERVICES

VISITOR INFORMATION

Free Travel Literature

Free travel literature is loaded with tips, discounts, maps, happenings, and more. Found at the airport arrival lounge and on some street stands, they include the narrow-format *This Week Maui, Maui Gold, Maui Magazine, Maui Beach and Activity Guide, Maui Activities and Attractions,* and the magazine-style *Maui Drive Guide,* with excellent maps and tips, provided free by many car-rental agencies. A great resource for activities is *101 Things to Do in Maui;* it also has money-saving coupons.

Visitors Bureaus

The **Hawaii Visitors and Convention Bureau** (HVCB; www.hvcb.org) is a top-notch organization providing help and information to Hawaii's visitors. Anyone contemplating a trip to Hawaii should visit a nearby office or check out its website for specific information that might be helpful or required.

The best information on Maui is dispensed by the **Maui Visitors Bureau** (427 Ala Makani St., Kahului; 808/244-3530; www.gohawaii.com). Additional online information pertaining to Maui County can be found at the official **County of Maui website** (www.mauicounty.gov).

Weather Reports and Surfing Conditions

Remember that Maui has microclimates with weather unlike that on the mainland. To check what the weather is going to be in a certain part of the island, refrain from using large national websites such as Weather.com and instead opt for a local site more in tune with the island nuances. For weather, the best site around is www.mauiweathertoday.com by Glenn James, which offers both weather and surf conditions, with surf heights in the Hawaiian scale.

Consumer Protection

If you encounter problems with accommodations, bad service, or downright rip-offs, try the following: **Maui Chamber of Commerce** (62 N. Market

BOOK ONLINE

If you want to save some serious cash when booking activities on Maui, virtually every activity operator on the island offers discounts for booking directly online. Oftentimes these discounts are in the range of 10-15 percent, which saves them money in the long run since concierge commissions can be as high as 30 percent (really). Granted, concierges work hard to earn that commission by educating themselves on exactly which activity will be right for you and your family, but if you've already decided on the activity you want, bust out that laptop and save some money by making your own reservation. Be sure to read the fine print: Sometimes the deal is only valid if booked at least seven days in advance.

St. #302, Wailuku; 808/244-0081; www.mauichamber.com), the state **Office of Consumer Protection** (808/243-4648; www.hawaii.gov), or the **Better Business Bureau** (808/244-0081).

MONEY
Currency
Only US currency (the dollar) is accepted in Hawai'i.

Credit Cards
Credit cards are accepted for virtually all business transactions on Maui. Almost every form of lodging, shop, restaurant, and amusement takes them, although a handful of local mom-and-pop shops only accept cash.

COMMUNICATIONS AND MEDIA
Telephone
The telephone system on the main islands is modern and comparable to any system on the mainland. For landlines, any phone call to a number on that island is a local call; it's long-distance when dialing to another island or beyond the state. Cell (mobile) phone reception is good throughout Hawaii. Like anywhere, however, there are pockets where reception is poor or nonexistent.

For directory assistance, dial 1-411 (local), 1-555-1212 (interisland), 1-area code/555-1212 (mainland), 1-800/555-1212 (toll-free). The area code for all of Hawaii is 808.

WEIGHTS AND MEASURES
Hawaii, like the rest of the United States, employs the US system of measurements. Dry weights are in ounces and pounds; liquid measures are in ounces, quarts, and gallons; and distances are measured in inches, feet, yards, and miles. The metric system is known but not in general use.

Electricity
The same electric system is in use in Hawaii as on the US mainland. The system functions on 110 volts, 60 hertz alternating current (AC); type A (two-pin) and type B (three-pin) plugs are used. Appliances from Japan will work, but there is some danger that they will burn out, while those requiring the normal European 220 volts, with other types of plugs, will not work.

Time Zones
There is no daylight saving time in Hawaii. In winter, Hawaii is two hours earlier than the West Coast's Pacific standard time, four hours earlier than central standard time, five hours earlier than eastern standard time, and 11 hours earlier than Germany. During the mainland's daylight saving time, Hawaii is three hours earlier than

Pacific daylight time and six hours earlier than eastern standard time.

Because Hawaii is just east of the International Date Line, it is almost a full day behind Asian and Pacific cities. Hawaii is 19 hours earlier than Japan, 18 hours earlier than Singapore, 21 hours earlier than Sydney, and 23 hours earlier than New Zealand and Fiji.

GLOSSARY

While English is the official language of tourism and daily life, the following list provides a basic vocabulary of words you are likely to hear. You might even discover some Hawaiian words that are so perfectly expressive they'll become regular parts of your vocabulary.

'a'a: rough clinker lava; 'a'a has become the geological term to describe this type of lava found anywhere in the world.

'ae: yes

aikane: friend; pal; buddy

'aina: land; the binding spirit to all Hawaiians. Love of the land is paramount in traditional Hawaiian beliefs.

ali'i: a Hawaiian chief or noble

aloha: the most common greeting in the islands; can mean both hello and good-bye, welcome and farewell. It can also mean romantic love, affection, or best wishes.

'a'ole: no

halau: school, as in hula school

hale: house or building; often combined with other words to name a specific place, such as Haleakalā (House of the Sun)

hana: work; combined with pau means end of work or quitting time

haupia: a coconut custard dessert often served at a luau

he'enalu: surfing

heiau: a platform made of skillfully fitted rocks, upon which temporary structures were built as temples and offerings were made to the gods

hono: bay, as in Honolulu (Sheltered Bay)

ho'olaule'a: any happy event, but especially a family outing or picnic

hula: indigenous Hawaiian dance in which the rhythm of the islands is captured by swaying hips and stories told by lyrically moving hands. A hula halau is a hula group or school.

huli huli: barbecue, as in huli huli chicken

kai: the sea. Many businesses and hotels employ kai as part of their names.

kalua: roasted underground in an imu. A favorite island food is kalua pork.

kane: man, but used to signify a relationship such as husband or boyfriend. Written on a restroom door, it means "men's room."

kapu: forbidden; taboo; keep out; do not touch

kaukau: slang word meaning food or chow. Some of the best food in Hawaii comes from the kaukau wagons, trucks that sell plate lunches and other morsels.

keiki: child or children; used by all ethnic groups. "Have you hugged your keiki today?"

kokua: help. "Your kokua is needed to keep Hawaii free from litter."

ko'olau: windward side of the island

la: the sun. Often combined with other words to be more descriptive, such as Lahaina (Merciless Sun) or Haleakalā (House of the Sun).

378 ESSENTIALS

lanai: veranda or porch. You'll pay more for a hotel room if it has a lanai with an ocean view.

lani: sky or the heavens

lei: a traditional garland of flowers or vines. One of Hawaii's most beautiful customs. Given at any auspicious occasion, but especially when arriving or leaving Hawaii.

lele: the stone altar at a heiau

limu: edible seaweed of various types. Gathered from the shore, it makes an excellent salad. It's used to garnish many island dishes and is a favorite at luau.

lomilomi: traditional Hawaiian massage; also, raw salmon made into a vinegared salad with chopped onion and spices (usually spelled lomi lomi)

lua: the toilet; the bathroom

luau: a Hawaiian feast featuring poi, imu baked pork, and other traditional foods. Good ones provide gastronomic delights. The correct plural form is luau.

mahalo: thank you. Mahalo nui means "big thanks" or "thank you very much."

mahimahi: a favorite eating fish. It's often called "dolphin," but mahimahi is a true fish, not a cetacean.

makai: toward the sea; used by islanders when giving directions

malihini: what you are if you have just arrived: a newcomer; a tenderfoot; a recent arrival

mauka: toward the mountains; used by islanders when giving directions

mauna: mountain. Often combined with other words to be more descriptive, such as Mauna Kea (White Mountain).

moa: chicken; fowl

moana: the ocean; the sea

moe: sleep

nani: beautiful

nui: big; great; large; as in mahalo nui (thank you very much)

'ohana: a family; the fundamental social division; extended family. Now often used to denote a social organization with grassroots overtones.

'ono: delicious; delightful; the best

pahoehoe: smooth, ropy lava that looks like burned pancake batter. It is now the geological term used to describe this type of lava found anywhere in the world.

pakalolo: "crazy smoke"; marijuana

pali: a cliff; precipice. Hawaii's geology makes them quite common. The most famous are the pali of O'ahu, where a major battle was fought.

pau: finished; done; completed. Often combined into pau hana, which means the end of work or quitting time.

poi: a glutinous paste made from the pounded corm of taro, which ferments slightly and has a light sour taste. Purplish in color, it's a staple at luau, where it is called one-, two-, or three-finger poi, depending on its thickness.

pono: righteous or excellent

pua: flower

pupu: an appetizer; a snack; hors d'oeuvres; can be anything from cheese and crackers to sushi. Often, bars or nightclubs offer complimentary pupu. The correct plural form is pupu, although you will sometimes see pupus used.

pupule: crazy; nuts; out of your mind

pu'u: hill, as in Pu'u 'Ula'ula (Red Hill)

ukulele: uku means "flea" and lele means "jumping," so "jumping flea." This is the way the Hawaiians perceived the quick finger movements used on the banjo-like Portuguese folk instrument called a cavaquinho.

wahine: young woman; female; girl;

GLOSSARY 379

wife. Used by all ethnic groups. When written on a restroom door, it means "women's room."

wai: freshwater; drinking water

wela: hot

wiki: quickly; fast; in a hurry. Often seen as wiki wiki (very fast), as in Wiki Wiki Messenger Service.

USEFUL PHRASES

Aloha kakahiaka Good morning
Aloha ahiahi Good afternoon
E komo mai Welcome
Mahalo nui loa Thank you very much

INDEX

A

accessibility: 370–371

accommodations; *see* lodging

adventure sports: 33, 136–137, 222, 268–270; *see also* biking; paragliding; zip-lining

'ahinahina (silversword): 361–362

air travel: 368; *see also specific place*

'akohekohe: 363

Ala Malama Avenue: 326

Ale House: 184–185, 186

Alexander and Baldwin Sugar Museum: 162–163

Ali'i Fishpond: 333–334

Ali'i Kula Lavender Farm: 209

'amakihi: 363

Andaz Maui: 48, 90

arts and crafts: 21, 38, 223–224

ATV rides: 137

B

Bailey House Museum: 40, 155, 160, 163–164

Baldwin Beach: 26, 243, 257

Bamboo Inn: 276–277

banyan trees: 110, 112, 360

bars and nightlife: 88–89, 91–92, 144–149, 184–186, 308

beaches: best 26; black-sand 354; Central Maui 167–169; clothing-optional 372; Lana'i 298–300; Moloka'i 335–338; Road to Hana and East Maui 257–261; South Maui 57–64; West Maui 113–116

beach yoga: 82

Big Beach (Oneloa): 60

Big Lefts: 172

biking: Central Maui 173–174; Haleakalā and Upcountry 33, 218–220; Lana'i 306–307; Moloka'i 344; Road to Hana and East Maui 267–268; South Maui 78–79; as transportation 369

birds / bird-watching: 80–81, 175, 221–222, 344, 362–364

black-sand beaches: 354

Blue Ginger Café: 286, 310–311, 312

booking online: 377

Braddah Hutts BBQ Grill: 241, 274–275

bus travel: 369; *see also specific place*

C

Café des Amis: 273, 274–275

Café O'Lei at the Plantation: 158, 166, 182–184

calendar of events: 21–23

camping: 203

canoes / canoeing: 23, 38–39, 78, 132

Captain Woody's: 104, 122–123

car travel and rentals: 20–21, 368, 369; *see also specific place*

carving: 39

Celebration of the Arts: 21

Central Maui: 153–189; bars and nightlife 184–186; beaches 167–169; best views 29; bird-watching 175; cultural information 40; food and dining 181–184; general discussion 18; golf 178–180; helicopter and flightseeing tours 177–178; highlights 162–167; hikes and walks 170–171; horseback riding 174–175; itineraries 156–160; lodging 186–187; map 154; orientation 162; other water sports 172–173, 174–175; planning your time 162; scenic drives 169–170; shopping 180–181; surfing and stand-up paddleboarding 32, 172; top 3 activities 155; travel and transport 188–189; volunteer work 372; zip-lining 176

children, traveling with: 371; *see also* family fun, best

Chinese New Year: 23

Circle M Ranch: 160, 174

Coffee Works: 290, 310

Colleen's: 238, 274

color, people of: 371–372

communications and media: 377

Cook pines: 361

coral / coral reefs: 355, 373–374

Cove, The: 57, 76–77

craters: 354

credit card: 377

crime: 376

crowds, avoiding: Central Maui 160; Haleakalā and Upcountry 198; Lana'i 292; Moloka'i 328; Road to Hana and East Maui 243; South Maui 50; West Maui 104 culture: 36–40; *see also* festivals and holidays

currency: 377

DE

disabilities, travelers with: 370–371

distilleries; *see* wineries and distilleries

diving; *see* snorkeling and diving

Dixie Maru Beach: 342

dolphins: 365

dragon fruit: 111–112

Dragon's Teeth (Makaluapuna Point): 99, 101, 105

drives; *see* scenic drives

D. T. Fleming Beach Park: 26, 32, 113

Duke's: 101, 142

East Moloka'i: 19, 333–335, 336–338, 340, 350

Ed Robinson's: 70–71, 74

808 Boards: 128–129

808 on Main: 28, 158, 182–183, 184

808 Wellness Spa & Healing Center: 50

electricity: 377

environmentalism: 41

Esters Fair Prospect: 184–185, 186

Extended Horizons: 126–127

FG

Fagan Memorial: 253

family fun, best: 34; *see also* children, traveling with

ferry travel: 315

festivals and holidays: 21–23

fires (2023): 111

First Cathedral: 304–305

fish, feeding: 41, 72

fishing: 78, 136, 345

fish tacos: 28

flightseeing tours; *see* helicopter and flightseeing tours

Flyin Hawaiian Zipline: 176

food and dining: 28; *see also specific place*

food trucks: 28

free activities: 370

Front Street: 110–111

Ganotisi's Pacific Rim Cuisine: 290, 308, 310–311, 312

Garden of Eden: 238, 245–246

gas: 351

Gather on Maui: 50, 88–89, 92

Gazebo, The: 102, 141, 142–143

geography and landscapes: 353–357

glossary: 378–380

golf: 79–80, 138–139, 178–180, 308–310

Goofy Foot: 128–129

Grandma's Coffee House: 196, 226–228

Grand Wailea: 90, 93

H

Ha'iku: 243, 266, 268, 271

Halawa Bay: 338

Halawa Valley: 19, 335, 338–339, 344

Halawa Valley Falls Cultural Hike: 27, 40, 321, 326, 340

Haleakalā and Upcountry: 191–231; adventure sports 33, 222; best views 29; biking 218–220; bird-watching 221–222; cultural information 40; food and dining 225–228; general discussion 18; highlights 199–211; hikes and walks 27, 213–217; horseback riding 220–221; itineraries 194–198; lodging 228–230; map 192; orientation 199; planning your time 199; scenic drives 213; shopping 223–225; spas and wellness 222–223; stargazing 211–212; top 3 activities 193; tours 211; volunteer work 372

Haleakalā National Park: 193, 195, 199–203; bird-watching 221; hikes and walks 213–215; map 200; Pools of 'Ohe'o (Seven Sacred Pools) 18, 237, 241, 254–256; sunrise or sunset at 10, 16, 202

Hale Ho'okipa Inn: 228–229

Haleki'i and Pihana Heiau: 166–167

Halemau'u Trail (Switchback Trail): 195, 203, 214

Hale O Lono: 343

Hali'imaile Distillery: 204

Hali'imaile General Store: 196, 225

Hamoa Beach: 26, 32, 241, 260, 266

Hana: beaches 259–261; food and dining 273; highlights 251–254; Highway 31 255; hikes and walks 262; lodging 276–277; map 252; shopping 272; surfing 266; *see also* Road to Hana; Road to Hana and East Maui

Hana Bay Beach Park: 251, 261

Hana Courthouse: 254

Hana Cultural Center: 253–254

Hana Farms Roadside Stand: 250, 267

382 INDEX

Hanakao'o Beach Park: 125
Hana-Maui Resort: 276–277
Hana to Kipahulu: 254–257
Haneo'o Fishpond: 260
hang gliding: 270
Haole rot: 375–376
Harold W. Rice Memorial Park: 198, 206, 207, 212
Haui's Life's a Beach: 88–89, 92
Hawaiian coot ('alea ke'oke'o): 364
Hawaiian Islands Humpback Whale National Marine Sanctuary Visitor Center: 56
Hawaiian Paddle Sports: 76–78, 130–131
Hawaiian Regional Cuisine: 28
Hawaiian Sailboard Techniques: 173, 174–175
Hawaiian stilt (ae'o): 363–364
health and safety: 372–376
helicopter and flightseeing tours: 177–178, 270
Helldiver: 73
Highway: 31 255
hikes and walks: best 27, Central Maui 170–171; Haleakalā and Upcountry 213–217; Lana'i 300–303; Moloka'i 339–340; Road to Hana and East Maui 18, 261–264; safety 374, 375; South Maui 65–68; tours 264; West Maui 117–118; wildlife 375
hili lei: 39–40
Hiro's Ohana Grill: 326, 346–347
Hoapili Trail and La Perouse: 27, 48, 66–68
Holiday Lighting of the Banyan Tree: 23
holidays; see festivals and holidays
Holua: 203
Honokowai; see Kapalua, Napili, and Honokowai
Honolua Bay: 31, 32, 102, 105–106, 119–120, 124, 127–128
Honolua Store: 102, 142
Honomanu Bay: 246
Ho'okipa Beach Park: 32, 245, 258–259, 264–265
Ho'olehua: 330–331
Ho'olehua Post-A-Nut: 330–331
horseback riding: 174–175, 220–221, 307
Hosmer's Grove: 203
Hosmer's Grove Nature Trail: 196, 214

hospitals: 376
Hotel Moloka'i: 350
Huelo Point Lookout: 275–277
Hui No'eau Visual Arts Center: 40, 204
hula: 21, 36–38
Hula Girl: 134
Hulopo'e Bay: 299, 302–303
Hulopo'e Beach Park: 28, 31, 290, 299, 304, 306
humpback whales: 364–365
humuhumu leis: 39–40

IJ
'Iao Valley: 18
Iao Valley Inn: 186–187
'Iao Valley State Monument: 29, 155, 157, 158, 165–166
'i'iwi: 363
information and services: 376–378
Inn at Mama's Fish House, The: 274–275, 276–277
insects: 375
Island Art Party: 88–89, 91–92
Island Fresh Café: 243
itineraries: 10–16; see also specific place
jacaranda trees: 360–361
Jaws (Pe'ahi): 265, 266
jewelry: 35

K
Ka'ahumanu Church: 164
Ka'anapali: accommodations 149; adventure sports 137; bars and nightlife 147–148; food and dining 141; highlights 108–110; hikes and walks 118; kayaking and stand-up paddle boarding 131; map 109; shopping 140; snorkeling and diving 120–122, 124–125, 126; spas and wellness 139
Ka'anapali Beach: 10, 26, 114
Ka'anapali Beach Hotel: 146–147, 149
Ka'anapali Beach Walk Trail: 118
Ka'anapali Point: 121
Ka'eleku Caverns: 249–250
Ka'ena Iki Heiau: 297
Kahakapao Loop Trail: 215–216
Kahakuloa: 167, 169–170, 173–174
Kahanu Garden: 240, 250
Kahekili Beach Park: 124–125
Kahoma Ranch: 137
Kahului: bars and nightlife 185–186; beaches 167–169; bike shops and

INDEX **383**

rentals 174; bird-watching 175; food and dining 182; golf 178; highlights 162–163; map 163; shopping 180; surfing and stand-up paddle-boarding 172

Kahului Airport: 20, 188, 368

Kaihalulu Beach (Red Sand Beach): 259–261

Kai Kanani: 70–71, 73–74

Kaiolohia (Shipwreck Beach): 298

Kalaupapa National Historical Park: 332

Kalaupapa Overlook Trail: 332, 339

Kalaupapa Peninsula: 321, 332–333

Kalaupapa Trail: 326, 339–340

Kalepolepo Beach Park: 57

Kama'alaea Bay: 338

Kamaole Beach: 50

Kamaole Beach Parks: 58

Kamaole Beach Walk: 65–66

Kanaha Beach Park: 18, 168, 172–173

Kanaha Pond State Wildlife Sanctuary: 175

Kanemitsu Bakery & Coffee Shop: 326, 346–347

Kanepu'u Preserve: 295–296

Kapalaoa: 203

Kapalua, Napili, and Honokowai: accommodations 149; adventure sports 136–137; bars and nightlife 146–147; beaches 113–114; food and dining 141; golf 138–139; highlights 105–108; hikes and walks 117–118; kayaking and stand-up paddle boarding 129–130; map 106; snorkeling and diving 119–120, 121, 124; spas and wellness 139; sunsets 29; surfing 127–129

Kapalua Bay: 31, 104, 113–115, 120, 124

Kapalua Bay Course: 138

Kapalua Coastal Trail: 27, 99, 102, 117–118

Kapalua Plantation Course: 138

Kapalua-West Maui Airport: 150

Kapalua Wine & Food Festival: 22

Kapalua Ziplines: 104, 136–137

Kapiha'a Fisherman's Trail: 286, 299, 303

Karen Lei's Gallery: 167

Ka'uiki Hill: 251

Ka Ule O Nanahoa (Phallic Rock): 332

Kaunakakai: 329, 336, 342, 343, 345, 347, 348–349

Kaunakakai to Halawa Valley: 338–339, 344

Kaunakakai Wharf: 342

Kaupo Gap: 215

Kawela Plantation: 334

Kawili Beach: 338

kayaking: 78, 129–131, 343

Keahiakawelo (Garden of the Gods): 285, 290, 296–297

Keahiakawelo Rock Garden Ride: 306

Kealia Pond National Wildlife Refuge: 54, 80

Ke'anae Peninsula: 246–249

Keawakapu Beach: 58

Keawala'i Congregational Church: 56–57

Keokea and Ulupalakua: 209–211, 217, 224, 227–228, 230

Keokea Park: 207, 209, 212

Kepaniwai Heritage Gardens: 18, 158, 165

Kepuhi Beach: 333, 336

Kiehi Boat Ramp: 77

Kihei: accommodations 93; bars and nightlife 91–92; beaches 57–58; bike shops and rentals 79; food and dining 85–88; golf 79; highlights 54–56; hikes and walks 65–66; map 55; shopping 83–84; spas and wellness 81; surfing 76–77

Kihei Caffe: 50, 86

Kihei Coastal Ride: 78

Kihei Kalama Village: 35

Kihei to Makena: 65, 78–79

King Kamehameha Day: 22

King's Highway Coastal Trail: 262

Kiowea Beach Park: 336

Kipahulu and Beyond: 262–264

Kite Beach: 32, 173

kitesurfing: 173

koa: 360

Ko'ie'ie Loko I'a Fishpond: 50, 54–56

Koki Beach: 266

Koloiki Ridge: 300–301, 302

Koloiki Ridge Trail: 292, 301–302, 306

Kuau Cove: 258

Kula: 18, 205–209, 211, 216–217, 220–221, 223–224, 225–226, 230

Kula Bistro: 225–227

Kula Botanical Garden: 209

Kula Country Farms: 198, 208–209

Kula Highway: 213

Kula Lodge: 195, 228–229, 230

384 INDEX

Kuloa Point Loop Trail: 256
Kumimi Beach: 338, 342
Kumu Farms: 326, 330

L

Lahaina: bars and nightlife 148–149; food and dining 141–144; highlights 110–111; map 110; snorkeling and diving 121, 122–123, 125, 126; surfing 129; updates following 2023 fires 111

Lahaina, south of: beaches 115–116; food and dining 144–145; highlights 111–113; kayaking and stand-up paddle boarding 130, 131; snorkeling and diving 121, 125; surfing 128

Lana'i: 281–315; bars and nightlife 308; beaches 298–300; Best Week itinerary 13; biking 306–307; cultural information 40; food and dining 310–311, 312–313; general discussion 19; golf 308–310; highlights 294–298; hikes and walks 300–303; horseback riding 307; itineraries 286–292; lodging 312–313, 314; map 282–283; orientation 294; planning your time 294; shopping 310–312; snorkeling and diving 31, 304–305; surfing 306; top 3 activities 285; travel and transport 315

Lana'i Cat Sanctuary: 297

Lana'i City: 290, 294–295, 300–302, 310–312; map 295

Lana'i Culture and Heritage Center: 19, 40, 285, 290, 294

Lana'ihale: 301

Lana'i Ocean Sports: 292

Lana'i Pineapple Festival: 22–23

La Perouse: 66–68

La Provence: 198, 226

lau lau: 28

Launiupoko Beach Park: 116

lava flows: 354

Lei Day: 21

lei making: 39–40

Leoda's Kitchen and Pie Shop: 142–143, 144–145

leptospirosis: 374

LGBTQ travelers: 371

Little Beach: 61, 372

Local Fishing Knowledge: 76–78

local-style food: 28

lodging: 20–21; *see also specific place*

lokelani flower: 362

Lopa: 306

Luahiwa Petroglyphs: 294–295

Luckey Strike: 134–135, 136

Lumeria Maui: 212

M

Ma'alaea: 52–54, 68–69, 70–73, 75–76, 83

mai tai: 28

Makaluapuna Point (Dragon's Teeth): 99, 101, 105

Makamaka'ole Valley Trail: 171

Makani Olu Ranch: 174–175

Makawao: 196, 204–205, 211, 221–224, 225, 229–230

Makawao Forest Reserve: 33, 193, 215–216, 218

Makawao History Museum: 204

Makawao Rodeo: 22

Makena and beyond: 56–57, 60–61, 65, 66–68, 69, 78–79

Makena Landing: 69–70

Makena State Park: 26, 45, 48, 60–61

Mala Ocean Tavern: 104, 141–143

Mala Wharf: 121, 125

Maliko Run, The: 267

Maluaka Beach: 13, 26, 48, 64

Mama's Fish House: 245, 272, 274–275

Mana'e Goods & Grindz: 346–347, 348

Manele Bay: 304

Manoli's Pizza Company: 86–87, 89–90

marinelife; *see* fish, feeding; plants and wildlife

Market Street: 160, 180

Marlow: 196, 225, 226–227

Masters of Slack Key: 144–145, 146–147

Maui Arts and Cultural Center: 184–185

Maui Brewing Company: 88–89, 92

Maui Dragon Fruit Farm: 111–112

Maui Film Festival: 22

Maui Friday Town Parties: 184–185, 186

Maui Mango Cottages: 90, 93

Maui Master Jewelers: 35

Maui Nui Botanical Gardens: 162

Maui Nui Luau at Black Rock: 144–145, 148

Maui Ocean Center: 34, 45, 47, 52–53, 73
Maui Pineapple Tour: 211
Maui Spearfishing Academy: 134–135, 136
Maui Stargazing: 211, 212
Maui Surfer Girls: 128–129
Maui Swap Meet: 180
Maui Tropical Plantation: 155, 157, 166
Maui Wave Riders: 74–75, 77
Maui Whale Festivals: 23
Maui Wine: 210–211
Maui Zipline: 176
Maunalei Gulch: 302
McGregor Point: 32, 76
medical services: 376
Merriman's: 28, 102, 141, 142–143
Mile Marker 31.8: 257
Mile Marker 39: 256–257
Mile Marker 51: 254
Moa'ula Falls: 340
Mokapu Beach: 31, 59, 69
Moku Ho'oniki: 342
Mokulei'a Bay (Slaughterhouse): 102, 115
Moloka'i: 317–351; adventure sports 33; beaches 335–338; biking 344; bird-watching 344; cultural information 40; fishing 345; food and dining 346–348; general discussion 19; highlights 329–335; hikes and walks 339–340; hikes / hiking 27; itineraries 322–328; kayaking and stand-up paddle boarding 343; lodging 348–350; map 318–319; orientation 329; planning your time 329; scenic drives 338–339; shopping 345–346; snorkeling and diving 342–343; surfing 342–343; top 3 activities 321; travel and transport 351
Moloka'i Airport: 351
Moloka'i Burger: 326, 346
Moloka'i Forest Reserve: 19, 33, 321, 331–332, 344
Moloka'i Hula Piko: 21
Moloka'i Museum and Cultural Center: 322, 331
Moloka'i Pizza Café: 322, 346
Moloka'i Plumerias: 329
Moloka'i Shores Resort: 348–350
Molokini Crater: 10, 31, 34, 45, 48, 68–69, 70–73, 80–81

money: 377
Monkeypod Kitchen: 86–87, 88–89
monk seals: 364
moray eels: 374
motorcycles and mopeds: 95, 151, 189; see also scooters
mountain biking: 33, 218–220; see also biking
Mulligan's On the Blue: 88–89, 92
Munro Trail: 300–301

NO
Naio Gulch: 302
Nakalele Blowhole: 102, 106–107
Nalu's South Shore Grill: 47, 85–88
Namalu Bay: 120
Napili; see Kapalua, Napili, and Honokowai
Napili Bay: 31, 113–115
Napili Kai Beach Resort: 146–147, 149
Native Hawaiian Culture: 36–40
Native Intelligence: 40, 181
nature, respecting: 373
nene goose: 364
No Ka 'Oi Grindz Lana'i: 292, 310
Northeast Lana'i: 298
northwestern coast: 117
Northwest Lana'i: 295–297, 300
Nuka: 243, 274
Ocean Vodka Organic Farm and Distillery: 193, 207–208
Off the Wall: 75–76
'ohi'a: 360
Old Lahaina Luau: 34, 144–145, 148–149
Old Wailuku Inn at Ulupono: 186–187
Olivine Pools: 107–108
Olowalu: 121, 125
Olowalu Petroglyphs: 112–113
One Forty: 310–311, 313
Oneloa Bay (Ironwoods): 115
Oneuli Beach: 61, 81
online booking: 377
Ono Organic Farms: 256
O'o Farm Gourmet Luncheon Tour: 211
Outrigger Canoe Races: 23
outrigger canoes: 132

P
Pacific Whale Foundation: 34, 35, 53–54
paddleboarding: 129–131, 172, 267, 343
Paddler's Restaurant and Bar: 346–347, 348

Pa'ia: 18, 257–259, 264–265, 266, 268, 271, 272–273, 274–275; map 258
Pa'ia Bay: 257–258
Paia Bay Coffee & Bar: 240, 274
Paia Fishmarket: 47, 85, 86–87, 272, 274–275
Pa'ia Inn: 274, 276–277
Pa'iloa Beach (Black-Sand Beach): 250, 259
Pala'au State Park: 332, 339
Palauea Beach (White Rock): 60
Palliku: 203
Paniolo Hale: 348–349, 350
Papohaku Beach: 19, 322, 326, 337
Paraglide Maui: 33
paragliding: 33, 222
parasailing: 136
parking: 94, 188
Paukukalo Beach: 172
Peace of Maui: 228–230
Pe'ahi (Jaws): 265, 266
Pele's Other Garden: 28, 308
people of color: 371–372
petroglyphs: 112–113, 294–295
Phallic Rock (Ka Ule O Nanahoa): 332
Pi'ilanihale Heiau: 250
Pipiwai Trail: 27, 262–263
planning tips: 20–23, 370–372; see also specific place
Plantation House: 104, 141, 142–143
Plantation Museum: 110
plants and wildlife: 359–365, 373–374, 375
Pohaku Beach Park: 127
Polihua Beach: 285, 290, 300
Polipoli: 18, 216–217, 218–220
Polipoli Spring State Recreation Area: 216–217
Polo Beach: 60
Po'olenalena Beach: 60
Pools of 'Ohe'o (Seven Sacred Pools): 18, 237, 241, 254–256
Portuguese men-of-war: 373
Prince Kuhio Day: 21
protea: 362
Punalau Beach (Windmills): 99, 101, 115
Purdy's Na Hua O Ka 'Aina Farm (Macadamia Nut Farm): 330
Pu'u Keka'a (Black Rock): 31, 108, 120–121, 125
Pu'u O Hoku Ranch: 328, 334–335, 348–349, 350

Pu'u Pehe Overlook Trail: 299, 302–303
Pu'u 'Ula'ula (Red Hill): 196, 201–203

QR

Queen Ka'ahumanu Shopping Center: 180
Rainbow Eucalyptus Trees: 245
rainforests: 355–357
rappelling: 268–270
red-sand beaches: 354–355
Request Music: 181
Richard's Market: 290, 310
Ritz-Carlton Kapalua: 146–147, 149
Road to Hana: beaches 259; best views 29; Best Week itinerary 14; bike ride 267; highlights and scenic drives 30, 244–251; hikes and walks 261–262; lodging 275–276; shopping 272; tips for driving 247
Road to Hana and East Maui: 233–279; adventure sports 268–270; beaches 26, 257–261; biking 267–268; food and dining 272–273, 274–275; general discussion 18; helicopter tours 270; highlights and scenic drives 244–257; hikes and walks 261–264; lodging 273–277; map 234–235; orientation 244; planning your time 244; shopping 271–272; spas and wellness 271; stand-up paddleboarding 267; surfing 32, 264–266; top 3 activities 237; travel and transport 278–279
Road to Kahakuloa: 169–170
Roy's: 141, 142–143
R. W. Meyer Sugar Mill: 331

S

safety: 372–376
Sail Maui: 134
Sam Sato's: 157, 182
Sandalwood Measuring Pit: 331
Sandy Beach: 338
Sansei: 144–145, 147
scenic drives: 30; see also specific place
scooters: 369–370; see also motorcycles and mopeds
Seabury Hall Craft Fair: 21
Seafire: 70–71, 73
seasons: 20
sea turtles: 69, 115, 120–121, 124, 125, 130, 132, 258

INDEX 387

sea urchins: 374
Second Cathedral: 305
Secret Beach: 372
sharks: 373
Sheraton's: 343
shopping; see specific place
Shoreline Snorkel: 121, 122–123
shuttles: 369; see also specific place
skydiving: 270
Skyline Drive: 216–217, 218–220
Skyline Hawaii: 33, 137
Sliding Sands Trail: 27, 203, 214–215
snorkeling and diving: best 31; Lana'i 304–305; Moloka'i 342–343; South Maui 68–75; tours and rentals 70–71, 121–123; West Maui 119–127
South Maui: 43–95; accommodations 90–91, 92–93; bars and nightlife 88–89; beaches 26, 57–64; biking 78–79; bird-watching 80–81; family fun 34; food and dining 85–91; general discussion 17; golf 79–80; highlights 52–57; hikes and walks 27, 65–68; itineraries 46–50; map 44; orientation 52; other water sports 78; planning your time 52; scenic drives 65; shopping 83–85; snorkeling and diving 31, 68–75; spas and wellness 81–83; surfing 32, 75–78; top 3 activities 45; travel and transport 94–95
Southwest Lana'i: 297
souvenirs: 35
Spago: 86–87, 90
spas and wellness: 81–83, 139, 222–223, 271
Stable Road: 167–169
stand-up paddleboarding: 129–131, 172, 267, 343
stargazing: 108–110, 202, 211–212
Star Lookout: 228–229, 230
St. John's Episcopal Church: 207, 209
Sugar Beach: 47, 65
sunrises: 200, 202, 219
sunscreen: 374–375
sunsets: Central Maui 165; Haleakalā and Upcountry 201, 202, 206; Lana'i 295; Moloka'i 333; Road to Hana and East Maui 245, 251; South Maui 53; West Maui 107, 133–134
Sun Yat Sen Park: 207, 209–210
surfing: 32, 75–78, 127–129, 172, 264–266, 306, 342–343

Surfing Goat Dairy: 206
sustainable travel: 41

T
Tante's Island Cuisine: 28, 157, 182–183
Tasty Crust Restaurant: 160, 182–183, 184
taxis: 368–369; see also specific place
telephone: 377
Teralani Sailing Adventures: 134, 135
Thai Food by Pranee: 273, 274–275
Thompson Road: 196, 217
Three's Bar & Grill: 28, 85, 86–87
tide pools: 355
time zones: 377–378
Tiny Bubbles Scuba: 126–127
Topside: 331–332, 339–340
Tour of the Stars: 108–110
tours: Central Maui 177–178; general discussion 370; Lana'i 297–298, 305, 307; Moloka'i 333–335, 342, 345; Road to Hana and East Maui 264, 270, 278–279
travel and transport: 20–21, 368–370; see also specific place
trespassing: 41, 247
Trilogy Excursions: 70–71, 73, 121–123, 133–134
Turnbull Studios & Sculpture: 167
Twin Falls Trail: 27, 237, 238, 245, 261–262

UV
UFO Parasail: 134–135, 136
Ukumehame Beach Park: 116
Ultimate Snorkel Adventure: 122–123
Ulua Beach: 31, 53, 59, 69
Ulupalakua; see Keokea and Ulupalakua
Upcountry Farmers Market: 204–205
Upper Waikani Falls (Three Bears): 249
useful phrases: 380
views: best 29; Central Maui 165; Haleakalā and Upcountry 206; Lana'i 295; Moloka'i 333; Road to Hana and East Maui 245, 251; South Maui 53; West Maui 107; see also scenic drives; sunrises; sunsets
Village Walking Trails: 118
volunteer work: 372

WYZ
Waialua Beach: 338

388 INDEX

Wai'anapanapa State Park: 29, 237, 240, 250–251

Waiehu Beach Park: 165, 169, 172

Waiehu Beach Park to Kahakuloa: 173–174

Waihe'e Coastal Dunes and Wetlands Preserve Trail: 170

Waihe'e Ridge Trail: 158, 170–171

Waihou Spring Forest Reserve: 216

Waihou Spring Trail: 216

Waikamoi Preserve: 221–222

Waikolu Overlook: 332

Wailea: accommodations 93; bars and nightlife 92; beaches 59–60; food and dining 88–90; golf 80; hikes and walks 66; map 59; shopping 84–85; snorkeling and diving 69; spas and wellness 82–83

Wailea Beach: 59–60

Wailea Coastal Walk: 48, 66

Wailea Ekolu Village: 90, 93

Wailele Polynesian Luau: 144–145, 147–148

Wailua Falls: 254

Wailuku: bars and nightlife 100; beaches 169; food and dining 183–184; golf 180; highlights 163–167; hikes and walks 170–171; horseback riding 174–175; lodging 187; map 164; shopping 180–181; surfing and stand-up paddleboarding 172

Wailuku Coffee Company: 158, 182

Waimoku Falls: 18, 27, 264

Waioka Pond (Venus Pool): 254

walks; see hikes and walks

waterfalls: general discussion 355–357; Halawa Valley Falls Cultural Hike 27, 40, 321, 326, 340; Moa'ula Falls 340; Twin Falls 238, 245; Twin Falls Trail 27, 237, 261–262; Wailua Falls 254; Waimoku Falls 18, 27, 264

water safety: 373

weather: 201

weaving: 39

West Maui: 97–151; accommodations 146–147, 149; adventure sports 33, 136–137; bars and nightlife 144–149; beaches 26, 113–116; best views 29; family fun 34; food and dining 140–145; general discussion 17; golf 138–139; highlights 105–113; hikes and walks 27, 117–118; itineraries 100–104; kayaking and stand-up paddle boarding 129–131; map 98; orientation 105; other water sports 136; planning your time 105; shopping 140; snorkeling and diving 31, 119–127; sunset cruises 133–134; surfing 32, 127–129; top 3 activities 99; travel and transport 150–151; volunteer work 372; water sports tours and lessons 134–135; whale-watching 135

West Moloka'i: 336, 343, 346, 350

wetlands: 355–357

Whalers Village: 140

whales and whale-watching: 23, 34, 35, 135, 364–365

wildfires (2023): 111

wildlife; see plants and wildlife

Windmills: 129

windsurfing: 172–173

wineries and distilleries: Hali'imaile Distillery 204; Maui Wine 210–211; Ocean Vodka Organic Farm and Distillery 193, 207–208

wood carving: 39–40

yoga: 82

zip-lining: 33, 136–137, 176, 222, 268

LIST OF MAPS

Best of Maui
Maui, Lana'i, and Moloka'i: 2–3

Welcome to Maui
Regions of Maui: 17
The Road to Hana: 30

South Maui
South Maui: 44
South Maui 3 Ways: 46
Kihei: 55
Wailea: 59

West Maui
West Maui: 98
West Maui 3 Ways: 100
Kapalua, Napili, and Honokowai: 106
Ka'anapali: 109
Lahaina: 110

Central Maui
Central Maui: 154
Central Maui 3 Ways: 156
Kahului: 163
Wailuku: 164

Haleakalā and Upcountry
Haleakalā and Upcountry: 192
Haleakalā and Upcountry 3 Ways: 194
Haleakalā National Park: 200
Makawao: 205
Keokea: 210

The Road to Hana and East Maui
The Road to Hana and
    East Maui: 234–235
The Road to Hana and
    East Maui 3 Ways: 240–241
Vicinity of Hana: 252
Pa'ia: 258

Lana'i
Lana'i: 282–283
Lana'i 3 Ways: 288–289
Lana'i City: 295

Moloka'i
Moloka'i: 318–319
Moloka'i 3 Ways: 324–325

PHOTO CREDITS

All photos © Greg Archer except page 1 Steven Doty | Dreamstime.com; page 7 © Hawaii Tourism Authority (HTA) / Tor Johnson; page 9 © Alwoodphoto | Dreamstime.com; page 10 © Galyna Andrushko | Dreamstime.com; page 12 © Mike7777777 | Dreamstime.com; page 14 © Pierre Leclerc | Dreamstime.com; page 16 © Ibrester | Dreamstime.com; page 18 © Wirestock | Dreamstime.com; page 19 © Hawaii Tourism Authority (HTA) / Mathieu Duchier; Hawaii Tourism Authority (HTA) / Tor Johnson; page 22 © Hawaii Tourism Authority (HTA) / Tor Johnson; page 25 © Timarindo | Dreamstime.com; page 26 © Hawaii Tourism Authority (HTA) / Tor Johnson; page 27 © MNStudio | Dreamstime.com; page 28 © PaulaCobleigh | Dreamstime.com; page 29 © Galyna Andrushko | Dreamstime.com; page 31 © Hawaii Tourism Authority (HTA) / Tor Johnson; page 33 © Hawaii Tourism Authority (HTA) / Pierce M. Myers Photography; page 35 © Mav100 | Dreamstime.com; Johnsmith2k | Dreamstime.com; page 37 © Hawaii Tourism Authority (HTA) / Ben Ono; page 38 © Hawaii Tourism Authority (HTA) / Heather Goodman; page 39 © Hawaii Tourism Authority (HTA) / Mathieu Duchier; page 43 © Hawaii Tourism Authority (HTA) / Tor Johnson; page 45 © Dmitry Akhmetov | Dreamstime.com; Hawaii Tourism Authority (HTA) / Blake Bronstad; Hawaii Tourism Authority (HTA) / Daeja Fallas; page 47 © Igokapil | Dreamstime.com; page 49 © Kyle Ellison; Kyle Ellison; Billy Mc Donald | Dreamstime.com; page 53 © Billy Mc Donald | Dreamstime.com; page 54 © Rwiseimages | Dreamstime.com; Kyle Ellison; Hawaii Tourism Authority (HTA) / Daeja Fallas; page 56 © Mike7777777 | Dreamstime.com; James Crawford | Dreamstime.com; page 57 © Ivansabo | Dreamstime.com; page 58 © Kyle Ellison; page 61 © Mike7777777 | Dreamstime.com; page 62 © Kyle Ellison; page 64 © Mike7777777 | Dreamstime.com; page 65 © Manuel Balesteri | Dreamstime.com; page 66 © Hawaii Tourism Authority (HTA) / Tor Johnson; page 67 © Hawaii Tourism Authority (HTA) / Mathieu Duchier; page 68 © Marco Pitacco | Dreamstime.com; Greg Amptman | Dreamstime.com; page 69 © Kyle Ellison; Kyle Ellison; page 72 © Kyle Ellison; page 75 © Hawaii Tourism Authority (HTA) / Tor Johnson; Kyle Ellison; page 79 © Timrobertsaerial | Dreamstime.com; Michael Siluk | Dreamstime.com; page 81 © EQRoy | Shutterstock.com; page 82 © David Kay | Dreamstime.com; page 84 © Ritu Jethani | Dreamstime.com; page 85 © Hawaii Tourism Authority (HTA) / Mathieu Duchier; page 97 © Mikhail Dudarev | Dreamstime.com; page 99 © Alexander Krassel | Dreamstime.com; Alexander Krassel | Dreamstime.com; Hawaii Tourism Authority (HTA) / Max Wange; page 101 © John Raffaghello Ii | Dreamstime.com; Billy Mc Donald | Dreamstime.com; page 107 © Ricardo Reitmeyer | Dreamstime.com; page 108 © Irina88w | Dreamstime.com; Kyle Ellison; page 111 © Hawaii Tourism Authority (HTA) / Tor Johnson; page 112 © Hawaii Tourism Authority (HTA) / Tor Johnson; page 113 © Artboardman39 | Dreamstime.com; Eugene Kalenkovich | Dreamstime.com; page 116 © Vergarazane | Dreamstime.com; Mike7777777 | Dreamstime.com; page 119 © Kyle Ellison; page 124 © Gilney Lima | Dreamstime.com; Underwatermaui | Dreamstime.com; page 130 © Kyle Ellison; page 132 © Cstiteler | Dreamstime.com; page 133 © Kyle Ellison; Gilney Lima | Dreamstime.com; page 135 © Idreamphotos | Dreamstime.com; page 137 © Kyle Ellison; Kyle Ellison; page 138 © Artboardman39 | Dreamstime.com; page 140 © Iainhamer | Dreamstime.com; Kyle Ellison; page 153 © Mike7777777 | Dreamstime.com; page 155 © Hawaii Tourism Authority (HTA) / Tor Johnson; Hawaii Tourism Authority (HTA) / Ben Ono; Kyle Ellison; page 159 © Hawaii Tourism Authority (HTA) / Tor Johnson; Palms | Dreamstime.com; page 165 © Hawaii Tourism Authority (HTA);

page 167 © Ralf Broskvar | Dreamstime.com; page 168 © Pikappa | Dreamstime.com; page 169 © Steveheap | Dreamstime.com; page 171 © Mike7777777 | Dreamstime.com; Kyle Ellison; page 173 © Timrobertsaerial | Dreamstime.com; Creatista | Dreamstime.com; page 176 © Hawaii Tourism Authority (HTA) / Mathieu Duchier; Hawaii Tourism Authority (HTA) / Dana Edmunds; page 177 © Derrick Neill | Dreamstime.com; page 181 © Hawaii Tourism Authority (HTA) / Mathieu Duchier; page 191 © Vlue | Dreamstime.com; page 193 © Billy McDonald / Alamy Stock Photo; Hannah Brezack; Elise St.Clair | Unsplash; page 197 © Tommy Song | Dreamstime.com; Hawaii Tourism Authority (HTA) / Tor Johnson; Hawaii Tourism Authority (HTA) / Tor Johnson; page 198 © Kyle Ellison; Hawaii Tourism Authority (HTA) / Ben Ono; page 206 © Kyle Ellison; page 208 © Hawaii Tourism Authority (HTA) / Mathieu Duchier; MNStudio | Dreamstime.com; page 212 © Evan Austen | Dreamstime.com; page 213 © Hawaii Tourism Authority (HTA) / Mathieu Duchier; page 214 © MNStudio | Dreamstime.com; Derrick Neill | Dreamstime.com; page 219 © Lee Orr | Dreamstime.com; page 221 © Maomaotou | Dreamstime.com; page 233 © Glenn Hartz | Dreamstime.com; page 236 © Hawaii Tourism Authority (HTA) / Kirk Lee Aeder; page 237 © Hawaii Tourism Authority (HTA) / Tommy Lundberg; Hawaii Tourism Authority (HTA); Svecchiotti | Dreamstime.com; page 242 © Shirajdesilva | Dreamstime.com; page 244 © Pierre Leclerc | Dreamstime.com; Gilney Lima | Dreamstime.com; page 246 © Christopher Bellette | Dreamstime.com; TheInnocentBystander | Dreamstime.com; Digital94086 | Dreamstime.com; page 248 © Arkontostock | Dreamstime.com; page 249 © MikeBrake | Dreamstime.com; Pierre Leclerc | Dreamstime.com; page 251 © Mike Brake | Dreamstime.com; page 253 © Hawaii Tourism Authority (HTA) / Tor Johnson; Paulacobleigh | Dreamstime.com; page 256 © Nathan Ziemanski | unsplash.com; page 257 © George Cole | Dreamstime.com; page 259 © Crackersclips | Dreamstime.com; Pierre Leclerc | Dreamstime.com; page 260 © Mike7777777 | Dreamstime.com; page 261 © Gavril Margittai | Dreamstime.com; page 263 © Hawaii Tourism Authority (HTA) / Tor Johnson; page 264 © Hawaii Tourism Authority (HTA) / Mark Kushimi; Gavril Margittai | Dreamstime.com; page 265 © Epicstock | Dreamstime.com; page 269 © Hawaii Tourism Authority (HTA) / Tommy Lundberg; page 273 © Hawaii Tourism Authority (HTA) / Tor Johnson; page 281 © Hawaii Tourism Authority (HTA) / AJ Feducia; page 284 © Hawaii Tourism Authority (HTA) / Heather Goodman; page 285 © Hawaii Tourism Authority (HTA) / Pierce M. Myers Photography; Kyle Ellison; Hawaii Tourism Authority (HTA) / Dana Edmunds; page 291 © Hawaii Tourism Authority (HTA) / Pierce M. Myers Photography; Hawaii Tourism Authority (HTA); Hawaii Tourism Authority (HTA) / Dana Edmunds; page 296 © Nathangray60 | Dreamstime.com; page 297 © Hawaii Tourism Authority (HTA) / Pierce M. Myers Photography; KnelsenPhoto | Shutterstock.com; Kyle Ellison; page 298 © Hawaii Tourism Authority (HTA) / Pierce M. Myers PhotographyPhotography; page 299 © Hawaii Tourism Authority (HTA) / AJ Feducia; page 301 © Hawaii Tourism Authority (HTA) / Lanai Hospitality Partners; Hawaii Tourism Authority (HTA) / Blake Bronstad; page 302 © Hawaii Tourism Authority (HTA) / Tommy Lundberg; page 303 © Hawaii Tourism Authority (HTA) / Dana Edmunds; page 307 © Hawaii Tourism Authority (HTA) / Pierce M. Myers Photography; page 308 © Kyle Ellison; Hawaii Tourism Authority (HTA) / Heather Goodman; page 309 © Hawaii Tourism Authority (HTA) / Blake Bronstad; page 313 © Hawaii Tourism Authority (HTA) / Pierce M. Myers Photography; Hawaii Tourism Authority (HTA) / Blake Bronstad; page 317 © Hawaii Tourism Authority (HTA) / Tor Johnson; page 320 © Hawaii Tourism Authority (HTA) / Tor Johnson; page 321 © Kyle Ellison; Nickolas Warner | Shutterstock; Mike Brake | Dreamstime.com; page 327 © Hawaii Tourism Authority (HTA) / Brooke Dombroski; Hawaii Tourism Authority (HTA) / Tor Johnson; Hawaii

Tourism Authority (HTA) / Blake Bronstad; page 330 © Edytamlaw | Dreamstime.com; Kyle Ellison; page 331 © Walter Stiedenroth | Dreamstime.com; Glenn Hartz | Dreamstime.com; page 333 © Hawaii Tourism Authority (HTA) / Heather Goodman; page 334 © Hawaii Tourism Authority (HTA) / Heather Goodman; Hawaii Tourism Authority (HTA) / Brooke Dombroski; page 336 © Mike Brake | Dreamstime.com; Fischinger | Dreamstime.com; MikeBrake | Dreamstime.com; page 337 © Hawaii Tourism Authority (HTA) / Dana Edmunds; page 339 © Hawaii Tourism Authority (HTA) / Dana Edmunds; Hawaii Tourism Authority (HTA) / Tor Johnson; page 341 © Hawaii Tourism Authority (HTA) / Tor Johnson; page 350 © Hawaii Tourism Authority (HTA) / Dana Edmunds; page 353 © Hawaii Tourism Authority (HTA) / Tor Johnson; page 354 © Hawaii Tourism Authority (HTA) / Tor Johnson; page 355 © MrLis | Dreamstime.com; idreamphotos | Dreamstime.com; Mike7777777 | Dreamstime.com; page 356 © Hawaii Tourism Authority (HTA) / Tor Johnson; page 359 © Hawaii Tourism Authority (HTA) / Pierce M. Myers Photography; page 361 © Hawaii Tourism Authority (HTA) / Heather Goodman; Hawaii Tourism Authority (HTA) / Heather Goodman; Gary Riegel | Dreamstime.com; page 362 © Diianadimitrova | Dreamstime.com; Hawaii Tourism Authority (HTA) / Dana Edmunds; page 363 © Satheesh Rajh Rajagopalan | Dreamstime.com; Hawaii Tourism Authority (HTA) / Mathieu Duchier; Satheesh Rajh Rajagopalan | Dreamstime.com; page 364 © Hawaii Tourism Authority (HTA) / Pierce M. Myers Photography; Hawaii Tourism Authority (HTA) / Ben Ono; page 365 © Hawaii Tourism Authority (HTA) / Joe West

Foldout map photos, from left to right: © Pierre Leclerc | Dreamstime.com; © Digital94086 | Dreamstime.com; © Christopher Bellette | Dreamstime.com; Christopher Bellette | Dreamstime.com; © MikeBrake | Dreamstime.com; © Hawaii Tourism Authority (HTA) / Tommy Lundberg

National Parks Travel Guides from Moon

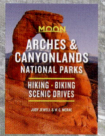

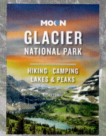

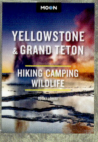

Get the bestselling all-parks guide, or check out Moon's new Best Of Parks series to make the most of a 1-3 day visit to top parks.

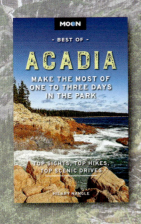
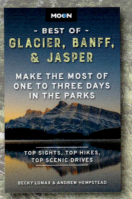
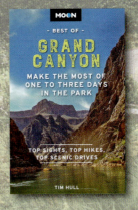

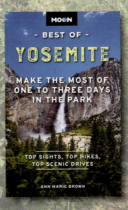

More Great Guides from Moon

 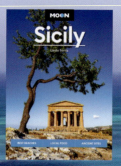 
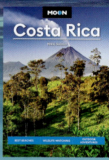 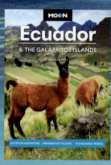 
  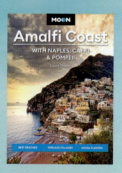
  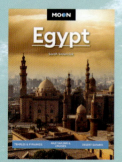

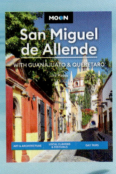
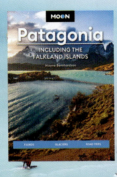
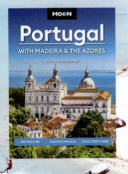

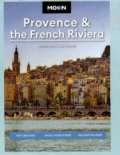

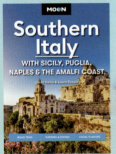

More Road Trip Guides from Moon

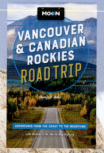 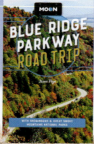  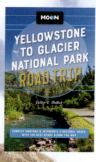

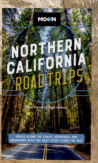 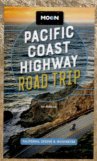 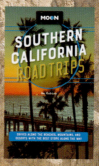 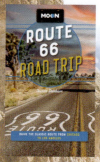

Road Trip USA

Criss-cross the country on classic two-lane highways with the new edition of Road Trip USA!

ROADTRIPUSA.COM | @MOONGUIDES

MAP SYMBOLS

═══	Highway	○	City/Town	P	Parking Area	▲	Small Park
═══	Primary Road	⊙	State Capital	T	Trailhead	▲	Mountain Peak
═══	Secondary Road	⊛	National Capital	B	Bike Trailhead	✦	Unique Natural Feature
-----	Unpaved Road	★	Top 3 Sight	△	Camping		
----	Trail	🏖	Top Beach	🏞	Picnic/Day Use Area	✦	Unique Hydro Feature
───	Paved Trail	★	Highlight/Sight	M	Mass Transit	〰	Waterfall
	Pedestrian Walkway	•	Accommodation	✈	Airport	🏄	Surfing
····	Ferry	▼	Restaurant/Bar	✈	Airfield		
┅┅	Railroad	■	Other Site	⛨	Place of Worship	🤿	Snorkeling/Diving

CONVERSION TABLES

°C = (°F − 32) / 1.8
°F = (°C x 1.8) + 32
1 inch = 2.54 centimeters (cm)
1 foot = 0.304 meters (m)
1 yard = 0.914 meters
1 mile = 1.6093 kilometers (km)
1 km = 0.6214 miles
1 fathom = 1.8288 m
1 chain = 20.1168 m
1 furlong = 201.168 m
1 acre = 0.4047 hectares
1 sq km = 100 hectares
1 sq mile = 2.59 square km
1 ounce = 28.35 grams
1 pound = 0.4536 kilograms
1 short ton = 0.90718 metric ton
1 short ton = 2,000 pounds
1 long ton = 1.016 metric tons
1 long ton = 2,240 pounds
1 metric ton = 1,000 kilograms
1 quart = 0.94635 liters
1 US gallon = 3.7854 liters
1 Imperial gallon = 4.5459 llters
1 nautical mile = 1.852 km

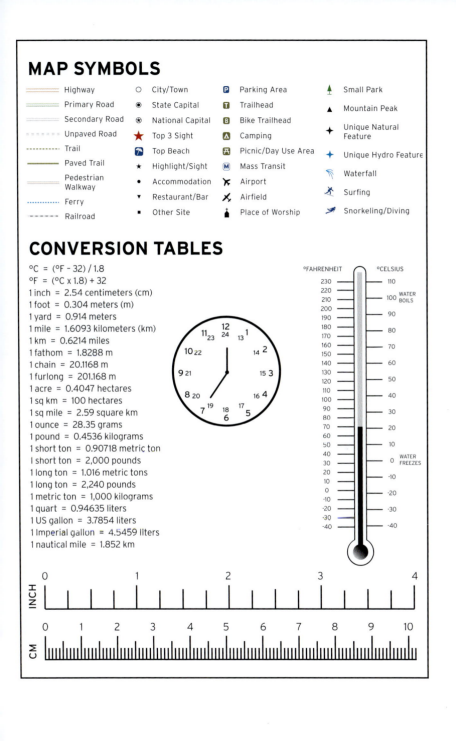

MOON BEST OF MAUI
Avalon Travel
Hachette Book Group, Inc.
555 12th Street, Suite 1850
Oakland, CA 94607, USA
www.moon.com

Editor: Vy Tran
Managing Editor: Courtney Packard
Copy Editor: Deana Shields
Graphics and Production Coordinator: Darren Alessi
Cover Design: Marcie Lawrence
Interior Design: Tabitha Lahr
Map Editor and Cartographer: John Culp
Proofreader: Hannah Brezack
Indexer: Rachel Lyon

ISBN-13: 979-8-88647-072-7

Printing History
1st Edition — August 2025
5 4 3 2 1

Text and maps © 2025 by Avalon Travel.
Some photos and illustrations are used by permission and are the property of the original copyright owners.

Hachette Book Group, Inc. supports the right to free expression and the value of copyright. The purpose of copyright is to encourage writers and artists to produce the creative works that enrich our culture. The scanning, uploading, and distribution of this book without permission is a theft of the author's intellectual property. If you would like permission to use material from the book (other than for review purposes), please contact permissions@hbgusa.com. Thank you for your support of the author's rights.

Front cover photo: Wailea, Maui © Design Pics Inc / Alamy Stock Photo
Back cover photos: Ka'anapali Beach (top) © Darren4155 | Dreamstime.com; Koki Beach (middle) © Arkantostock | Dreamstime.com; Sliding Sands Trail (bottom) © MNStudio | Dreamstime.com; hula dancers at Old Lahaina Luau (inside flap) © Mav100 | Dreamstime.com

Printed in China by RR Donnelley Dongguan

Avalon Travel is a division of Hachette Book Group, Inc. Moon and the Moon logo are trademarks of Hachette Book Group, Inc. All other marks and logos depicted are the property of the original owners.

All recommendations, including those for sights, activities, hotels, restaurants, and shops, are based on each author's individual judgment. We do not accept payment for inclusion in our travel guides, and our authors do not accept free goods or services in exchange for positive coverage.

Although every effort was made to ensure that the information was correct at the time of going to press, the author and Hachette Book Group, Inc. do not assume, and hereby disclaim, any liability to any party for any loss or damage caused by any information or recommendations contained in this book, including any errors or omissions regardless of whether such errors or omissions result from negligence, accident, or any other cause.

Hachette Book Group, Inc. is not responsible for websites (or their content) that are not owned by Hachette Book Group, Inc.